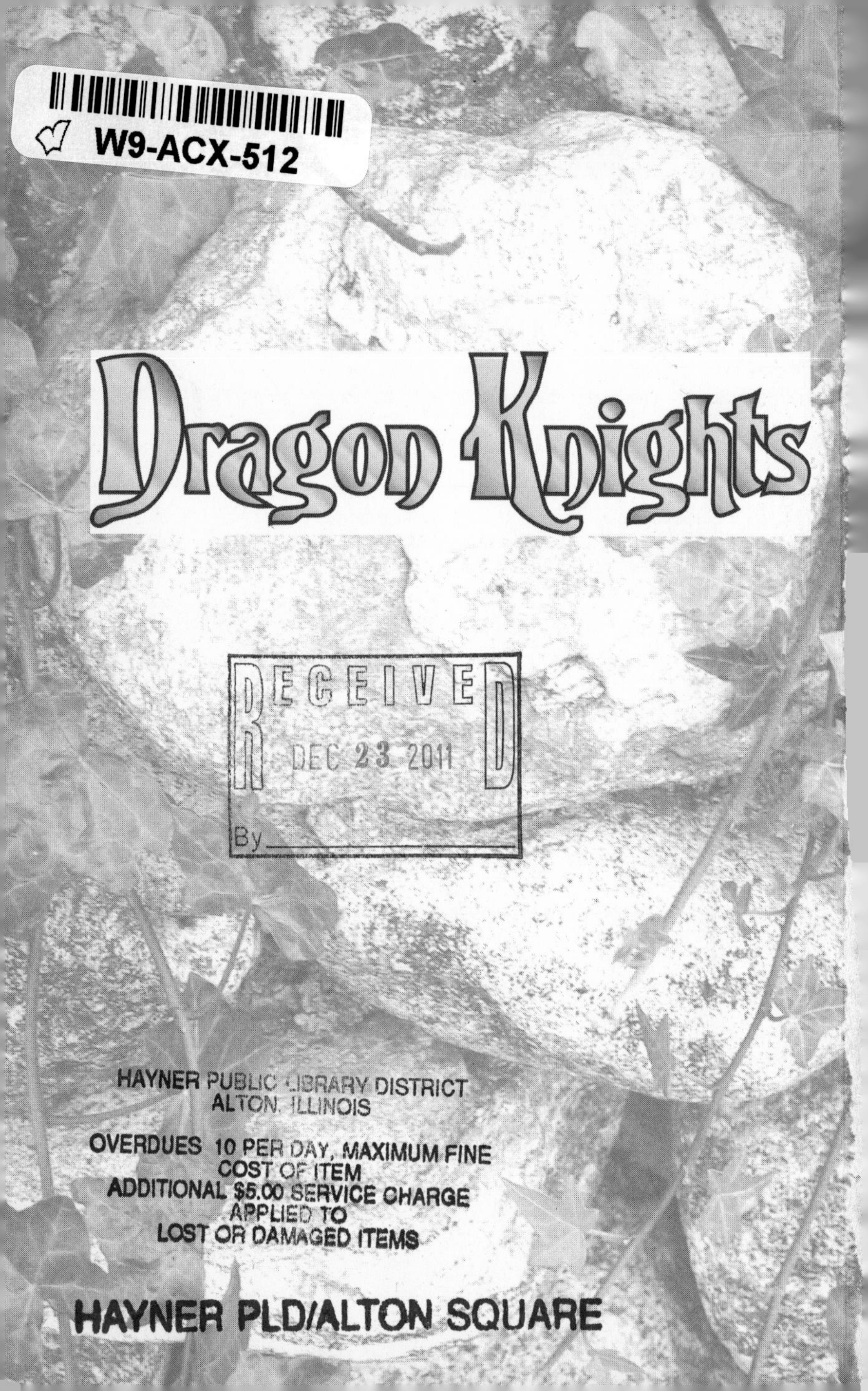

Dragon Knights

Other 100% Authentic Manga Available from TOKYOPOP®:

COWBOY BEBOP 1-3 (of 3)
All-new adventures of interstellar bounty hunting, based on the hit anime seen on Cartoon Network.

MARMALADE BOY 1-2 (of 8)
A tangled teen romance for the new millennium.

REAL BOUT HIGH SCHOOL 1-3 (of 4+)
At Daimon High, teachers don't break up fights…they grade them.

MARS 1-3 (of 15)
Biker Rei and artist Kira are as different as night and day, but fate binds them in this angst-filled romance.

GTO 1-4 (of 23+)
Biker gang member Onizuka is going back to school…as a teacher!

CHOBITS 1-2 (of 5+)
In the future, boys will be boys and girls will be…robots? The newest hit series from CLAMP!

SKULL MAN 1-3 (of 7+)
They took his family. They took his face. They took his soul. Now, he's going to take his revenge.

DRAGON KNIGHTS 1-3 (of 17)
Part dragon, part knight, ALL glam. The most inept knights on the block are out to kick some demon butt.

INITIAL D 1-2 (of 23+)
Delivery boy Tak has a gift for driving, but can he compete in the high-stakes world of street racing?

PARADISE KISS 1-2 (of 3+)
High fashion and deep passion collide in this hot new shojo series!

KODOCHA: Sana's Stage 1-2 (of 10)
There's a rumble in the jungle gym when child star Sana Kurata and bully Akito Hayama collide.

ANGELIC LAYER 1 (of 5)
In the future, the most popular game is Angelic Layer, where hand-raised robots battle for supremacy.

LOVE HINA 1-4 (of 14)
Can Keitaro handle living in a dorm with five cute girls…and still make it through school?

Coming Soon from TOKYOPOP®:

SHAOLIN SISTERS 1 (of 5)
The epic martial-arts/fantasy sequel to Juline, by the creator of Vampire Princess Miyu.

KARE KANO: He Says, She Says 1 (of 12+)
What happens when the smartest girl in school gets competition from the cutest guy?

TOKYOPOP®

Presents

Dragon Knights

Written and Illustrated by
Mineko Ohkami

TOKYOPOP®

Los Angeles – Tokyo

Translator – Yuki Ichimura
English Adaptation – Stephanie Sheh
Retouch and Layout – Monalisa De Asis
Graphic Designer – Anna Kernbaum
Cover Designer – Jeremy Canceko

Editor – Luis Reyes
Production Manager – Joaquin Reyes
Art Director – Matt Alford
VP Production – Ron Klamert
Publisher – Stuart Levy

Email: editor@TOKYOPOP.com
Come visit us online at www.TOKYOPOP.com

A  manga

5900 Wilshire Blvd. Ste 2000, Los Angeles, CA 90036

ISBN: 1-931514-42-9

First TOKYOPOP® printing: July 2002

10 9 8 7 6 5 4 3 2 1

Manufactured in the USA

From the Chronicles of the Dragon Knights ...

The First Battle Between Nadil and Lord Lykouleon ...
When the Yokai Nadil kidnapped the Dragon Queen Raseleane,
The Dragon Lord Lykouleon, against the advice of his Dragon
Officers, ventured to the Demon Realm to rescue her. He
defeats Nadil by cutting off his head, thereby saving Raseleane,
but not before the demon leader renders her barren, unable to
give Lykouleon a child ... and the Dragon Kingdom an heir.
(After the encounter with Lykouleon, Nadil did indeed retrieve
his own head and left the scene with a sardonic snarl at his
adversary. Volume Three suggests that the Dragon Knight
Rath cut off Nadil's head at a later date, and it was after
this that the Dragon Knights were dispatched to retrieve it.)

How The Dragon Knights Formed ...
Nadil has already destroyed many of the Dragon Officers and
Dragon Knights, driving Lykouleon to rebuild the Dragon army.
Rath, part Yokai himself, has already unlocked the seal for the
Dragon of Fire and readies himself to face the demon forces as
a Dragon Knight. Thatz, a human thief drawn thin on his luck,
decides to steal the Dragon Rock from the Dragon Castle and
inadvertently unlocks the seal for the Dragon of Earth. Rune,
in a battle with the Demon Fish Varawoo, heals the Water
Dragon, thereby unlocking its seal, and ascends to the ranks of
the Dragon Knights. With Lord Lykouleon possessed of the
Dragon of Light (Little Dues/Shin), only the Dragon of Wind
has yet to be unlocked.

The Conflict at Hand ...
Now, Nadil's hordes, led by the ominously enigmatic Shydeman
and Shyrendora, hope to retrieve Nadil's head from within the
Dragon Castle's walls, thereby resurrecting their fallen
leader. But this is a feat suited solely for the Yokai Bierrez,
the only demon thus far who has acquired the ability to pene-
trate the magical protective shield that Lykouleon has placed
around the castle grounds — an ability he has not yet
revealed to his demon compatriots. Bierrez has his own designs
on the demon leadership.

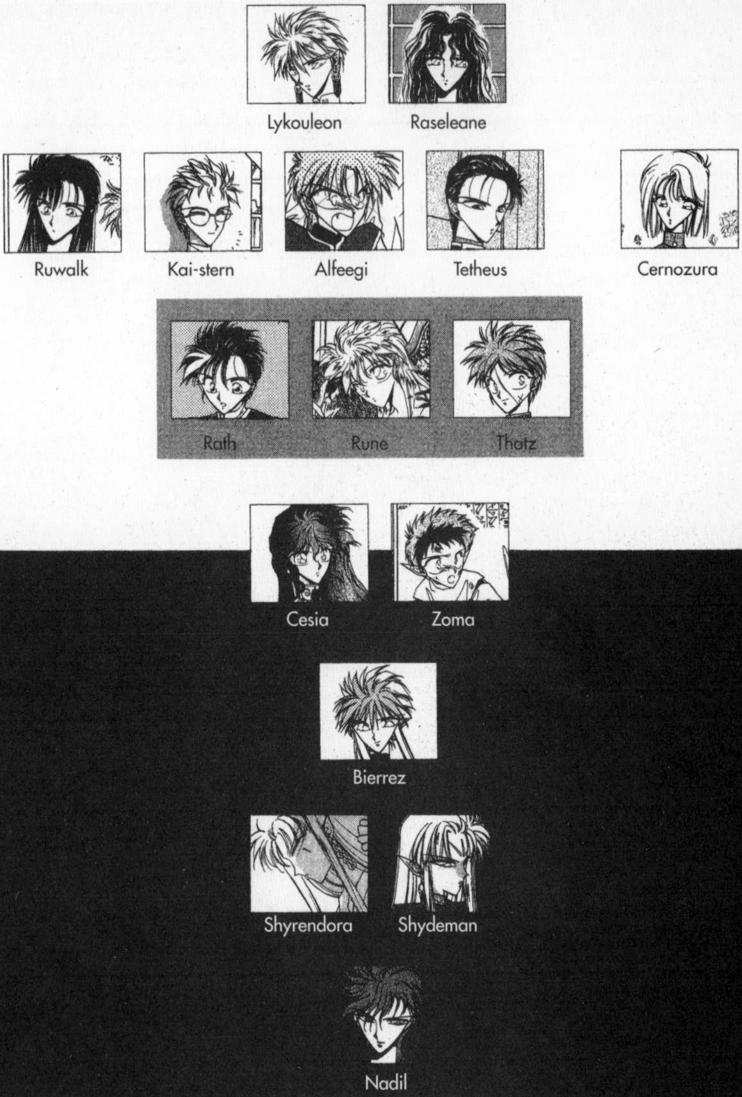
Lykouleon
Raseleane
Ruwalk
Kai-stern
Alfeegi
Tetheus
Cernozura
Rath
Rune
Thatz
Cesia
Zoma
Bierrez
Shyrendora
Shydeman
Nadil

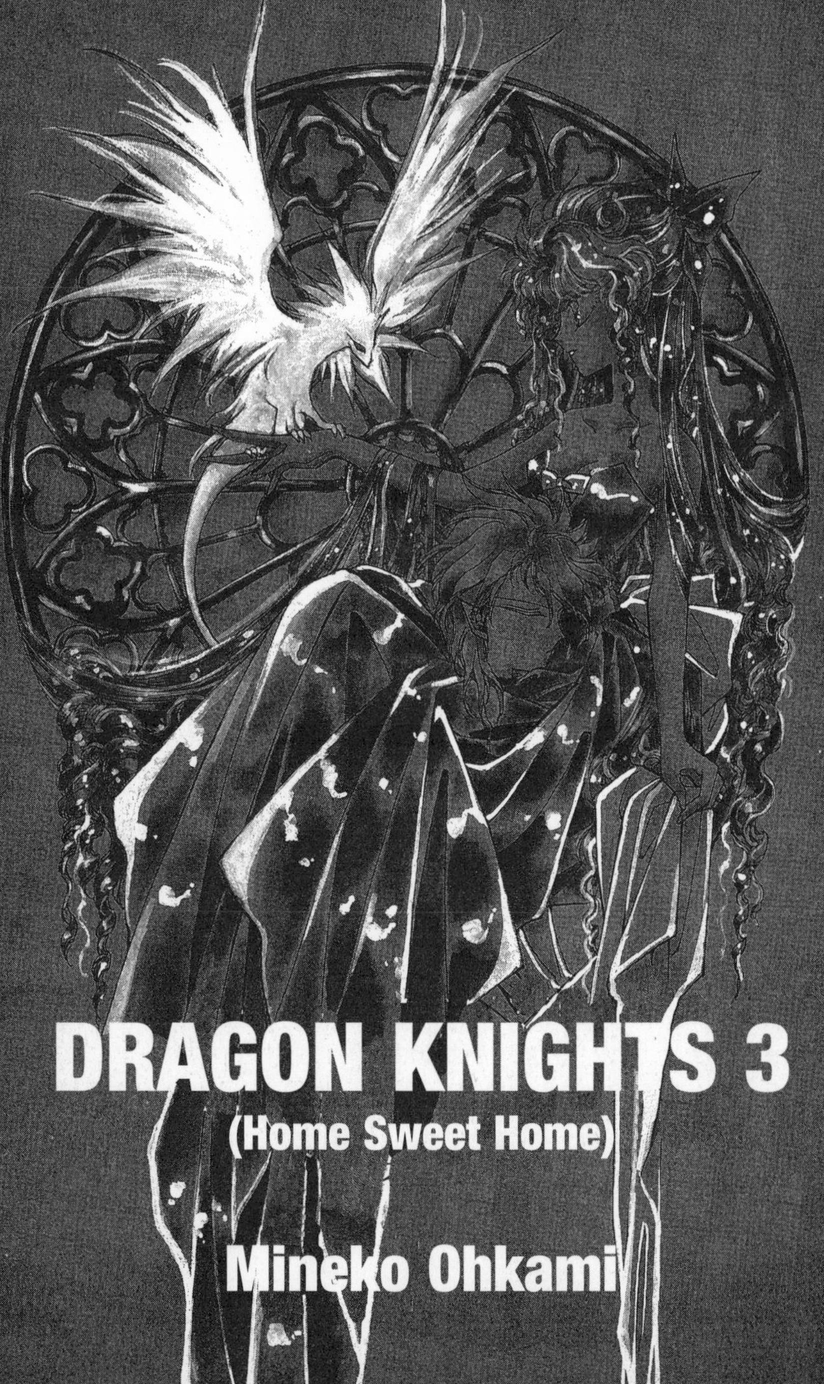

DRAGON KNIGHTS 3

(Home Sweet Home)

Mineko Ohkami

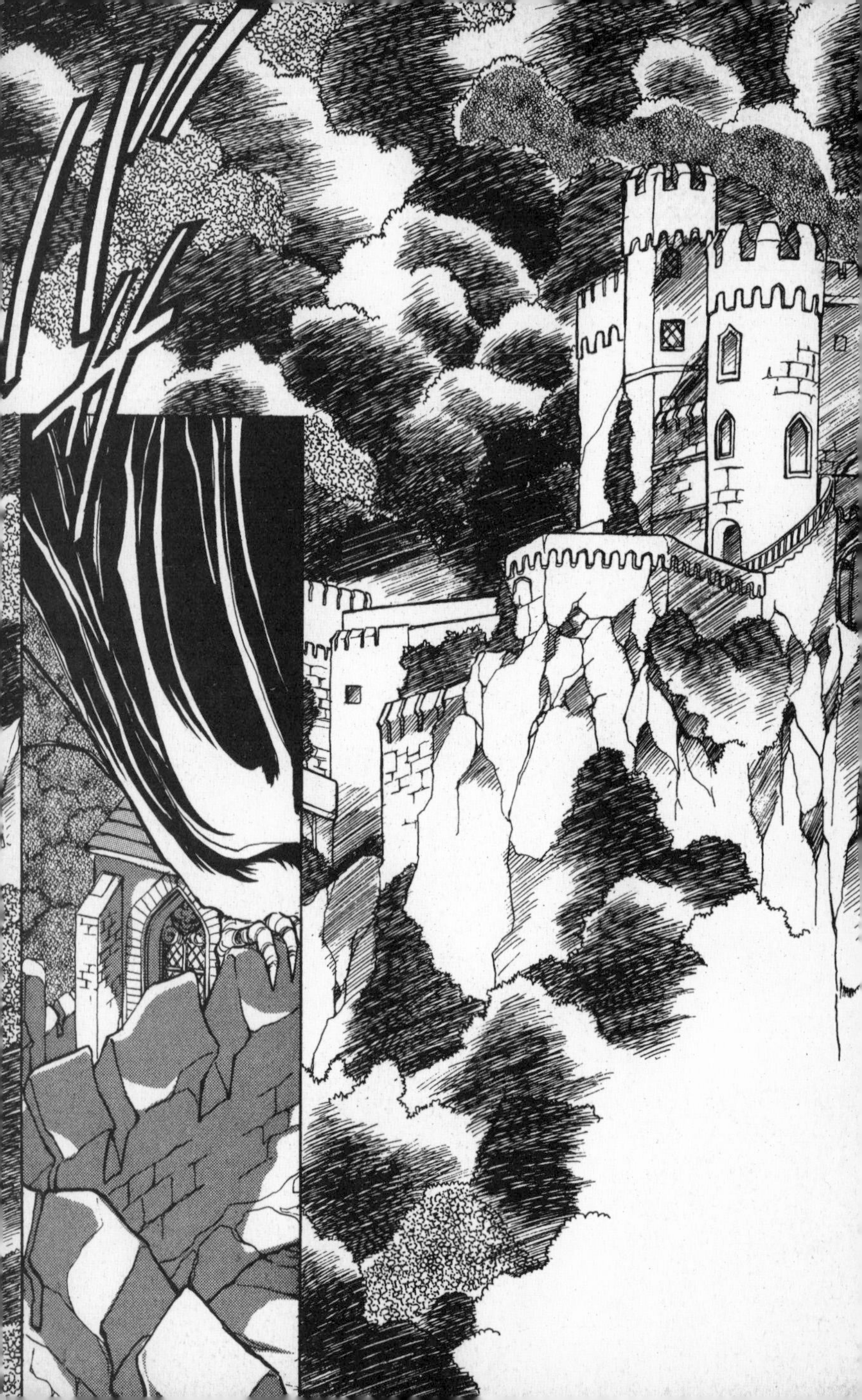

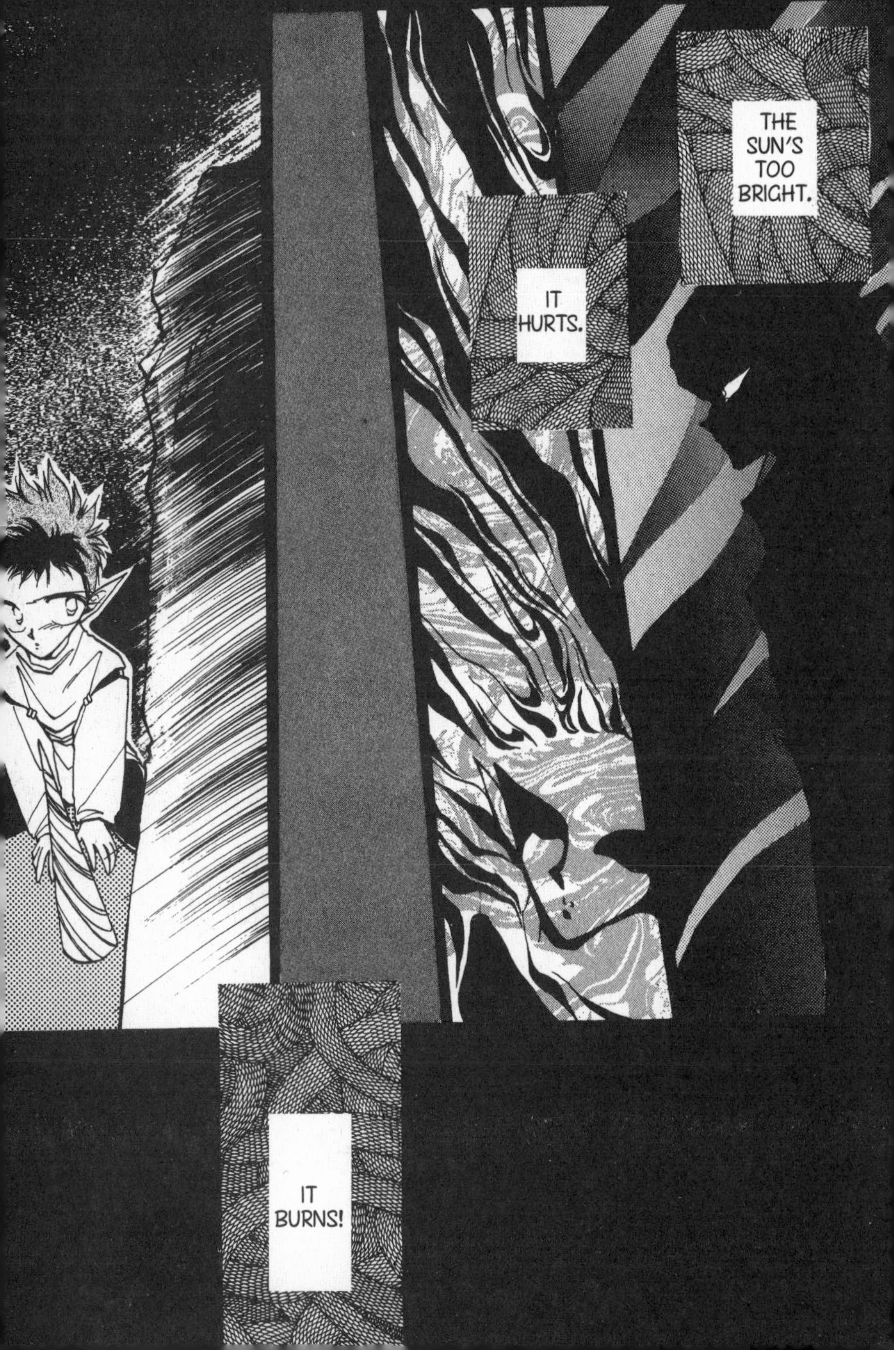
THE SUN'S TOO BRIGHT.
IT HURTS.
IT BURNS!

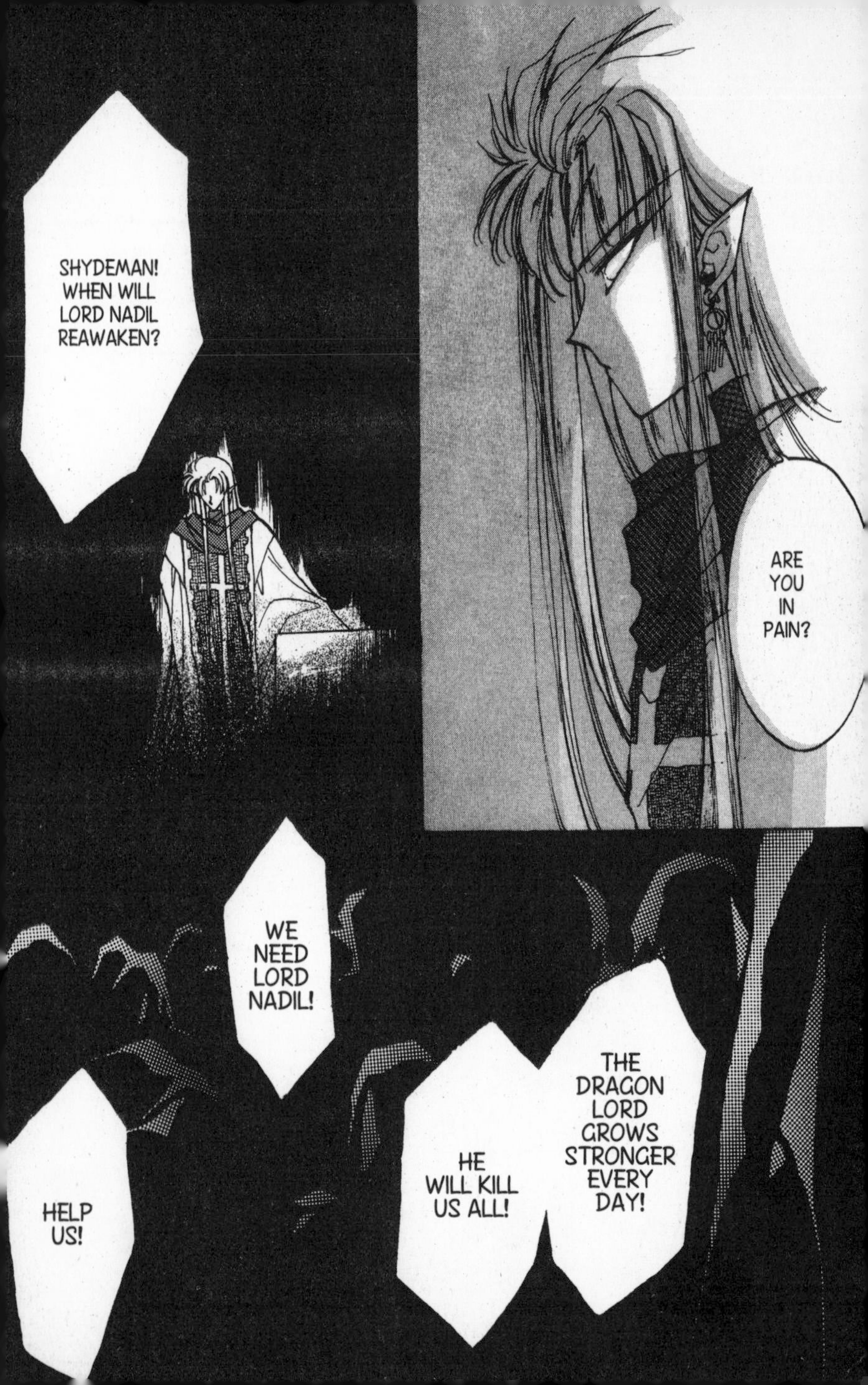
ARE YOU IN PAIN?
SHYDEMAN! WHEN WILL LORD NADIL REAWAKEN?
THE DRAGON LORD GROWS STRONGER EVERY DAY!
WE NEED LORD NADIL!
HE WILL KILL US ALL!
HELP US!

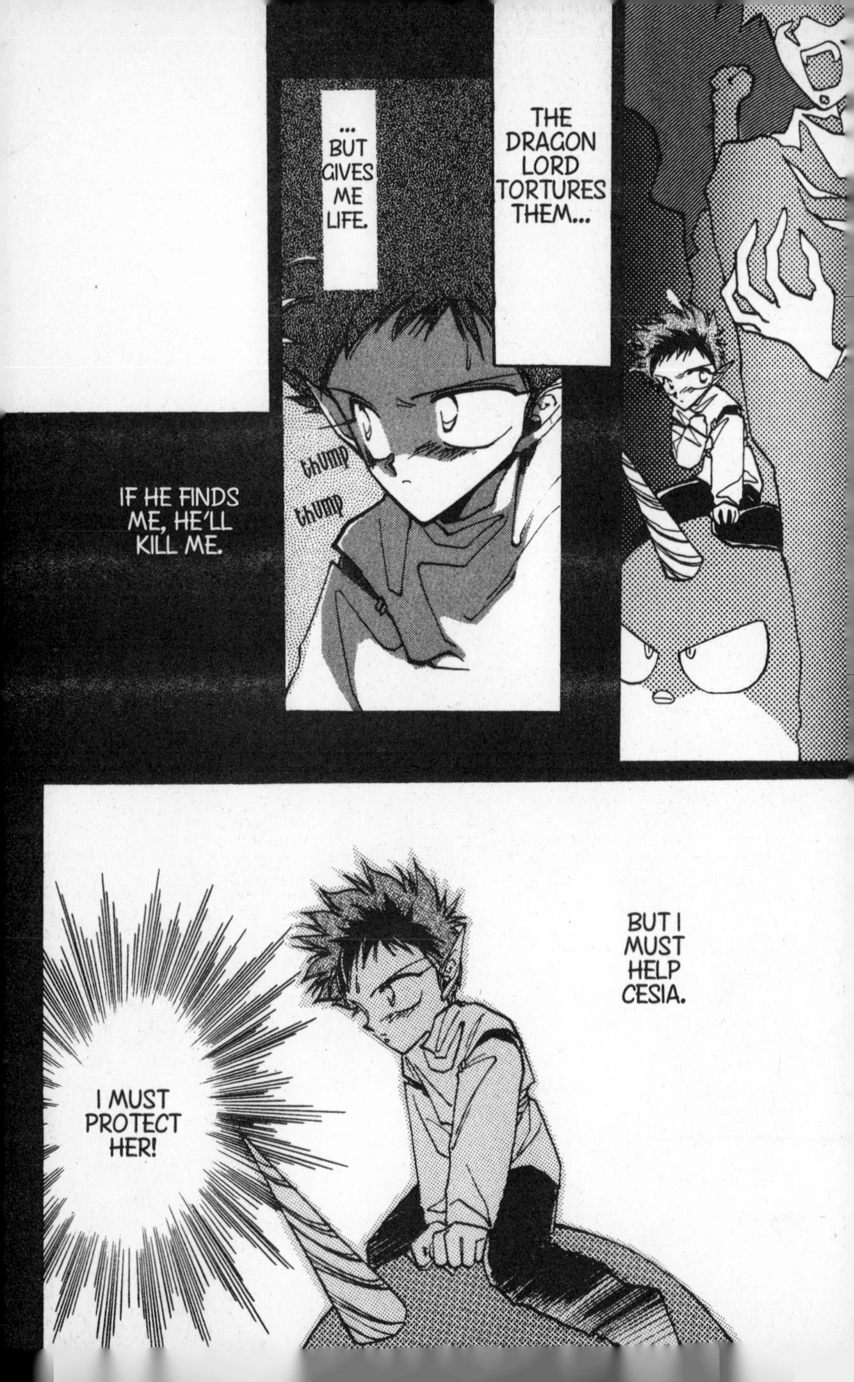
THE DRAGON LORD TORTURES THEM...
... BUT GIVES ME LIFE.
THUMP
THUMP
IF HE FINDS ME, HE'LL KILL ME.
BUT I MUST HELP CESIA.
I MUST PROTECT HER!

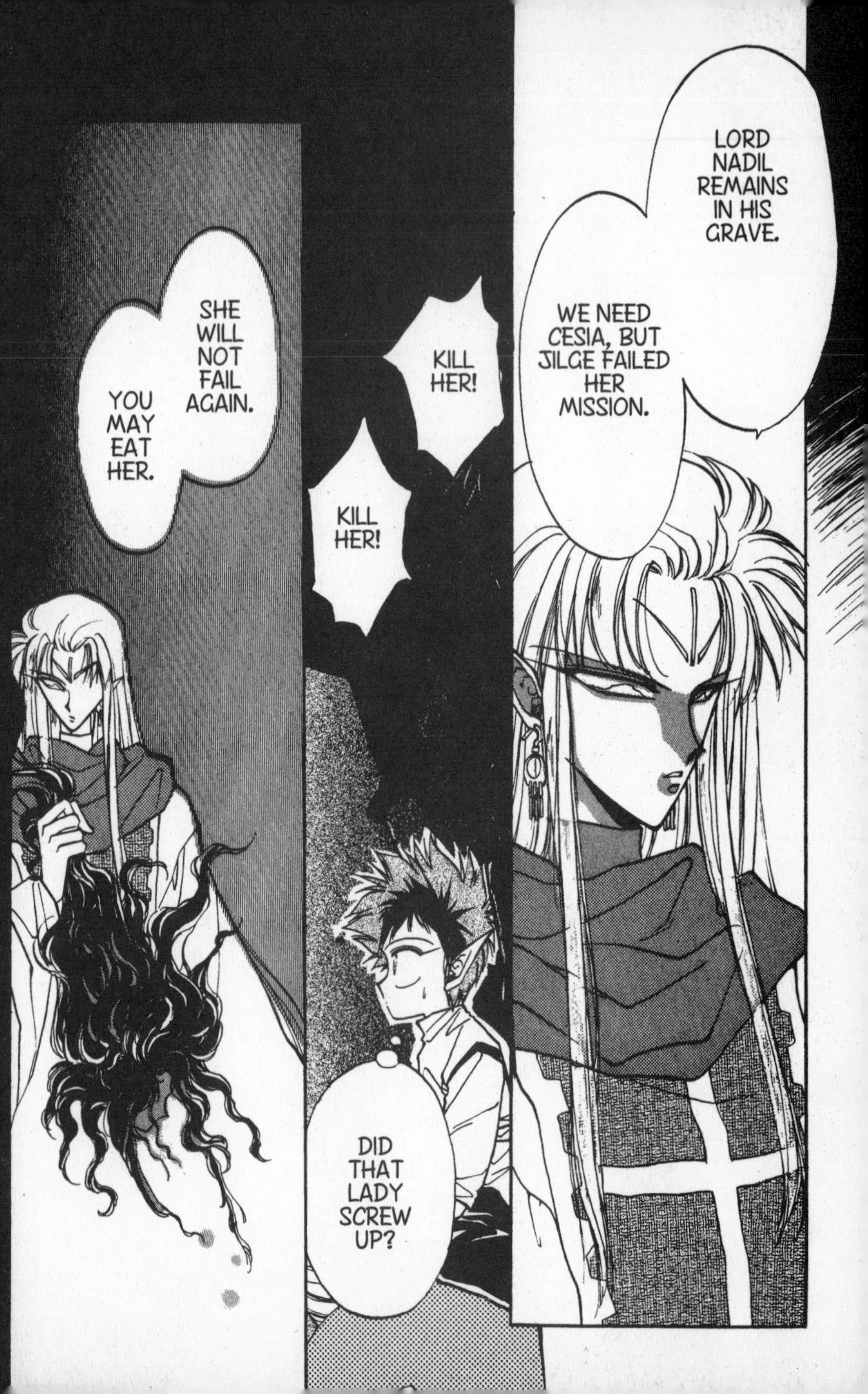
LORD NADIL REMAINS IN HIS GRAVE.
WE NEED CESIA, BUT JILGE FAILED HER MISSION.
KILL HER!
KILL HER!
DID THAT LADY SCREW UP?
SHE WILL NOT FAIL AGAIN.
YOU MAY EAT HER.

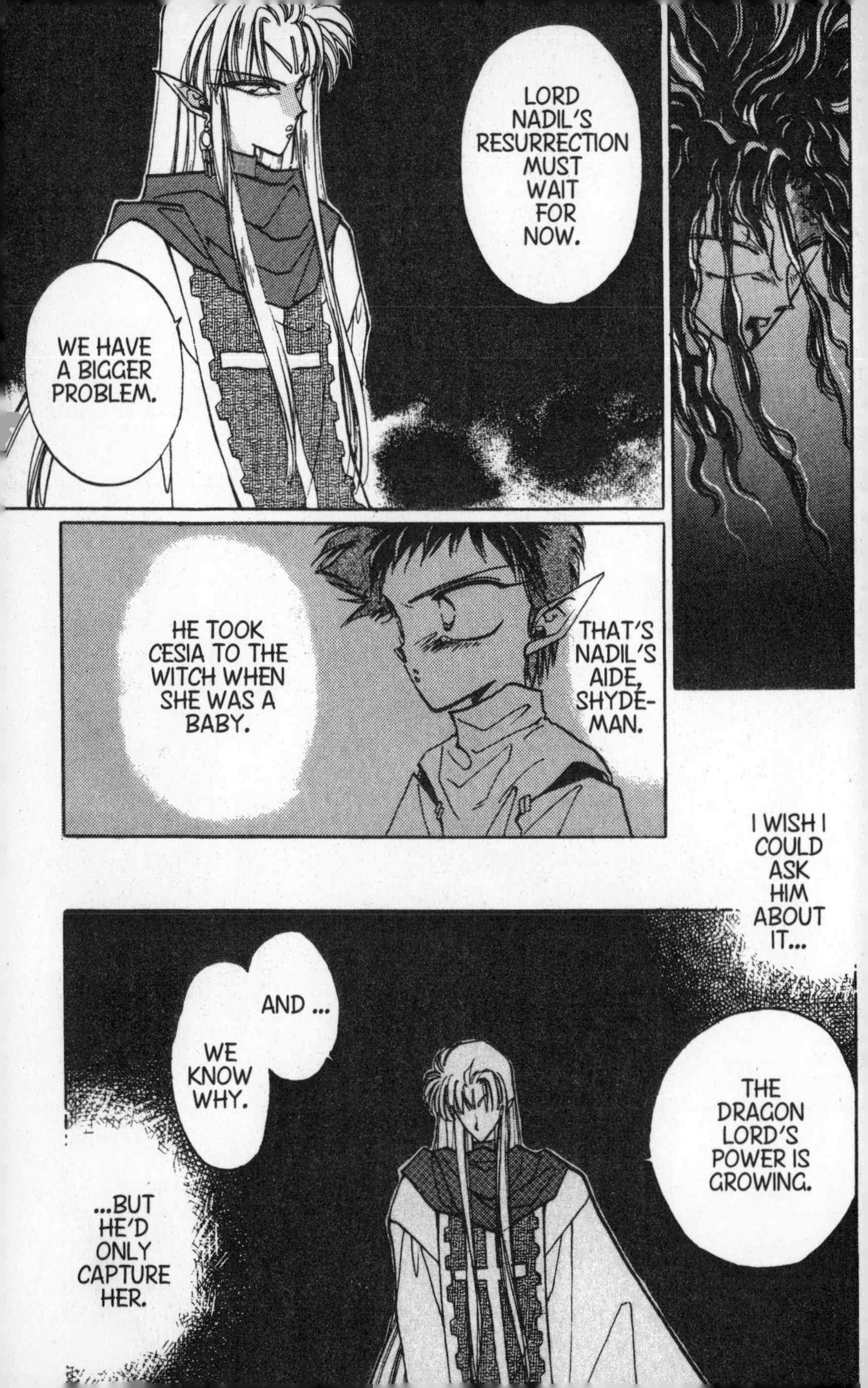
LORD NADIL'S RESURRECTION MUST WAIT FOR NOW.
WE HAVE A BIGGER PROBLEM.
THAT'S NADIL'S AIDE, SHYDE-MAN.
HE TOOK CESIA TO THE WITCH WHEN SHE WAS A BABY.
I WISH I COULD ASK HIM ABOUT IT...
THE DRAGON LORD'S POWER IS GROWING.
AND ...
WE KNOW WHY.
...BUT HE'D ONLY CAPTURE HER.

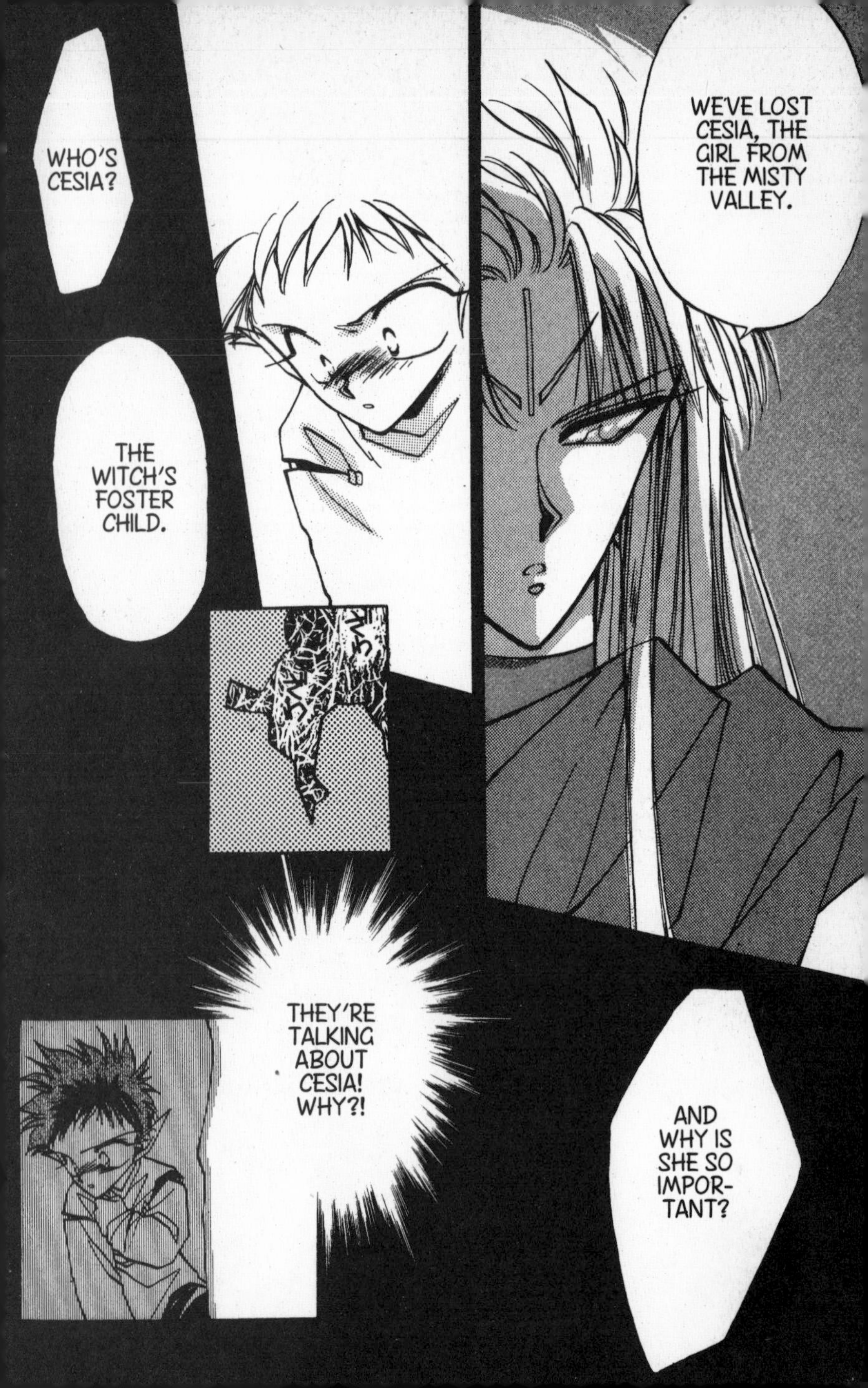
WE'VE LOST CESIA, THE GIRL FROM THE MISTY VALLEY.
WHO'S CESIA?
THE WITCH'S FOSTER CHILD.
THEY'RE TALKING ABOUT CESIA! WHY?!
AND WHY IS SHE SO IMPOR-TANT?

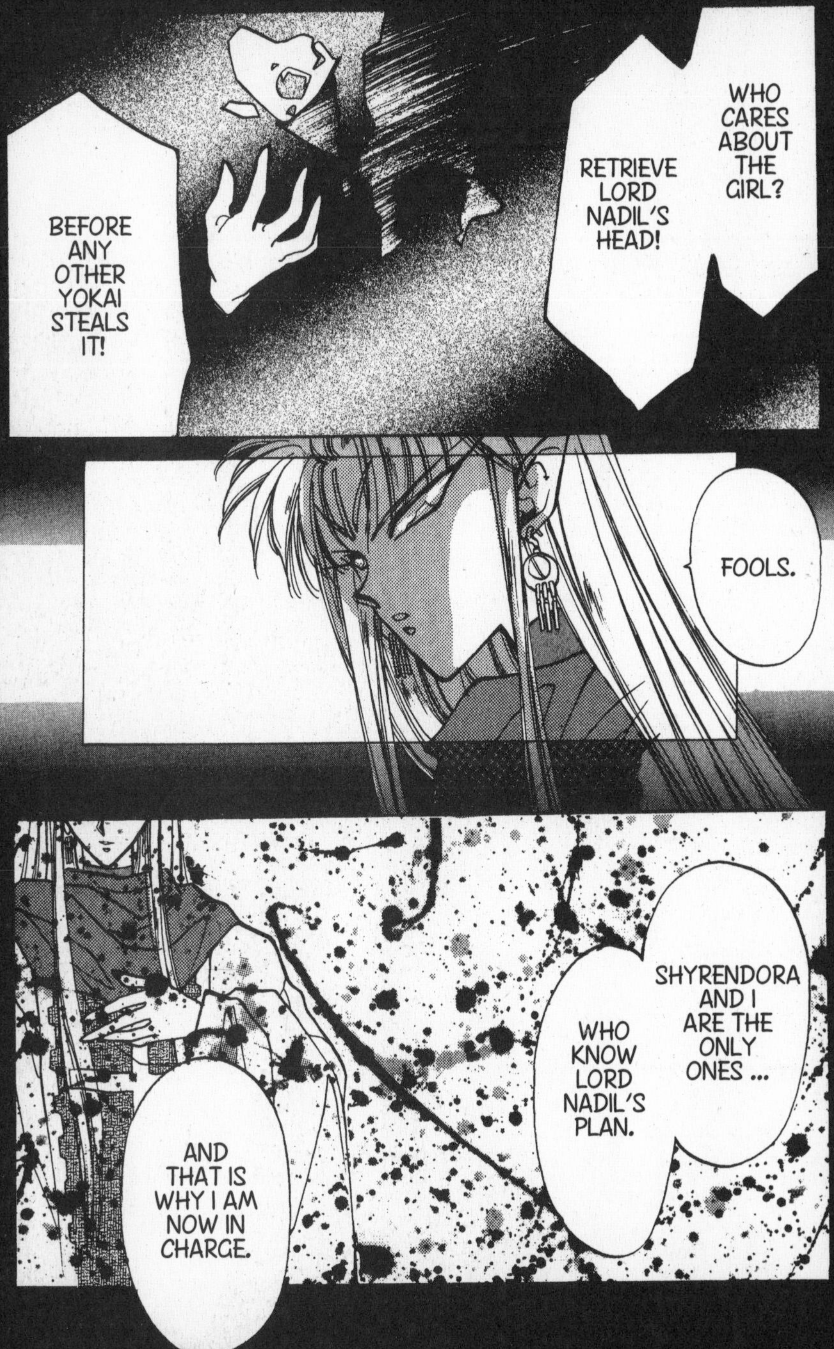
WHO CARES ABOUT THE GIRL?
RETRIEVE LORD NADIL'S HEAD!
BEFORE ANY OTHER YOKAI STEALS IT!
FOOLS.
SHYRENDORA AND I ARE THE ONLY ONES ...
WHO KNOW LORD NADIL'S PLAN.
AND THAT IS WHY I AM NOW IN CHARGE.

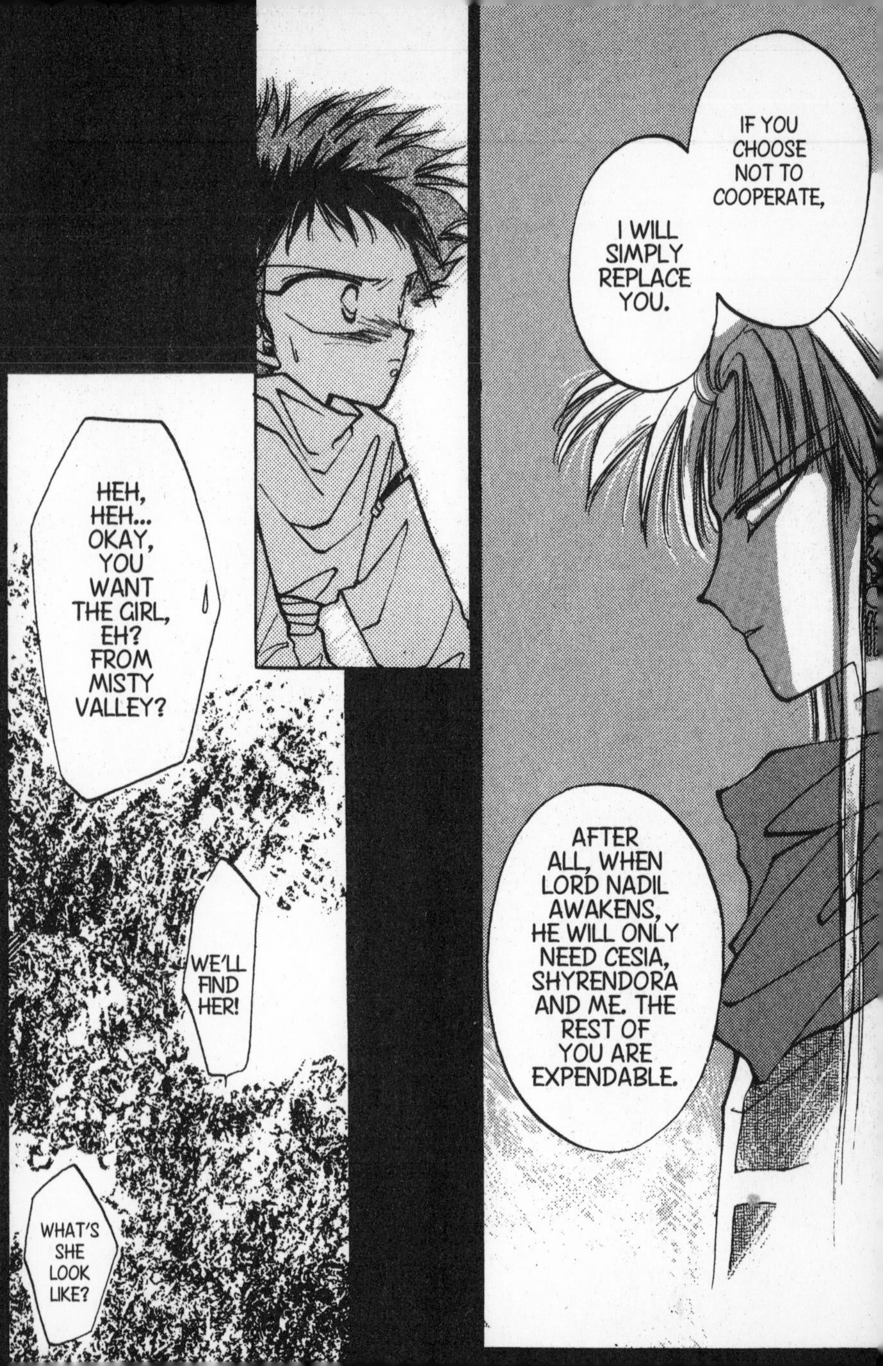
IF YOU CHOOSE NOT TO COOPERATE,
I WILL SIMPLY REPLACE YOU.
AFTER ALL, WHEN LORD NADIL AWAKENS, HE WILL ONLY NEED CESIA, SHYRENDORA AND ME. THE REST OF YOU ARE EXPENDABLE.
HEH, HEH... OKAY, YOU WANT THE GIRL, EH? FROM MISTY VALLEY?
WE'LL FIND HER!
WHAT'S SHE LOOK LIKE?

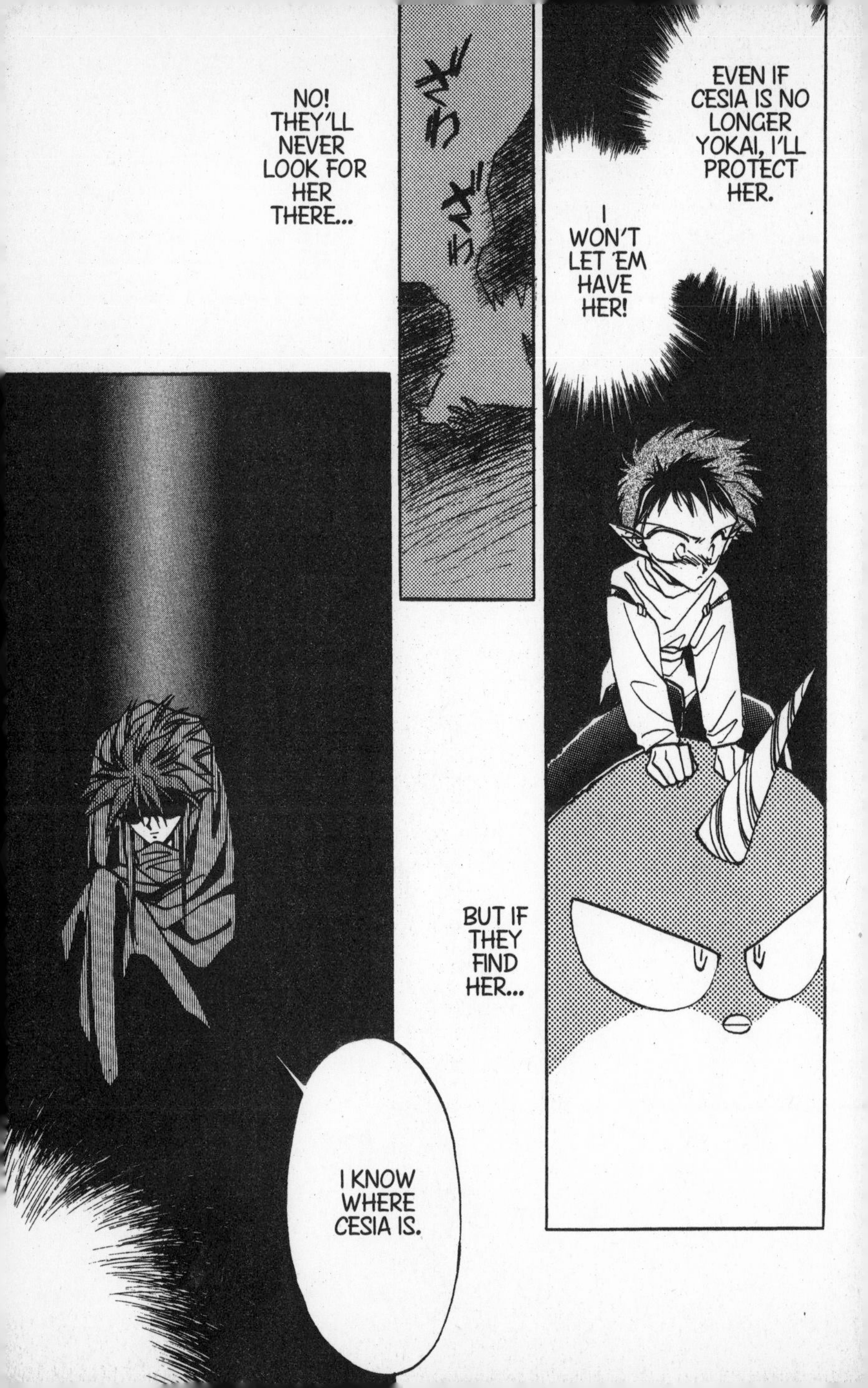
EVEN IF CESIA IS NO LONGER YOKAI, I'LL PROTECT HER.
I WON'T LET 'EM HAVE HER!
BUT IF THEY FIND HER...
ざわ ざわ
NO! THEY'LL NEVER LOOK FOR HER THERE...
I KNOW WHERE CESIA IS.

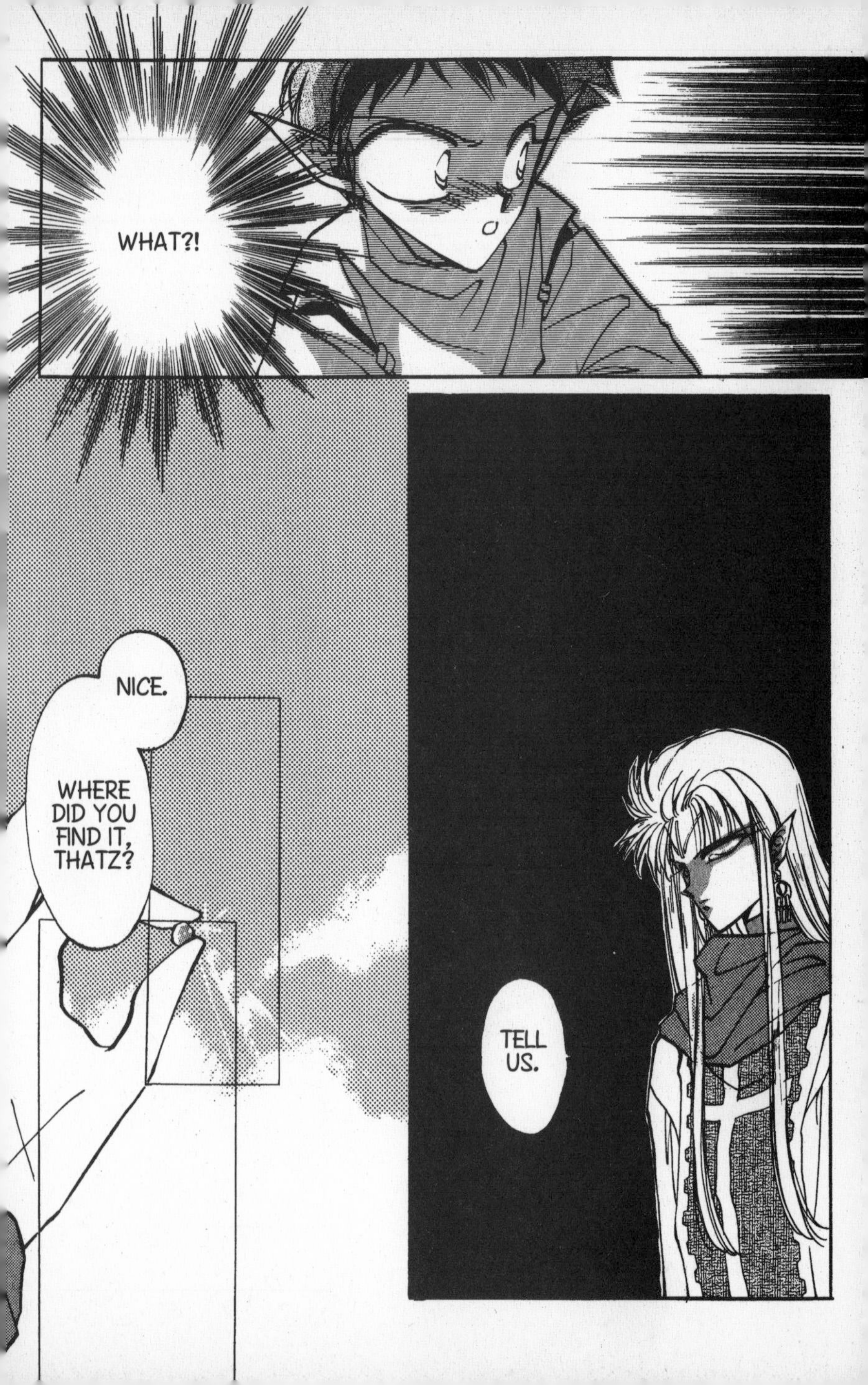
WHAT?!
NICE.
WHERE DID YOU FIND IT, THATZ?
TELL US.

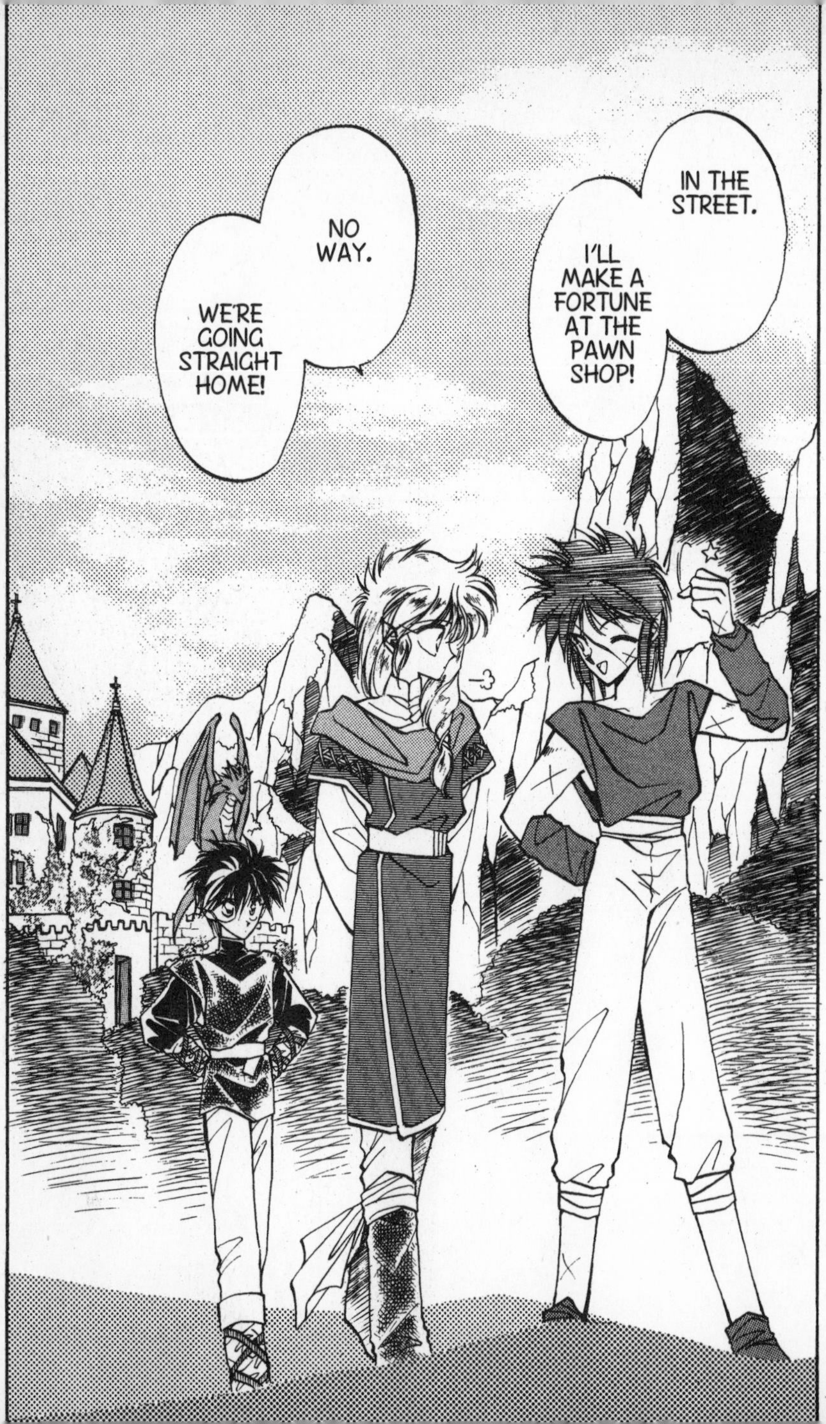
IN THE STREET.
I'LL MAKE A FORTUNE AT THE PAWN SHOP!
NO WAY.
WE'RE GOING STRAIGHT HOME!

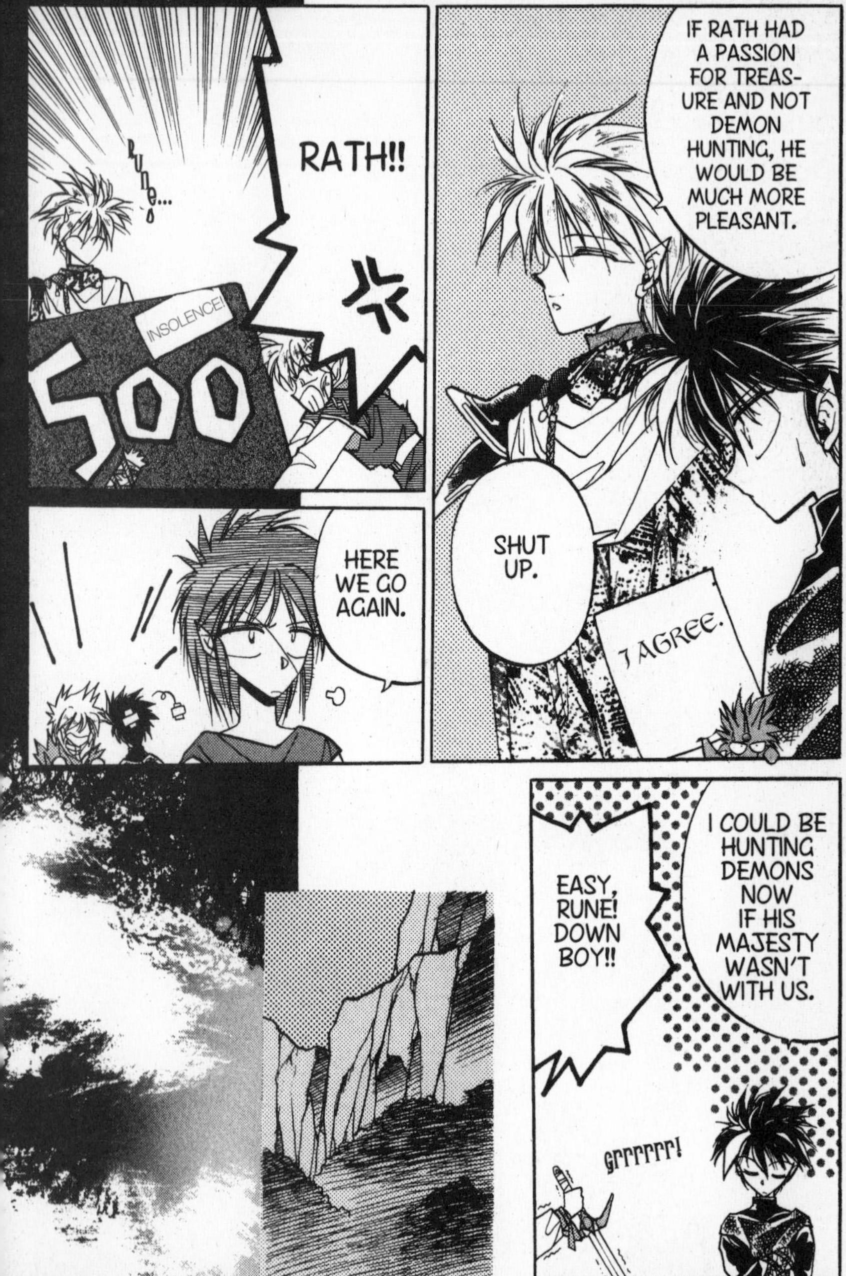
IF RATH HAD A PASSION FOR TREASURE AND NOT DEMON HUNTING, HE WOULD BE MUCH MORE PLEASANT.
SHUT UP.
I AGREE.
RATH!!
Rune...
INSOLENCE!
500
HERE WE GO AGAIN.
I COULD BE HUNTING DEMONS NOW IF HIS MAJESTY WASN'T WITH US.
EASY, RUNE! DOWN BOY!!
Grrrrrr!

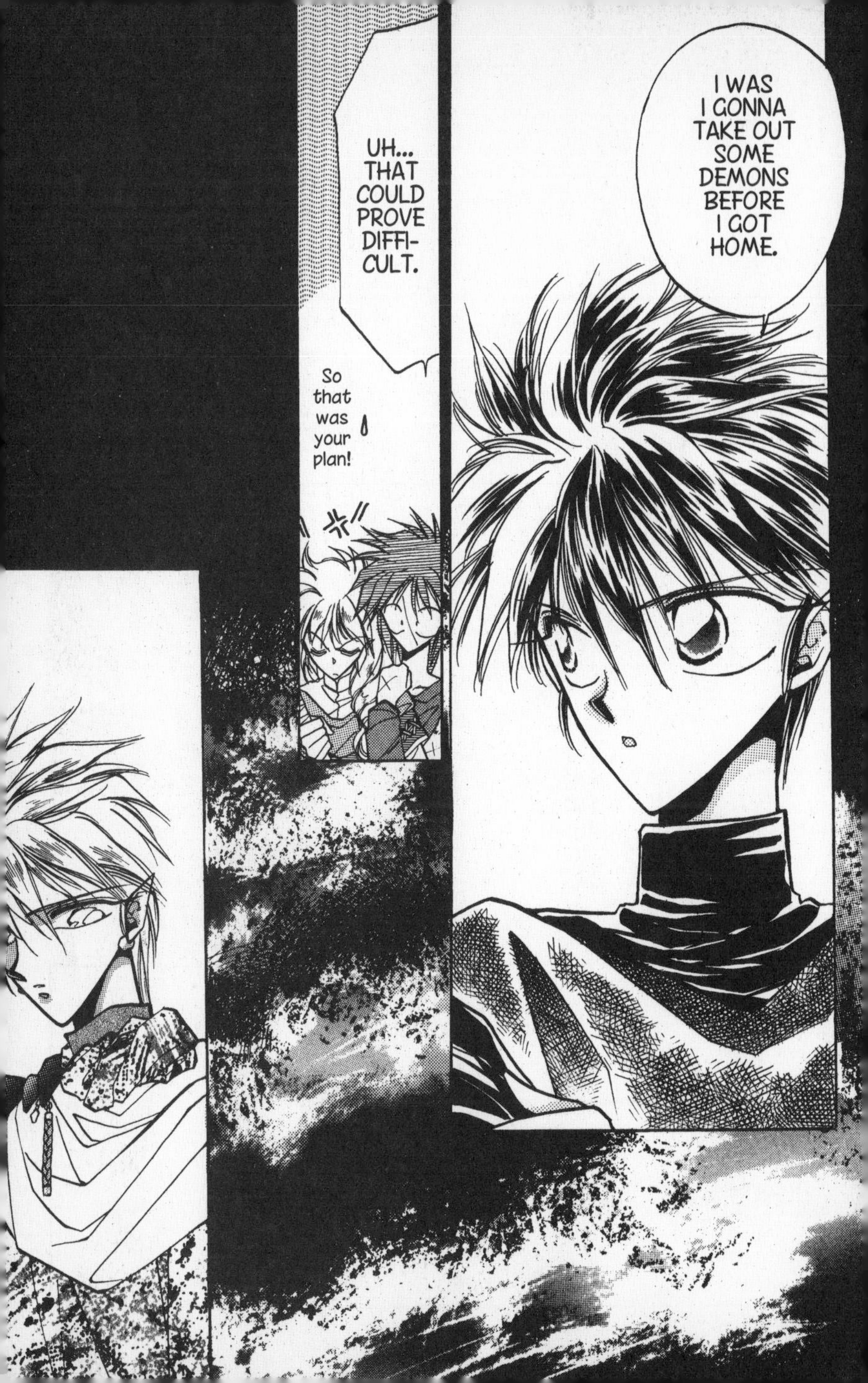
I WAS I GONNA TAKE OUT SOME DEMONS BEFORE I GOT HOME.
UH... THAT COULD PROVE DIFFI-CULT.
So that was your plan!

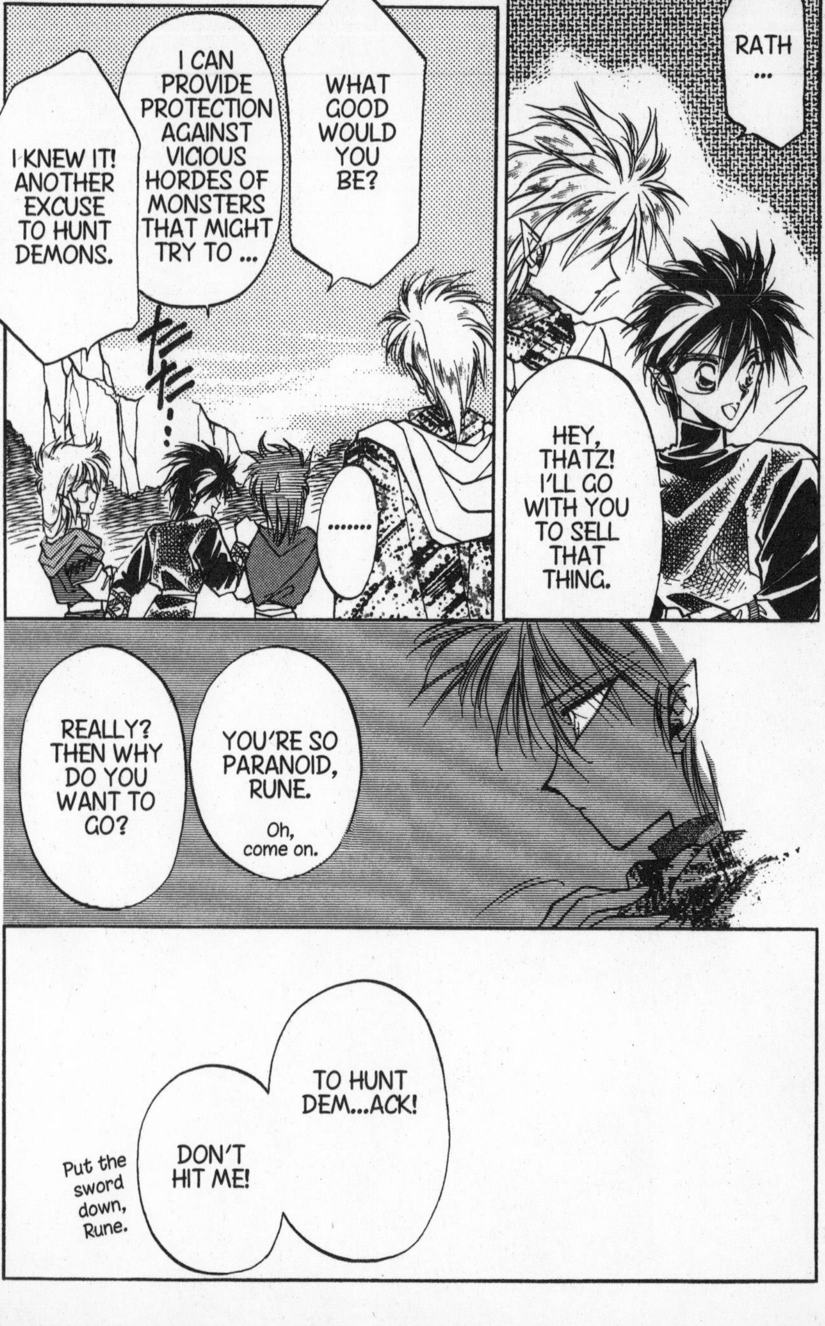
RATH ...
HEY, THATZ! I'LL GO WITH YOU TO SELL THAT THING.
WHAT GOOD WOULD YOU BE?
I CAN PROVIDE PROTECTION AGAINST VICIOUS HORDES OF MONSTERS THAT MIGHT TRY TO ...
I KNEW IT! ANOTHER EXCUSE TO HUNT DEMONS.
....
YOU'RE SO PARANOID, RUNE.
Oh, come on.
REALLY? THEN WHY DO YOU WANT TO GO?
TO HUNT DEM...ACK!
DON'T HIT ME!
Put the sword down, Rune.

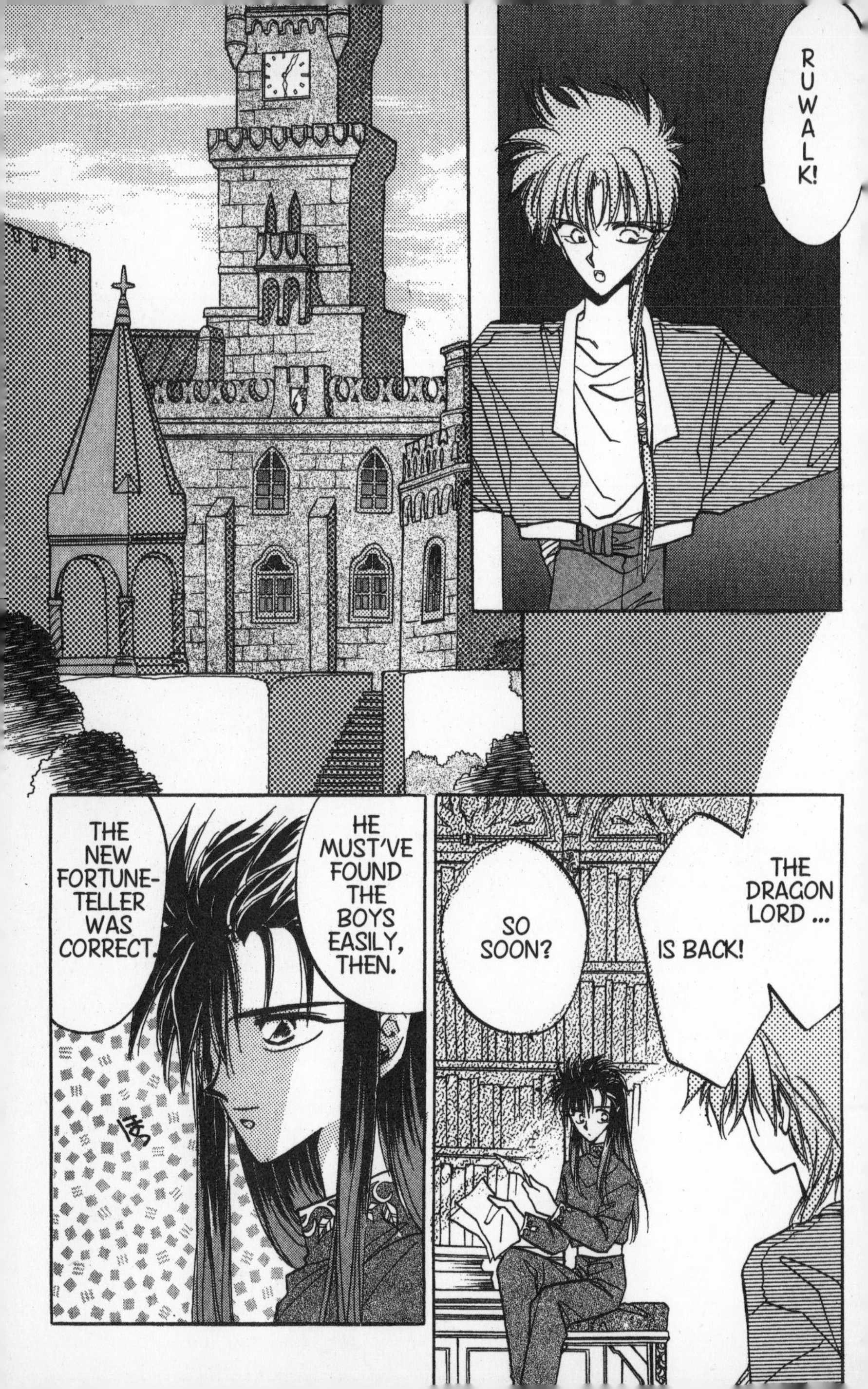
RUWALK!
THE DRAGON LORD ...
IS BACK!
SO SOON?
HE MUST'VE FOUND THE BOYS EASILY, THEN.
THE NEW FORTUNE-TELLER WAS CORRECT.

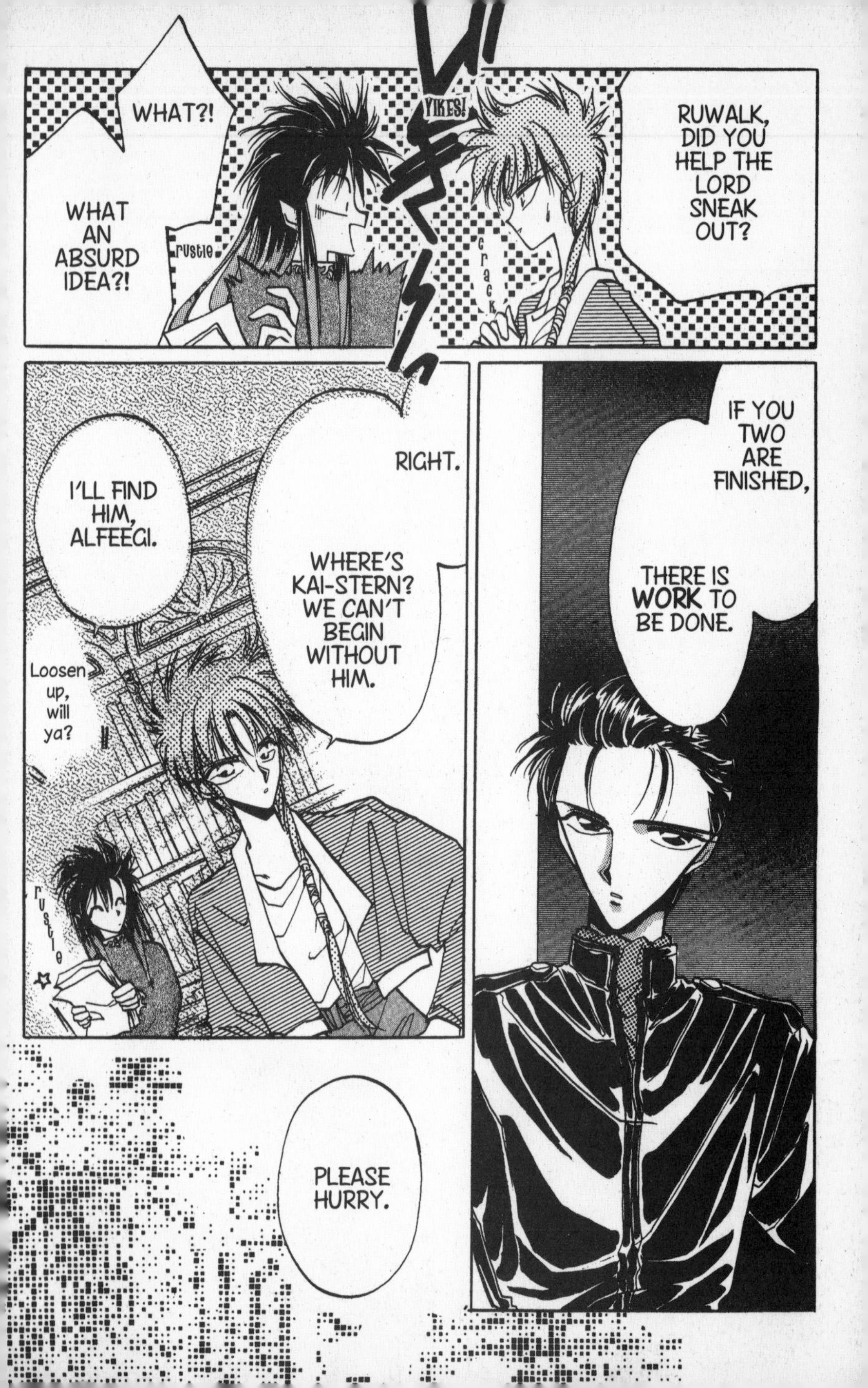
RUWALK, DID YOU HELP THE LORD SNEAK OUT?
YIKES!
crack
WHAT?!
WHAT AN ABSURD IDEA?!
rustle
IF YOU TWO ARE FINISHED,
THERE IS **WORK** TO BE DONE.
RIGHT.
WHERE'S KAI-STERN? WE CAN'T BEGIN WITHOUT HIM.
I'LL FIND HIM, ALFEEGI.
Loosen up, will ya?
rustle
PLEASE HURRY.

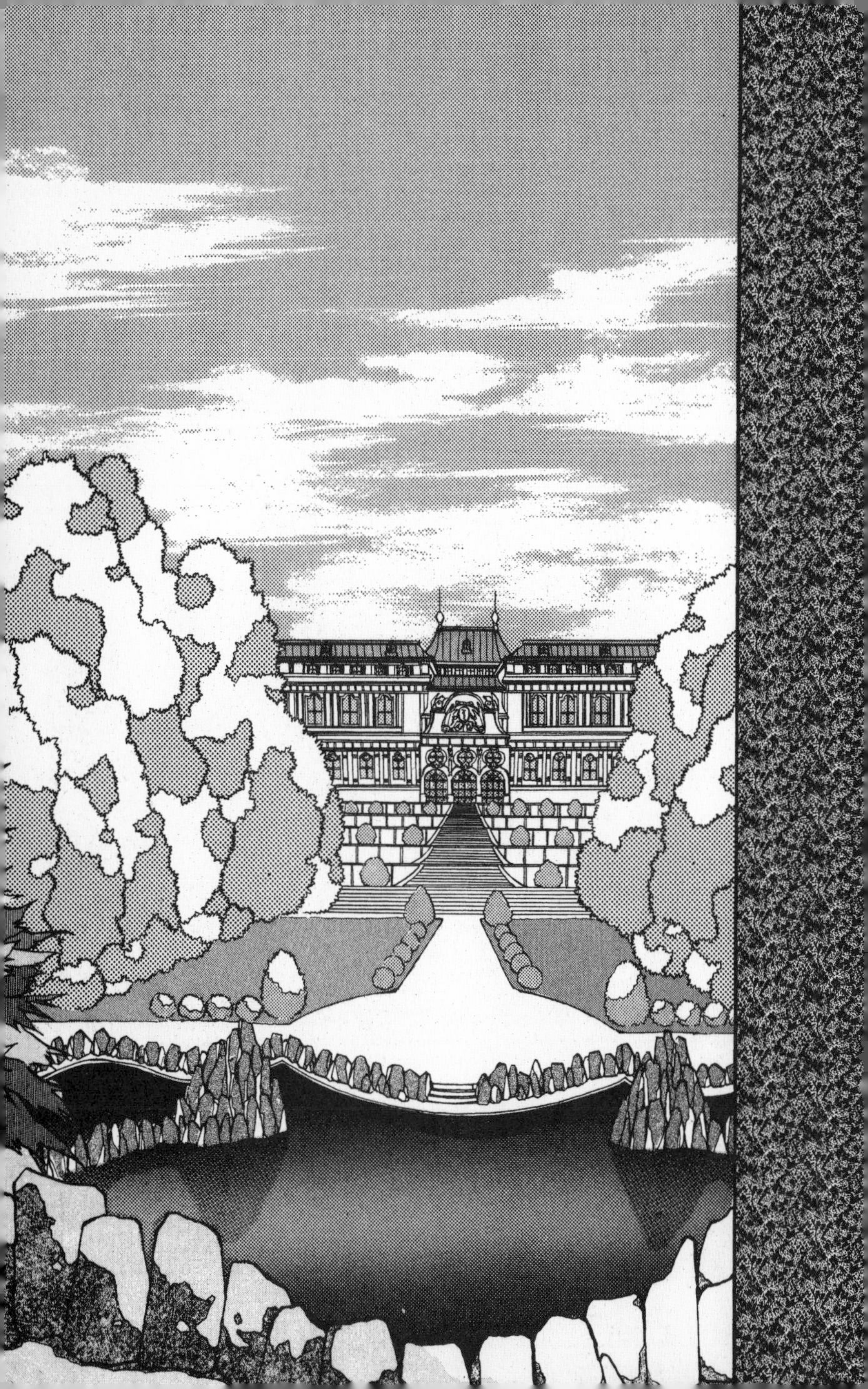

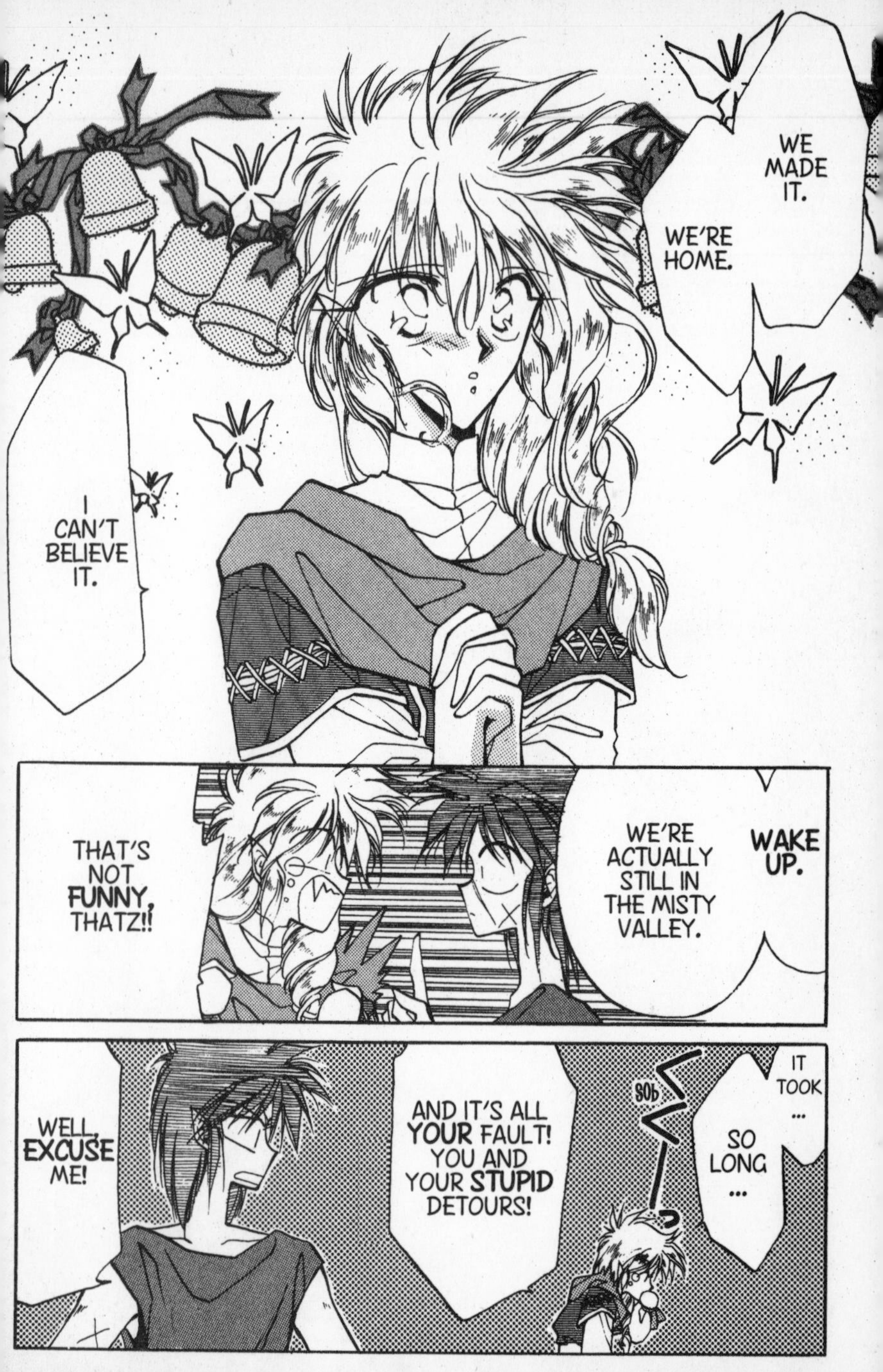
WE MADE IT.
WE'RE HOME.
I CAN'T BELIEVE IT.
WAKE UP.
WE'RE ACTUALLY STILL IN THE MISTY VALLEY.
THAT'S NOT FUNNY, THATZ!!
IT TOOK ...
SO LONG ...
SOB
AND IT'S ALL YOUR FAULT! YOU AND YOUR STUPID DETOURS!
WELL, EXCUSE ME!

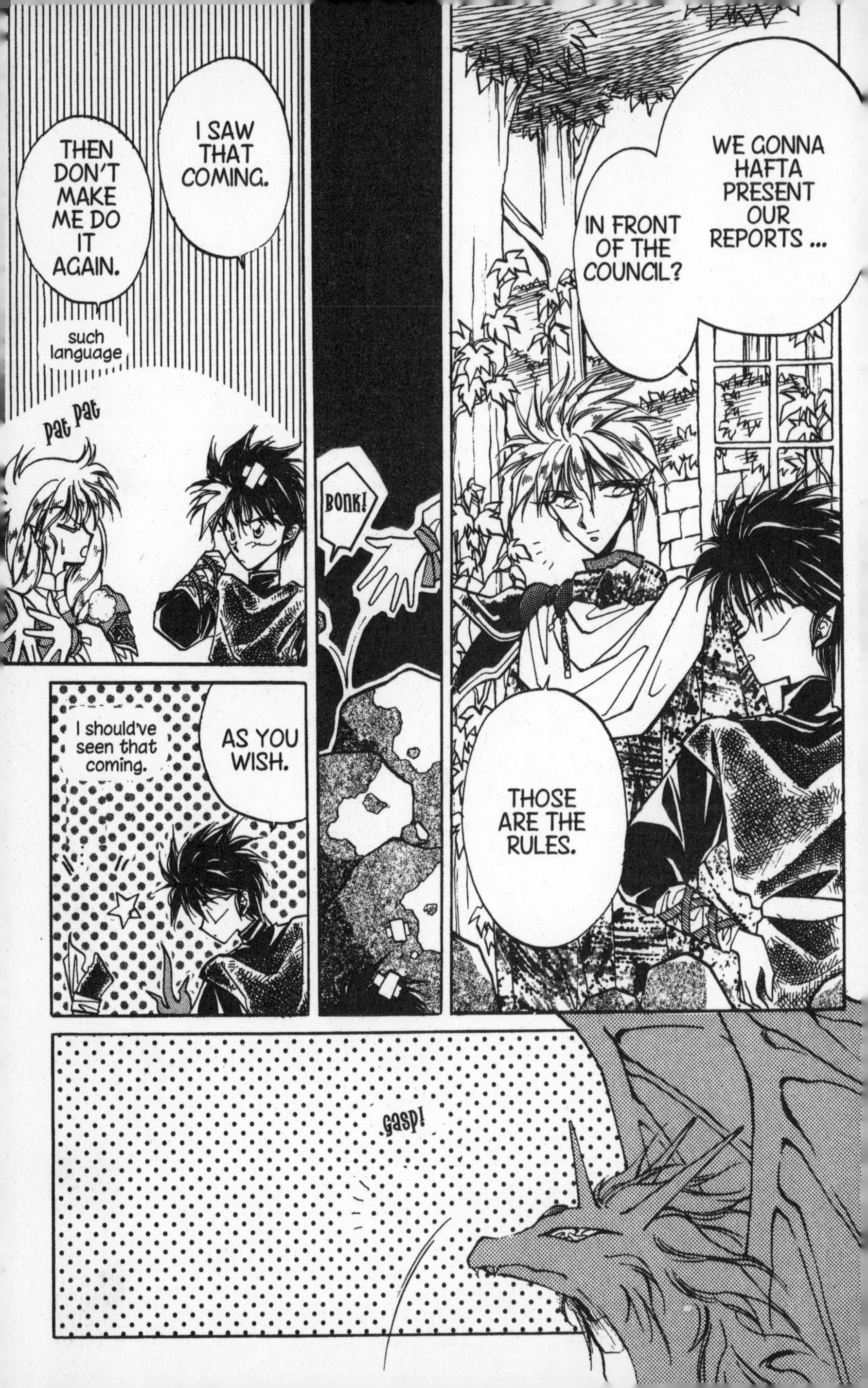
WE GONNA HAFTA PRESENT OUR REPORTS ...
IN FRONT OF THE COUNCIL?
THOSE ARE THE RULES.
BONK!
I SAW THAT COMING.
THEN DON'T MAKE ME DO IT AGAIN.
such language
pat pat
AS YOU WISH.
I should've seen that coming.
gasp!

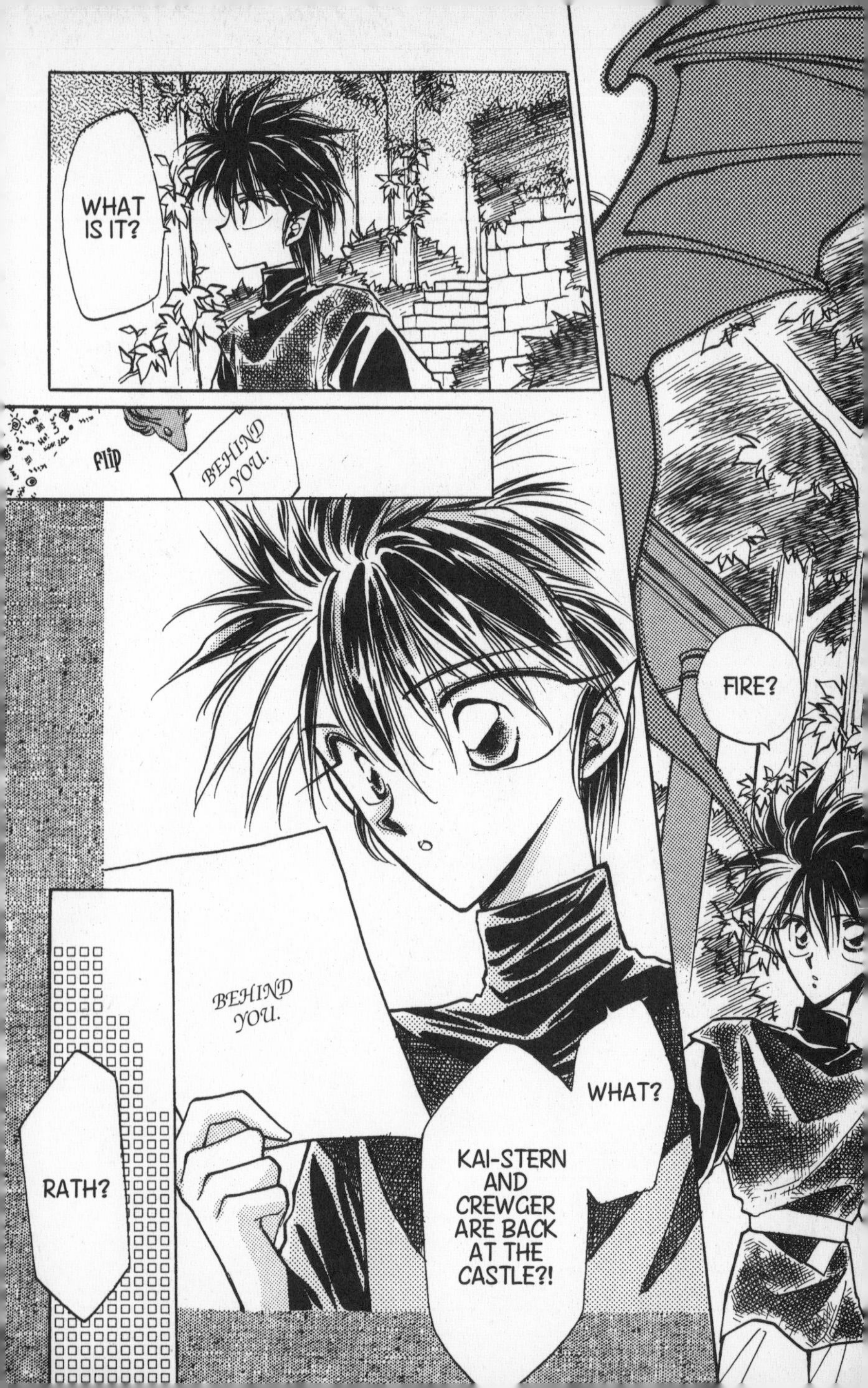
FIRE?
WHAT IS IT?
flip
BEHIND YOU.
BEHIND YOU.
WHAT?
KAI-STERN AND CREWGER ARE BACK AT THE CASTLE?!
RATH?

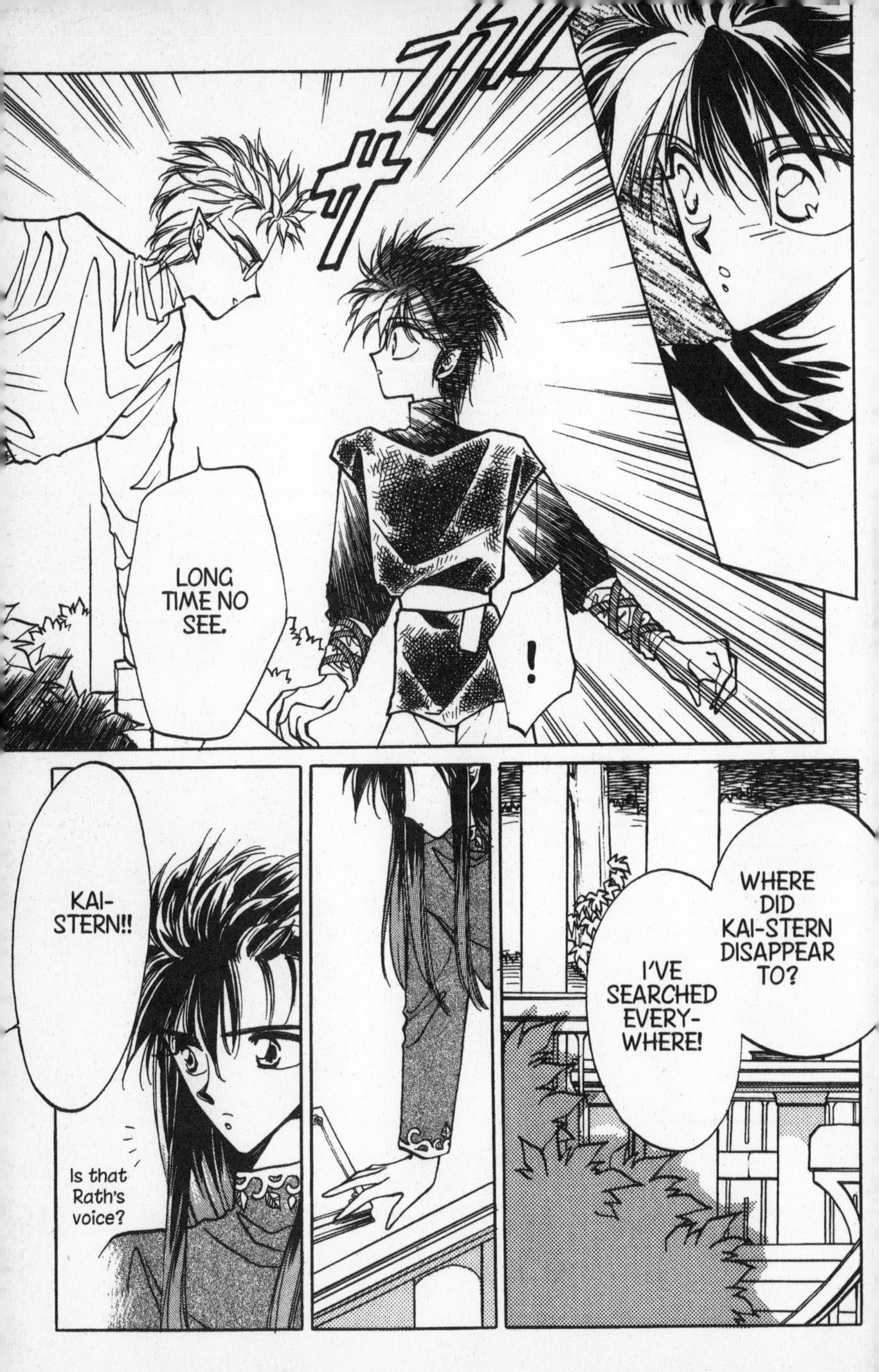
ガサ
!
LONG TIME NO SEE.
WHERE DID KAI-STERN DISAPPEAR TO?
I'VE SEARCHED EVERY-WHERE!
KAI-STERN!!
Is that Rath's voice?

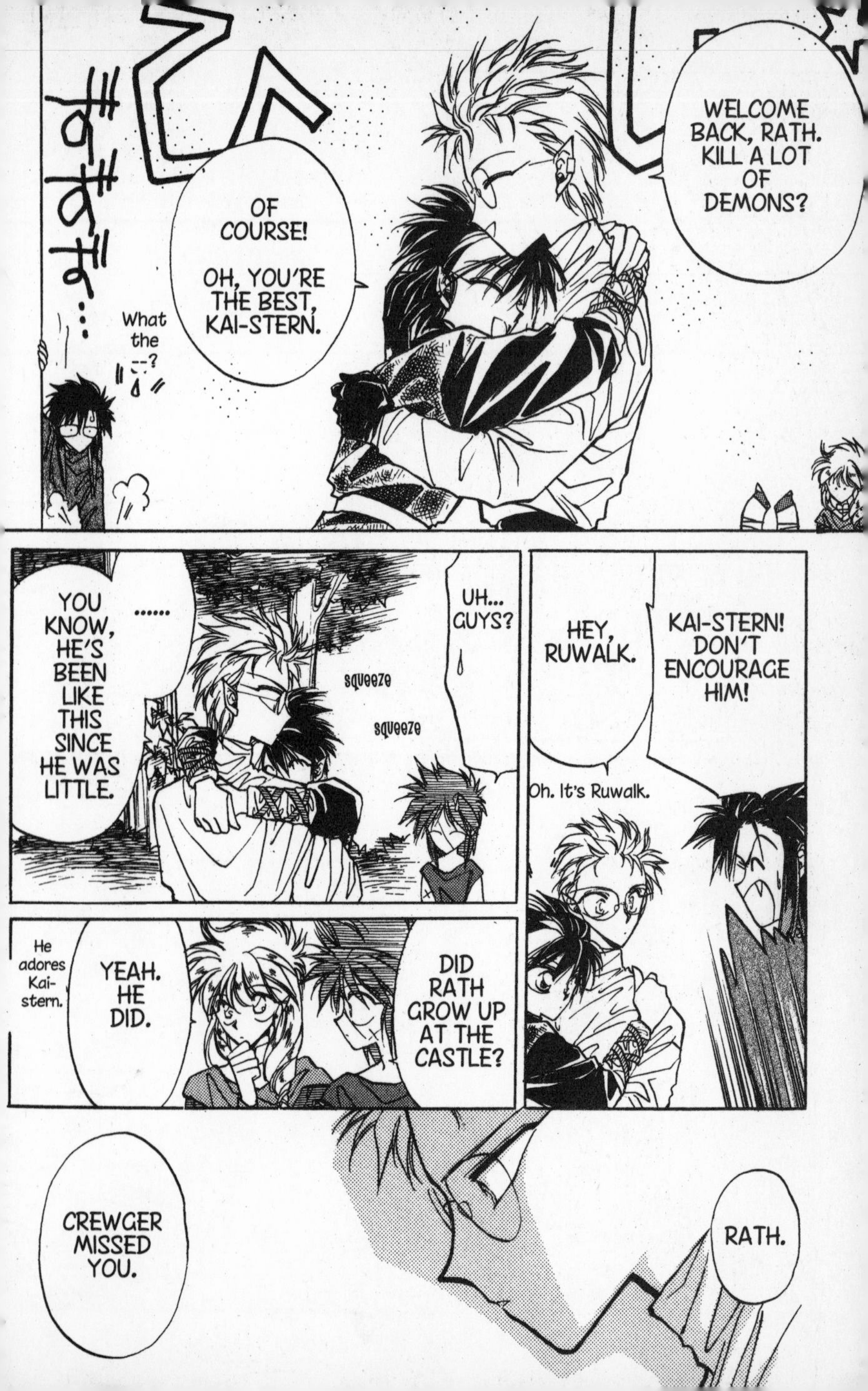
WELCOME BACK, RATH. KILL A LOT OF DEMONS?
OF COURSE!
OH, YOU'RE THE BEST, KAI-STERN.
ずずず…
What the --?
KAI-STERN! DON'T ENCOURAGE HIM!
HEY, RUWALK.
Oh. It's Ruwalk.
UH... GUYS?
squeeze
squeeze
......
YOU KNOW, HE'S BEEN LIKE THIS SINCE HE WAS LITTLE.
DID RATH GROW UP AT THE CASTLE?
YEAH. HE DID.
He adores Kai-stern.
RATH.
CREWGER MISSED YOU.

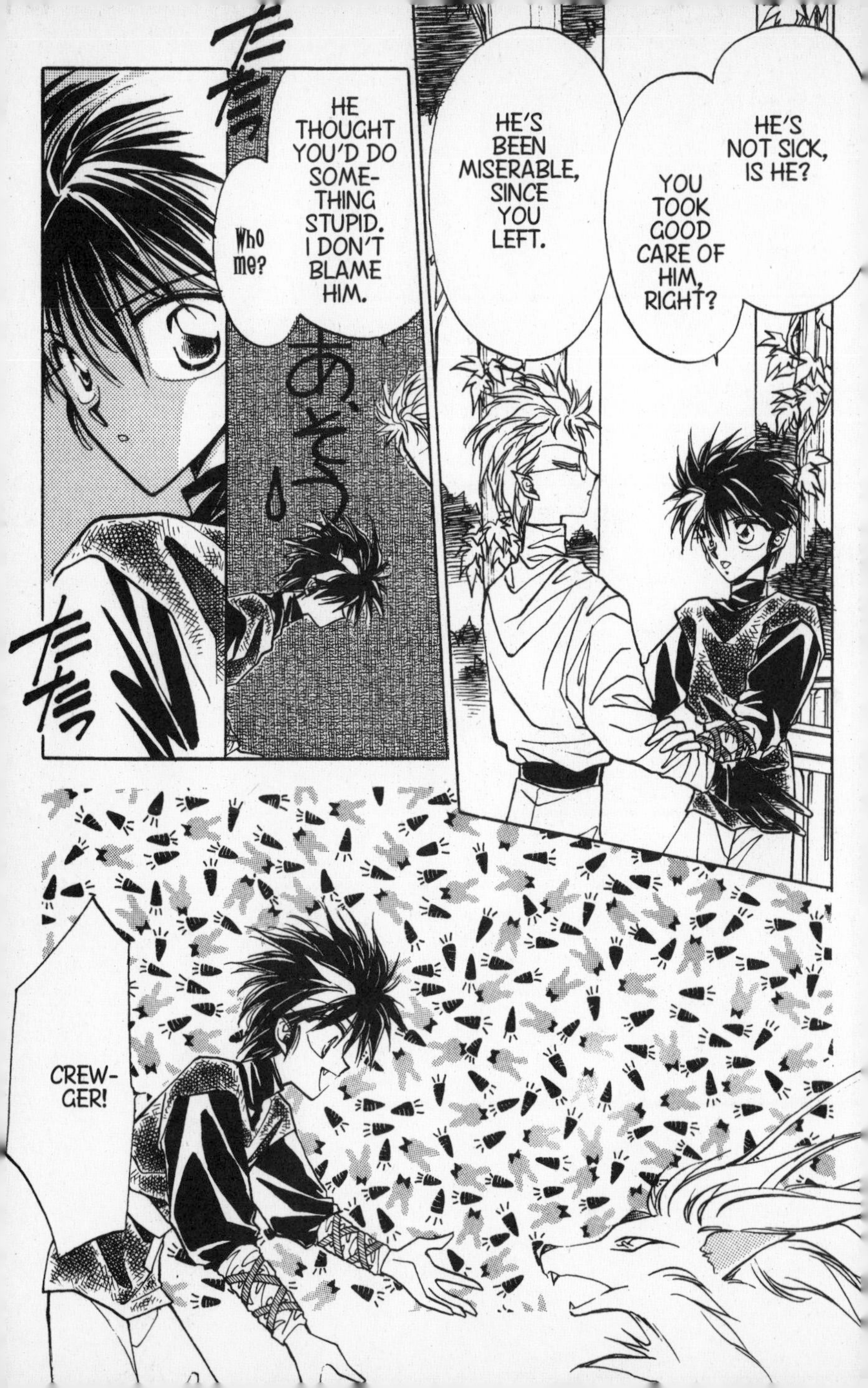
HE'S NOT SICK, IS HE?
YOU TOOK GOOD CARE OF HIM, RIGHT?
HE'S BEEN MISERABLE, SINCE YOU LEFT.
HE THOUGHT YOU'D DO SOME-THING STUPID. I DON'T BLAME HIM.
Who me?
あそう
CREW-GER!

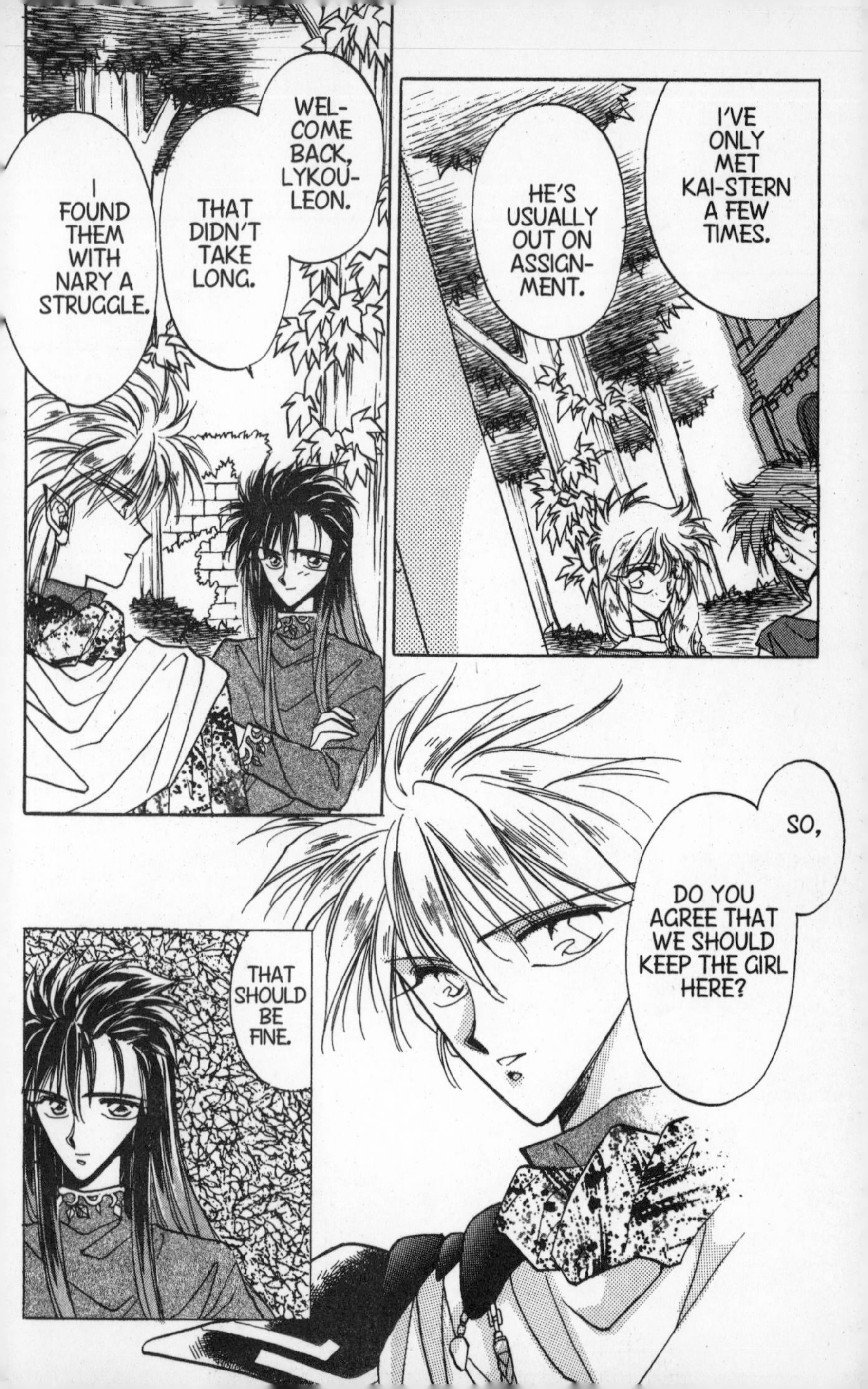
I'VE ONLY MET KAI-STERN A FEW TIMES.
HE'S USUALLY OUT ON ASSIGN-MENT.
WEL-COME BACK, LYKOU-LEON.
THAT DIDN'T TAKE LONG.
I FOUND THEM WITH NARY A STRUGGLE.
SO,
DO YOU AGREE THAT WE SHOULD KEEP THE GIRL HERE?
THAT SHOULD BE FINE.

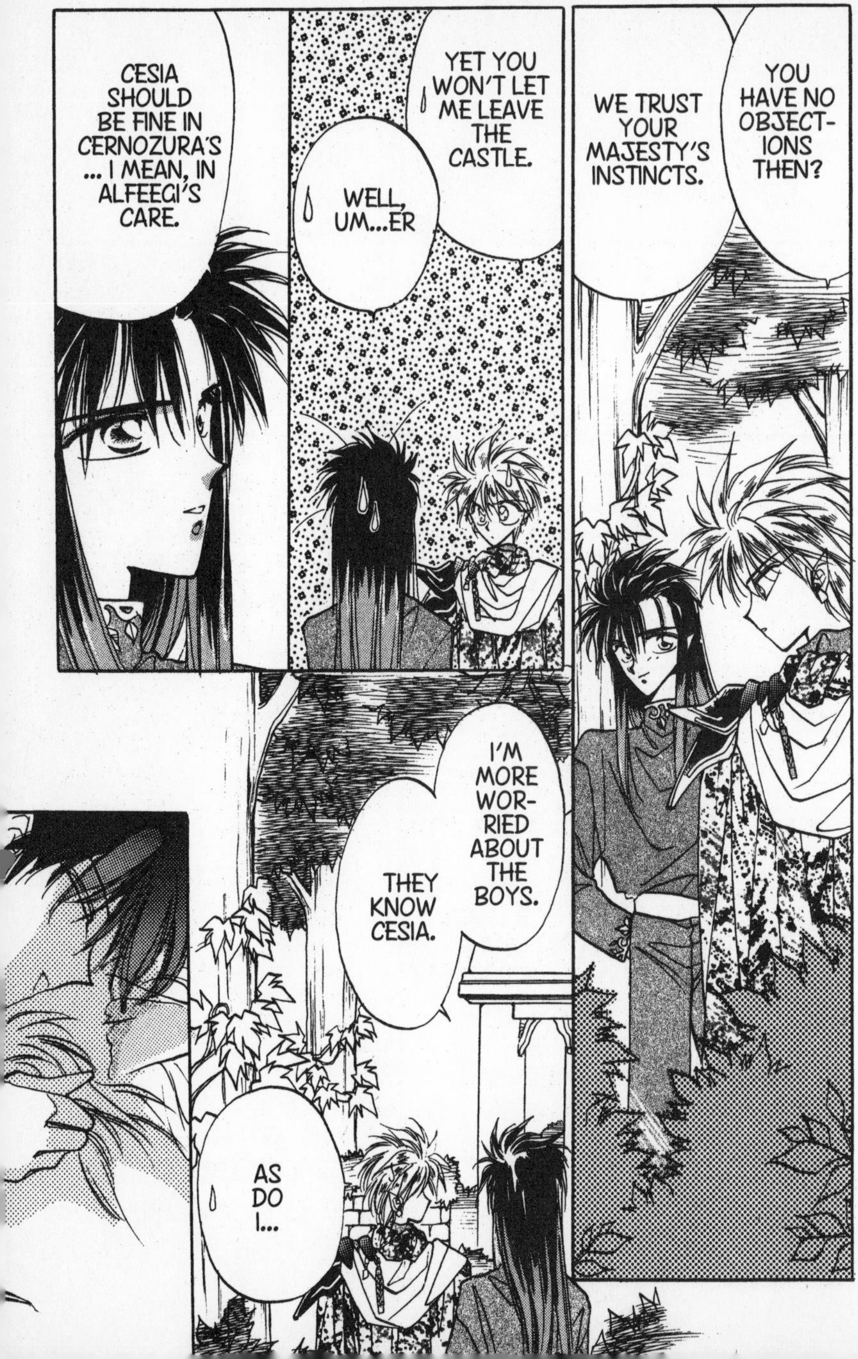
YOU HAVE NO OBJECTIONS THEN?
WE TRUST YOUR MAJESTY'S INSTINCTS.
YET YOU WON'T LET ME LEAVE THE CASTLE.
WELL, UM...ER
CESIA SHOULD BE FINE IN CERNOZURA'S ... I MEAN, IN ALFEEGI'S CARE.
I'M MORE WORRIED ABOUT THE BOYS.
THEY KNOW CESIA.
AS DO I...

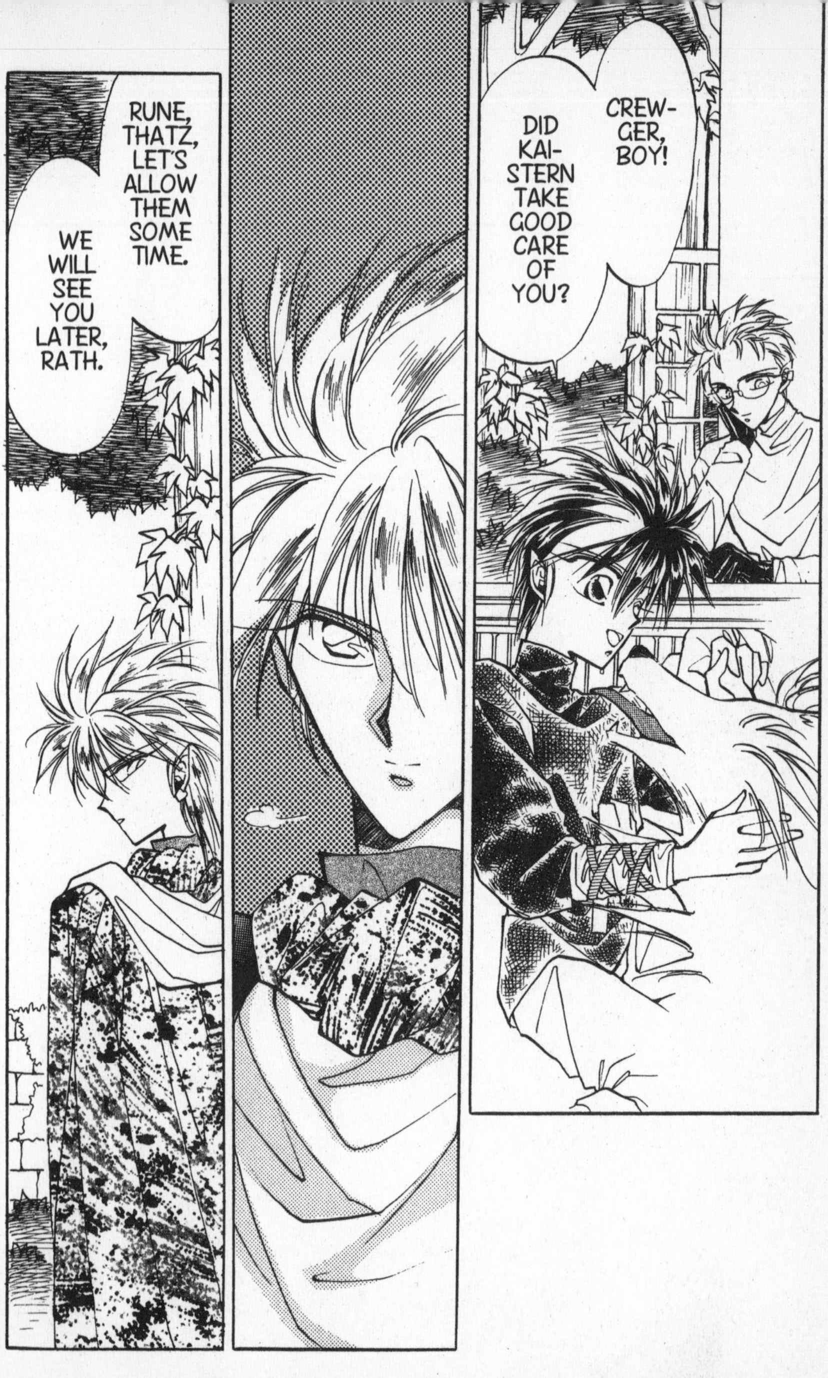
CREWGER, BOY!
DID KAISTERN TAKE GOOD CARE OF YOU?
RUNE, THATZ, LET'S ALLOW THEM SOME TIME.
WE WILL SEE YOU LATER, RATH.

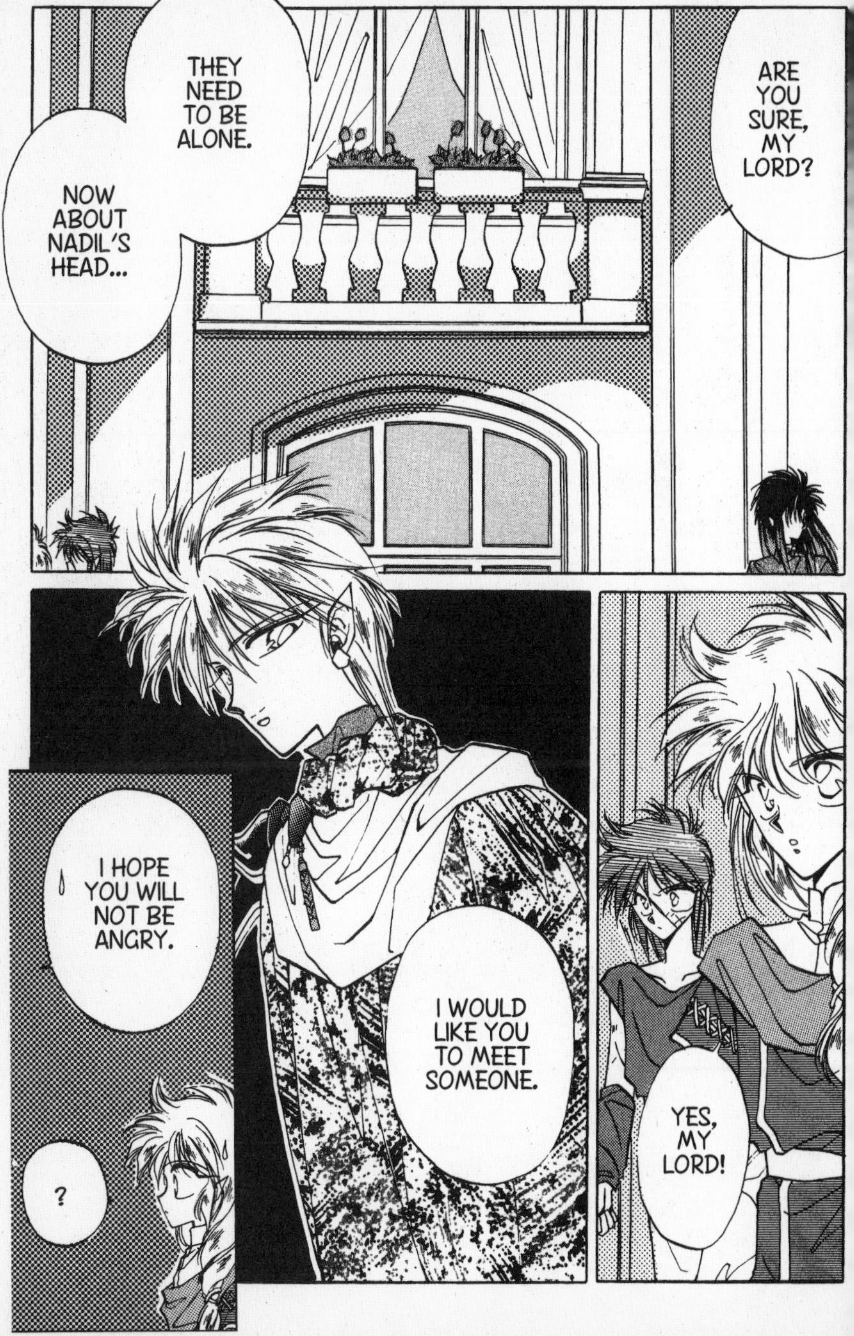
ARE YOU SURE, MY LORD?
THEY NEED TO BE ALONE.
NOW ABOUT NADIL'S HEAD...
YES, MY LORD!
I WOULD LIKE YOU TO MEET SOMEONE.
I HOPE YOU WILL NOT BE ANGRY.
?

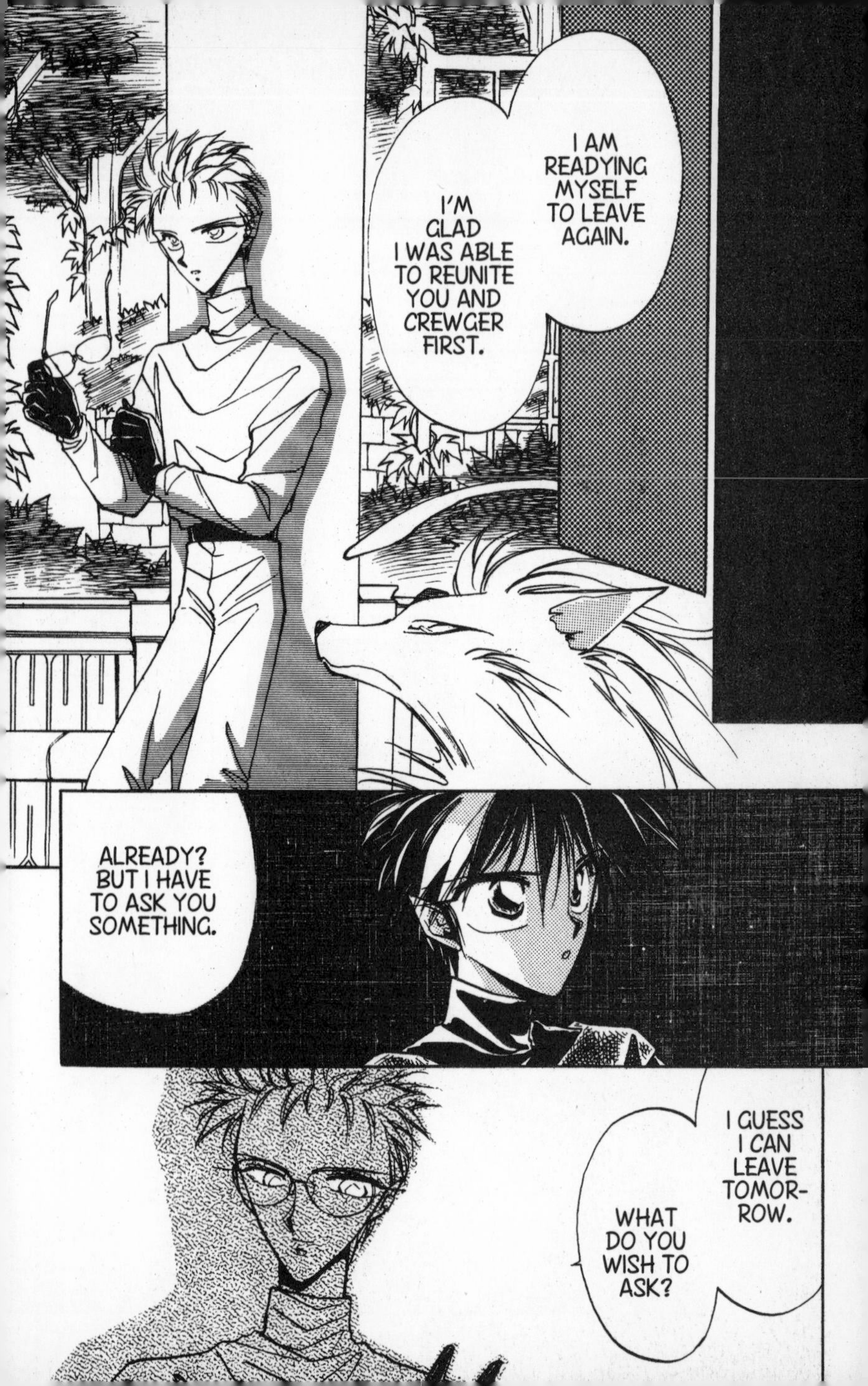
I AM READYING MYSELF TO LEAVE AGAIN.
I'M GLAD I WAS ABLE TO REUNITE YOU AND CREWGER FIRST.
ALREADY? BUT I HAVE TO ASK YOU SOMETHING.
I GUESS I CAN LEAVE TOMOR-ROW.
WHAT DO YOU WISH TO ASK?

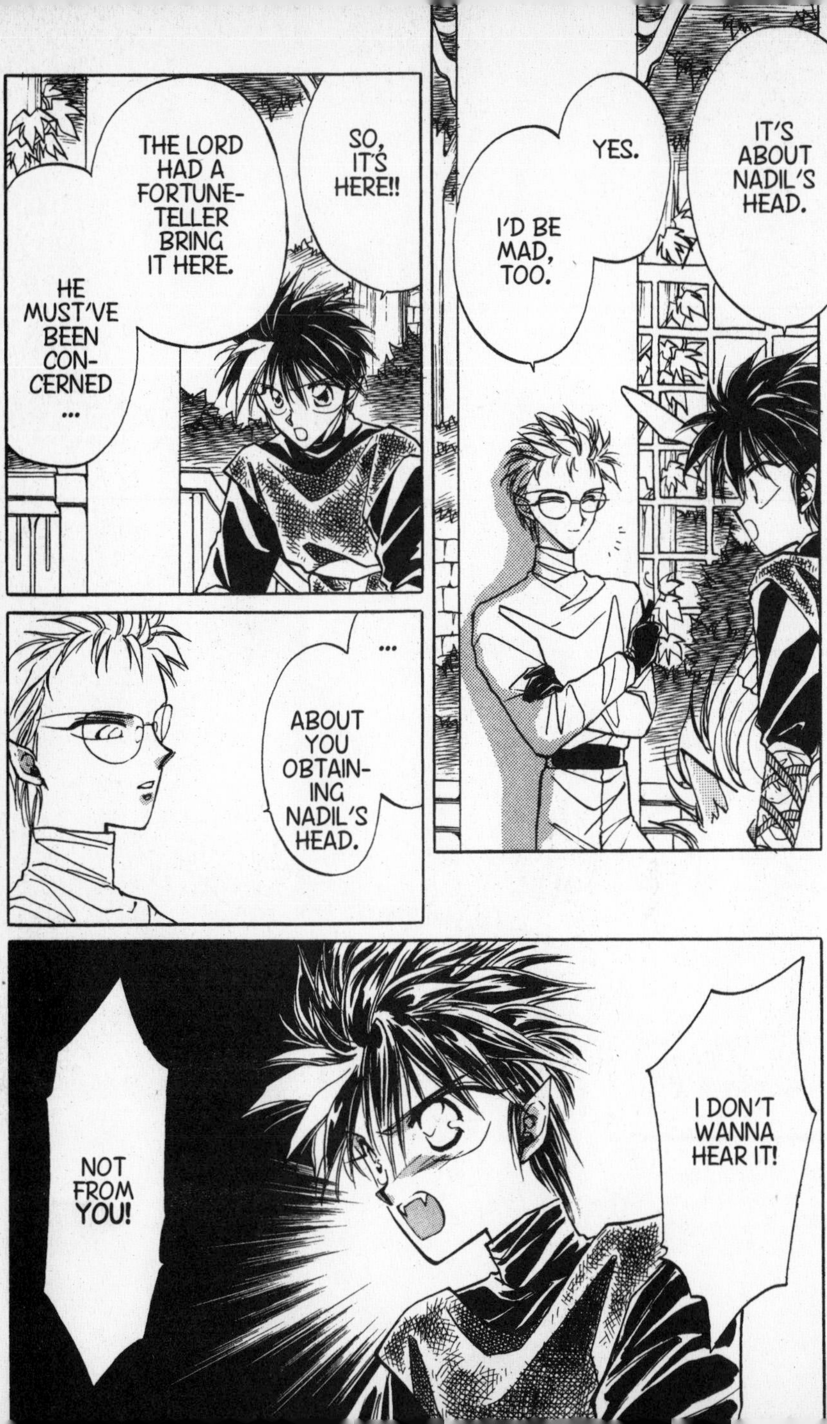
IT'S ABOUT NADIL'S HEAD.
YES. I'D BE MAD, TOO.
SO, IT'S HERE!!
THE LORD HAD A FORTUNE-TELLER BRING IT HERE.
HE MUST'VE BEEN CON-CERNED ...
... ABOUT YOU OBTAIN-ING NADIL'S HEAD.
I DON'T WANNA HEAR IT!
NOT FROM YOU!

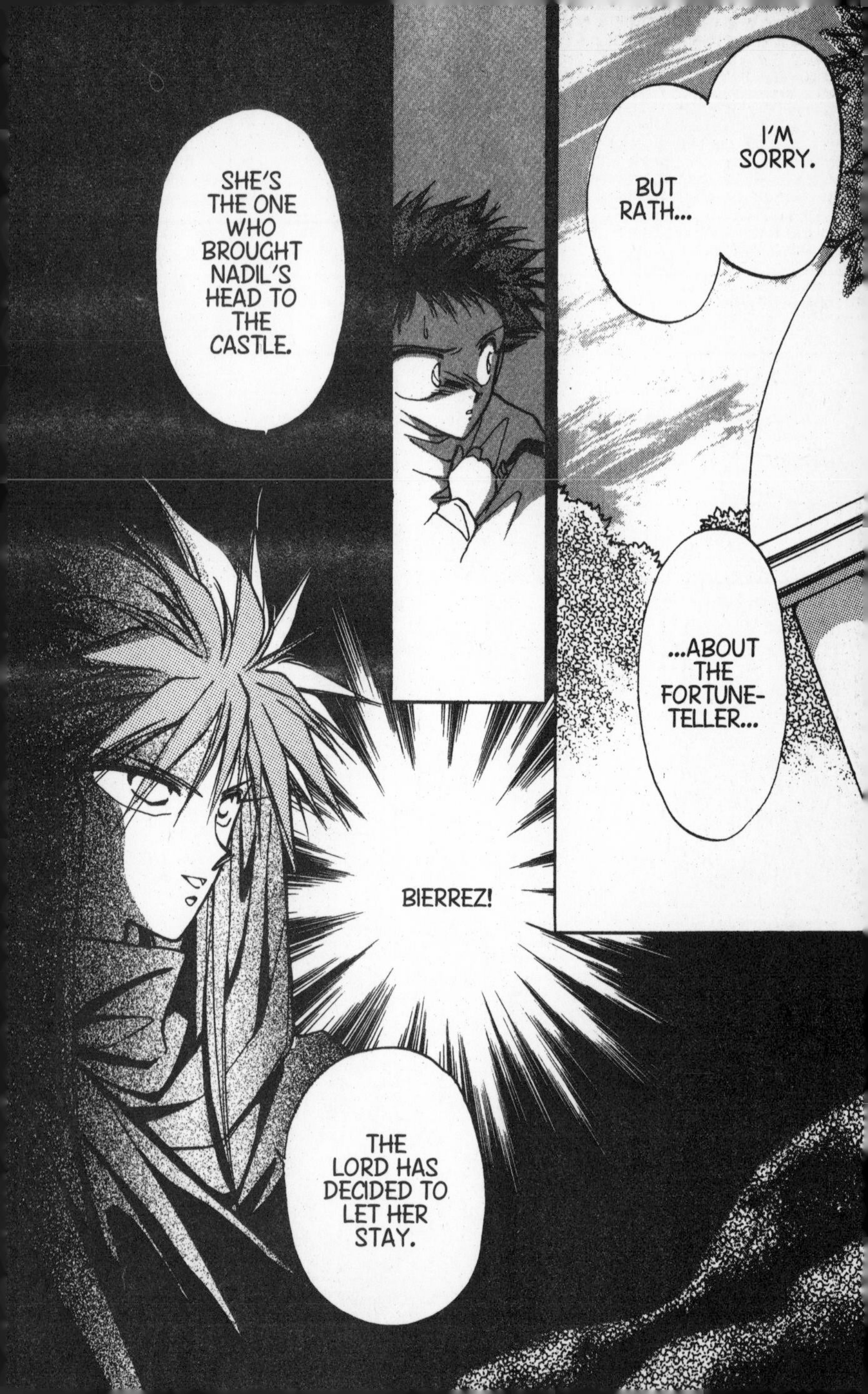
I'M SORRY.
BUT RATH...
...ABOUT THE FORTUNE-TELLER...
SHE'S THE ONE WHO BROUGHT NADIL'S HEAD TO THE CASTLE.
BIERREZ!
THE LORD HAS DECIDED TO LET HER STAY.

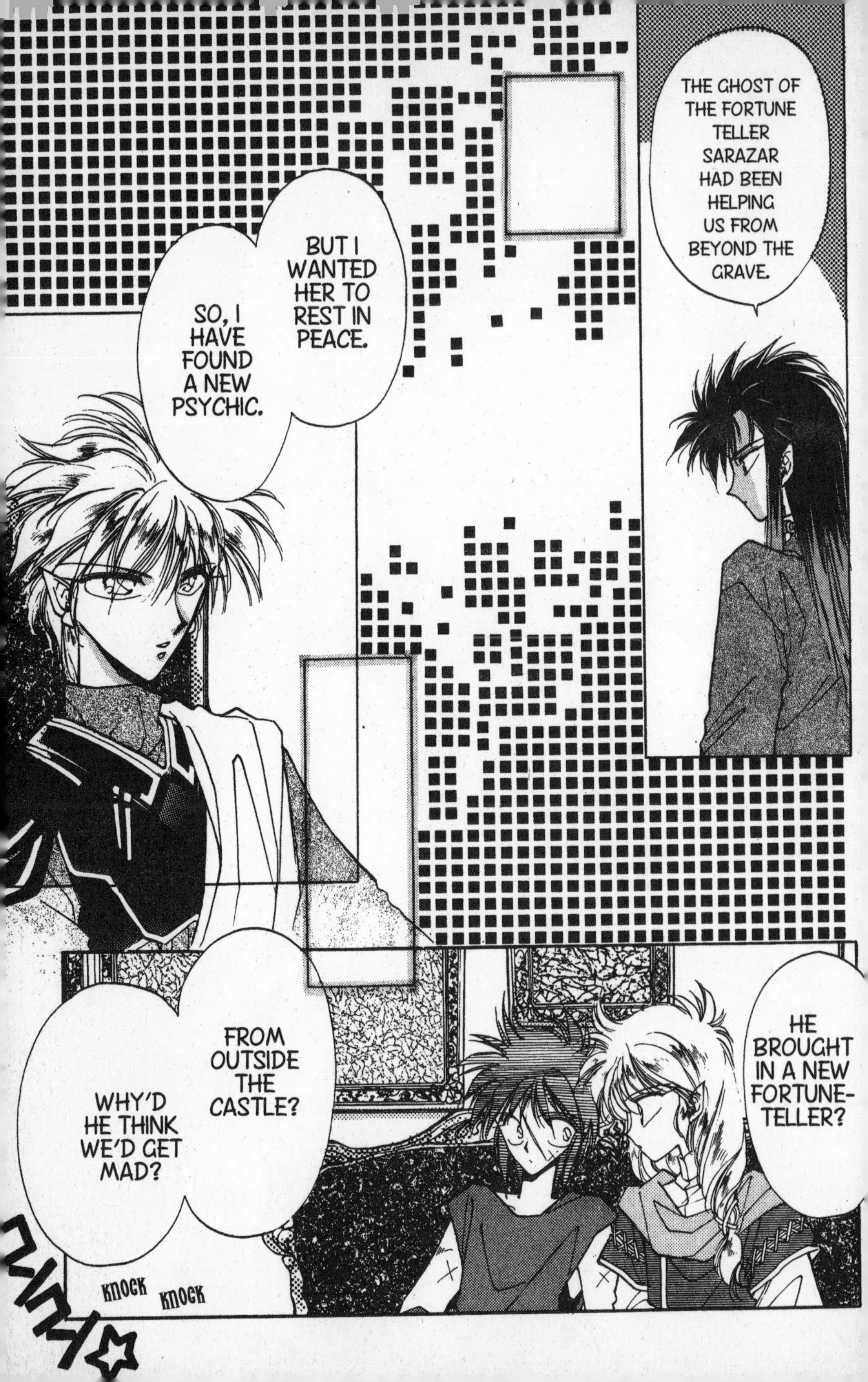
THE GHOST OF THE FORTUNE TELLER SARAZAR HAD BEEN HELPING US FROM BEYOND THE GRAVE.
BUT I WANTED HER TO REST IN PEACE.
SO, I HAVE FOUND A NEW PSYCHIC.
HE BROUGHT IN A NEW FORTUNE-TELLER?
FROM OUTSIDE THE CASTLE?
WHY'D HE THINK WE'D GET MAD?
KNOCK
KNOCK

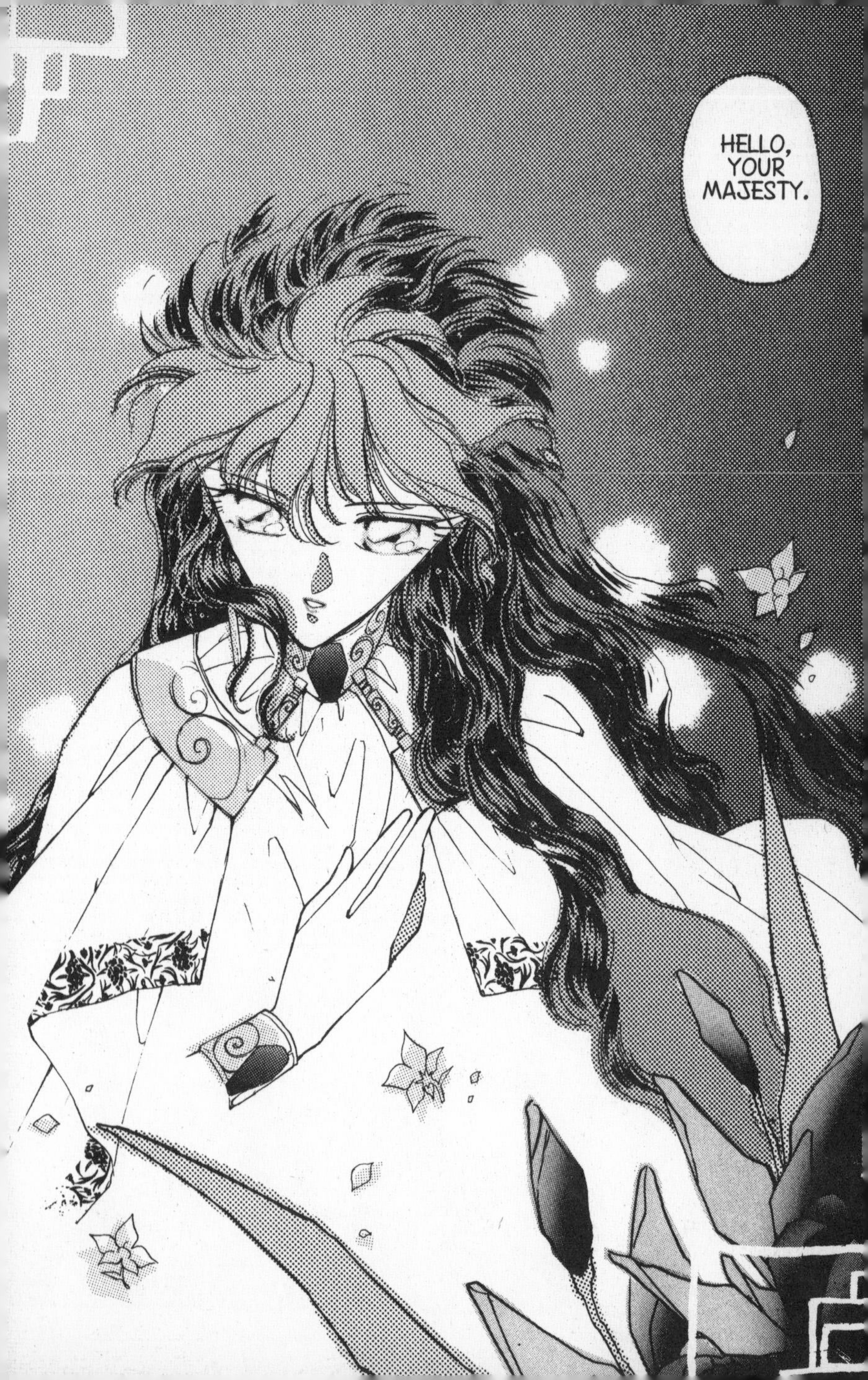
HELLO, YOUR MAJESTY.

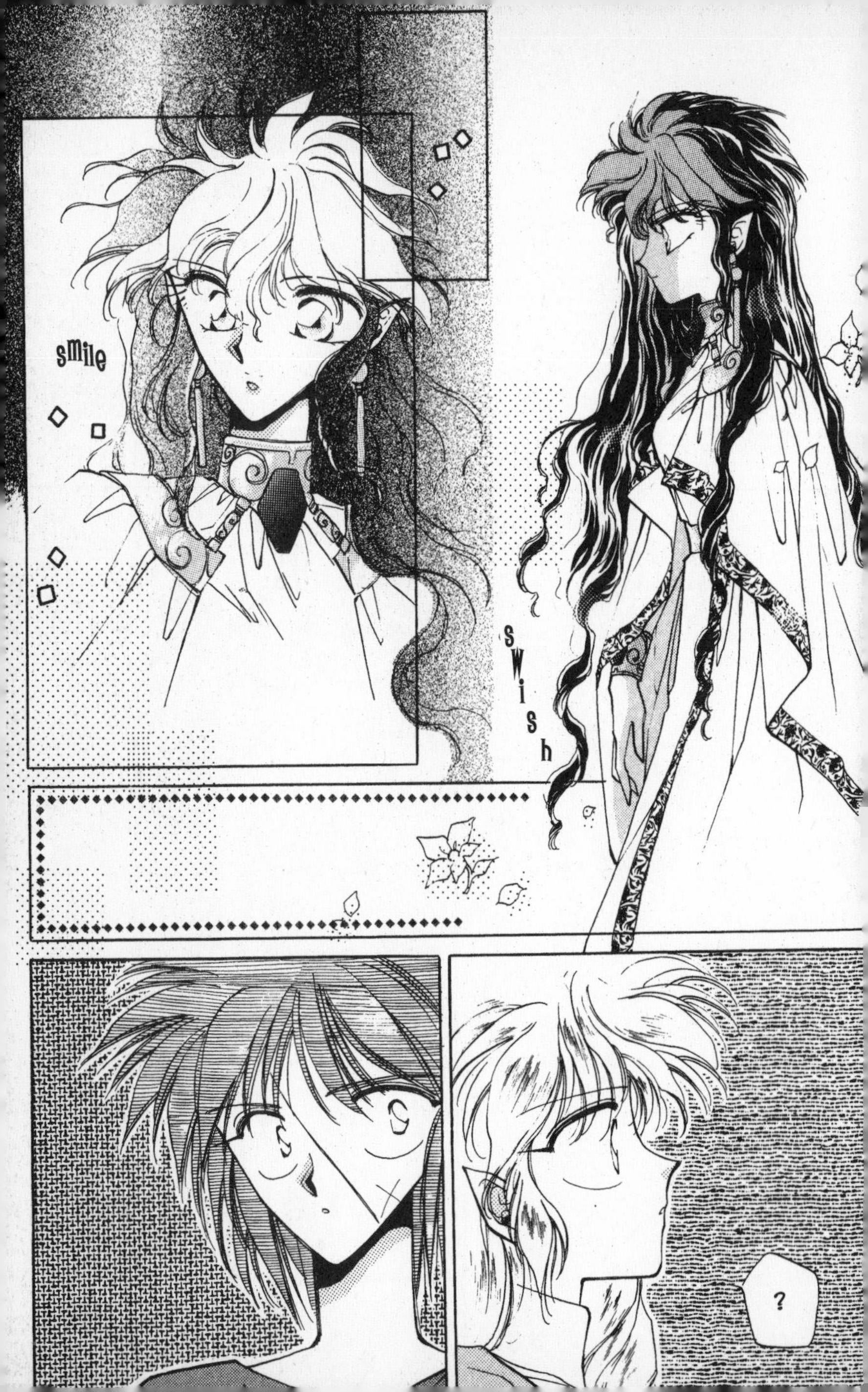
swish
smile
?

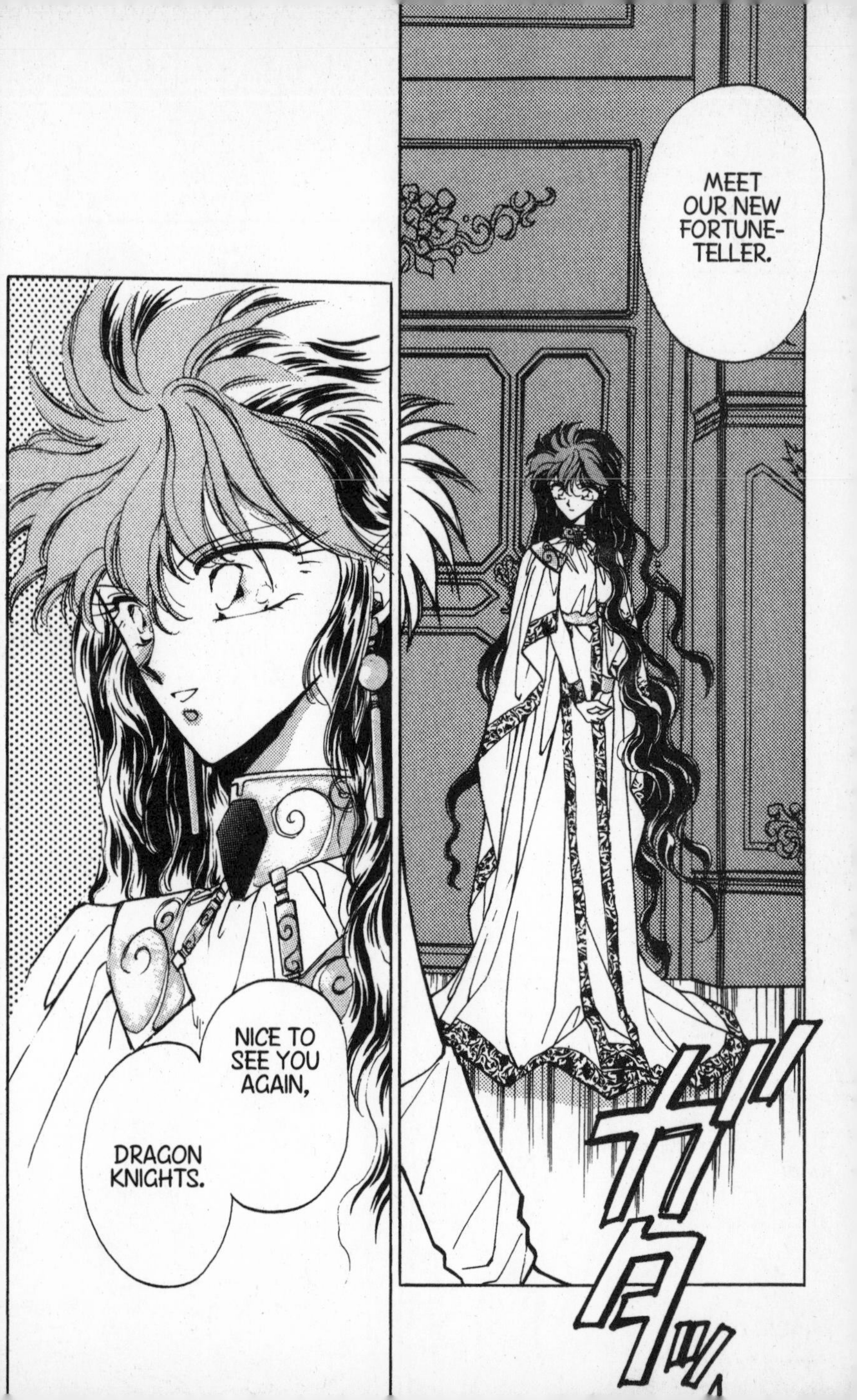
MEET OUR NEW FORTUNE-TELLER.
NICE TO SEE YOU AGAIN,
DRAGON KNIGHTS.

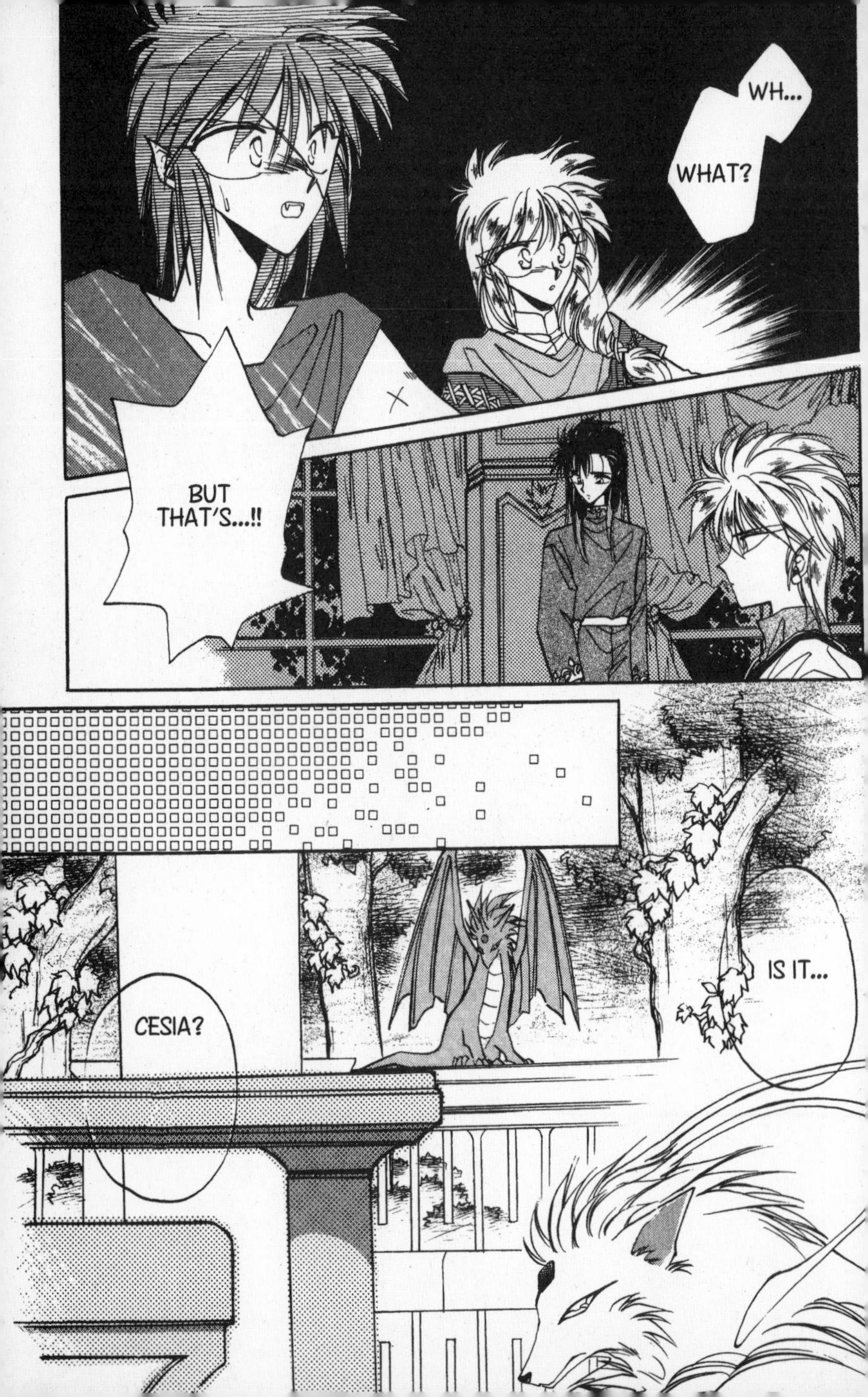
WH... WHAT?
BUT THAT'S...!!
IS IT...
CESIA?

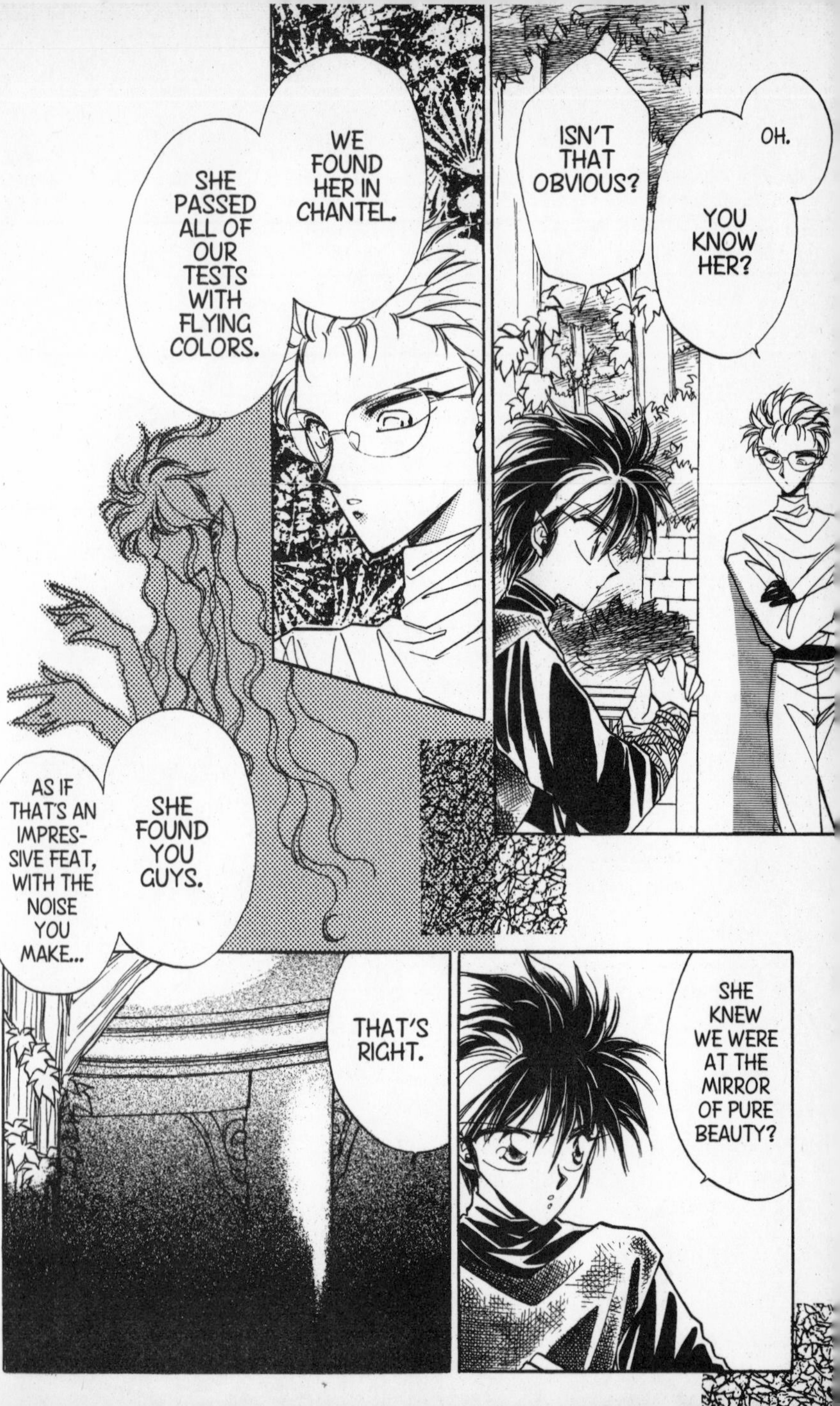
OH.
YOU KNOW HER?
ISN'T THAT OBVIOUS?
WE FOUND HER IN CHANTEL.
SHE PASSED ALL OF OUR TESTS WITH FLYING COLORS.
SHE FOUND YOU GUYS.
AS IF THAT'S AN IMPRES-SIVE FEAT, WITH THE NOISE YOU MAKE...
SHE KNEW WE WERE AT THE MIRROR OF PURE BEAUTY?
THAT'S RIGHT.

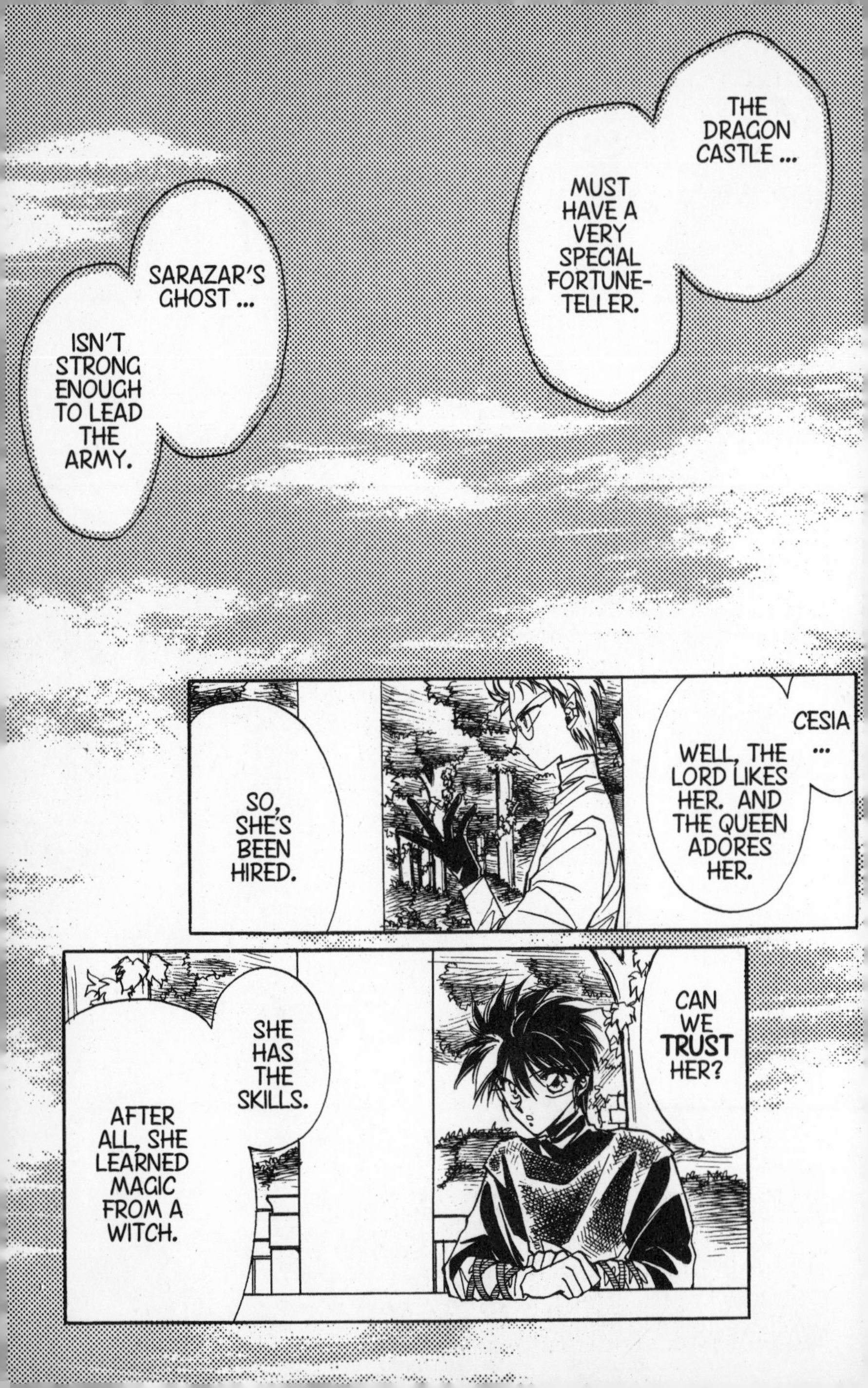
THE DRAGON CASTLE ...
MUST HAVE A VERY SPECIAL FORTUNE-TELLER.
SARAZAR'S GHOST ...
ISN'T STRONG ENOUGH TO LEAD THE ARMY.
CESIA ...
WELL, THE LORD LIKES HER. AND THE QUEEN ADORES HER.
SO, SHE'S BEEN HIRED.
CAN WE TRUST HER?
SHE HAS THE SKILLS.
AFTER ALL, SHE LEARNED MAGIC FROM A WITCH.

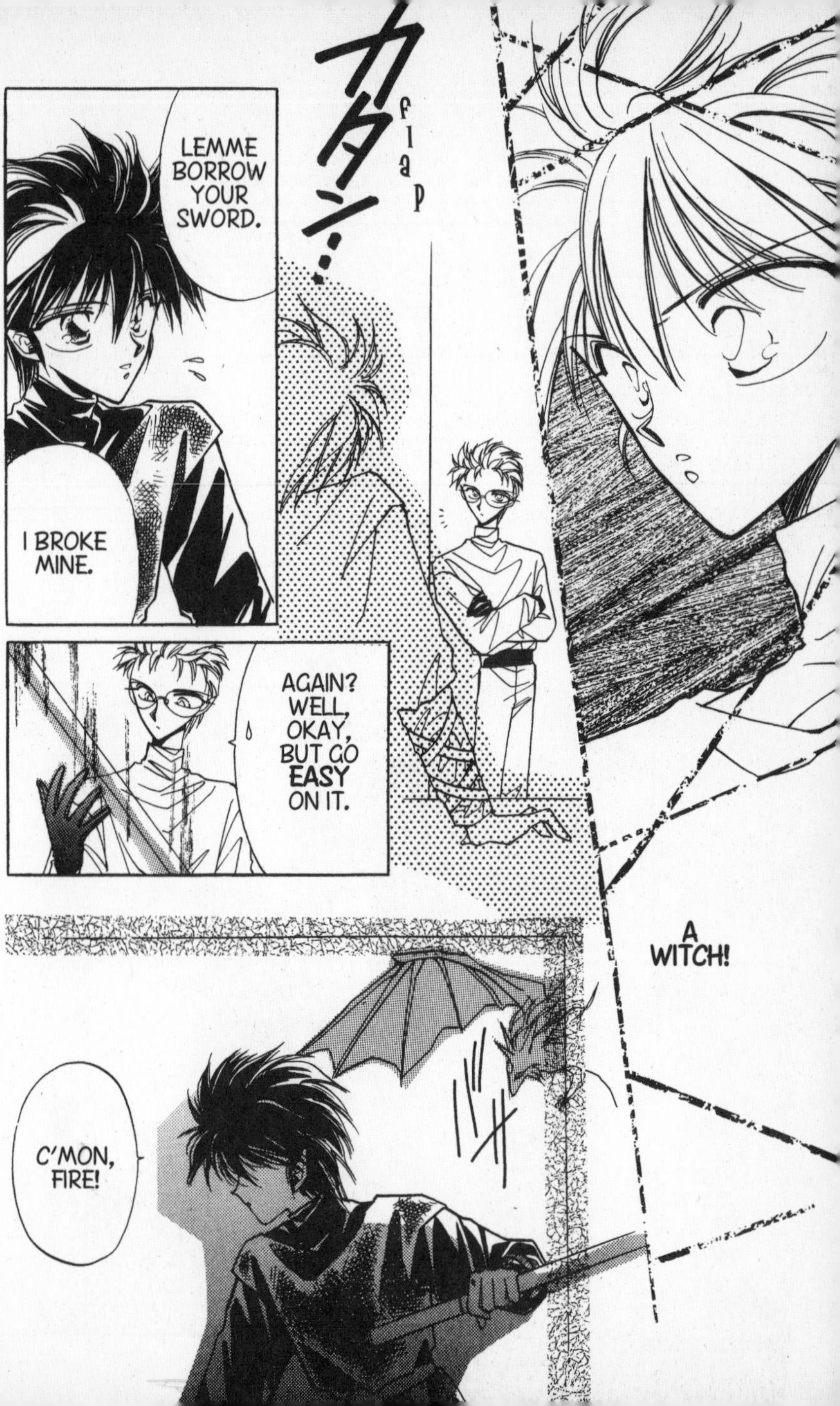
A WITCH!
カタン…
flap
LEMME BORROW YOUR SWORD.
I BROKE MINE.
AGAIN? WELL, OKAY, BUT GO EASY ON IT.
C'MON, FIRE!

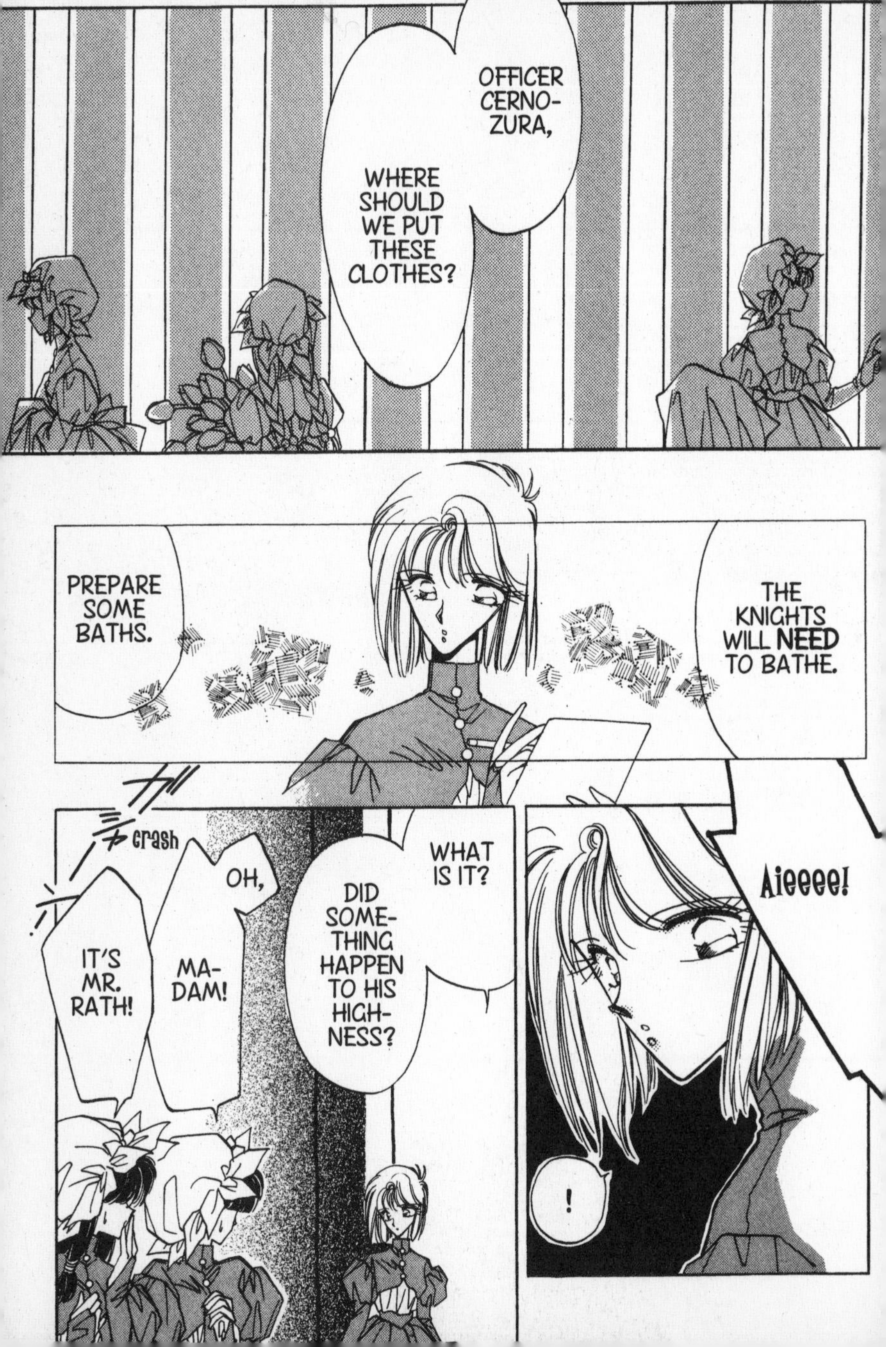
OFFICER CERNO-ZURA,
WHERE SHOULD WE PUT THESE CLOTHES?
THE KNIGHTS WILL **NEED** TO BATHE.
PREPARE SOME BATHS.
Aieeeee!
!
WHAT IS IT?
DID SOME-THING HAPPEN TO HIS HIGH-NESS?
OH,
MA-DAM!
crash
IT'S MR. RATH!

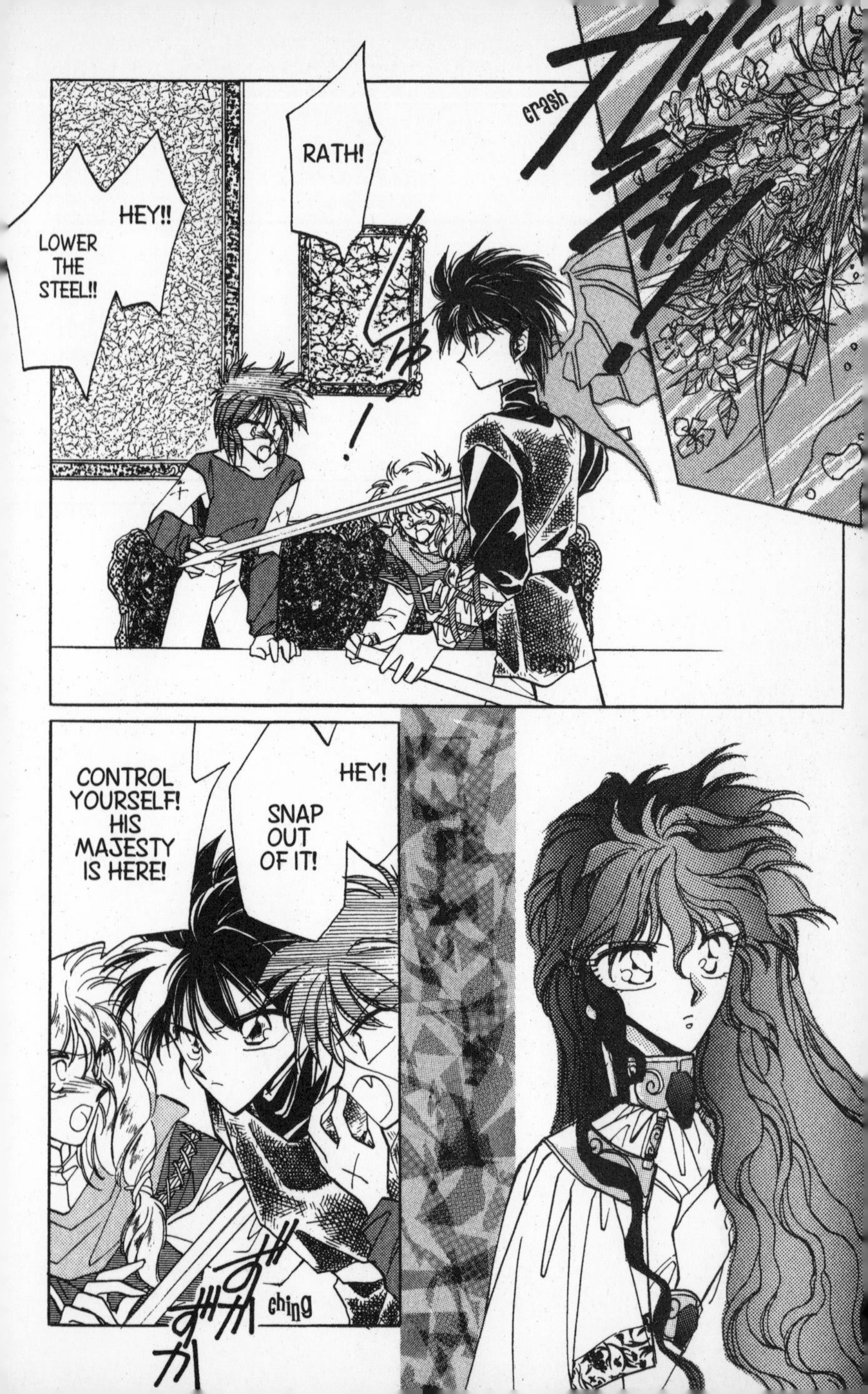
crash
RATH!
HEY!! LOWER THE STEEL!!
crash
HEY! SNAP OUT OF IT!
CONTROL YOURSELF! HIS MAJESTY IS HERE!
ching

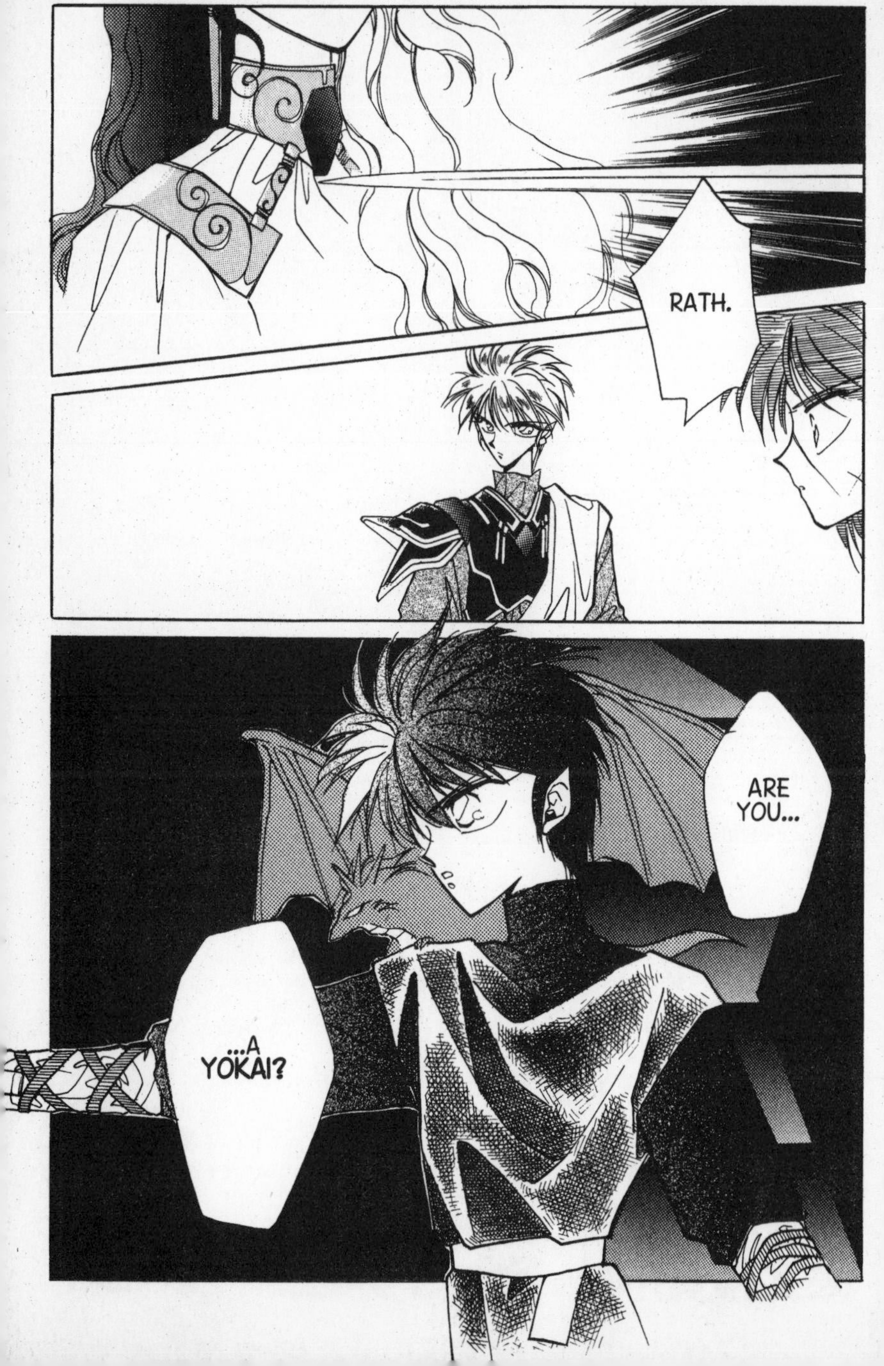
RATH.
ARE YOU...
...A YOKAI?

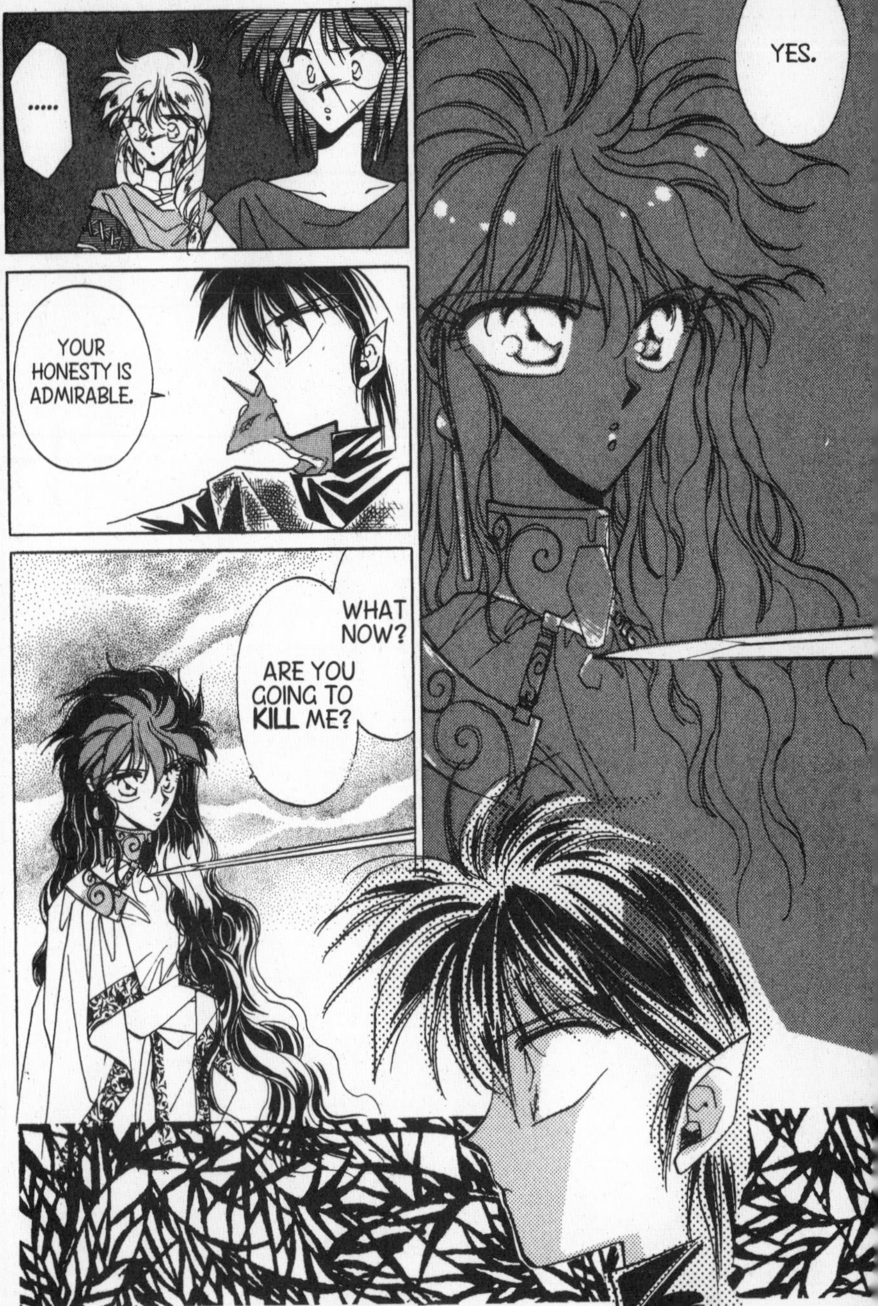
YES.
......
YOUR HONESTY IS ADMIRABLE.
WHAT NOW?
ARE YOU GOING TO KILL ME?

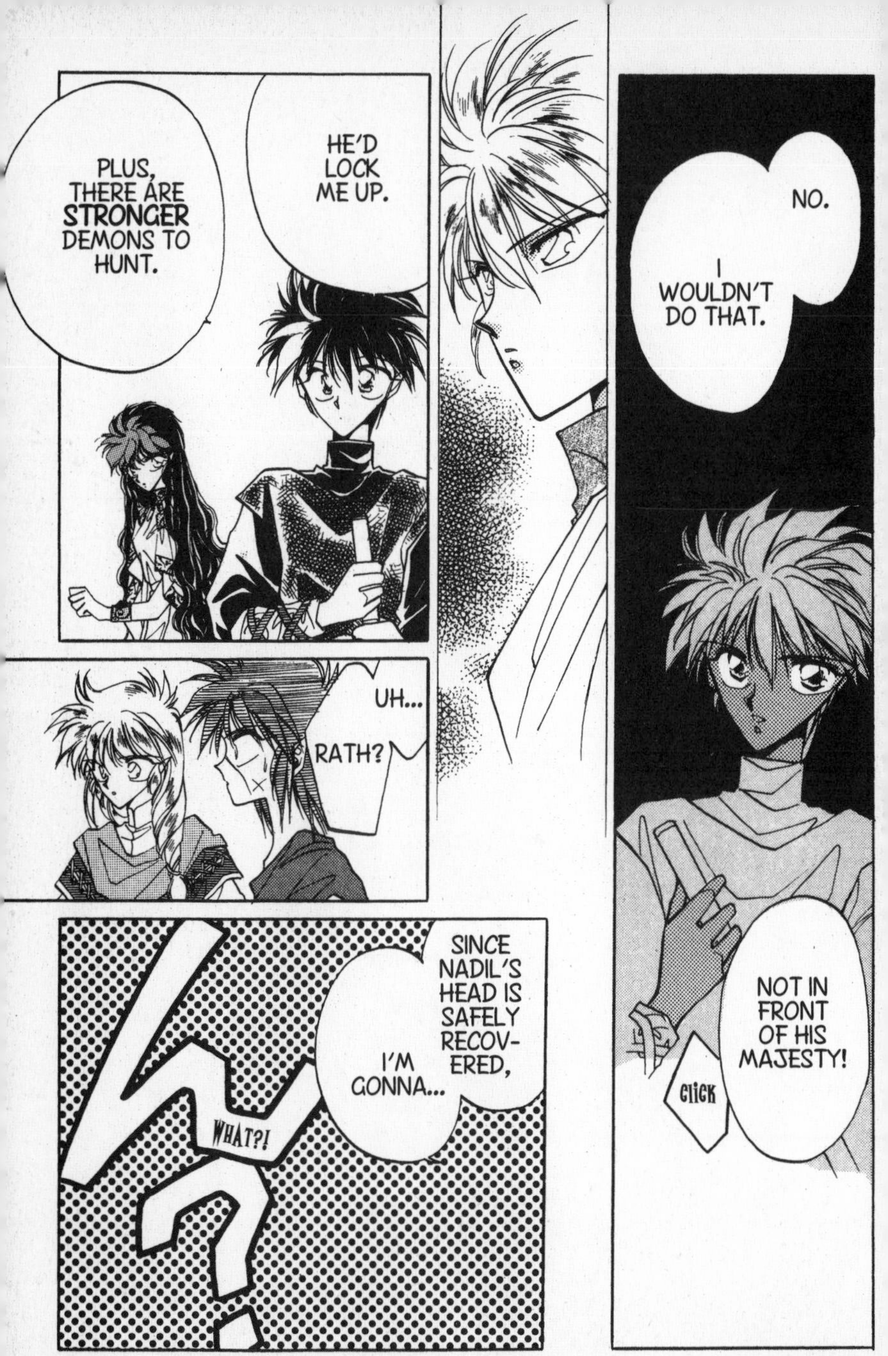
NO.
I WOULDN'T DO THAT.
CLICK
NOT IN FRONT OF HIS MAJESTY!
HE'D LOCK ME UP.
PLUS, THERE ARE **STRONGER** DEMONS TO HUNT.
UH...
RATH?
SINCE NADIL'S HEAD IS SAFELY RECOVERED,
I'M GONNA...
WHAT?!

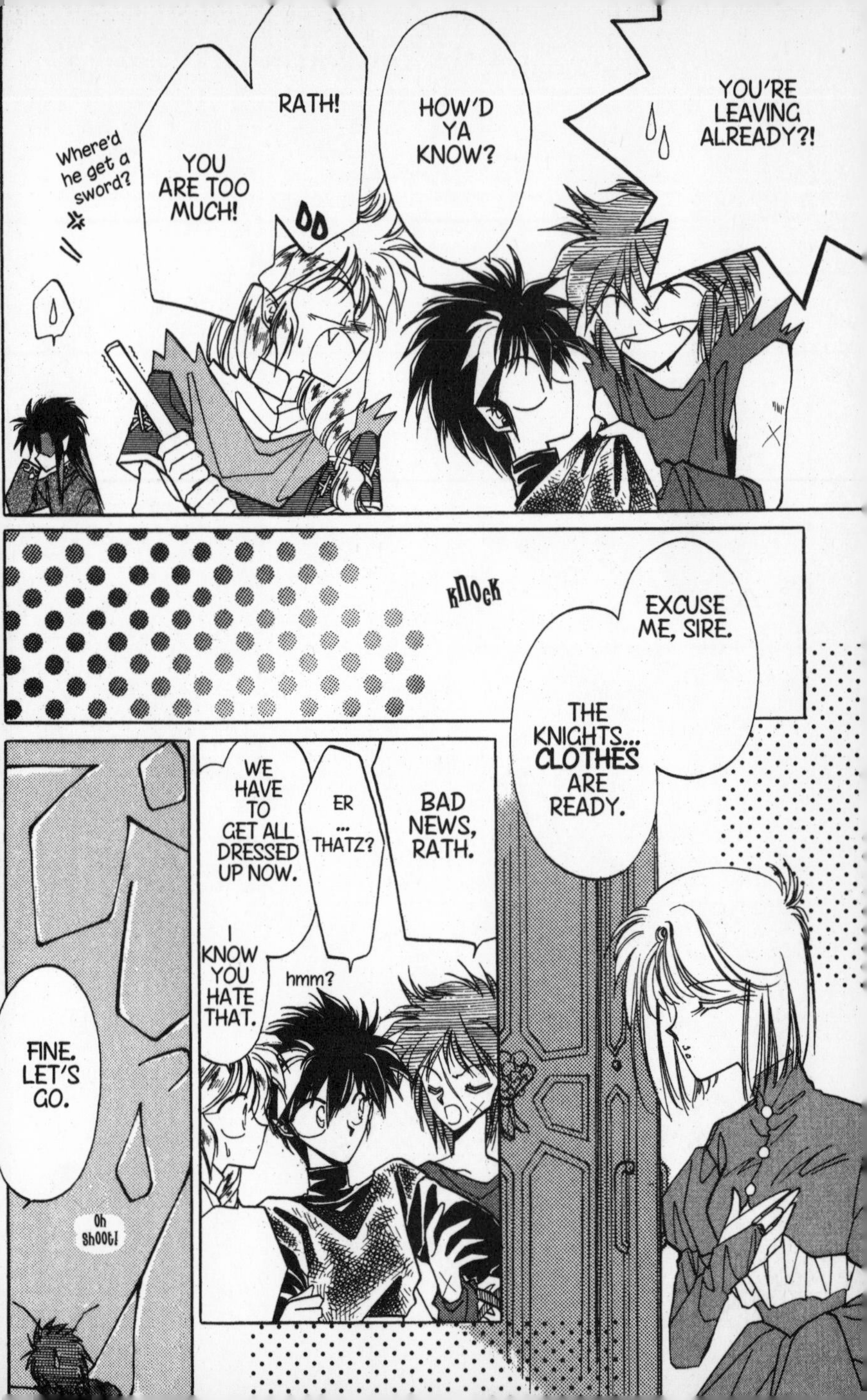
YOU'RE LEAVING ALREADY?!
HOW'D YA KNOW?
RATH!
YOU ARE TOO MUCH!
Where'd he get a sword?
KNOCK
EXCUSE ME, SIRE.
THE KNIGHTS... CLOTHES ARE READY.
BAD NEWS, RATH.
ER ... THATZ?
WE HAVE TO GET ALL DRESSED UP NOW.
hmm?
I KNOW YOU HATE THAT.
FINE. LET'S GO.
Oh shoot!

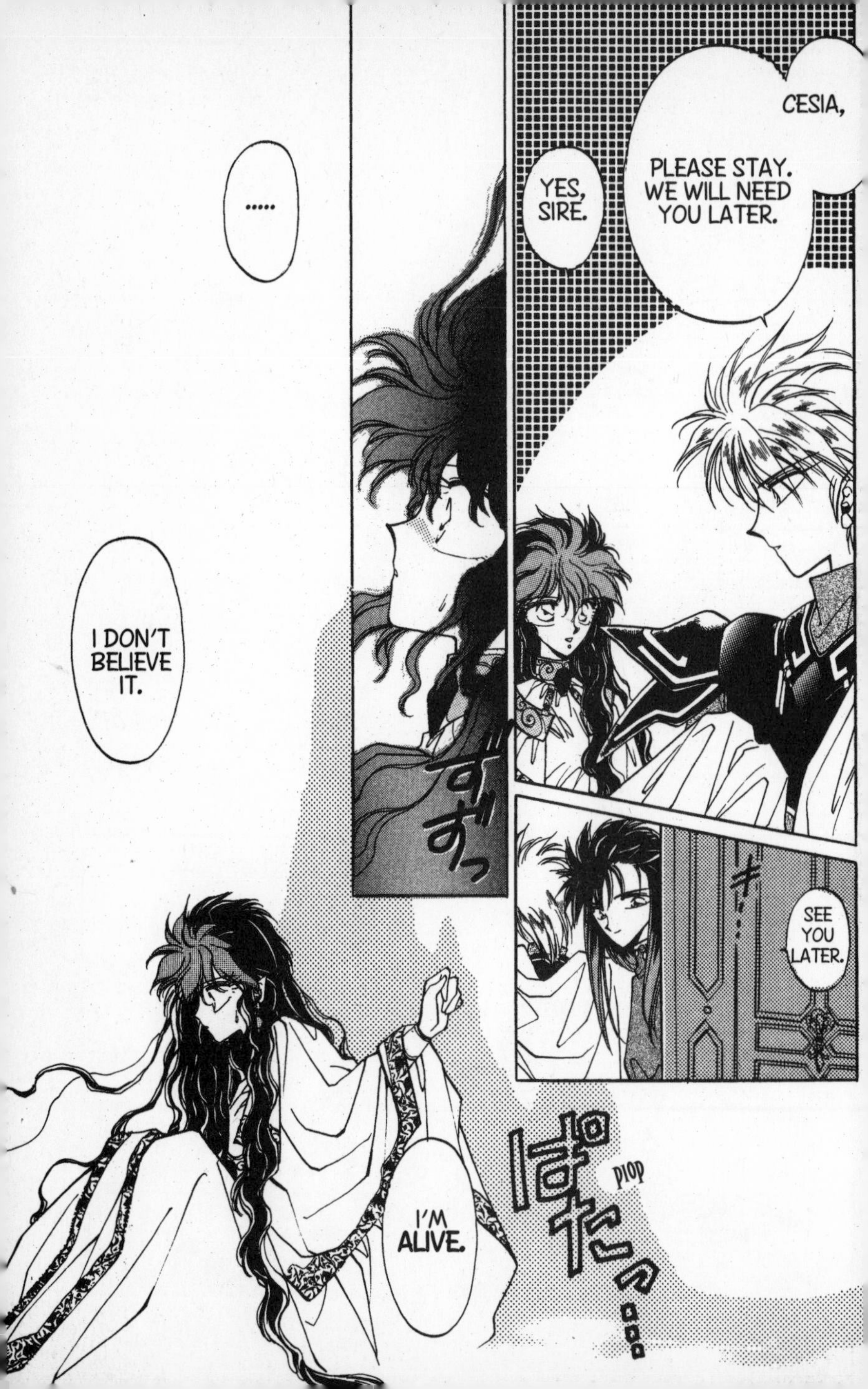
CESIA,
PLEASE STAY. WE WILL NEED YOU LATER.
YES, SIRE.
ギ…
SEE YOU LATER.
ずずっ
......
I DON'T BELIEVE IT.
ぱたっ…
plop
I'M ALIVE.

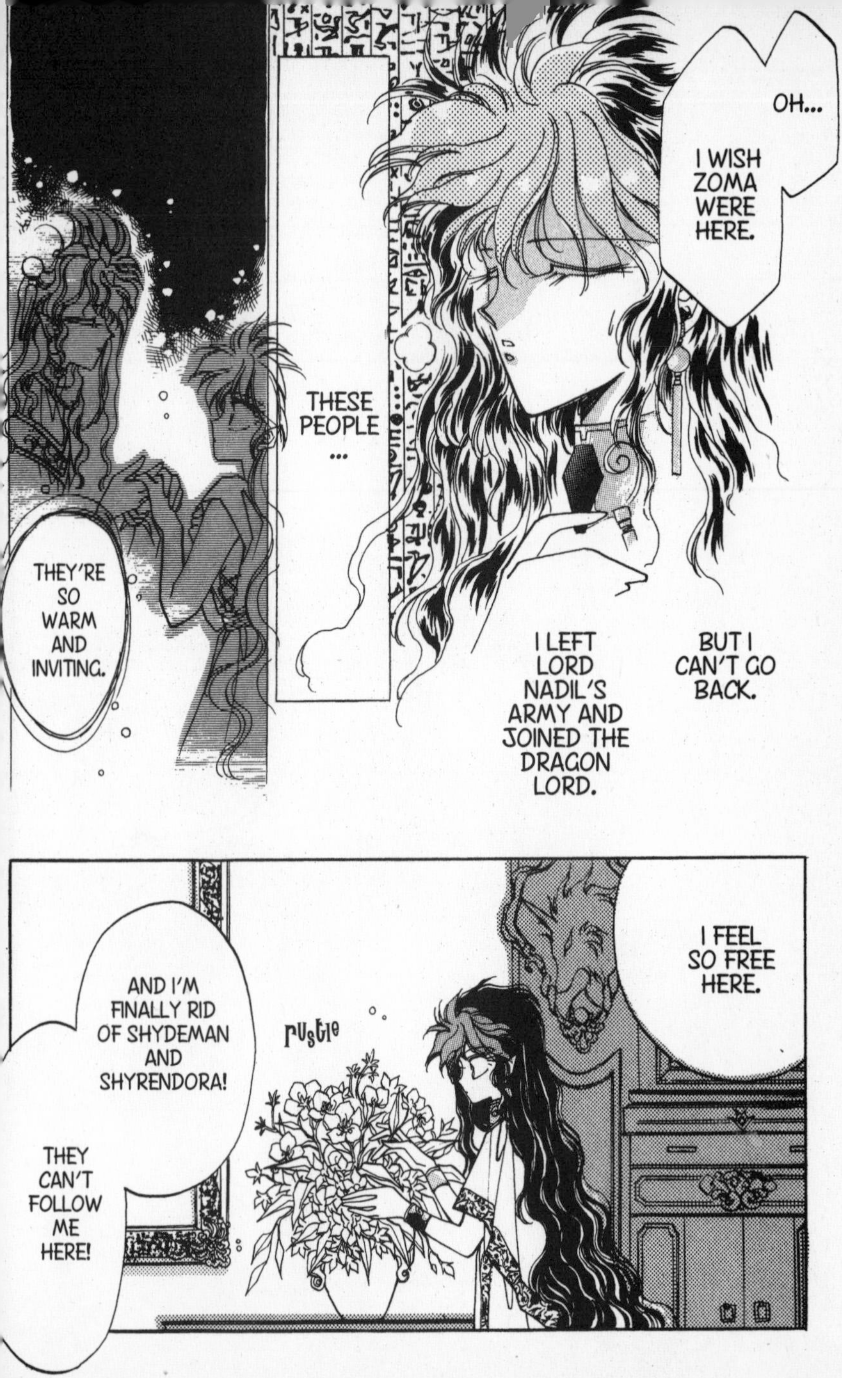

OH...
I WISH ZOMA WERE HERE.
BUT I CAN'T GO BACK.
I LEFT LORD NADIL'S ARMY AND JOINED THE DRAGON LORD.
THESE PEOPLE ...
THEY'RE SO WARM AND INVITING.
I FEEL SO FREE HERE.
rustle
AND I'M FINALLY RID OF SHYDEMAN AND SHYRENDORA!
THEY CAN'T FOLLOW ME HERE!

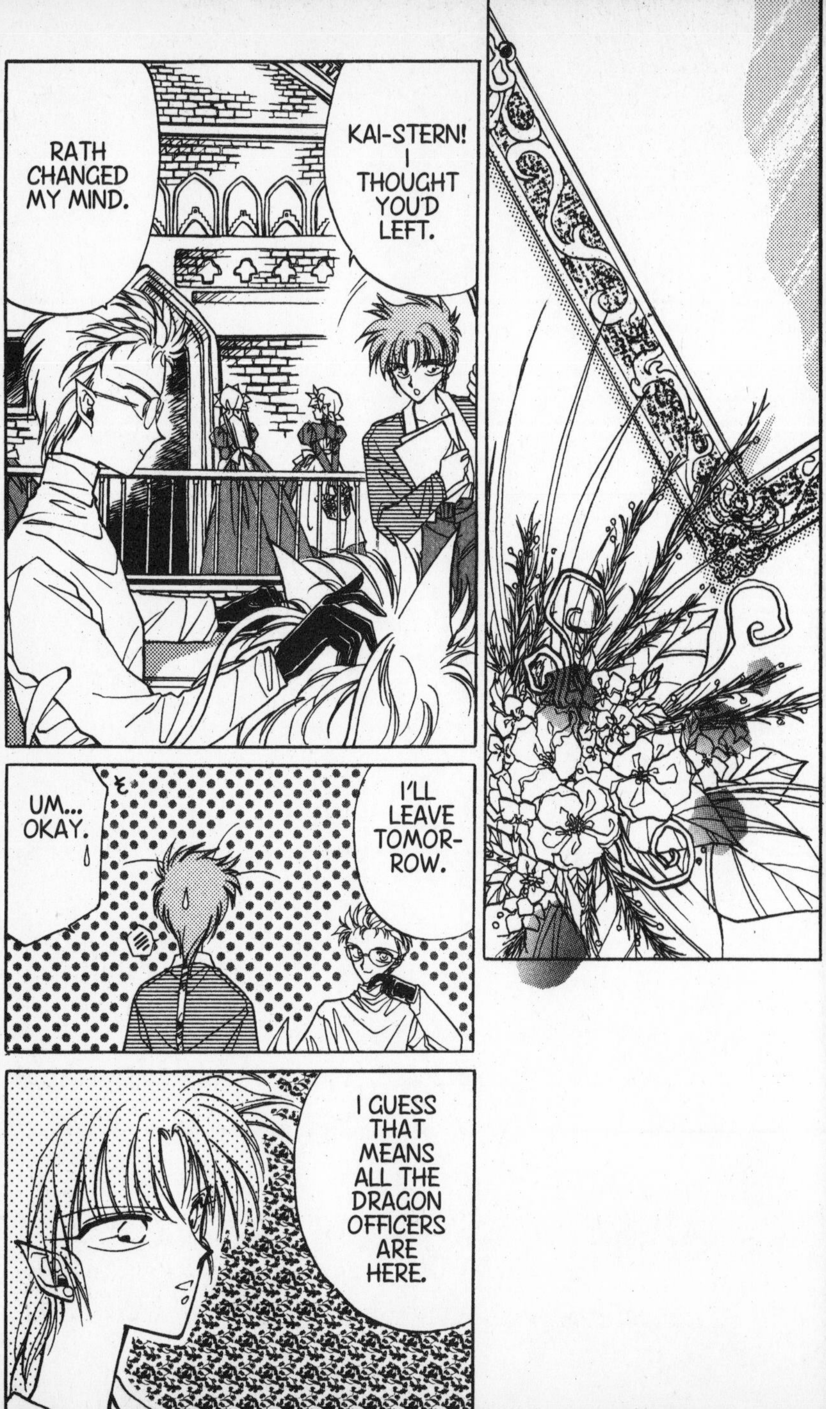
KAI-STERN! I THOUGHT YOU'D LEFT.
RATH CHANGED MY MIND.
I'LL LEAVE TOMOR-ROW.
UM... OKAY.
I GUESS THAT MEANS ALL THE DRAGON OFFICERS ARE HERE.

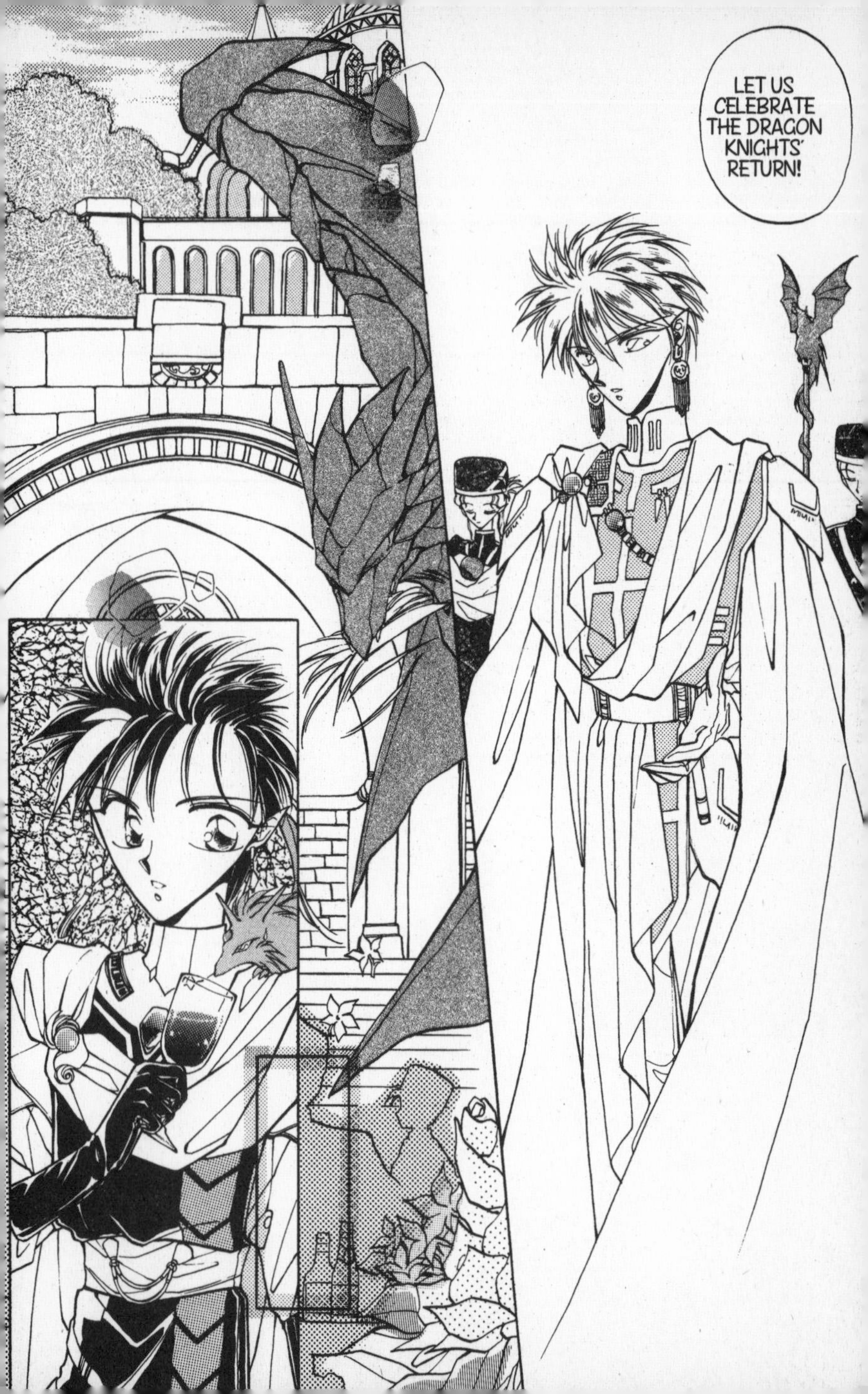
LET US CELEBRATE THE DRAGON KNIGHTS' RETURN!

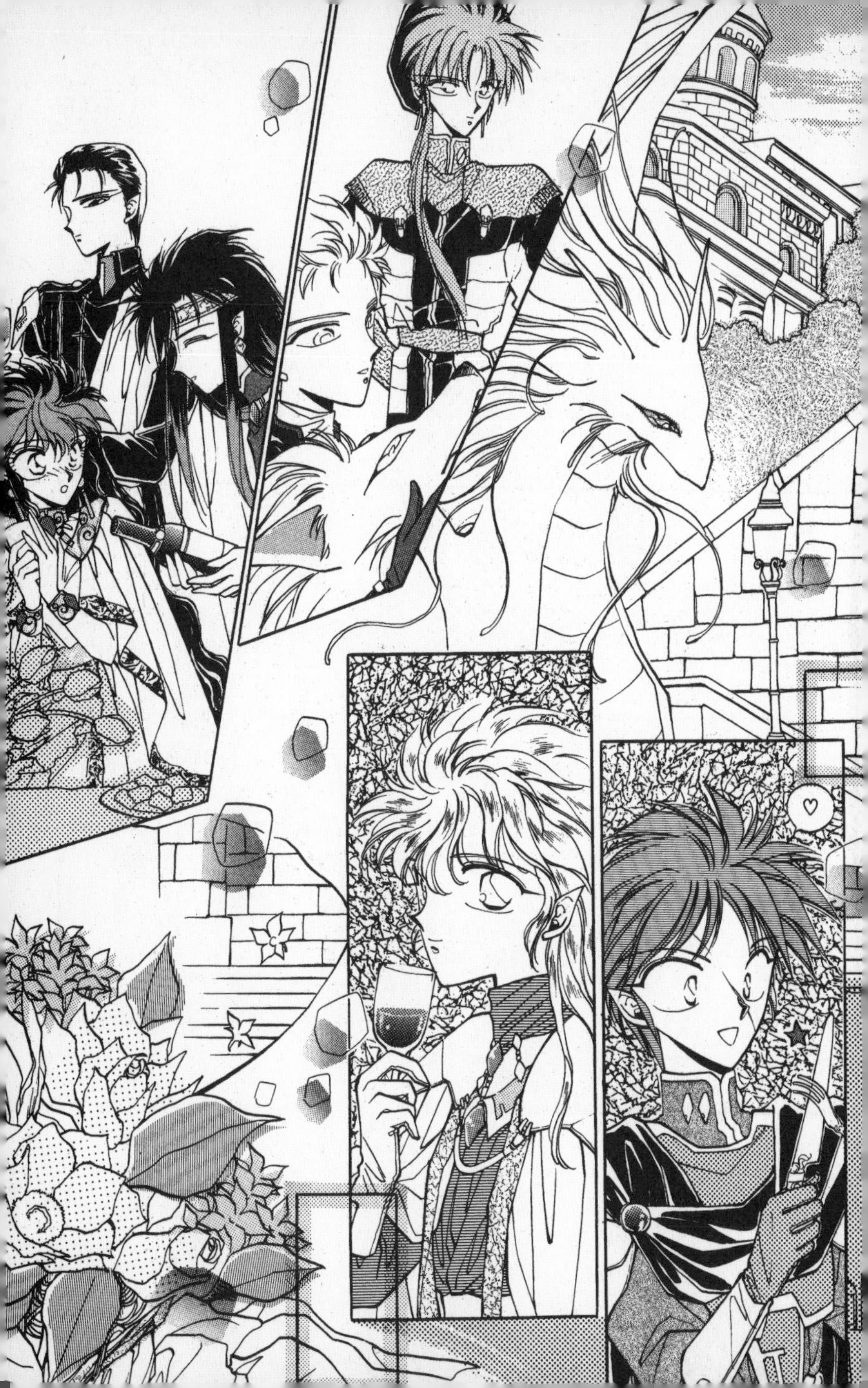

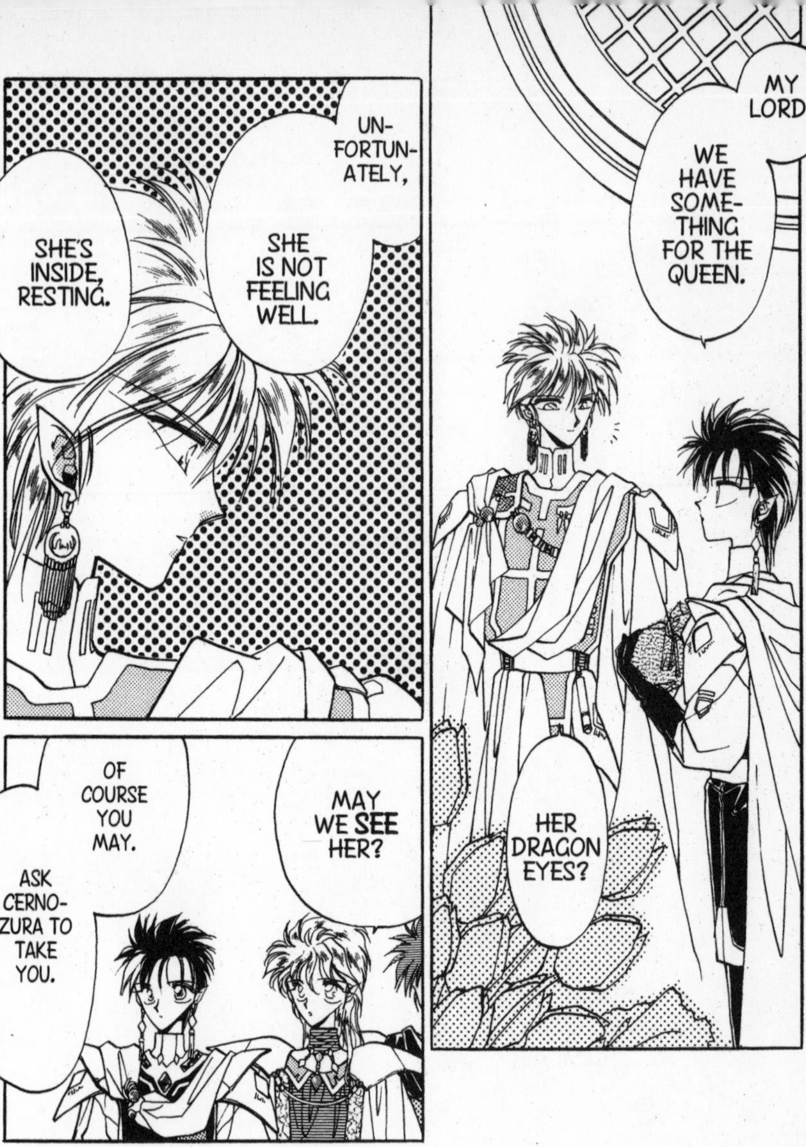
MY LORD,
WE HAVE SOME- THING FOR THE QUEEN.
HER DRAGON EYES?
UN- FORTUN- ATELY,
SHE IS NOT FEELING WELL.
SHE'S INSIDE, RESTING.
MAY WE SEE HER?
OF COURSE YOU MAY.
ASK CERNO- ZURA TO TAKE YOU.

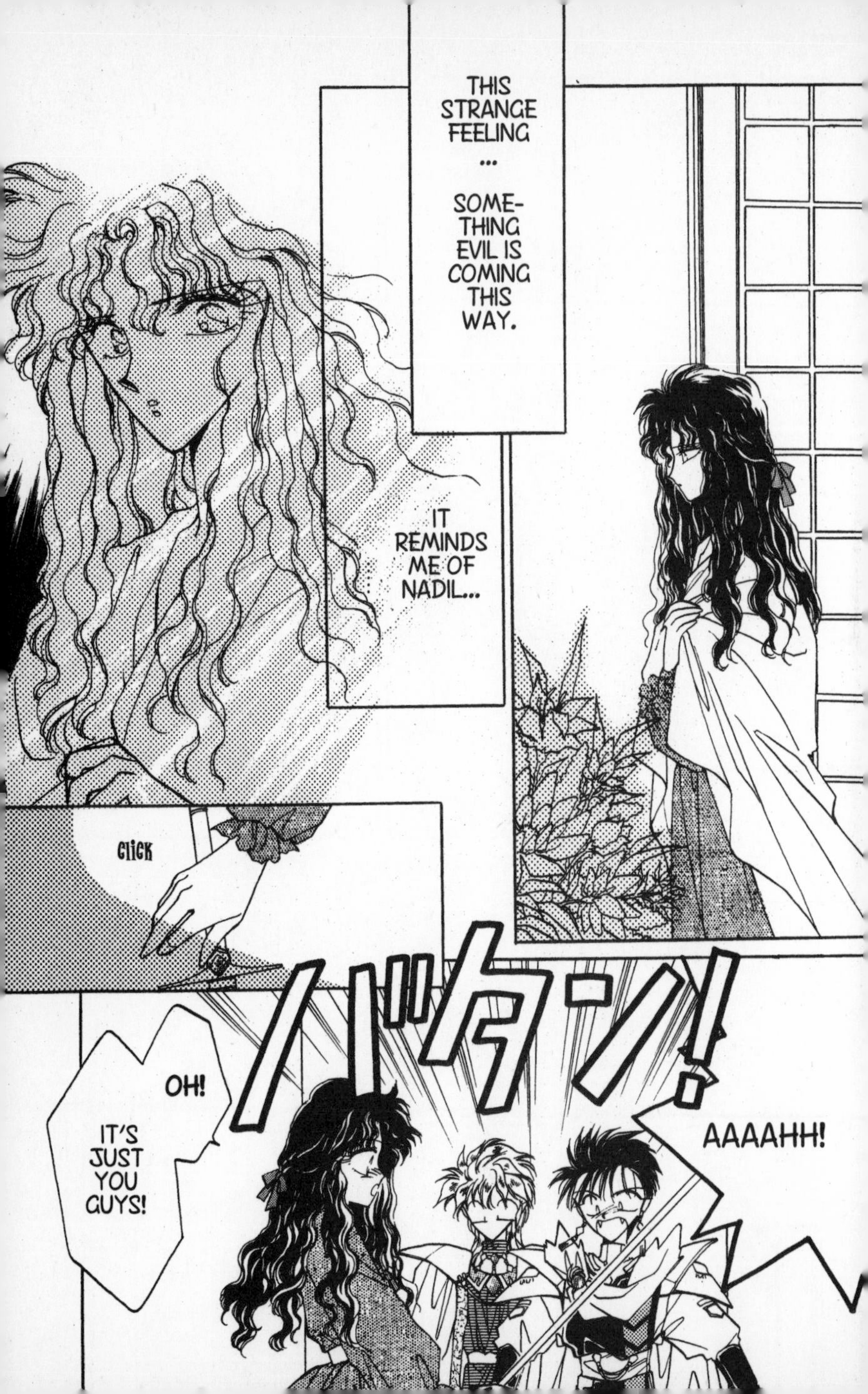
THIS STRANGE FEELING ... SOME-THING EVIL IS COMING THIS WAY.
IT REMINDS ME OF NADIL...
CliCK
バターン!
AAAAHH!
OH!
IT'S JUST YOU GUYS!

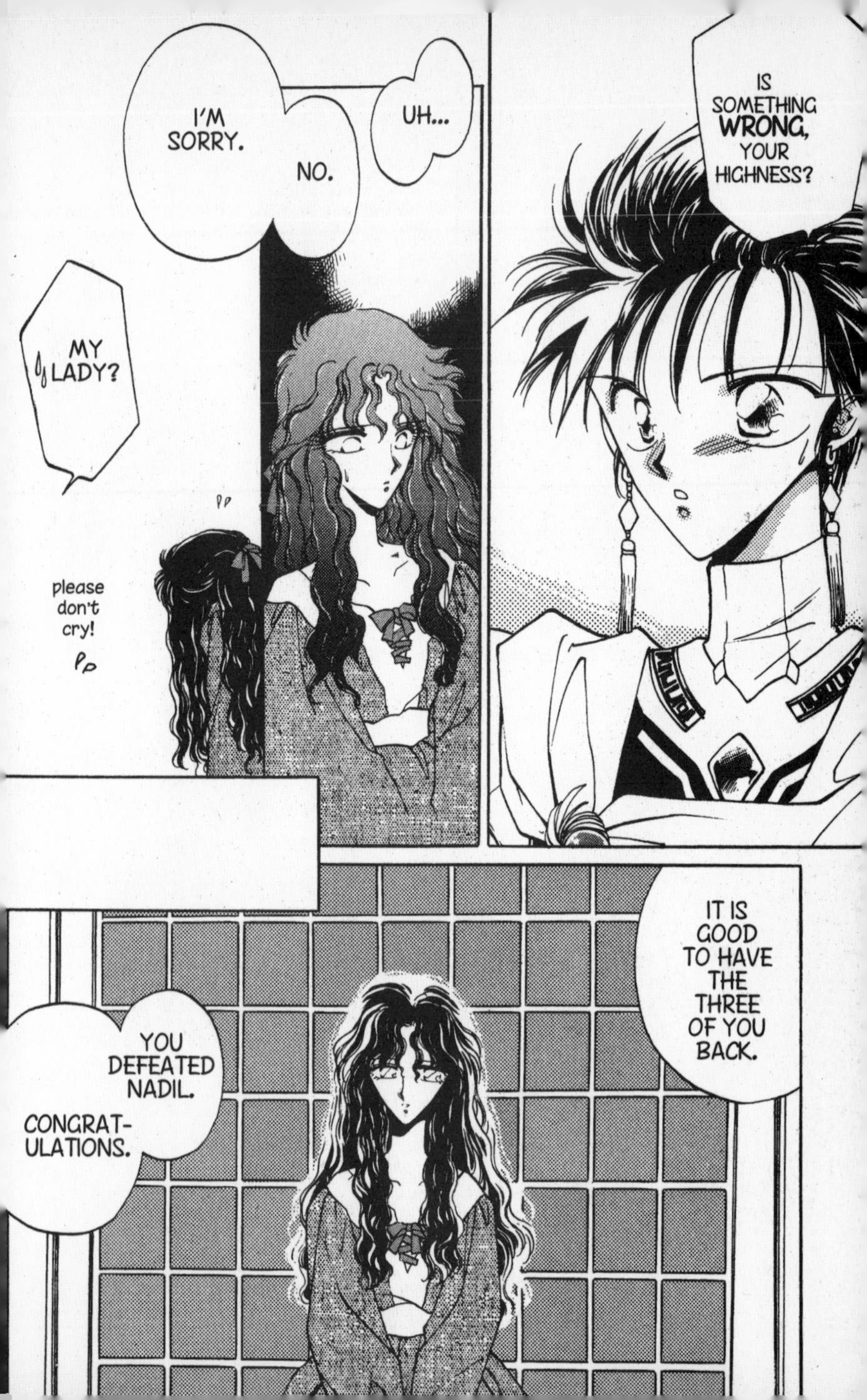
IS SOMETHING WRONG, YOUR HIGHNESS?
UH...
NO.
I'M SORRY.
MY LADY?
please don't cry!
IT IS GOOD TO HAVE THE THREE OF YOU BACK.
YOU DEFEATED NADIL.
CONGRAT-ULATIONS.

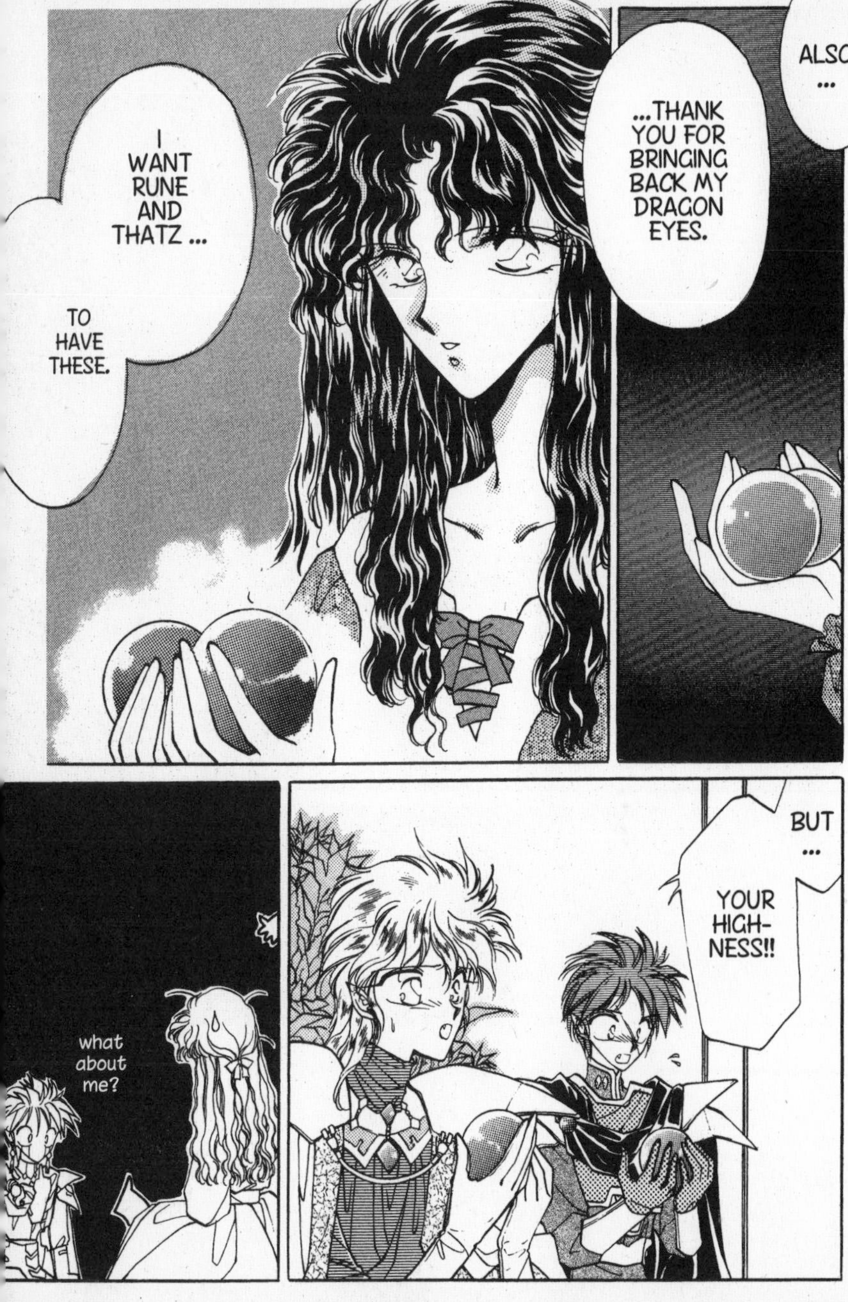
ALSO ...
...THANK YOU FOR BRINGING BACK MY DRAGON EYES.
I WANT RUNE AND THATZ ...
TO HAVE THESE.
BUT ...
YOUR HIGH-NESS!!
what about me?

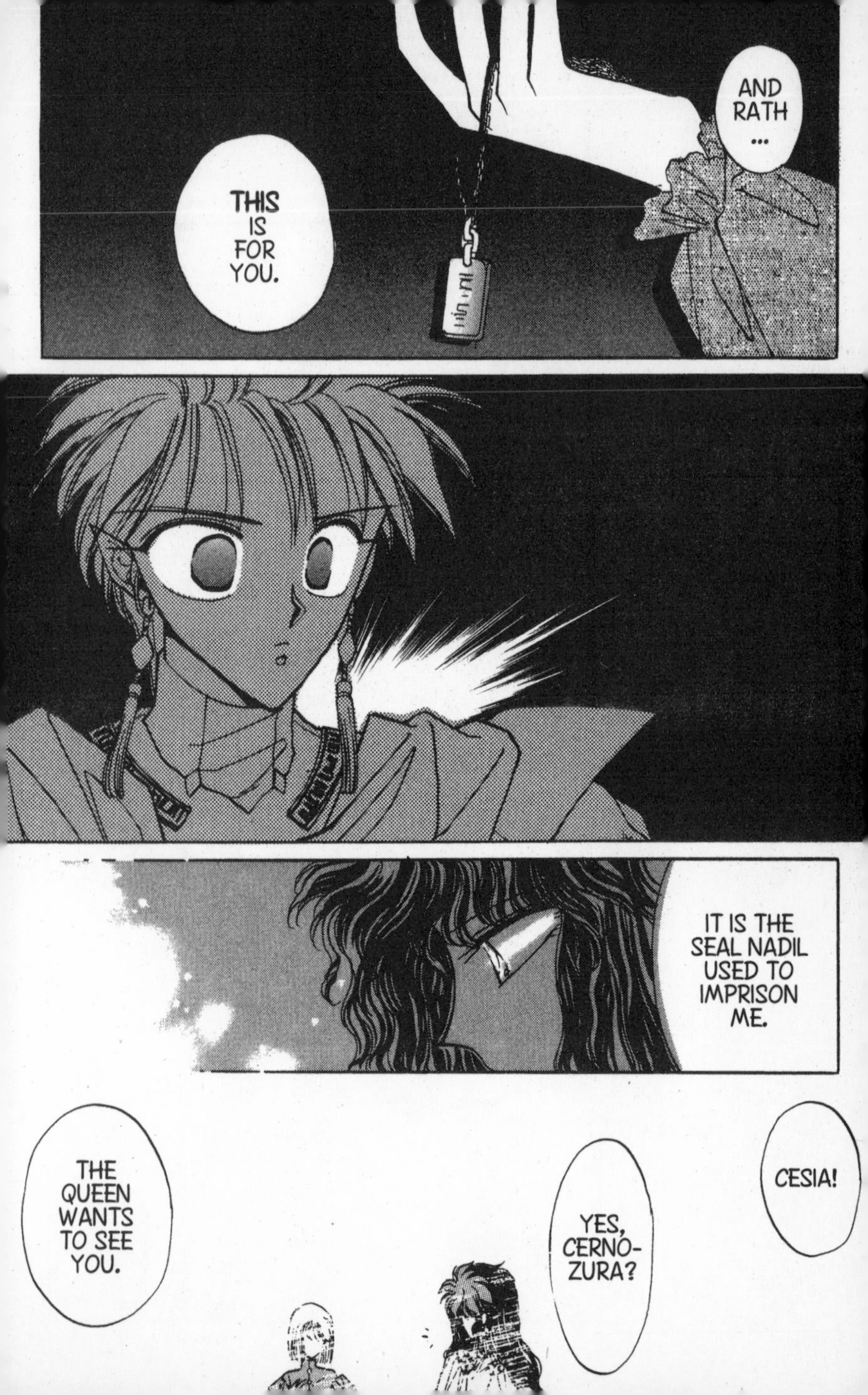
AND RATH ...
THIS IS FOR YOU.
IT IS THE SEAL NADIL USED TO IMPRISON ME.
CESIA!
YES, CERNO-ZURA?
THE QUEEN WANTS TO SEE YOU.

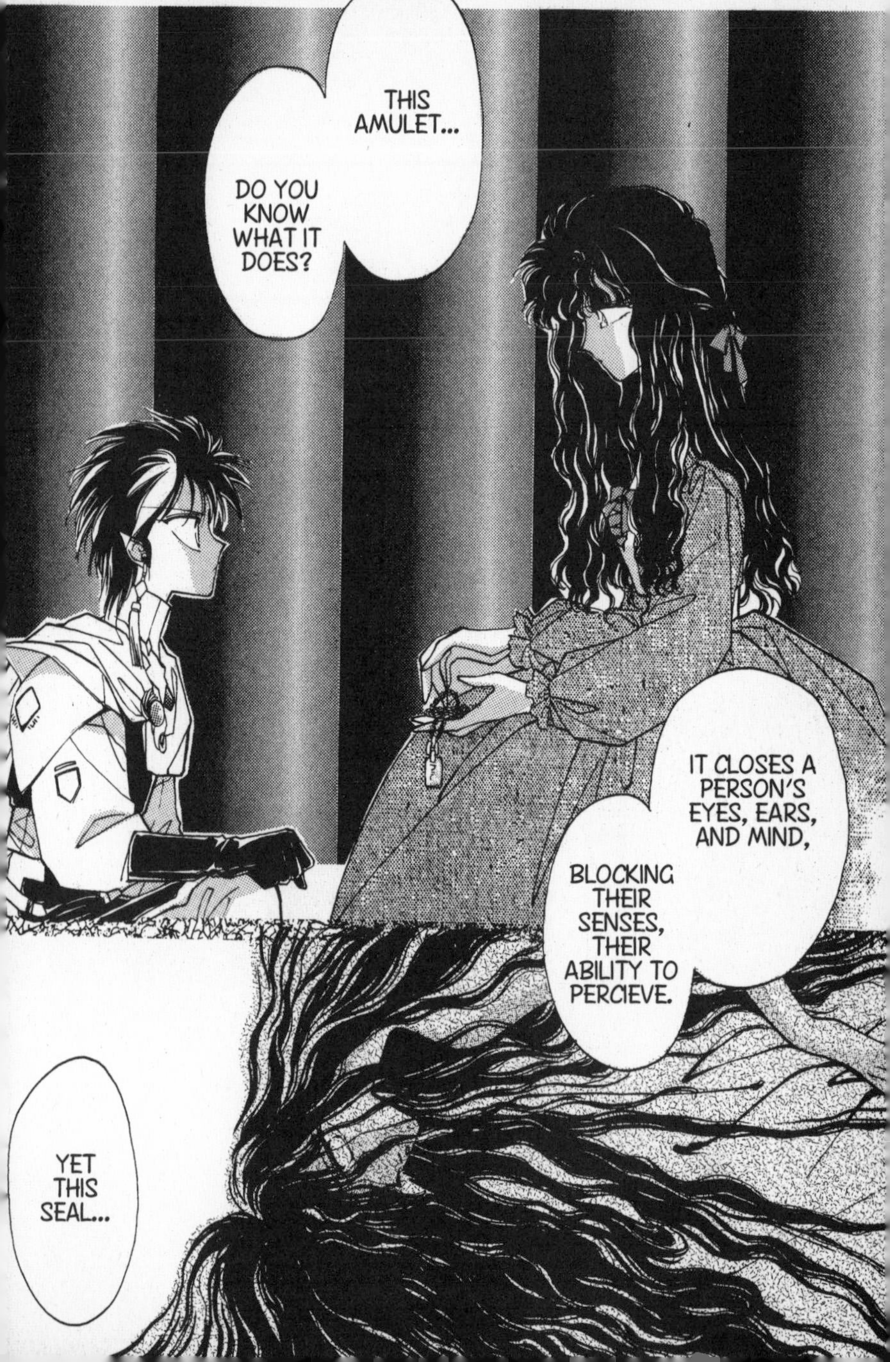
THIS AMULET...
DO YOU KNOW WHAT IT DOES?
IT CLOSES A PERSON'S EYES, EARS, AND MIND,
BLOCKING THEIR SENSES, THEIR ABILITY TO PERCIEVE.
YET THIS SEAL...

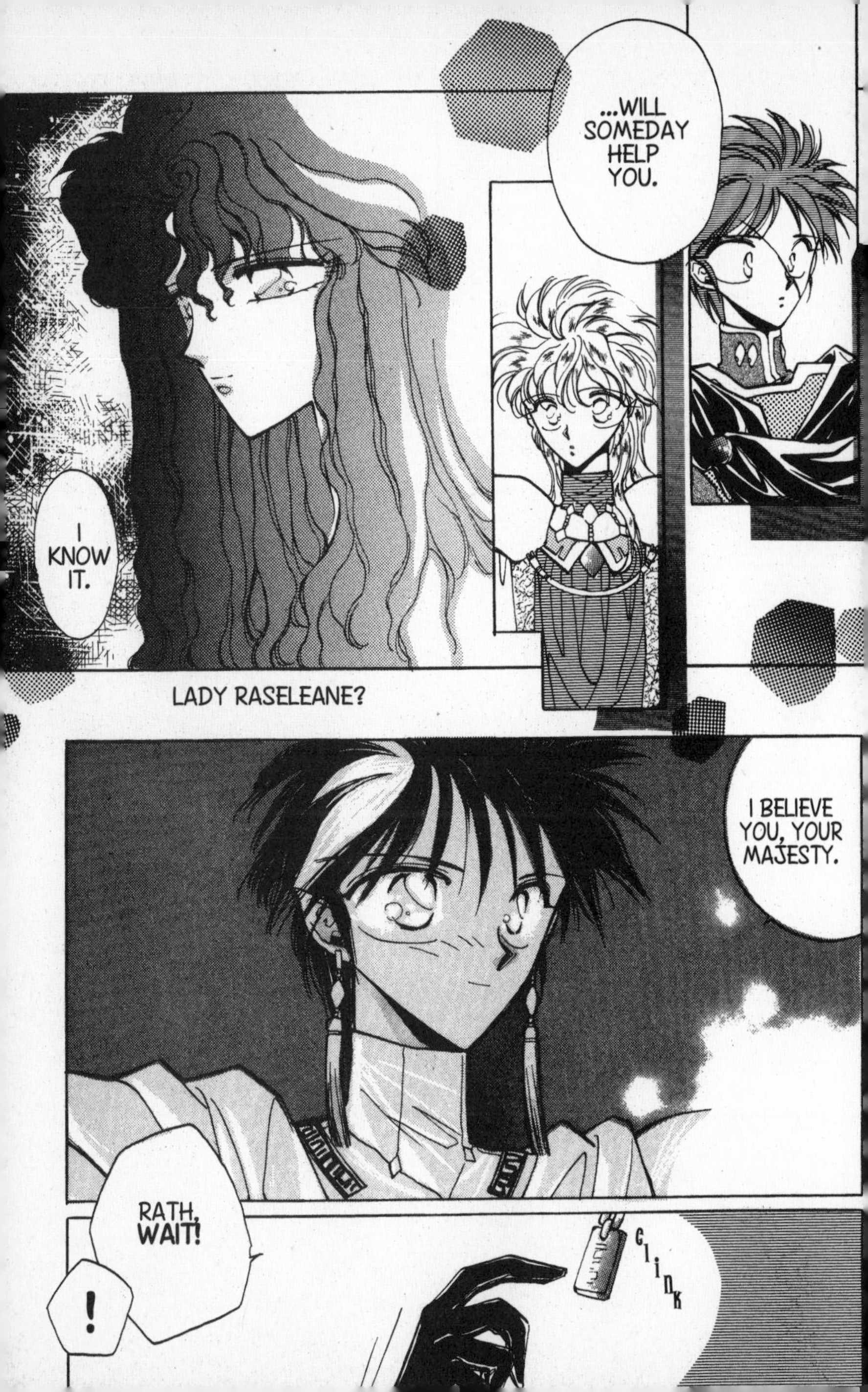
...WILL SOMEDAY HELP YOU.
I KNOW IT.
LADY RASELEANE?
I BELIEVE YOU, YOUR MAJESTY.
CLINK
RATH, WAIT!
!

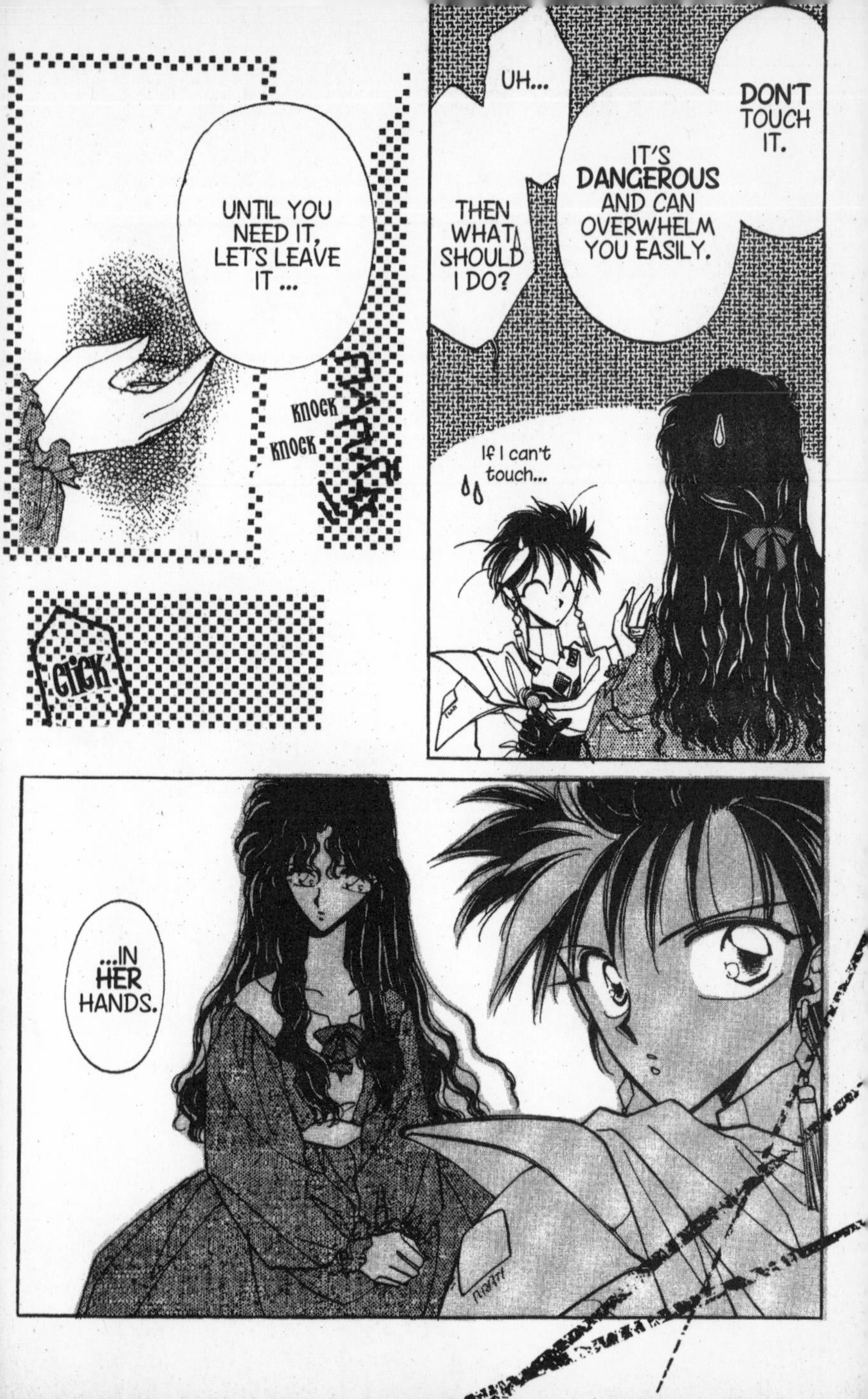
DON'T TOUCH IT.
UH...
IT'S DANGEROUS AND CAN OVERWHELM YOU EASILY.
THEN WHAT SHOULD I DO?
If I can't touch...
UNTIL YOU NEED IT, LET'S LEAVE IT ...
KNOCK
KNOCK
CLICK
...IN HER HANDS.

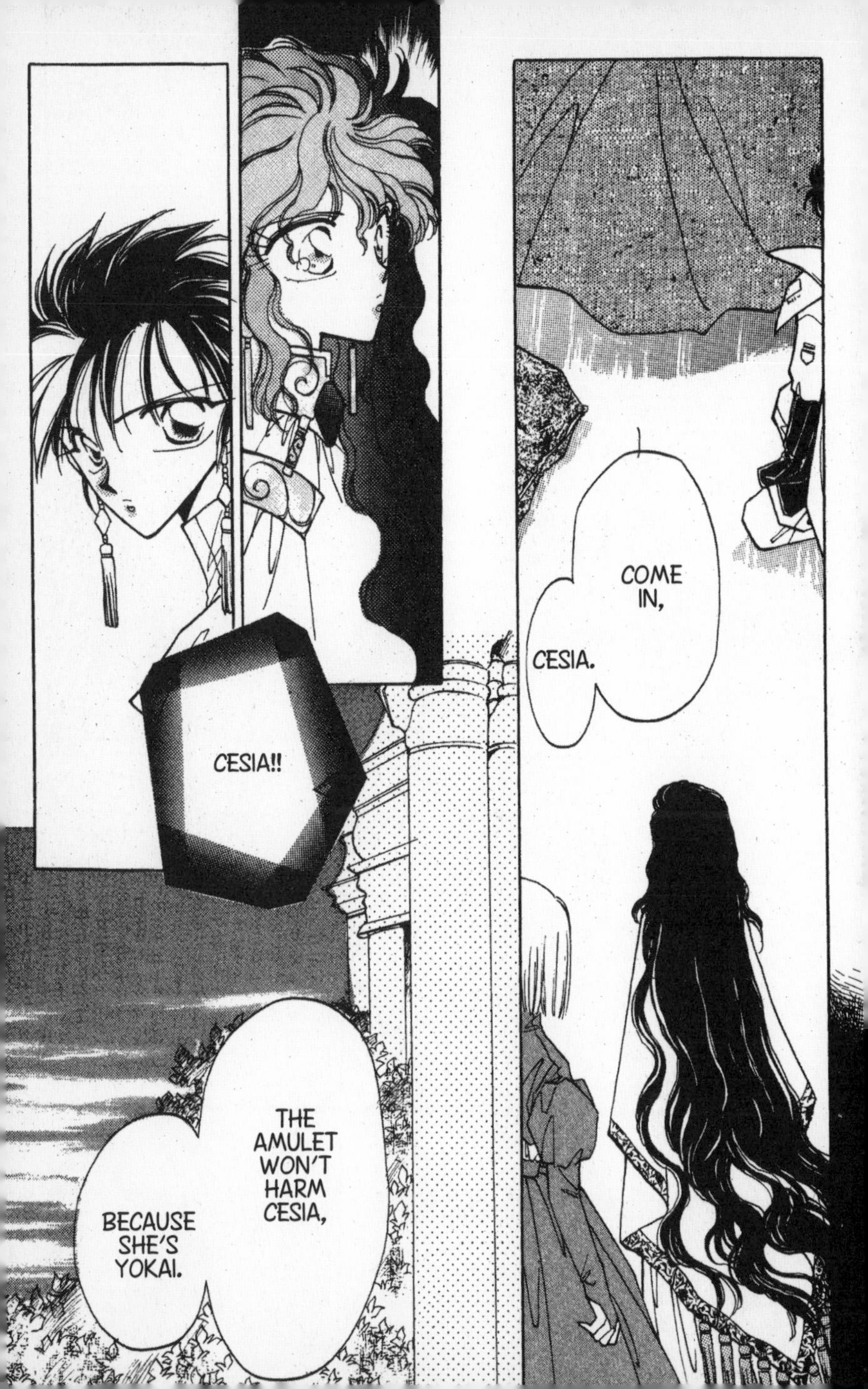
COME IN, CESIA.
CESIA!!
THE AMULET WON'T HARM CESIA, BECAUSE SHE'S YOKAI.

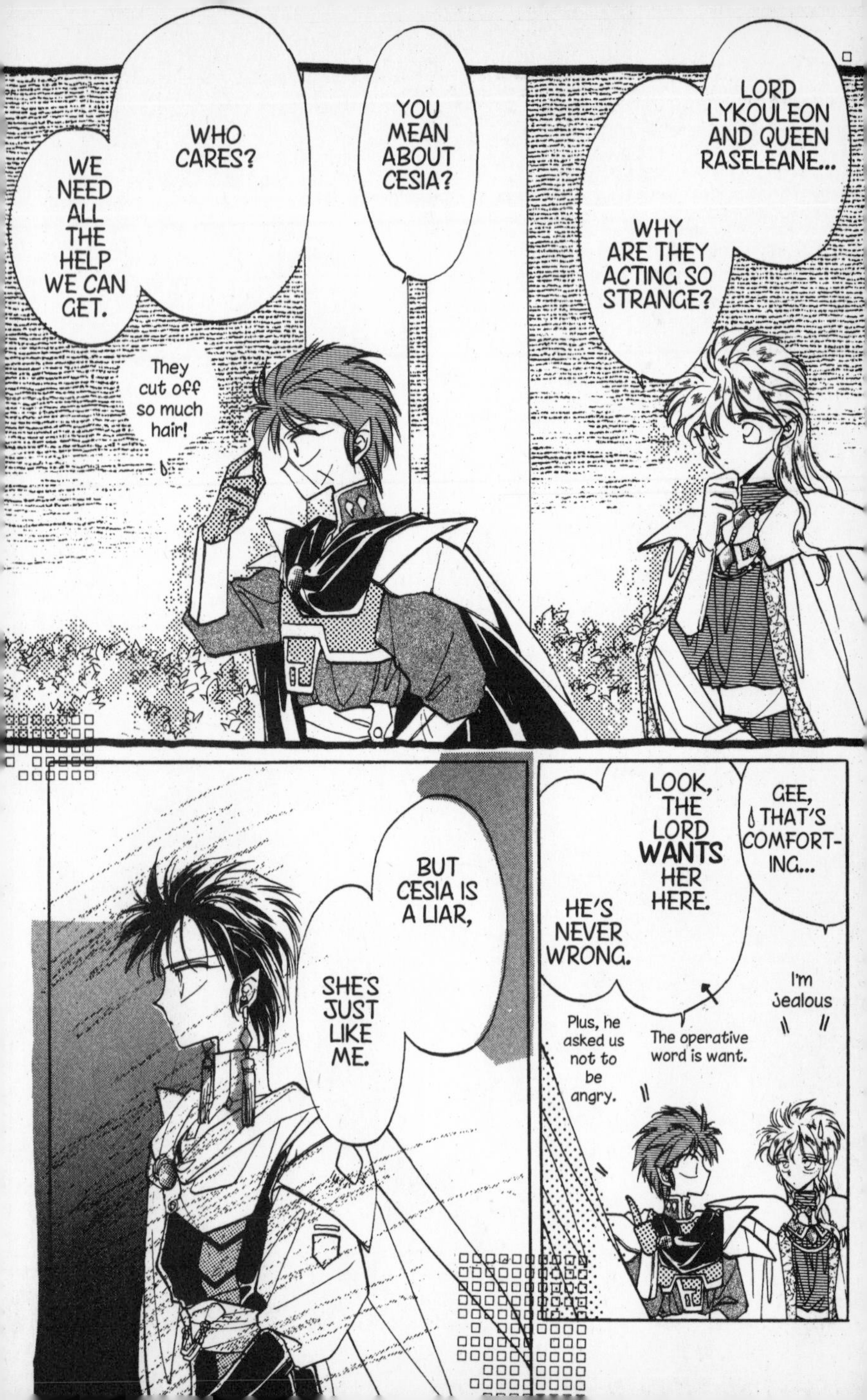
LORD LYKOULEON AND QUEEN RASELEANE...
WHY ARE THEY ACTING SO STRANGE?
YOU MEAN ABOUT CESIA?
WHO CARES?
WE NEED ALL THE HELP WE CAN GET.
They cut off so much hair!
GEE, THAT'S COMFORT-ING...
LOOK, THE LORD **WANTS** HER HERE.
HE'S NEVER WRONG.
I'm jealous
The operative word is want.
Plus, he asked us not to be angry.
BUT CESIA IS A LIAR,
SHE'S JUST LIKE ME.

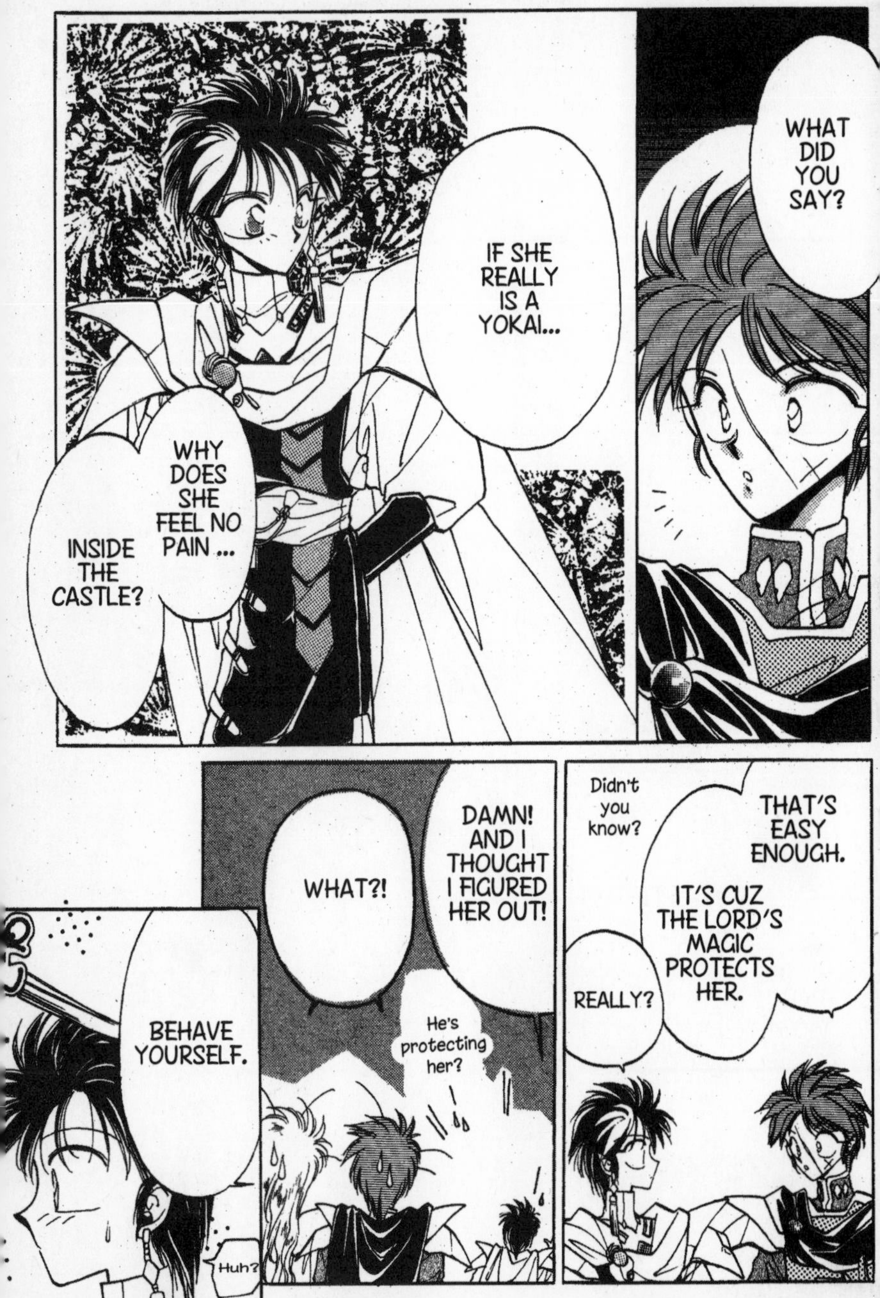
WHAT DID YOU SAY?
IF SHE REALLY IS A YOKAI...
WHY DOES SHE FEEL NO PAIN ...
INSIDE THE CASTLE?
THAT'S EASY ENOUGH.
IT'S CUZ THE LORD'S MAGIC PROTECTS HER.
Didn't you know?
REALLY?
DAMN! AND I THOUGHT I FIGURED HER OUT!
WHAT?!
He's protecting her?
BEHAVE YOURSELF.
Huh?

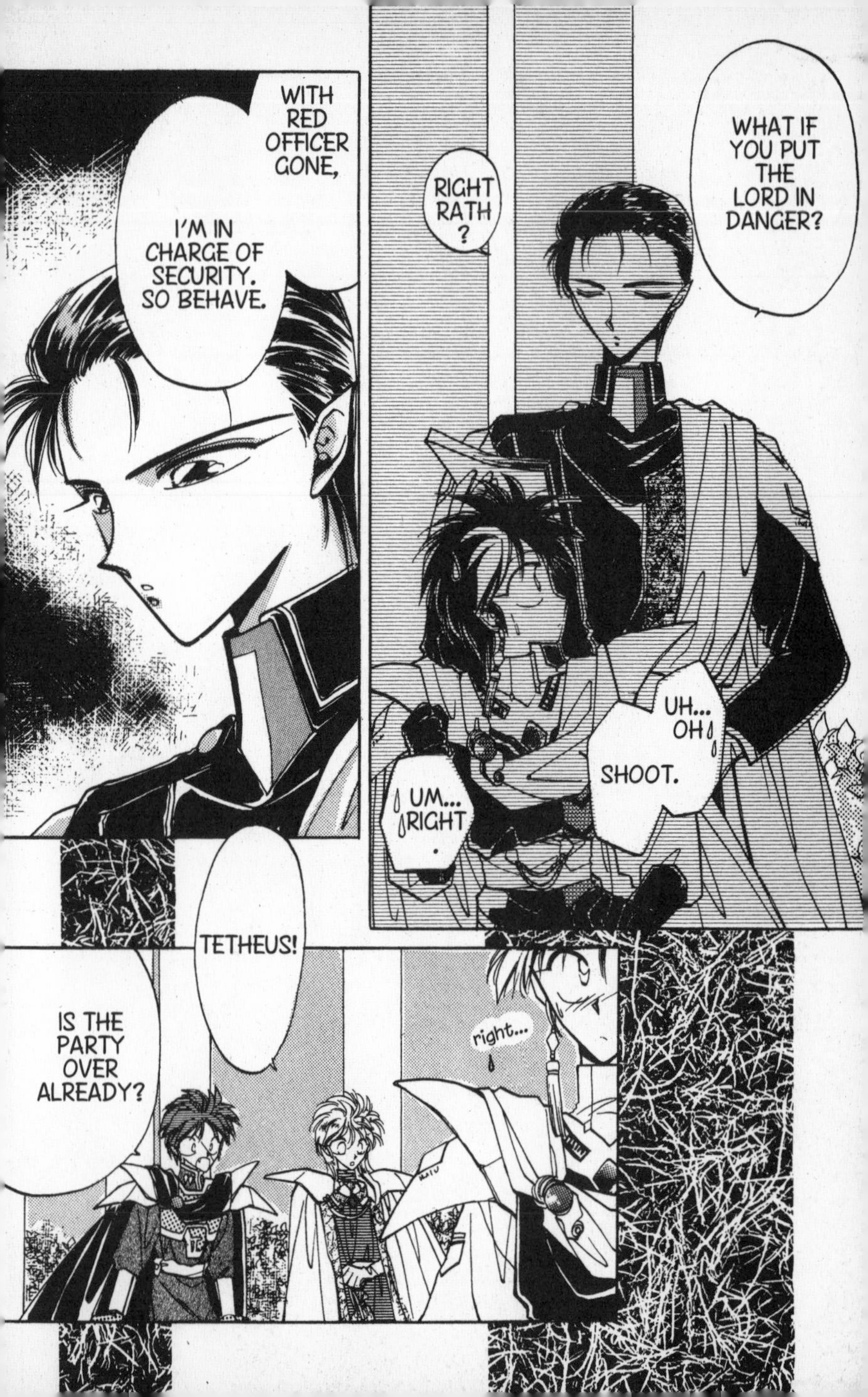
WHAT IF YOU PUT THE LORD IN DANGER?
RIGHT RATH?
UH... OH
SHOOT.
UM... RIGHT.
WITH RED OFFICER GONE,
I'M IN CHARGE OF SECURITY. SO BEHAVE.
right...
TETHEUS!
IS THE PARTY OVER ALREADY?

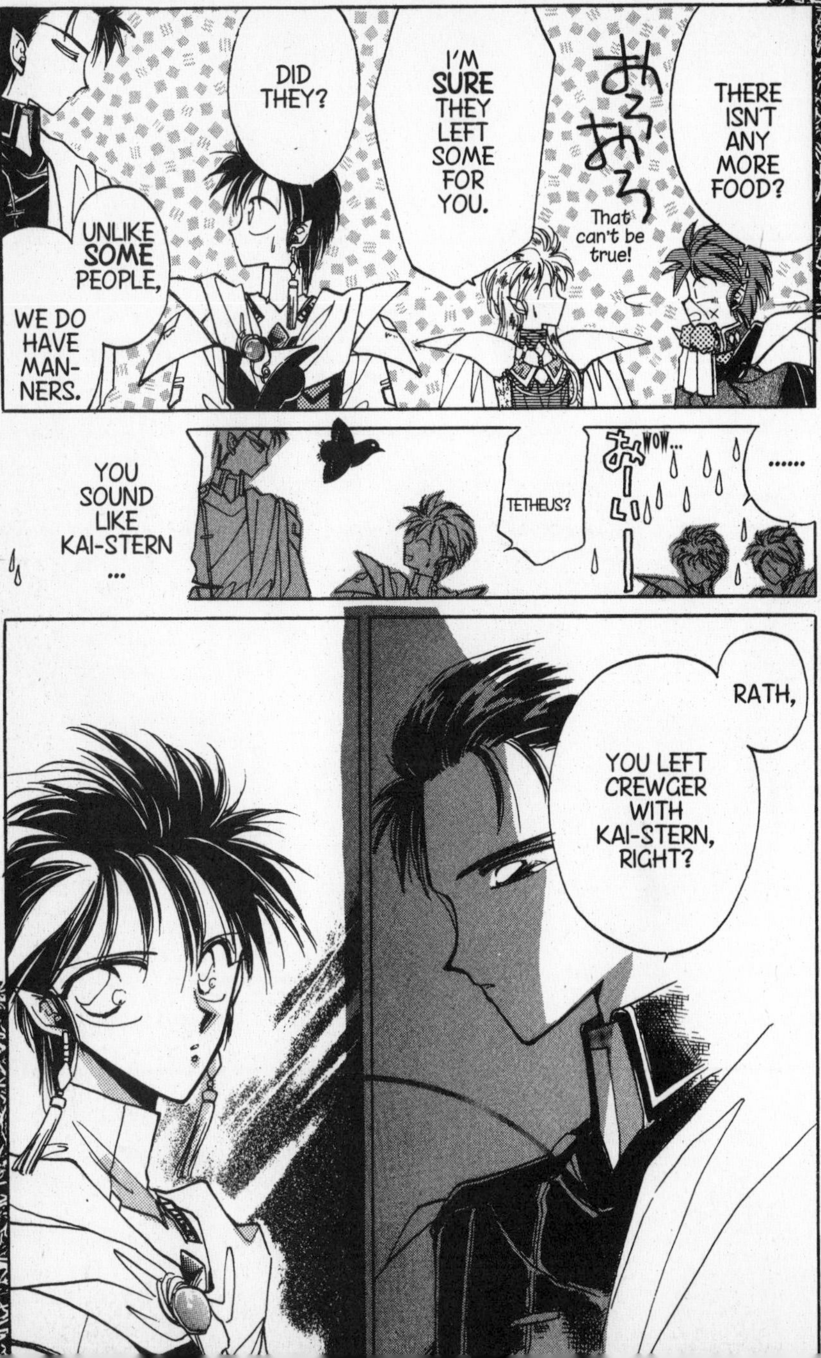
THERE ISN'T ANY MORE FOOD?
おろおろ
That can't be true!
I'M SURE THEY LEFT SOME FOR YOU.
DID THEY?
UNLIKE SOME PEOPLE,
WE DO HAVE MAN-NERS.
......
WOW...
TETHEUS?
YOU SOUND LIKE KAI-STERN ...
RATH,
YOU LEFT CREWGER WITH KAI-STERN, RIGHT?

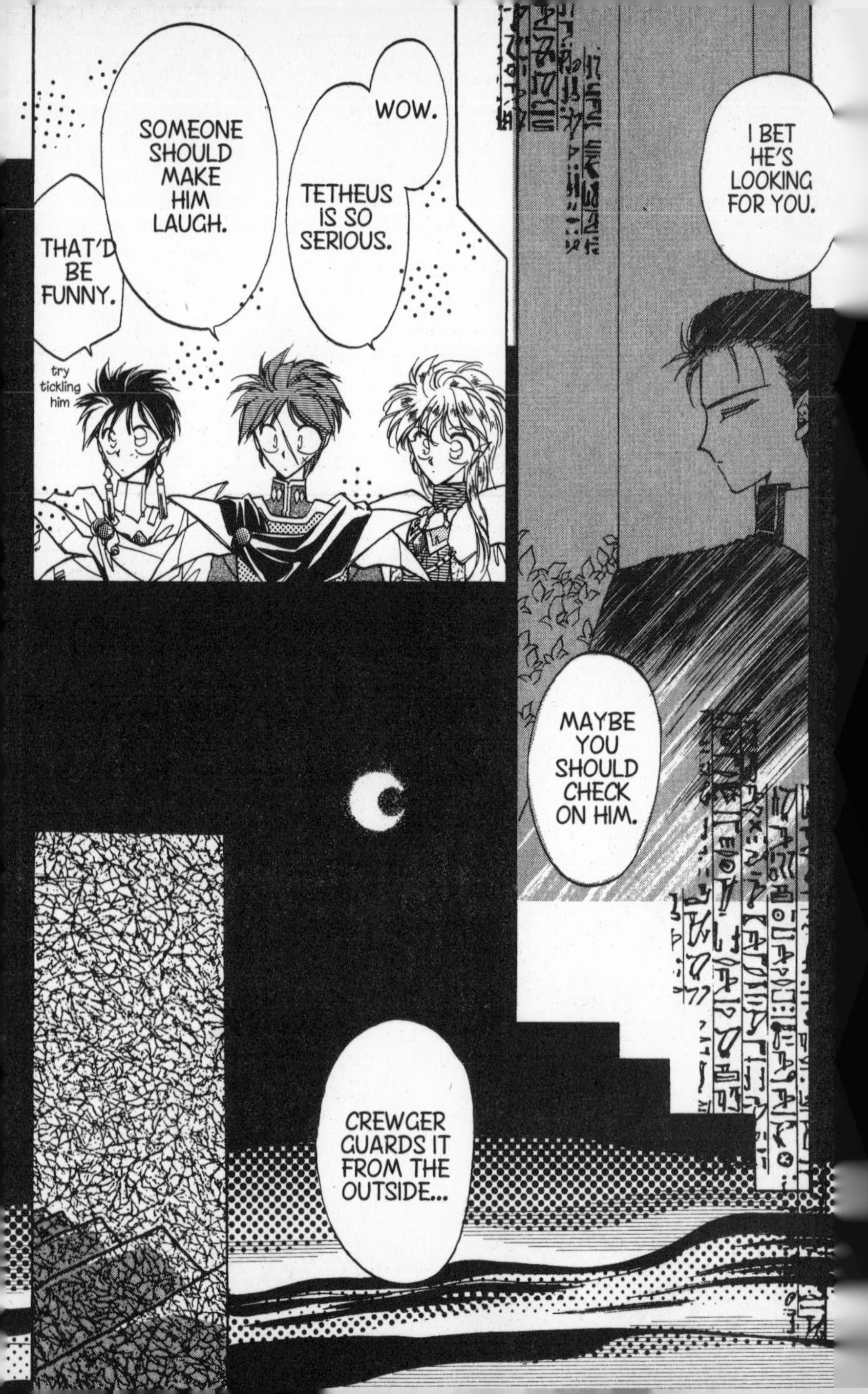
I BET HE'S LOOKING FOR YOU.
MAYBE YOU SHOULD CHECK ON HIM.
WOW.
TETHEUS IS SO SERIOUS.
SOMEONE SHOULD MAKE HIM LAUGH.
THAT'D BE FUNNY.
try tickling him
CREWGER GUARDS IT FROM THE OUTSIDE...

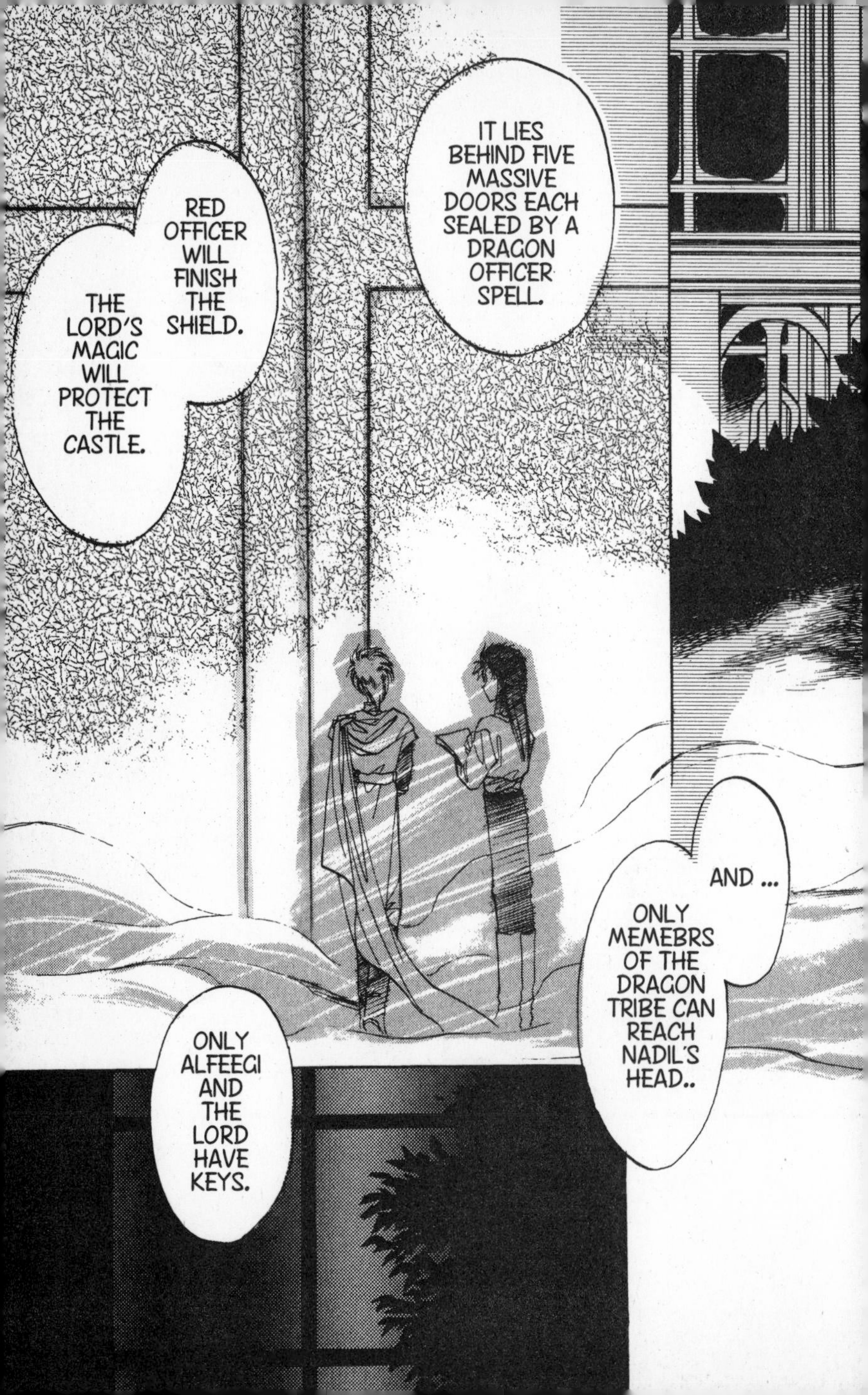
IT LIES BEHIND FIVE MASSIVE DOORS EACH SEALED BY A DRAGON OFFICER SPELL.
RED OFFICER WILL FINISH THE SHIELD.
THE LORD'S MAGIC WILL PROTECT THE CASTLE.
AND ...
ONLY MEMEBRS OF THE DRAGON TRIBE CAN REACH NADIL'S HEAD..
ONLY ALFEEGI AND THE LORD HAVE KEYS.

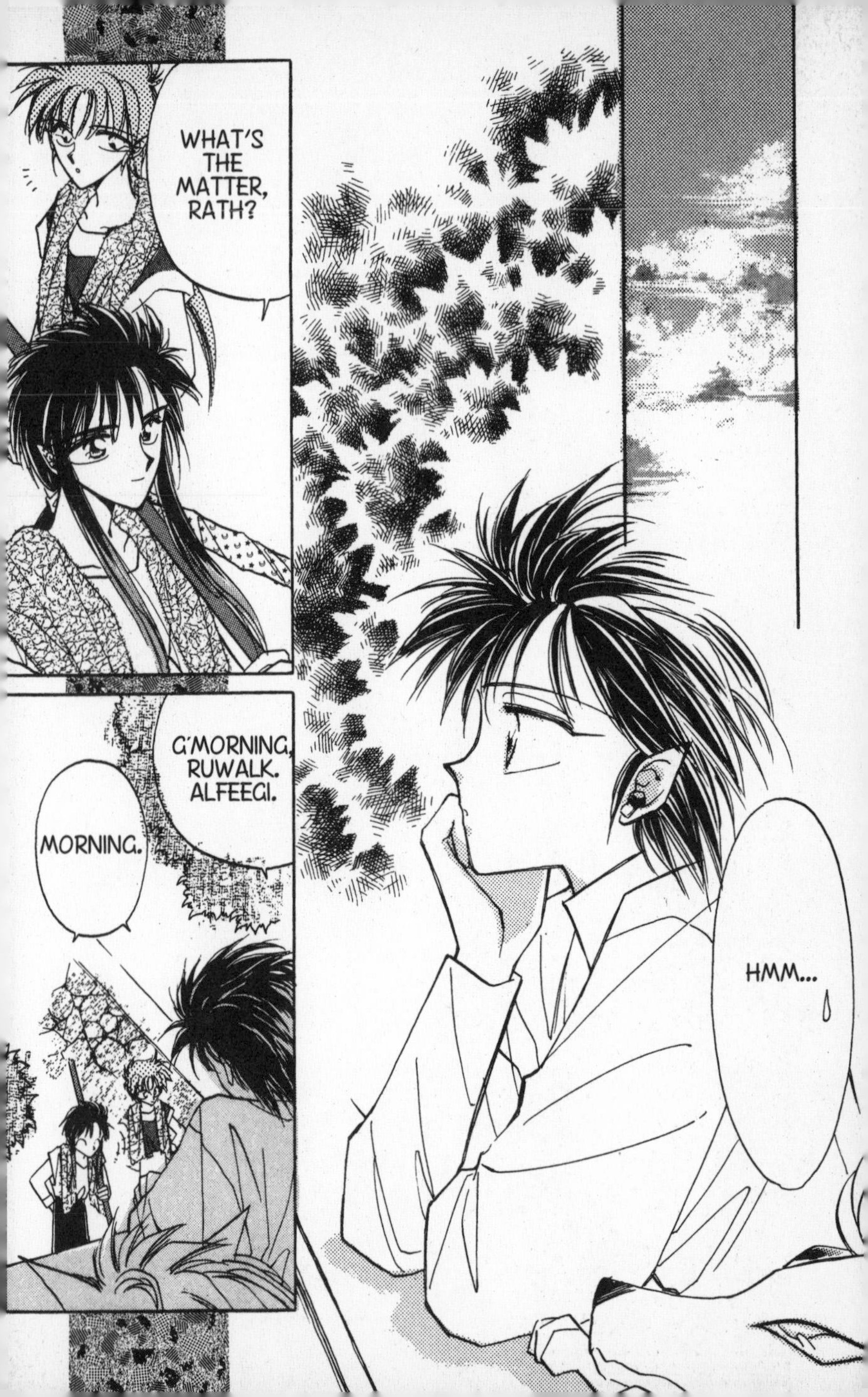
HMM...
WHAT'S THE MATTER, RATH?
G'MORNING, RUWALK. ALFEEGI.
MORNING.

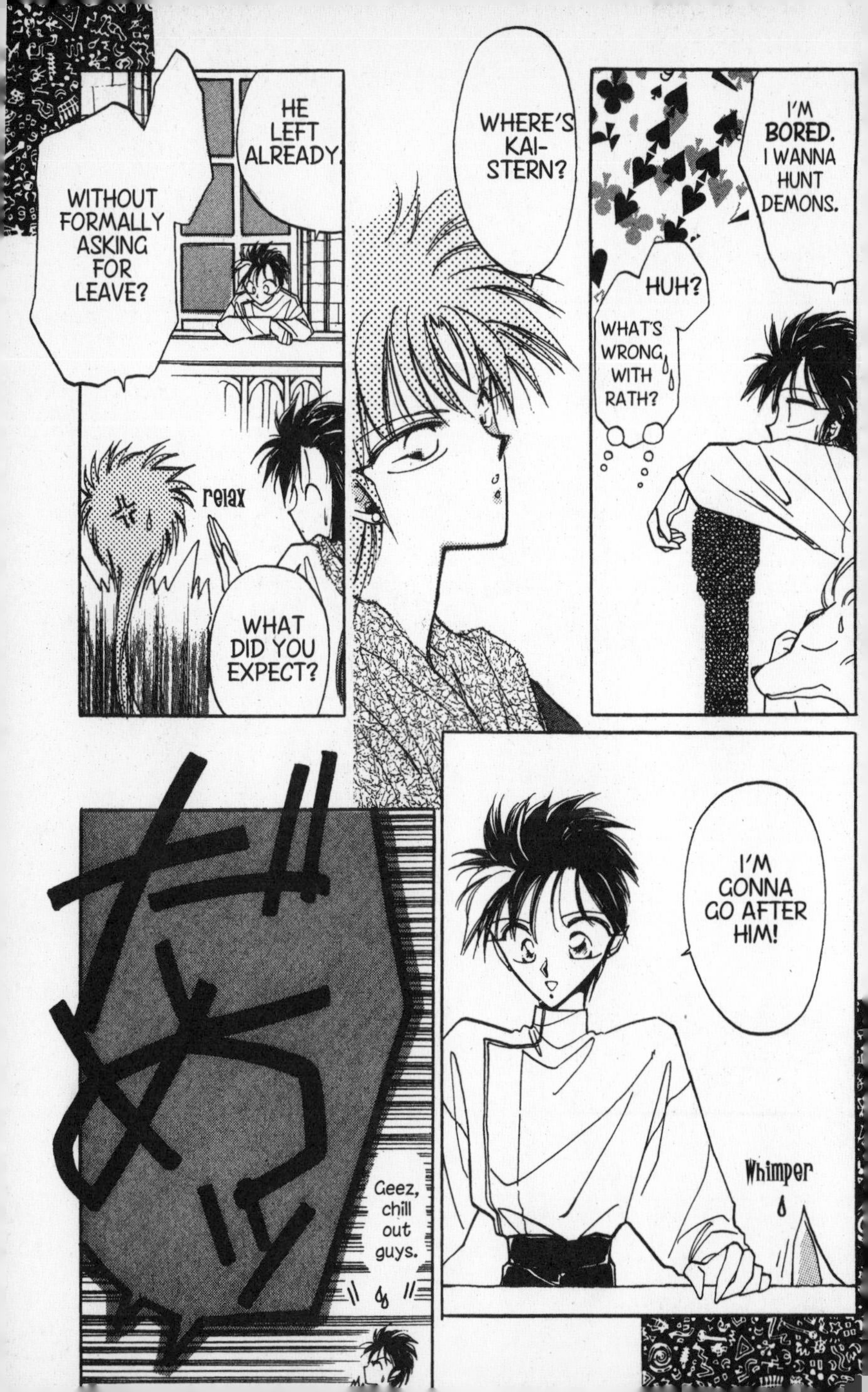
I'M BORED. I WANNA HUNT DEMONS.
HUH?
WHAT'S WRONG WITH RATH?
WHERE'S KAI-STERN?
HE LEFT ALREADY.
WITHOUT FORMALLY ASKING FOR LEAVE?
relax
WHAT DID YOU EXPECT?
I'M GONNA GO AFTER HIM!
Whimper
Geez, chill out guys.

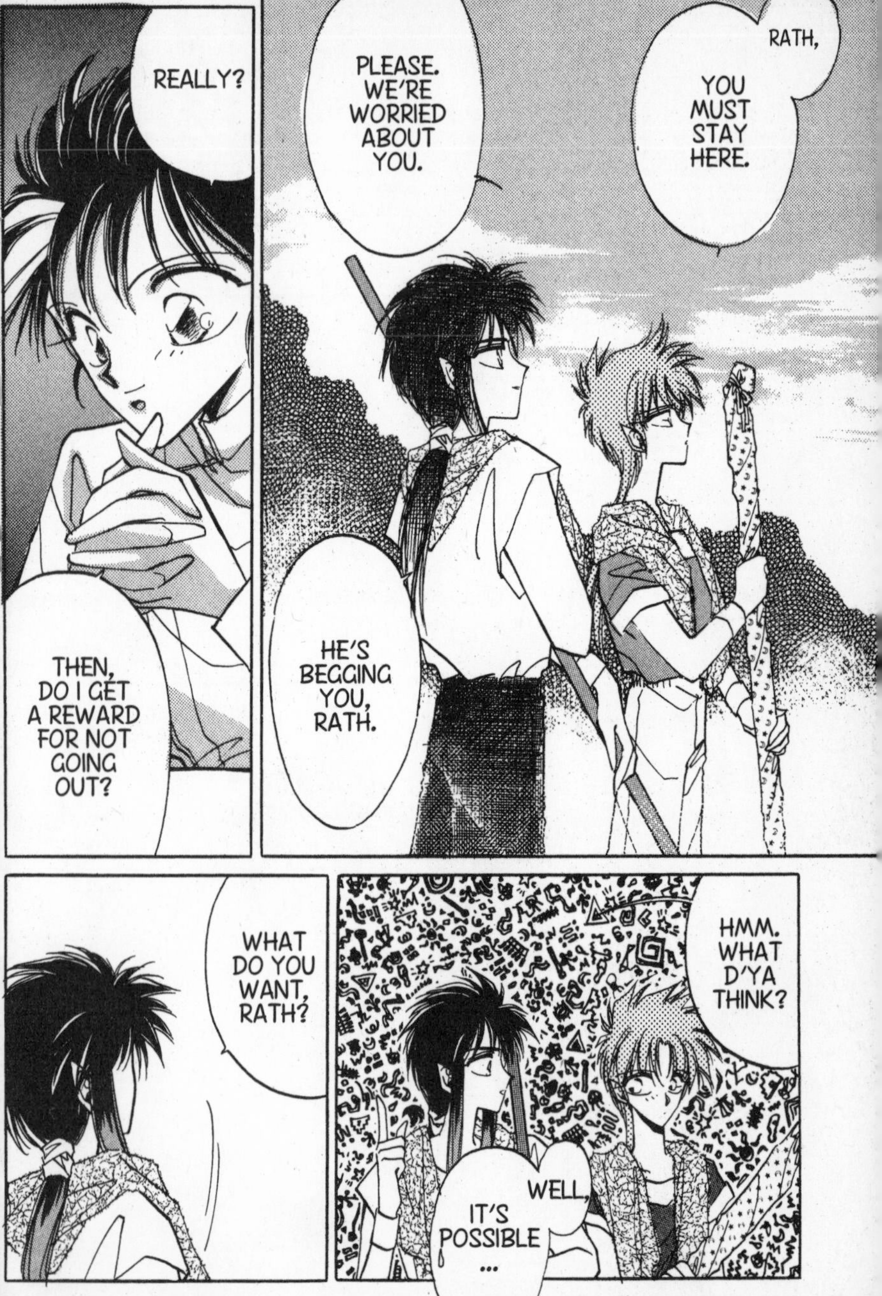
RATH,
YOU MUST STAY HERE.
PLEASE. WE'RE WORRIED ABOUT YOU.
HE'S BEGGING YOU, RATH.
REALLY?
THEN, DO I GET A REWARD FOR NOT GOING OUT?
HMM. WHAT D'YA THINK?
WELL,
IT'S POSSIBLE ...
WHAT DO YOU WANT, RATH?

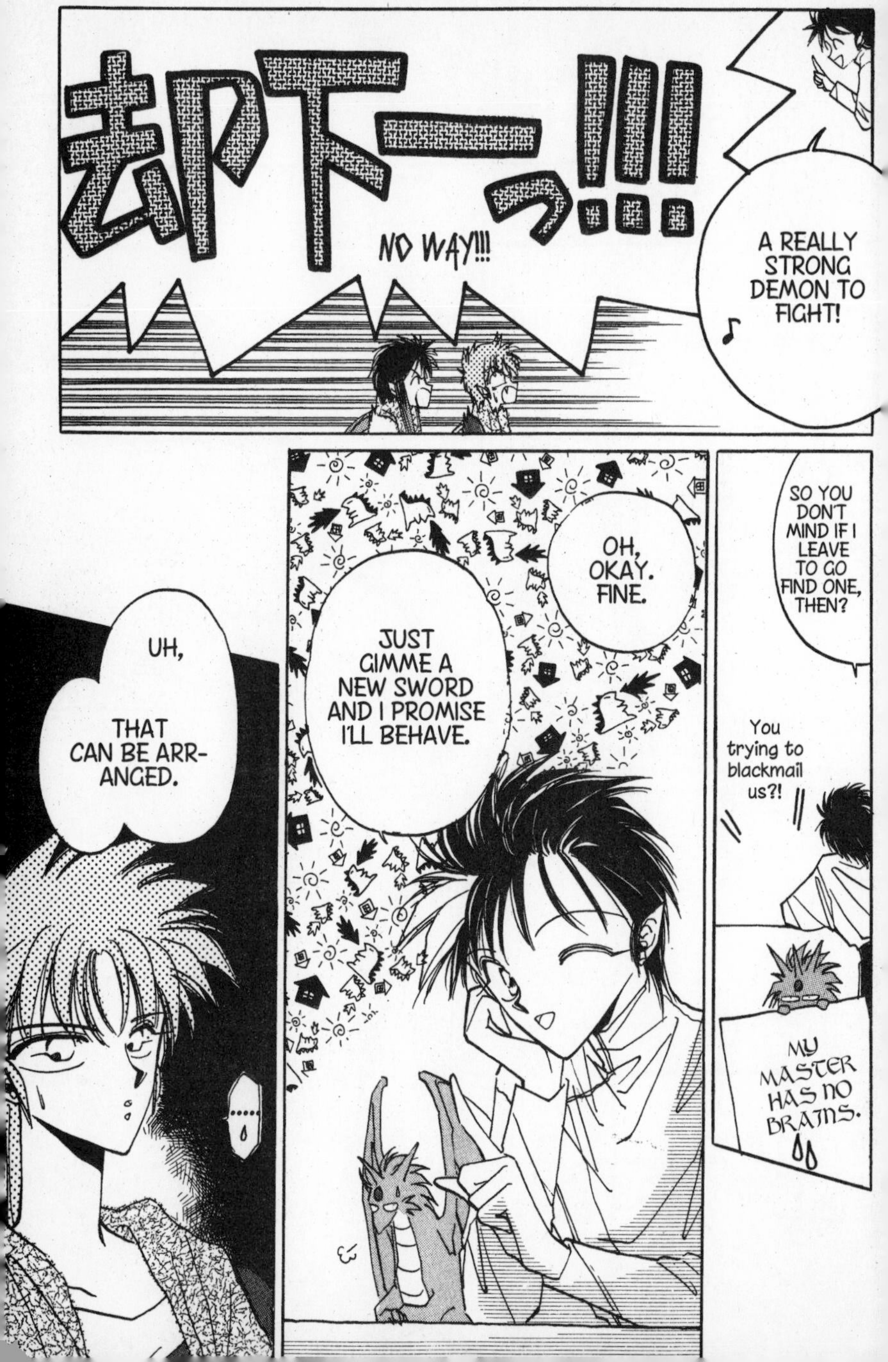
A REALLY STRONG DEMON TO FIGHT! ♪
却下っ!!!
NO WAY!!!
SO YOU DON'T MIND IF I LEAVE TO GO FIND ONE, THEN?
You trying to blackmail us?!
MY MASTER HAS NO BRAINS.
OH, OKAY. FINE.
JUST GIMME A NEW SWORD AND I PROMISE I'LL BEHAVE.
UH,
THAT CAN BE ARR-ANGED.
......

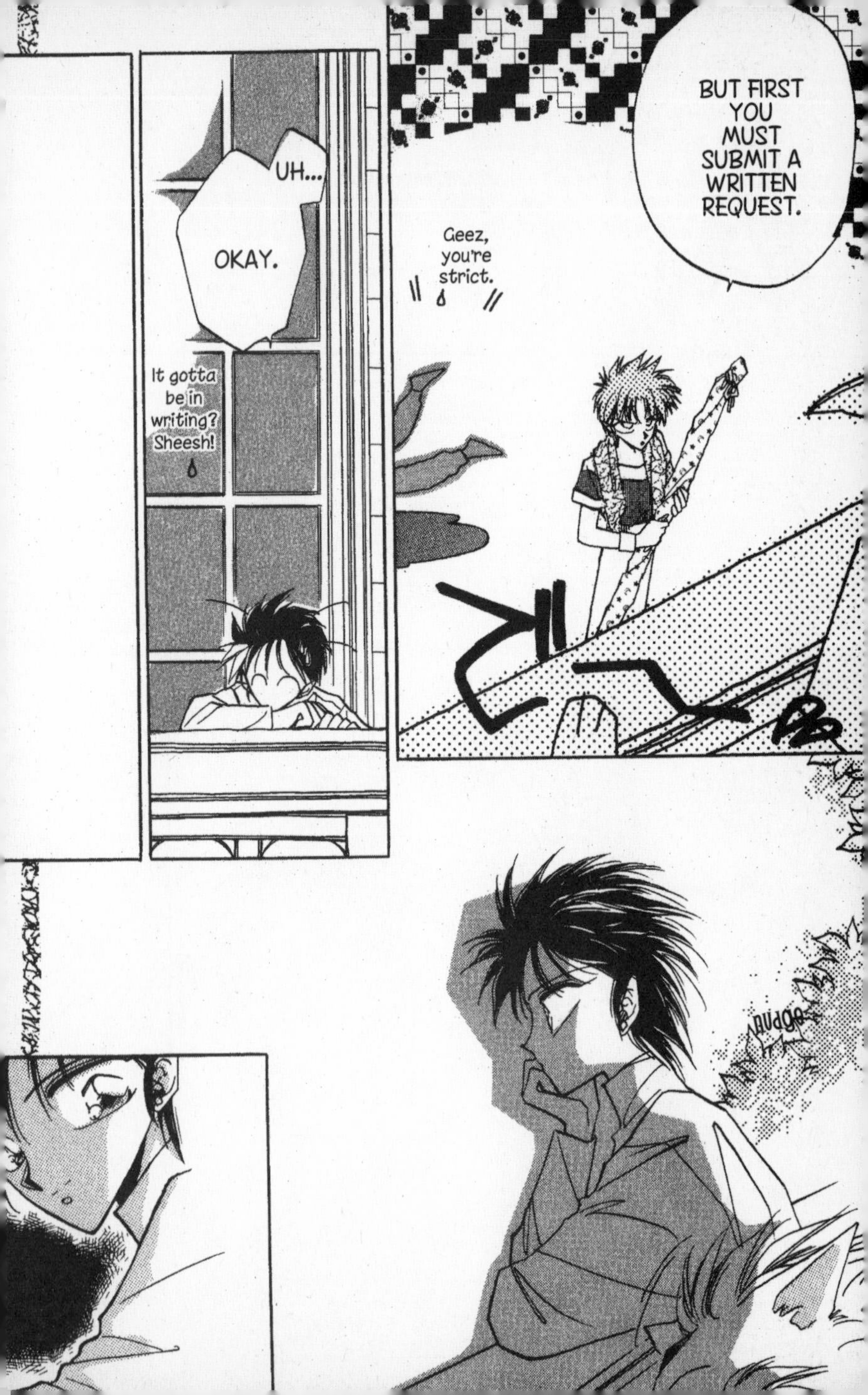
BUT FIRST YOU MUST SUBMIT A WRITTEN REQUEST.
Geez, you're strict.
UH...
OKAY.
It gotta be in writing? Sheesh!
nudge

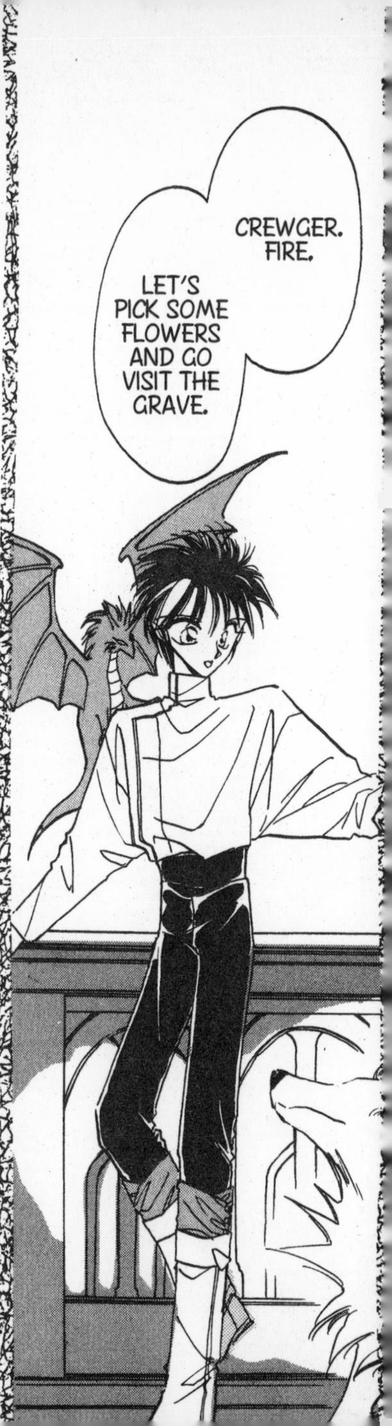
CREWGER. FIRE.
LET'S PICK SOME FLOWERS AND GO VISIT THE GRAVE.
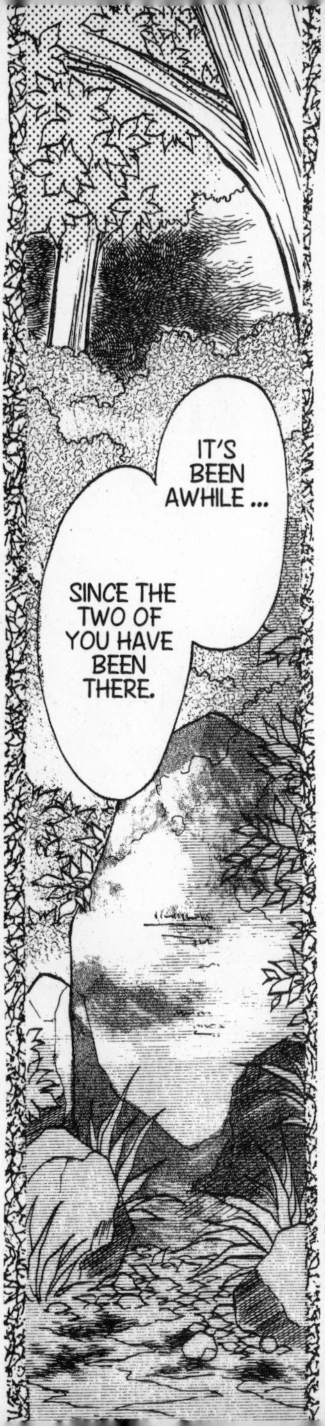
IT'S BEEN AWHILE ...
SINCE THE TWO OF YOU HAVE BEEN THERE.

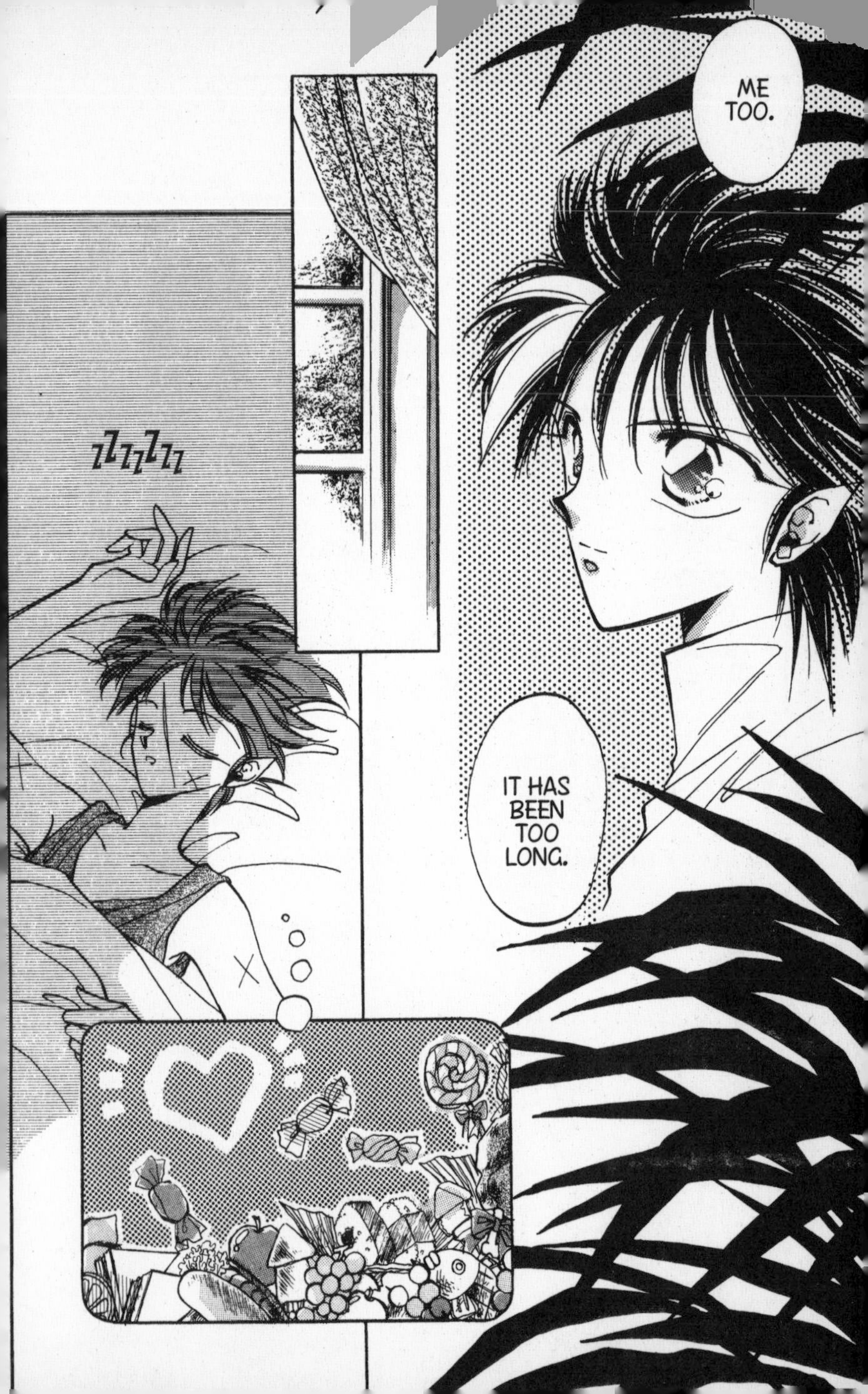
ME TOO.
IT HAS BEEN TOO LONG.
ZZZZZZ

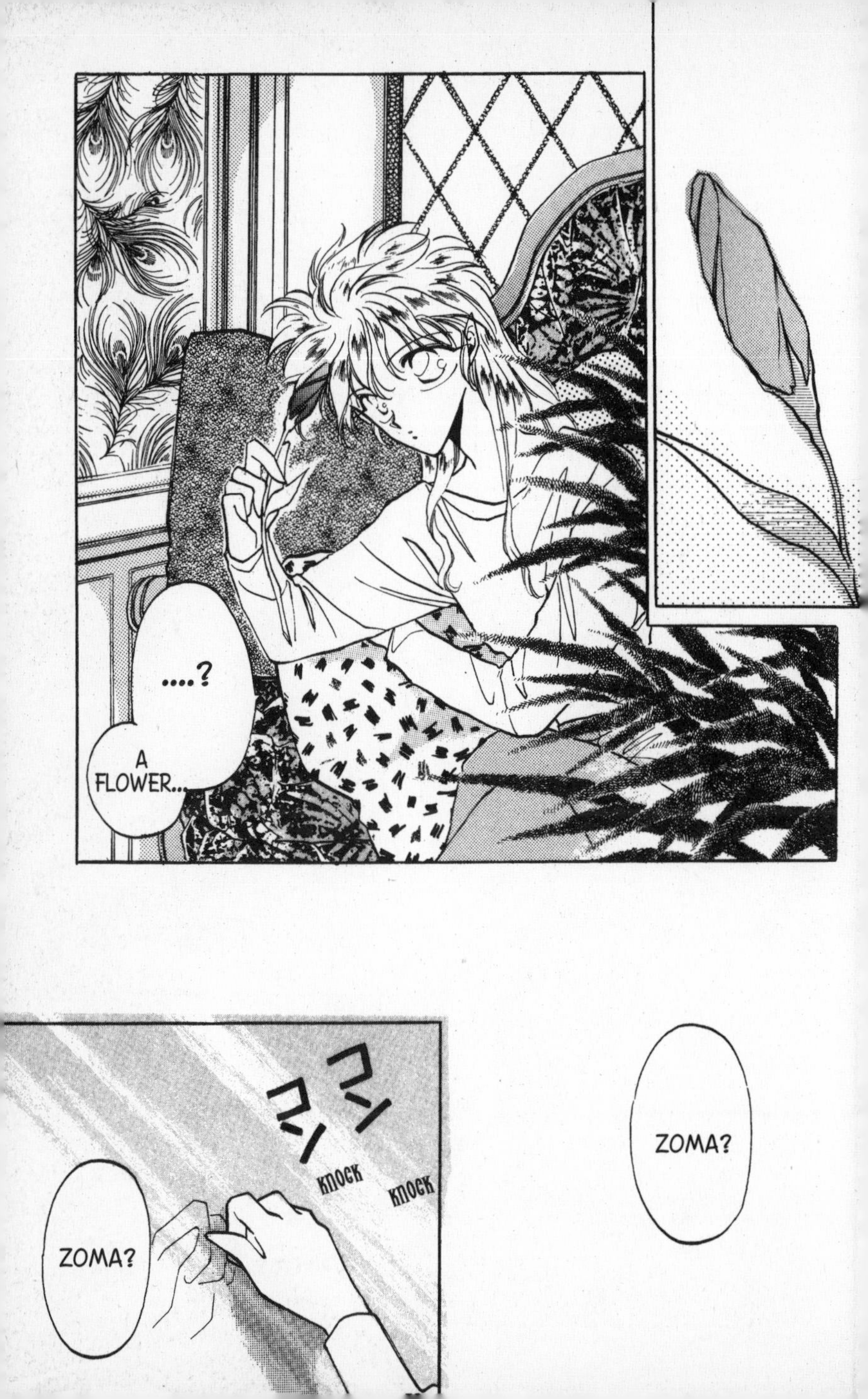
....?
A FLOWER...
ZOMA?
コン
コン
KNOCK
KNOCK
ZOMA?

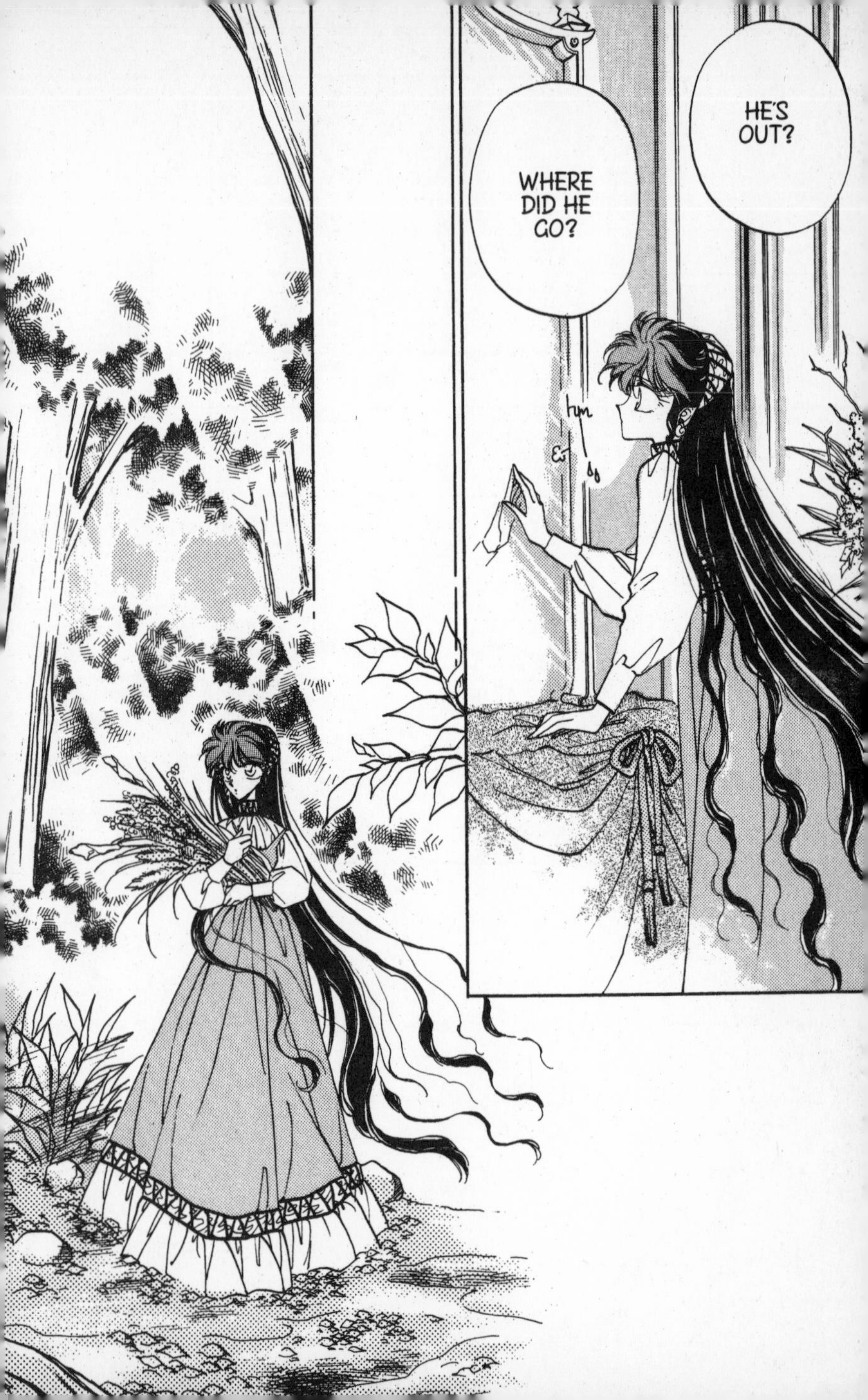
HE'S OUT?
WHERE DID HE GO?

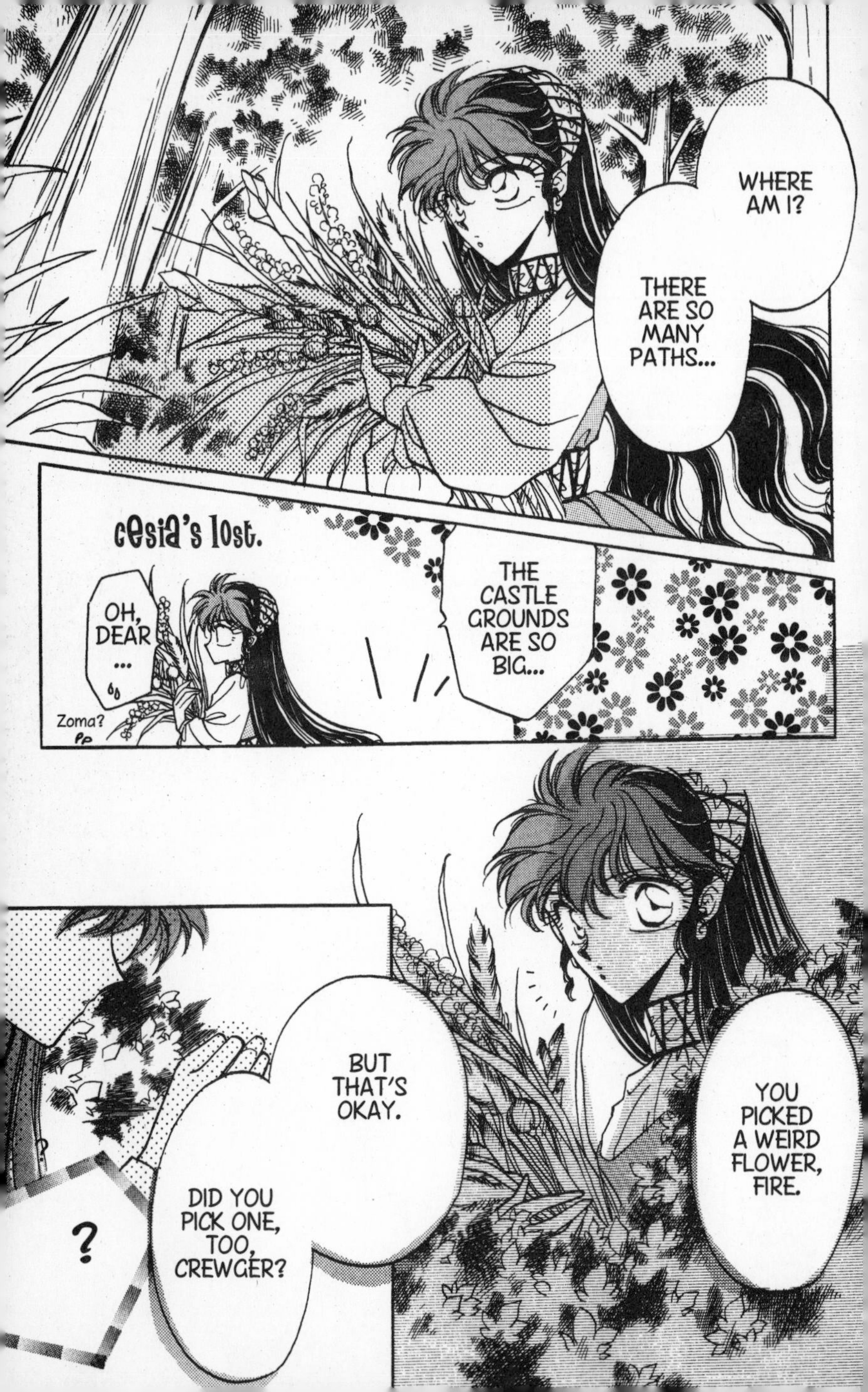
WHERE AM I?
THERE ARE SO MANY PATHS...
THE CASTLE GROUNDS ARE SO BIG...
cesia's lost.
OH, DEAR ...
Zoma?
YOU PICKED A WEIRD FLOWER, FIRE.
BUT THAT'S OKAY.
DID YOU PICK ONE, TOO, CREWGER?
?

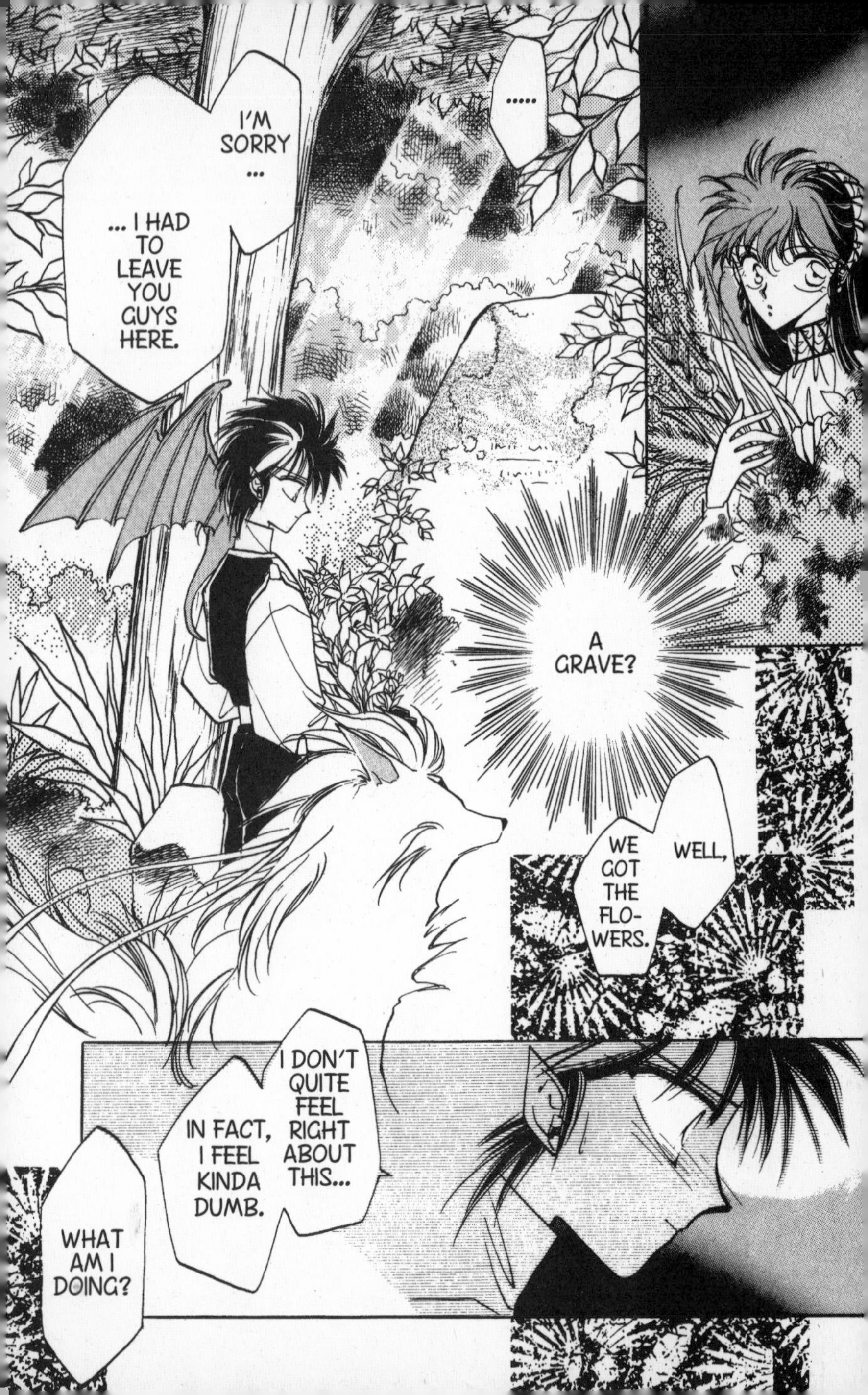
.....
I'M SORRY ...
... I HAD TO LEAVE YOU GUYS HERE.
A GRAVE?
WELL, WE GOT THE FLOWERS.
I DON'T QUITE FEEL RIGHT ABOUT THIS...
IN FACT, I FEEL KINDA DUMB.
WHAT AM I DOING?

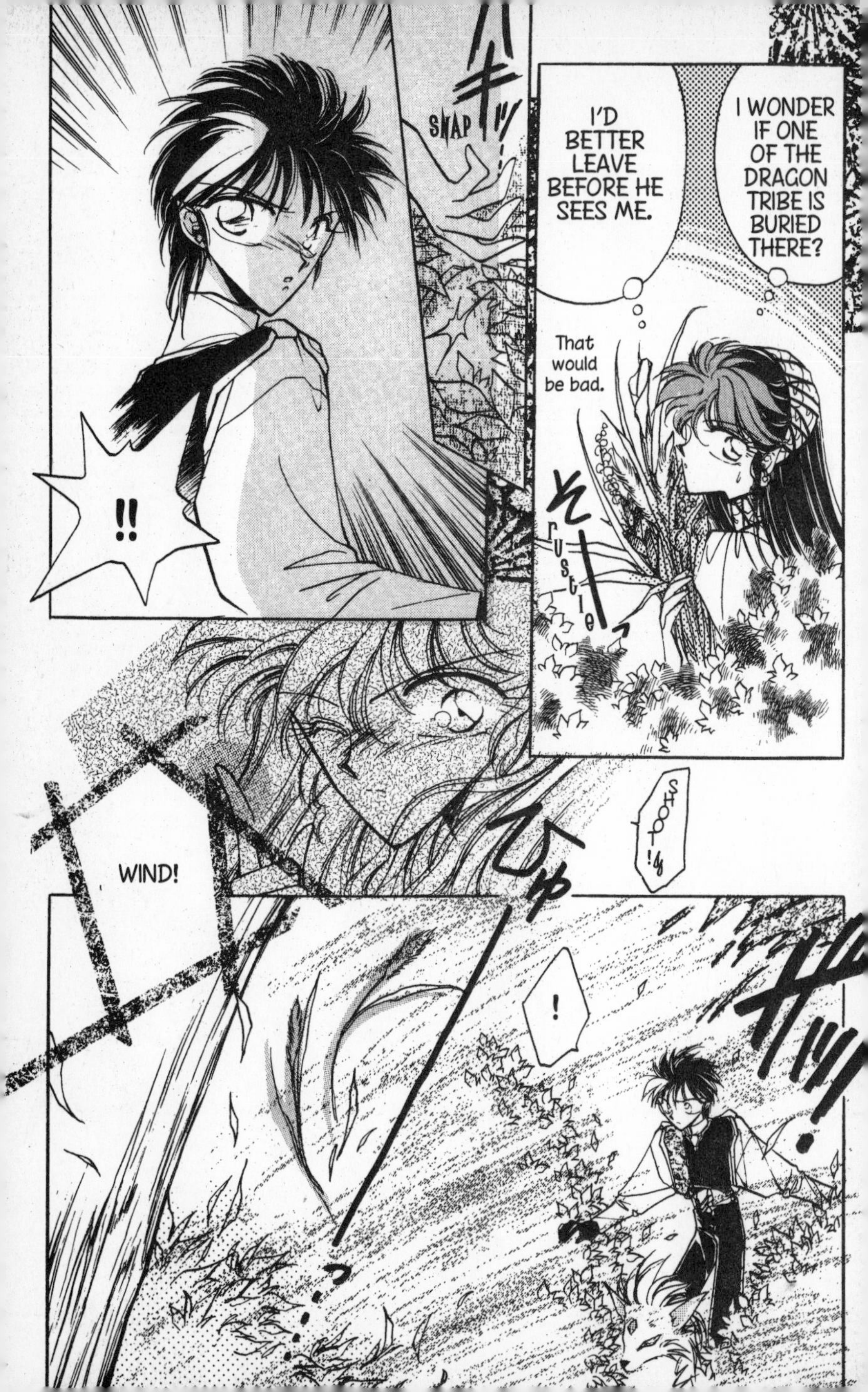
I WONDER IF ONE OF THE DRAGON TRIBE IS BURIED THERE?
I'D BETTER LEAVE BEFORE HE SEES ME.
That would be bad.
rustle
SNAP
!!
SHOOT!
WIND!
!

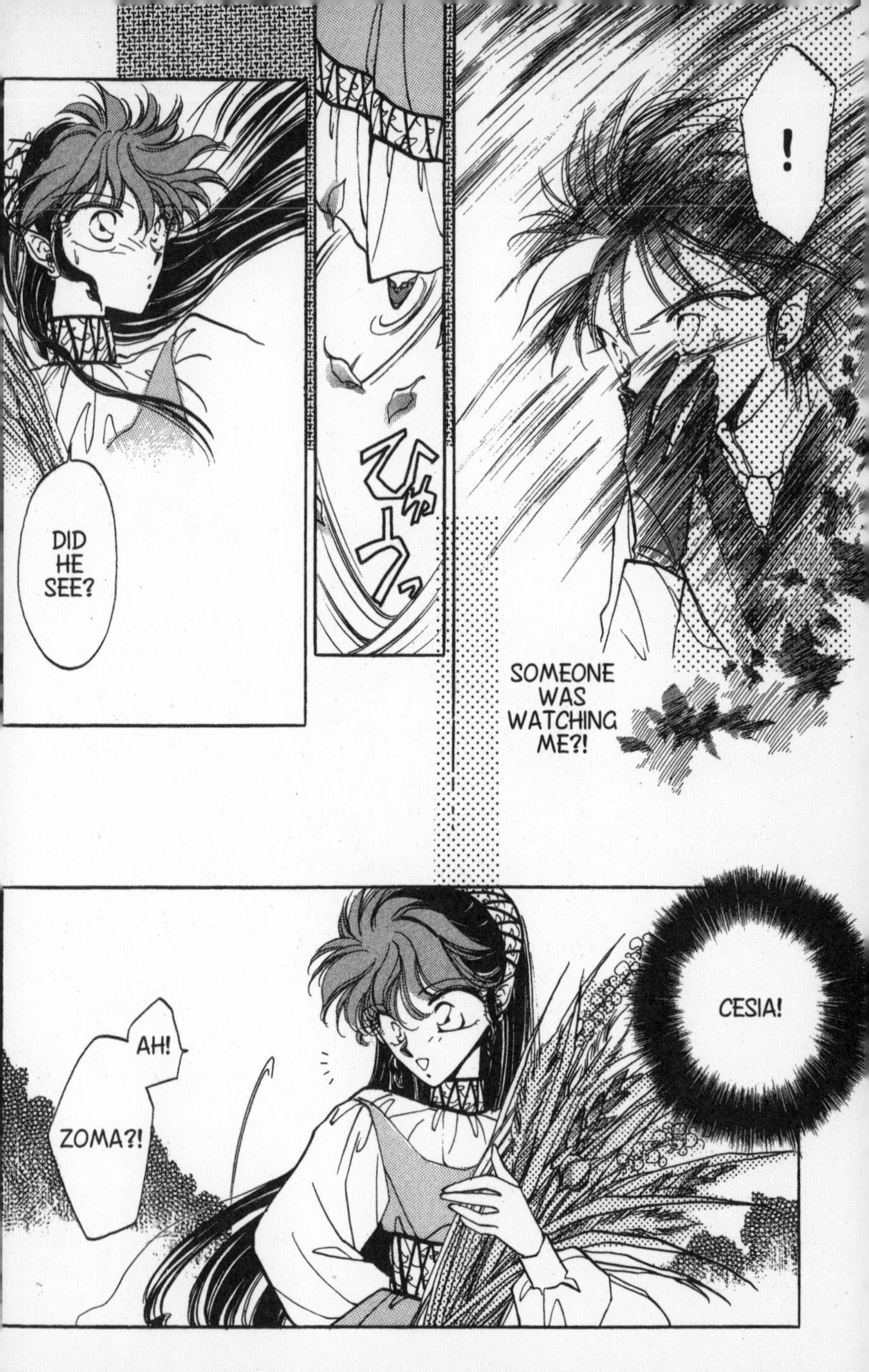
!
SOMEONE WAS WATCHING ME?!
ひゅーっ
DID HE SEE?
CESIA!
AH!
ZOMA?!

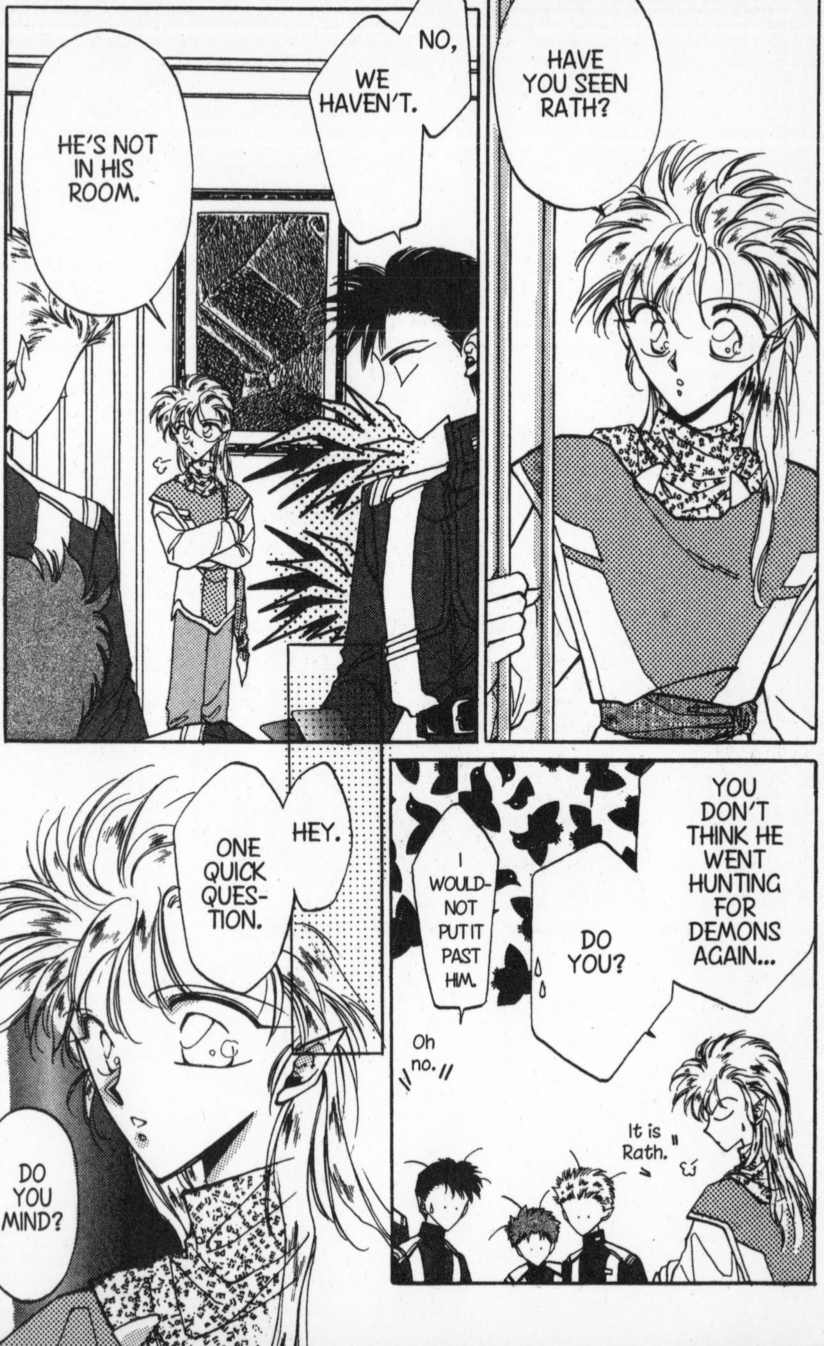
HAVE YOU SEEN RATH?
NO, WE HAVEN'T.
HE'S NOT IN HIS ROOM.
YOU DON'T THINK HE WENT HUNTING FOR DEMONS AGAIN...
DO YOU?
I WOULD-NOT PUT IT PAST HIM.
It is Rath.
Oh no.
HEY.
ONE QUICK QUES-TION.
DO YOU MIND?

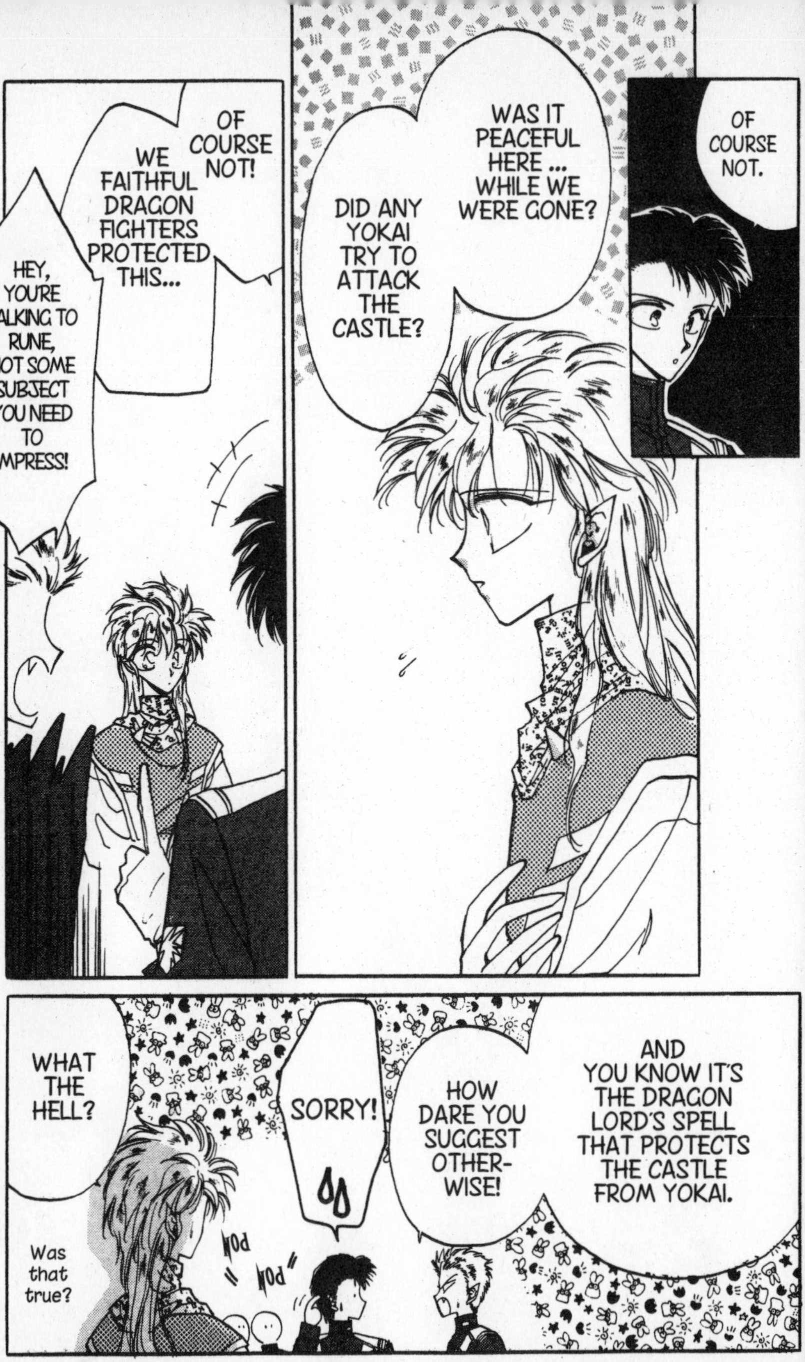
WAS IT PEACEFUL HERE ... WHILE WE WERE GONE?
DID ANY YOKAI TRY TO ATTACK THE CASTLE?
OF COURSE NOT.
OF COURSE NOT!
WE FAITHFUL DRAGON FIGHTERS PROTECTED THIS...
HEY, YOU'RE TALKING TO RUNE, NOT SOME SUBJECT YOU NEED TO IMPRESS!
AND YOU KNOW IT'S THE DRAGON LORD'S SPELL THAT PROTECTS THE CASTLE FROM YOKAI.
HOW DARE YOU SUGGEST OTHER-WISE!
SORRY!
NOD
NOD
WHAT THE HELL?
Was that true?

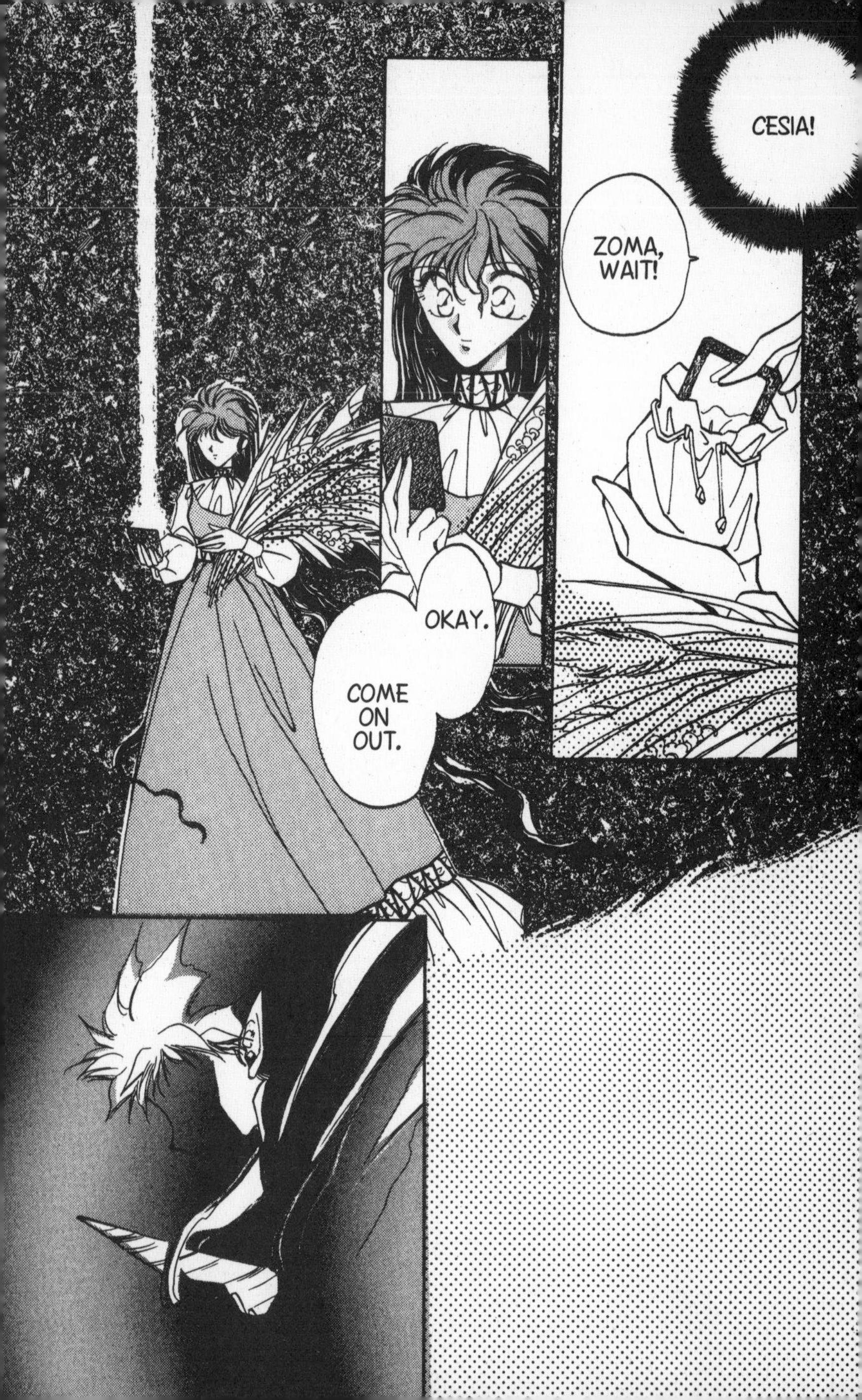
CESIA!
ZOMA, WAIT!
OKAY.
COME ON OUT.

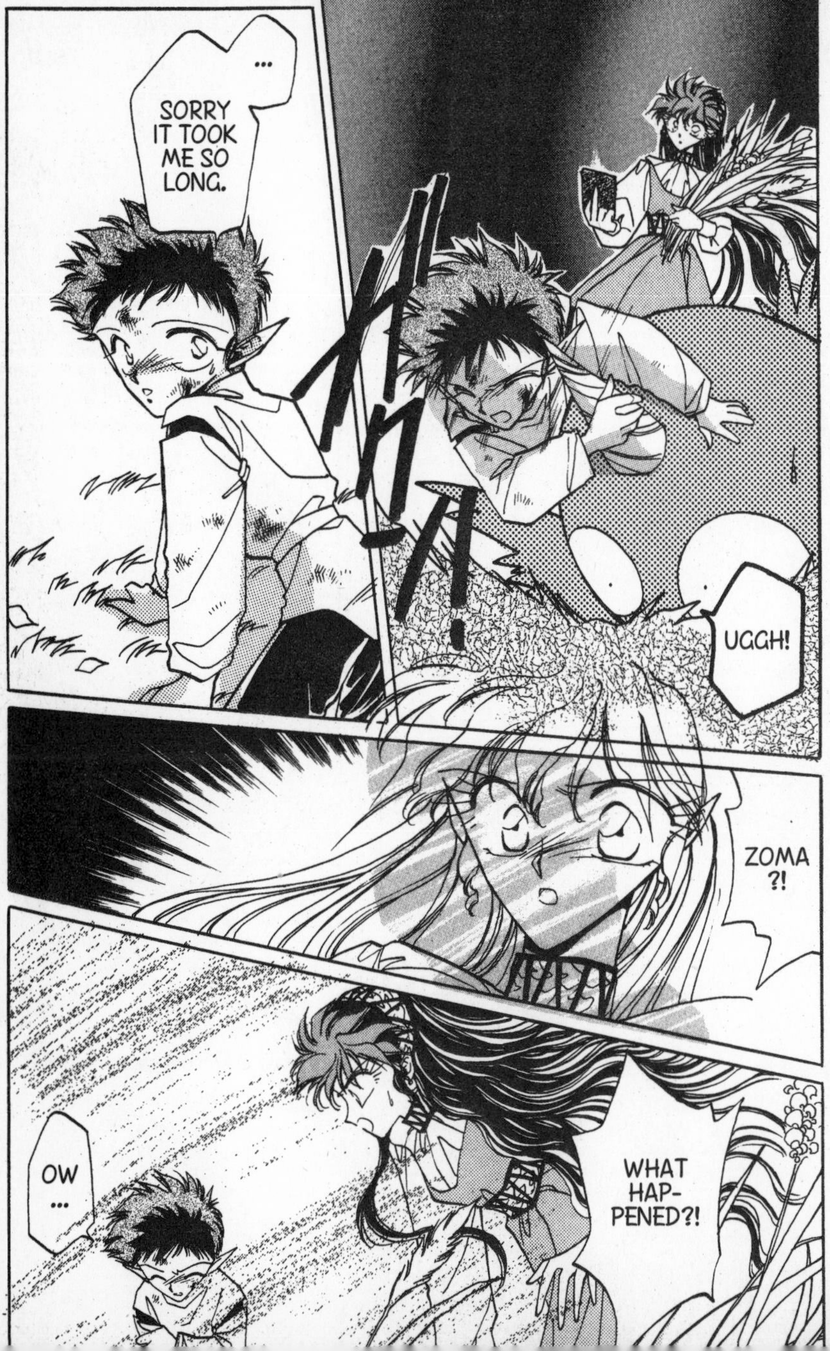
UGGH!
...
SORRY IT TOOK ME SO LONG.
ZOMA ?!
WHAT HAP-PENED?!
OW ...

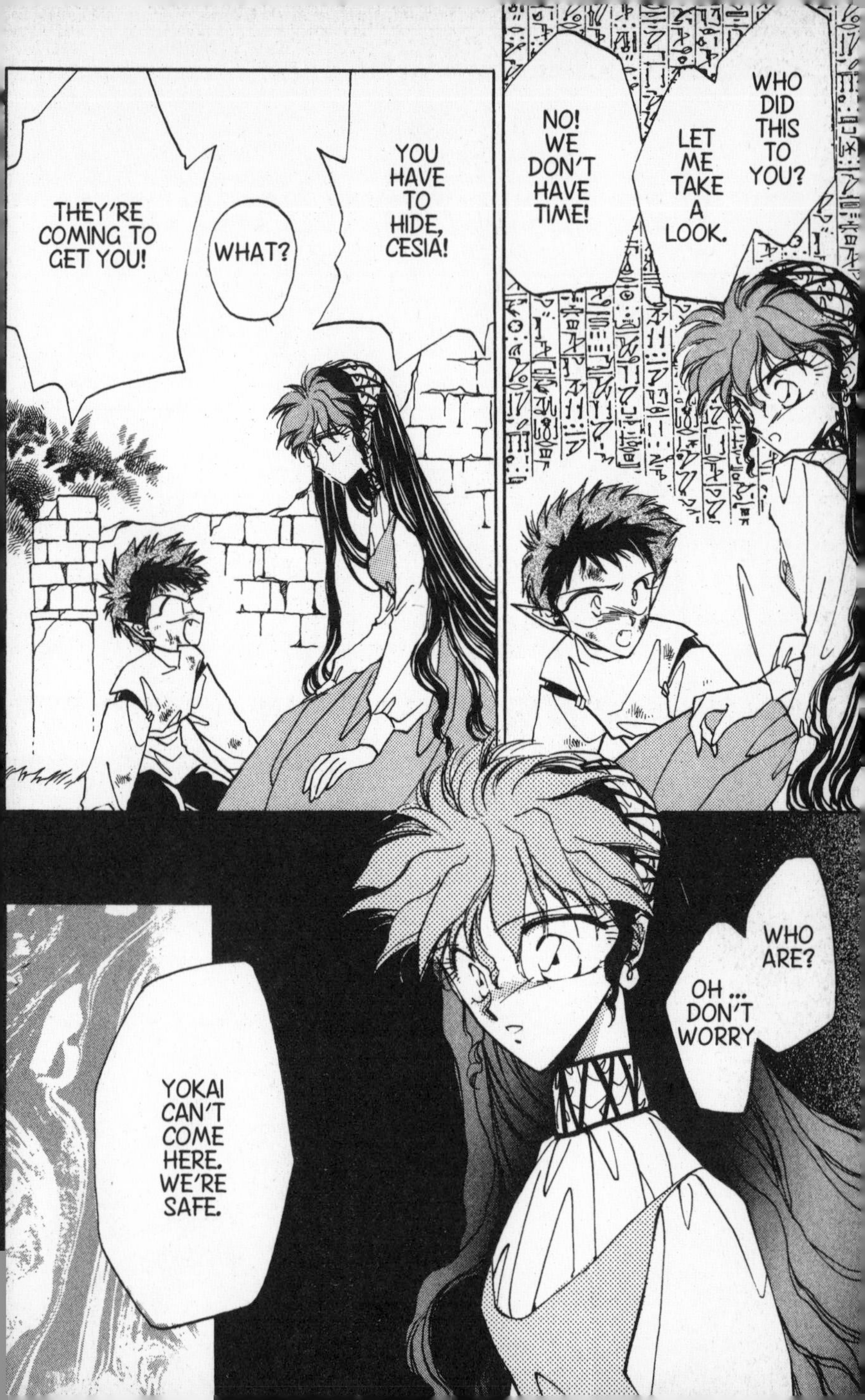
WHO DID THIS TO YOU?
LET ME TAKE A LOOK.
NO! WE DON'T HAVE TIME!
YOU HAVE TO HIDE, CESIA!
WHAT?
THEY'RE COMING TO GET YOU!
WHO ARE?
OH ... DON'T WORRY
YOKAI CAN'T COME HERE. WE'RE SAFE.

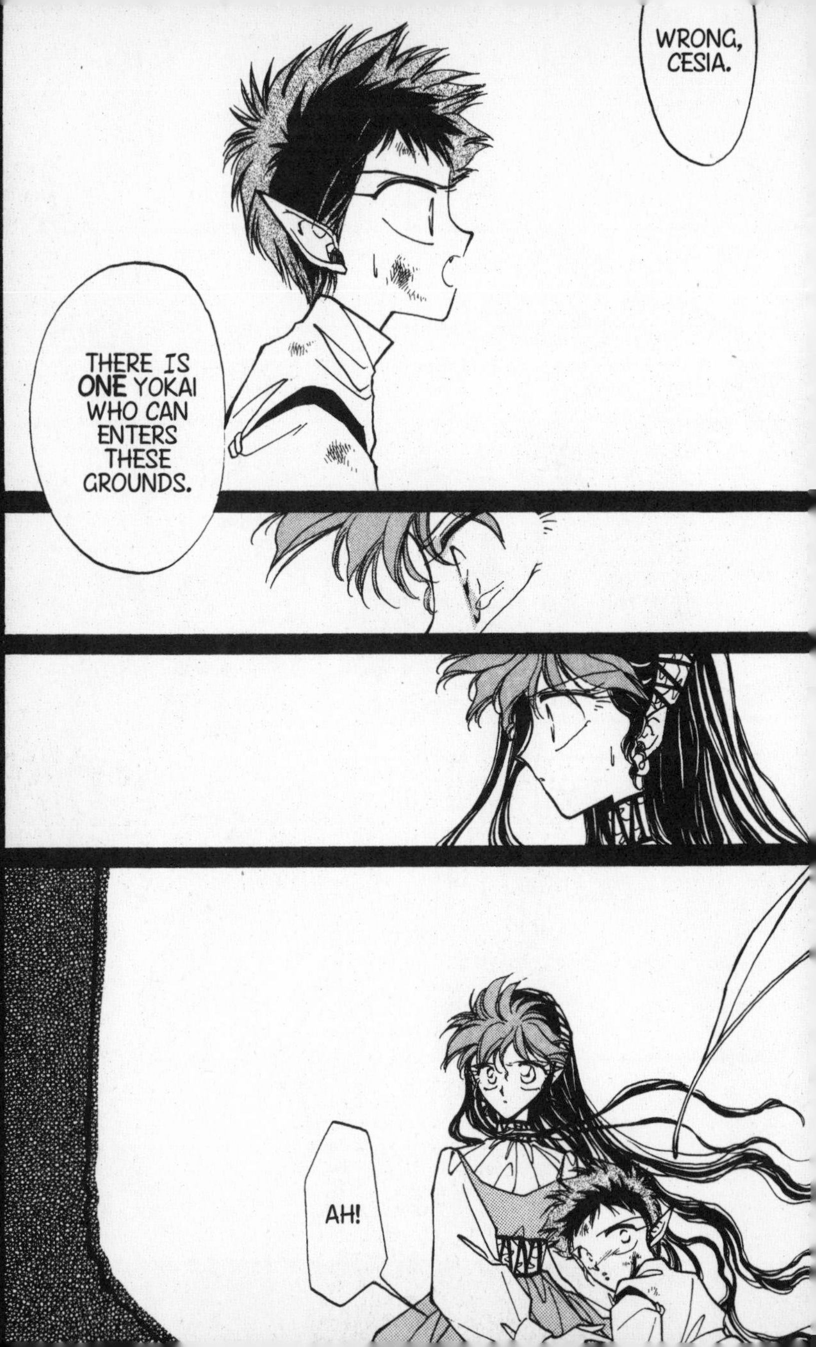
WRONG, CESIA.
THERE IS ONE YOKAI WHO CAN ENTERS THESE GROUNDS.
AH!

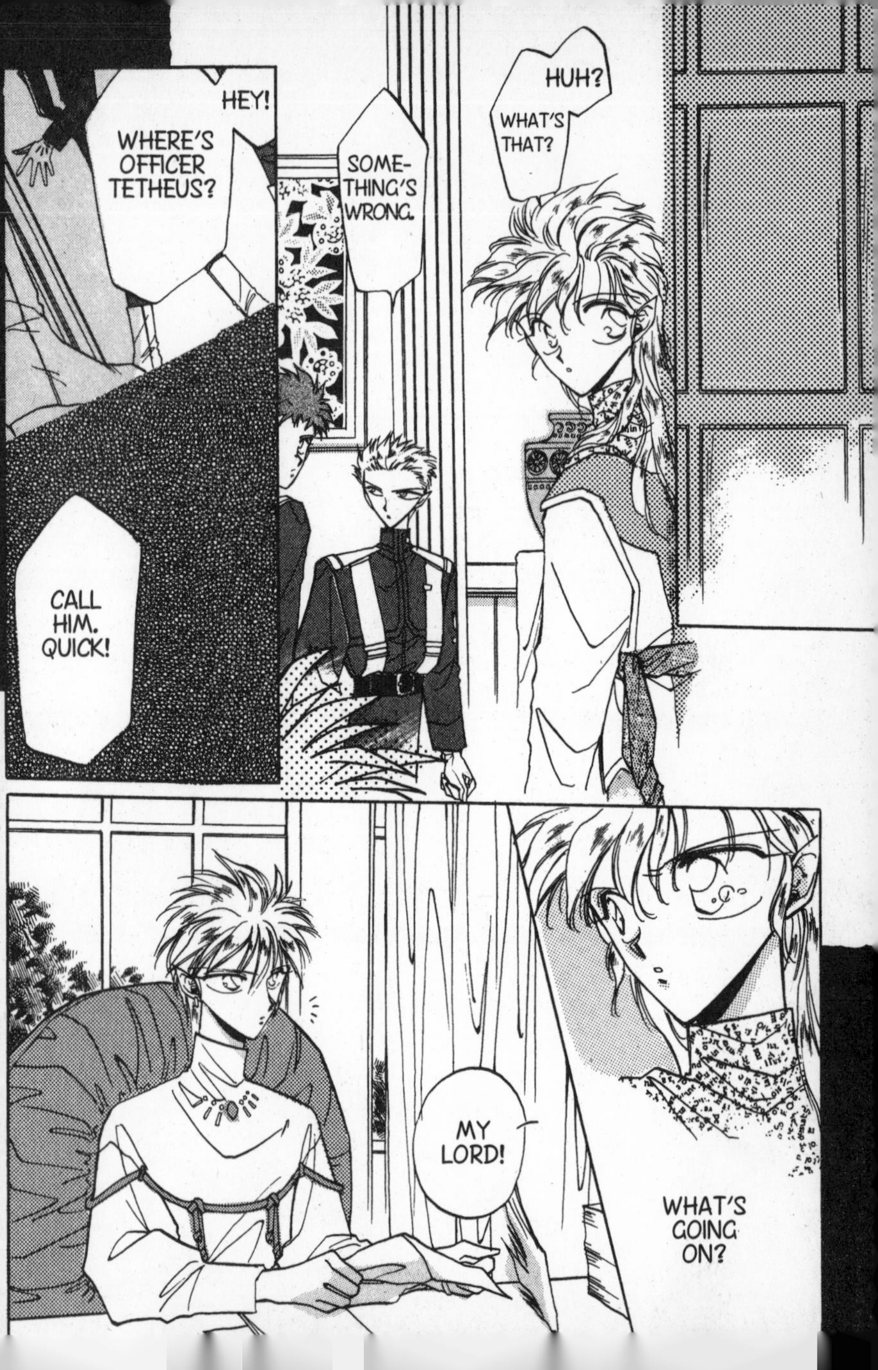
HUH?
WHAT'S THAT?
SOME-THING'S WRONG.
HEY!
WHERE'S OFFICER TETHEUS?
CALL HIM. QUICK!
WHAT'S GOING ON?
MY LORD!

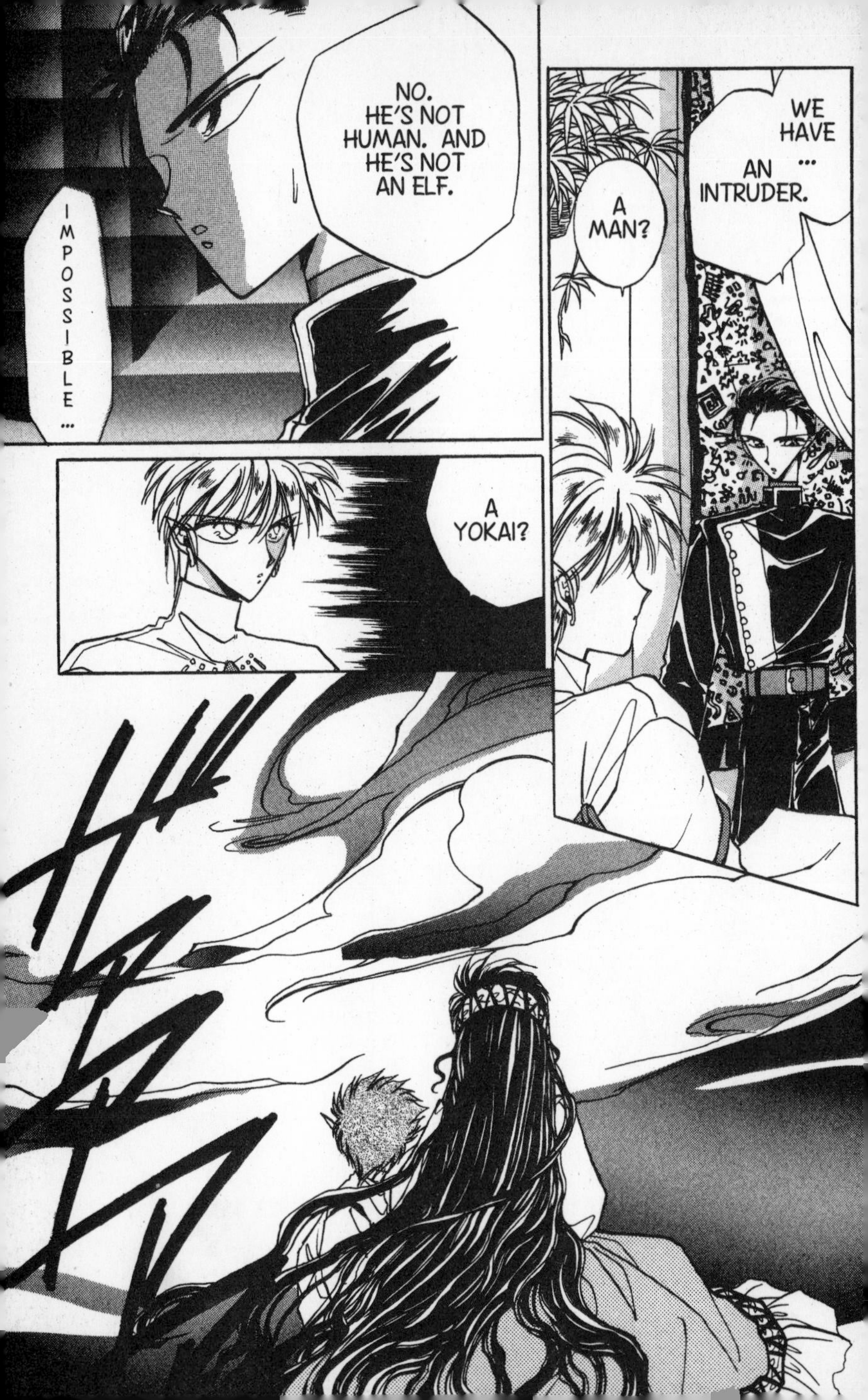
WE HAVE ... AN INTRUDER.
A MAN?
NO. HE'S NOT HUMAN. AND HE'S NOT AN ELF.
IMPOSSIBLE...
A YOKAI?

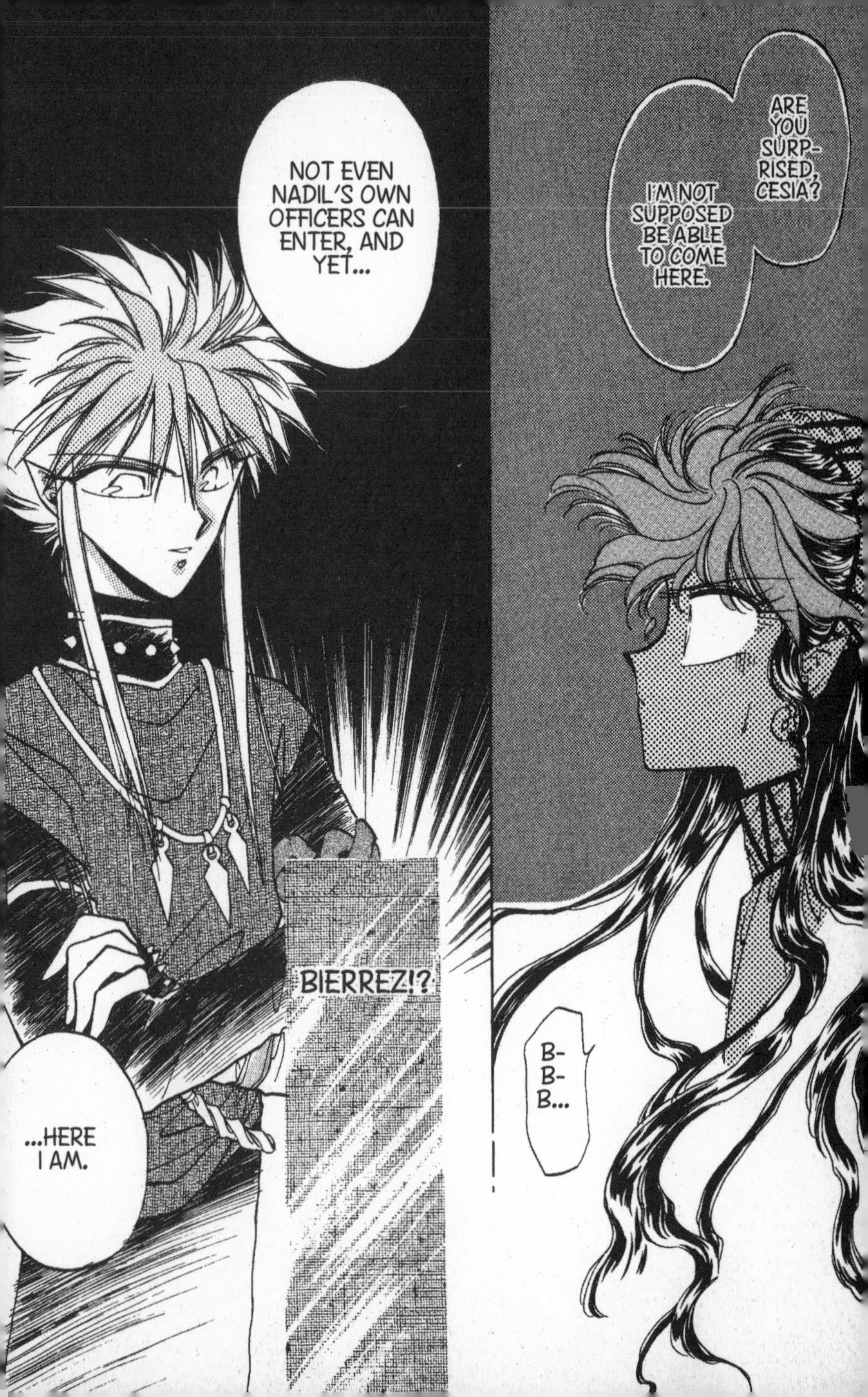
ARE YOU SURP-RISED, CESIA?
I'M NOT SUPPOSED BE ABLE TO COME HERE.
B-B-B...
NOT EVEN NADIL'S OWN OFFICERS CAN ENTER, AND YET...
BIERREZ!?
...HERE I AM.

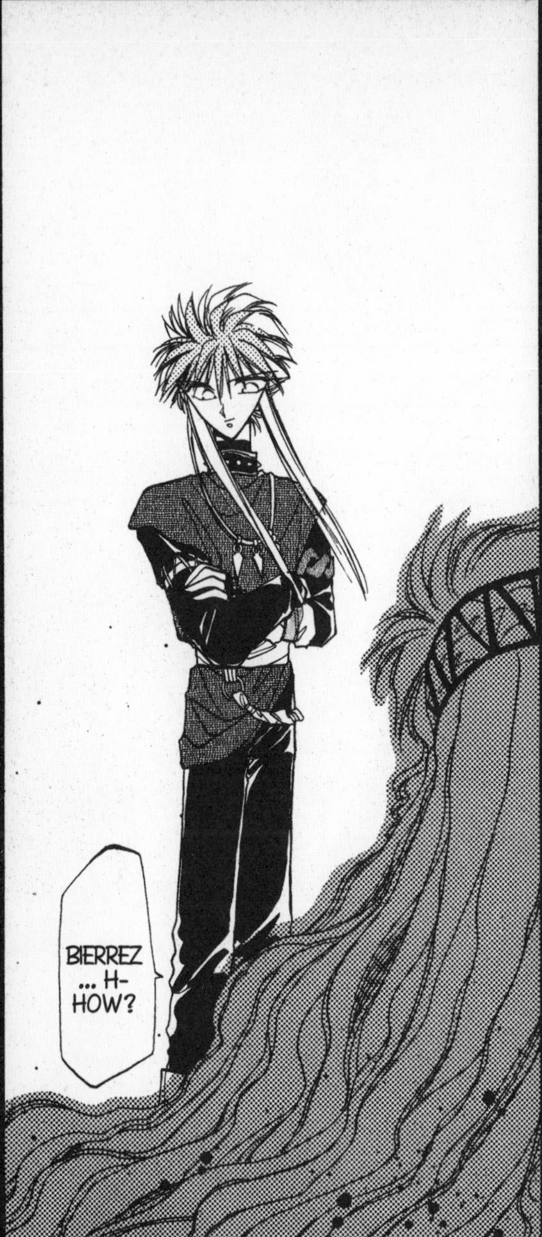
BIERREZ ... H-HOW?

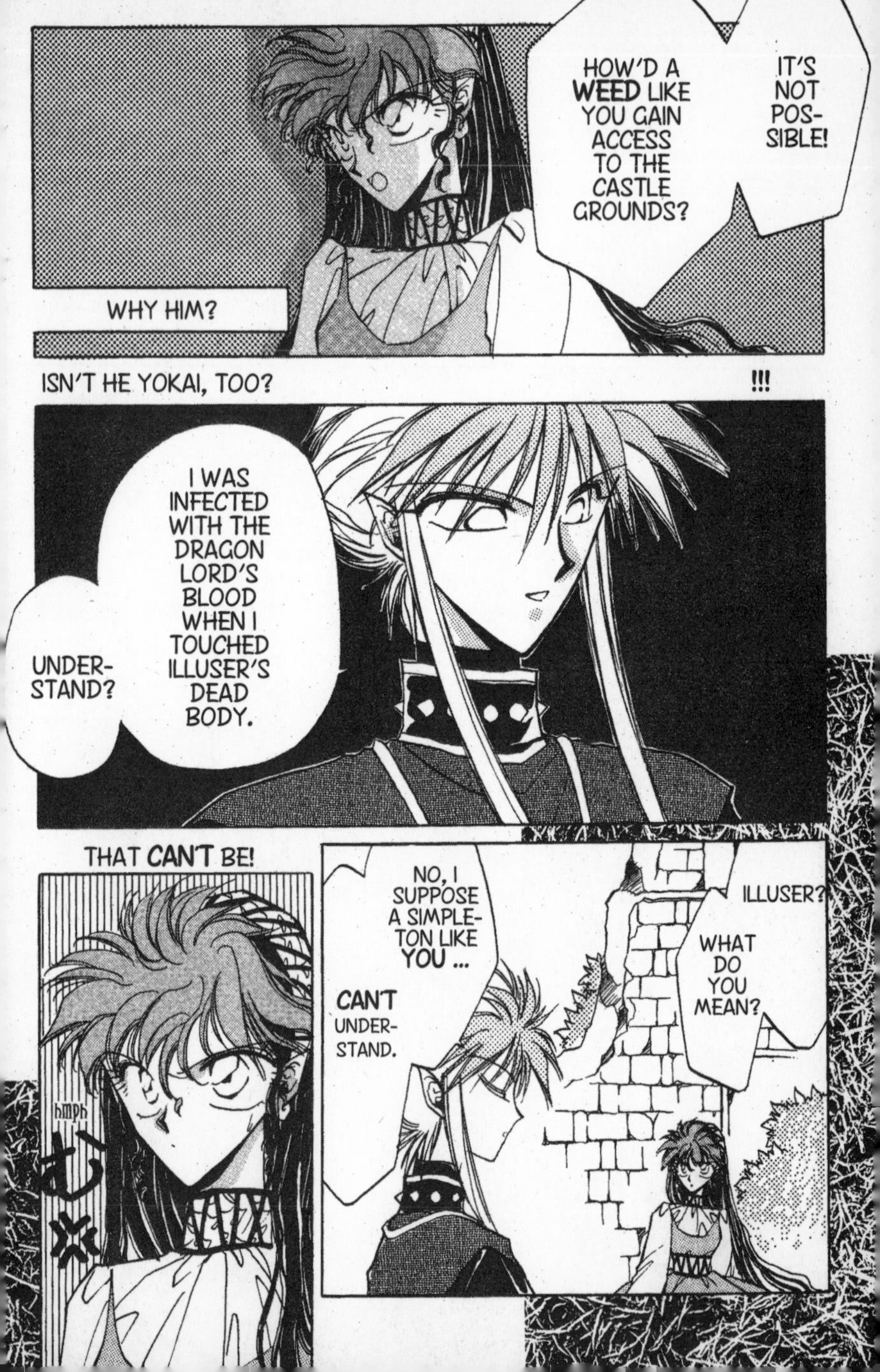
IT'S NOT POS-SIBLE!
HOW'D A **WEED** LIKE YOU GAIN ACCESS TO THE CASTLE GROUNDS?
WHY HIM?
!!!
ISN'T HE YOKAI, TOO?
I WAS INFECTED WITH THE DRAGON LORD'S BLOOD WHEN I TOUCHED ILLUSER'S DEAD BODY.
UNDER-STAND?
ILLUSER?
WHAT DO YOU MEAN?
NO, I SUPPOSE A SIMPLE-TON LIKE **YOU** ...
CAN'T UNDER-STAND.
THAT **CAN'T** BE!
hmph

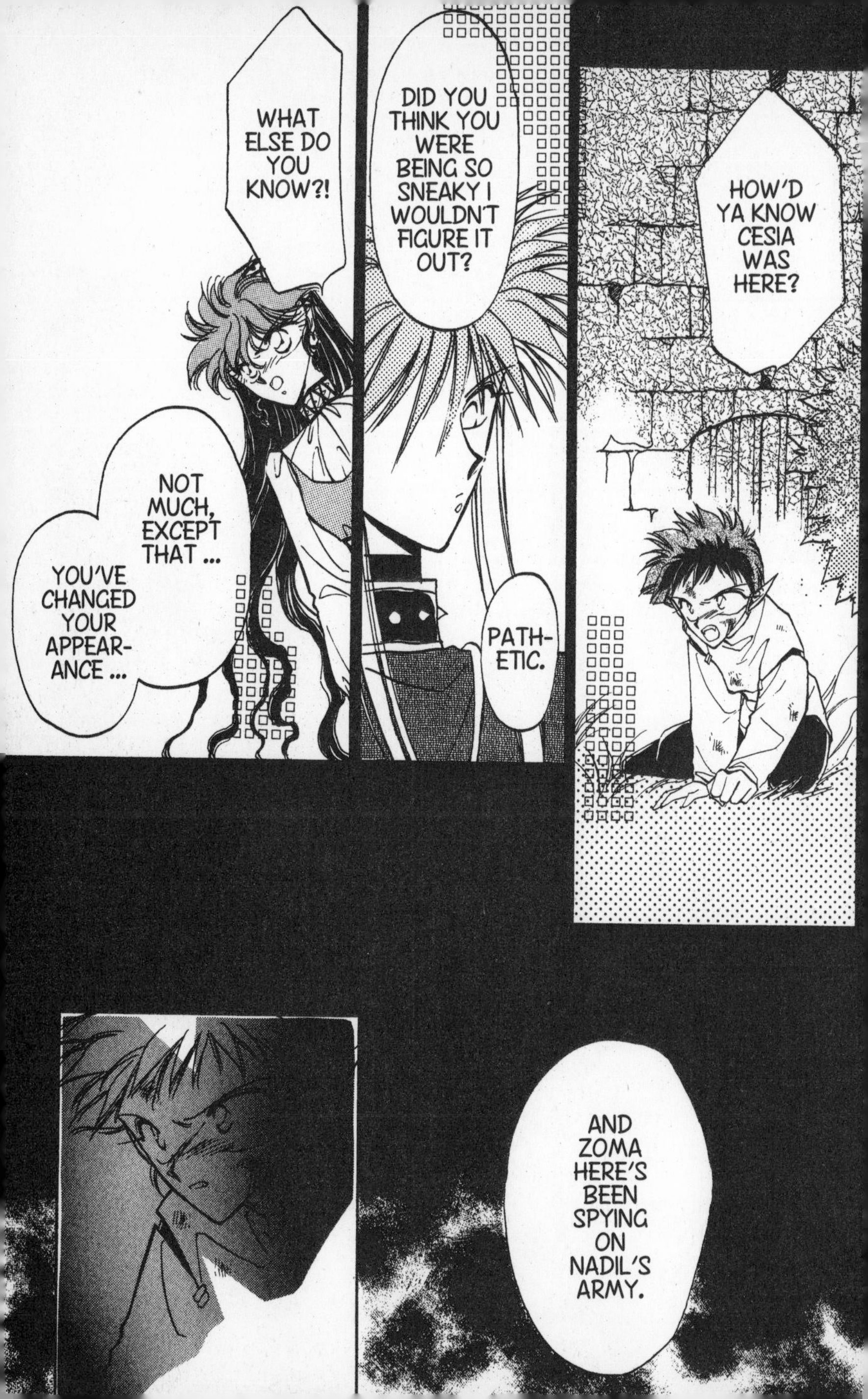
HOW'D YA KNOW CESIA WAS HERE?
DID YOU THINK YOU WERE BEING SO SNEAKY I WOULDN'T FIGURE IT OUT?
PATH-ETIC.
WHAT ELSE DO YOU KNOW?!
NOT MUCH, EXCEPT THAT ...
YOU'VE CHANGED YOUR APPEAR-ANCE ...
AND ZOMA HERE'S BEEN SPYING ON NADIL'S ARMY.

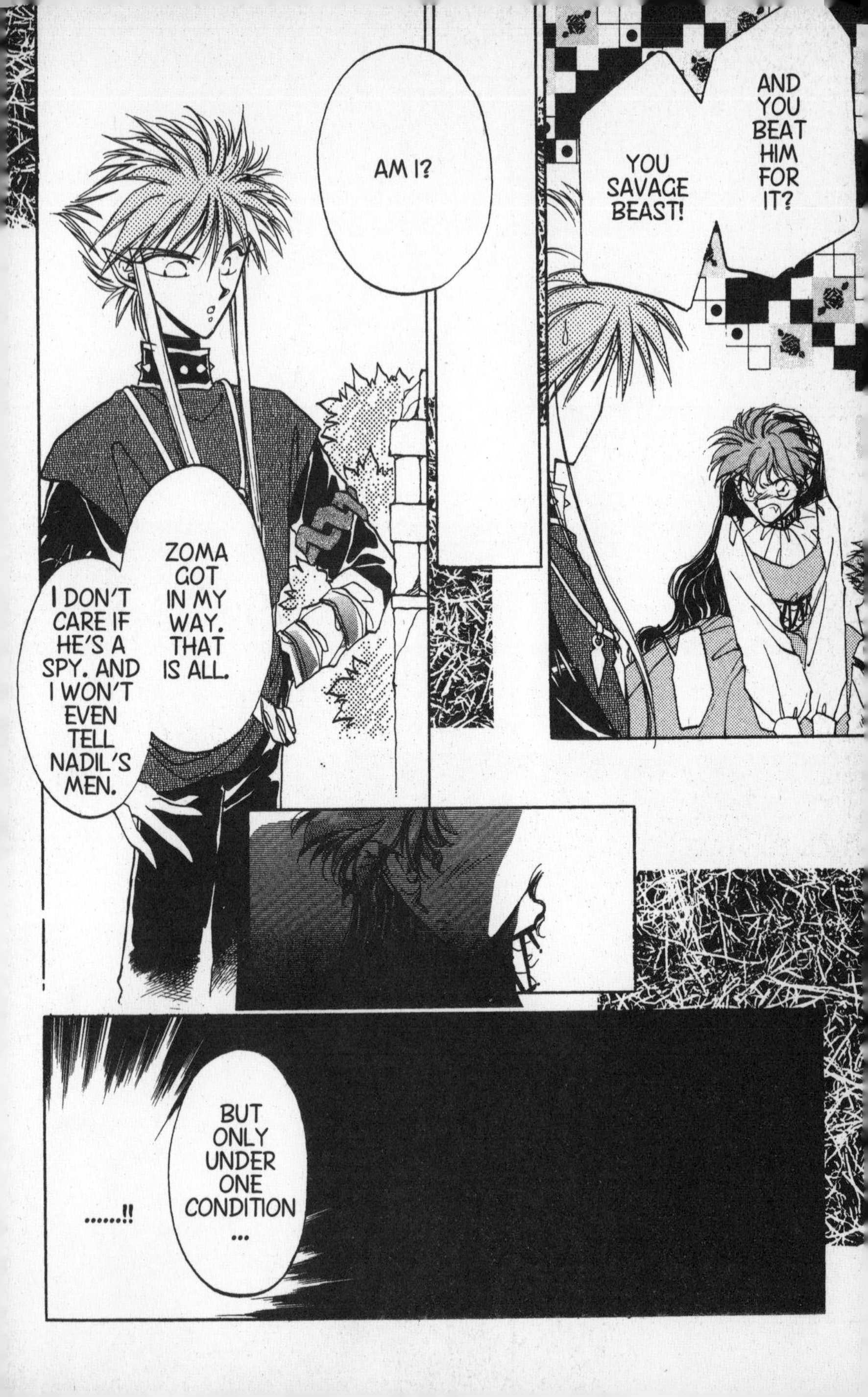
AND YOU BEAT HIM FOR IT?
YOU SAVAGE BEAST!
AM I?
ZOMA GOT IN MY WAY. THAT IS ALL.
I DON'T CARE IF HE'S A SPY. AND I WON'T EVEN TELL NADIL'S MEN.
BUT ONLY UNDER ONE CONDITION ...
......!!

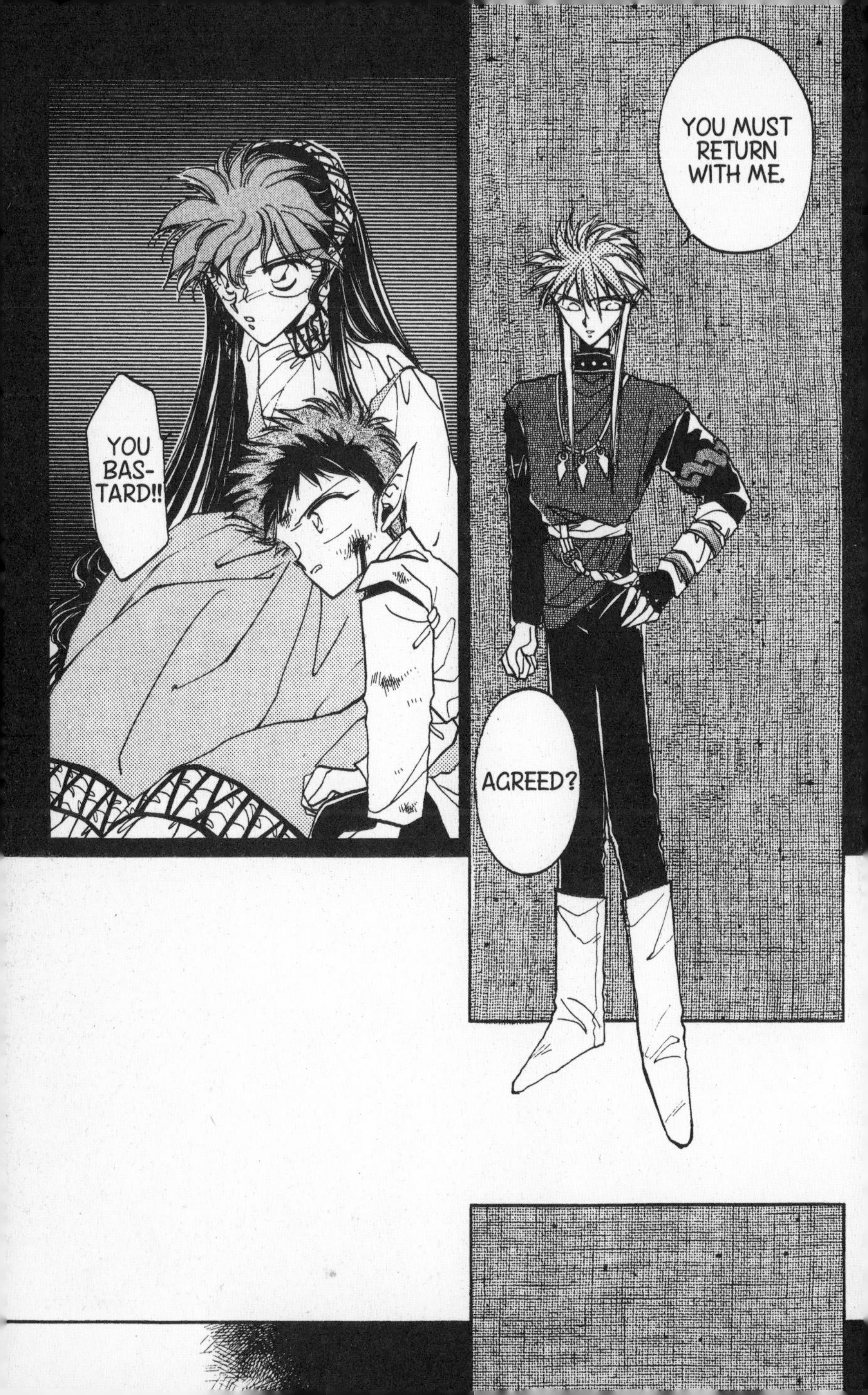
YOU MUST RETURN WITH ME.
AGREED?
YOU BAS-TARD!!

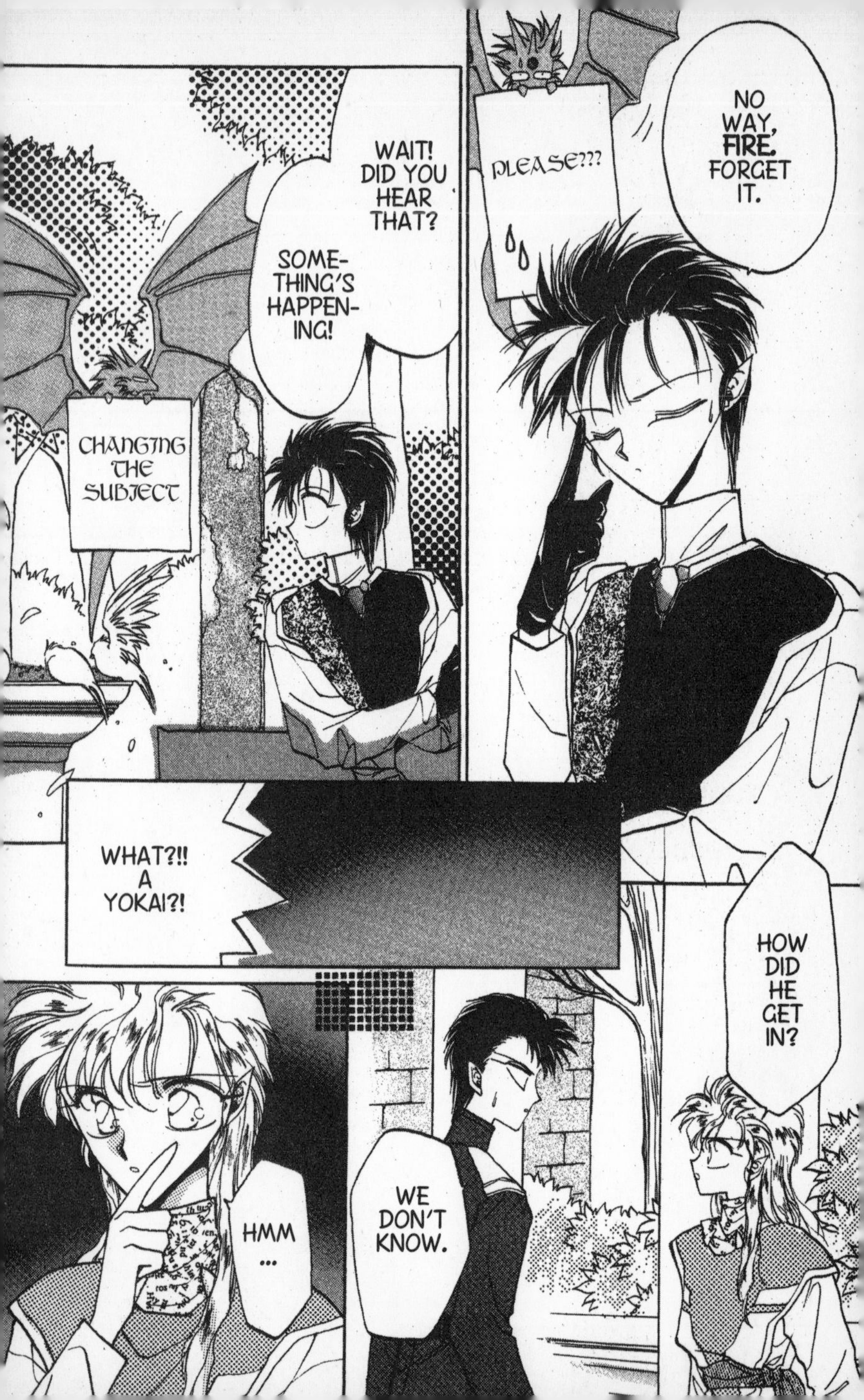
NO WAY, FIRE. FORGET IT.
PLEASE???
WAIT! DID YOU HEAR THAT?
SOMETHING'S HAPPENING!
CHANGING THE SUBJECT
WHAT?!! A YOKAI?!
HOW DID HE GET IN?
WE DON'T KNOW.
HMM ...

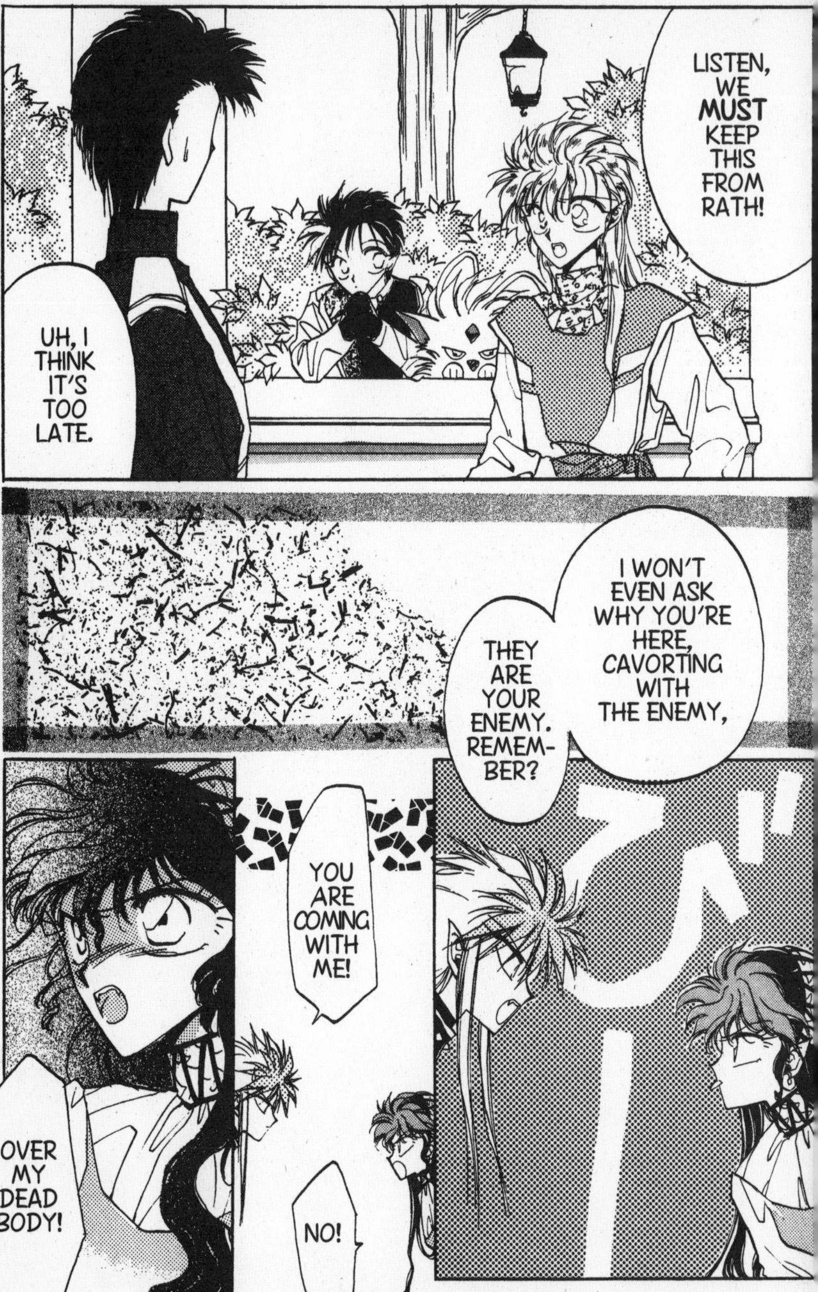

LISTEN, WE MUST KEEP THIS FROM RATH!
UH, I THINK IT'S TOO LATE.
I WON'T EVEN ASK WHY YOU'RE HERE, CAVORTING WITH THE ENEMY,
THEY ARE YOUR ENEMY. REMEMBER?
YOU ARE COMING WITH ME!
OVER MY DEAD BODY!
NO!

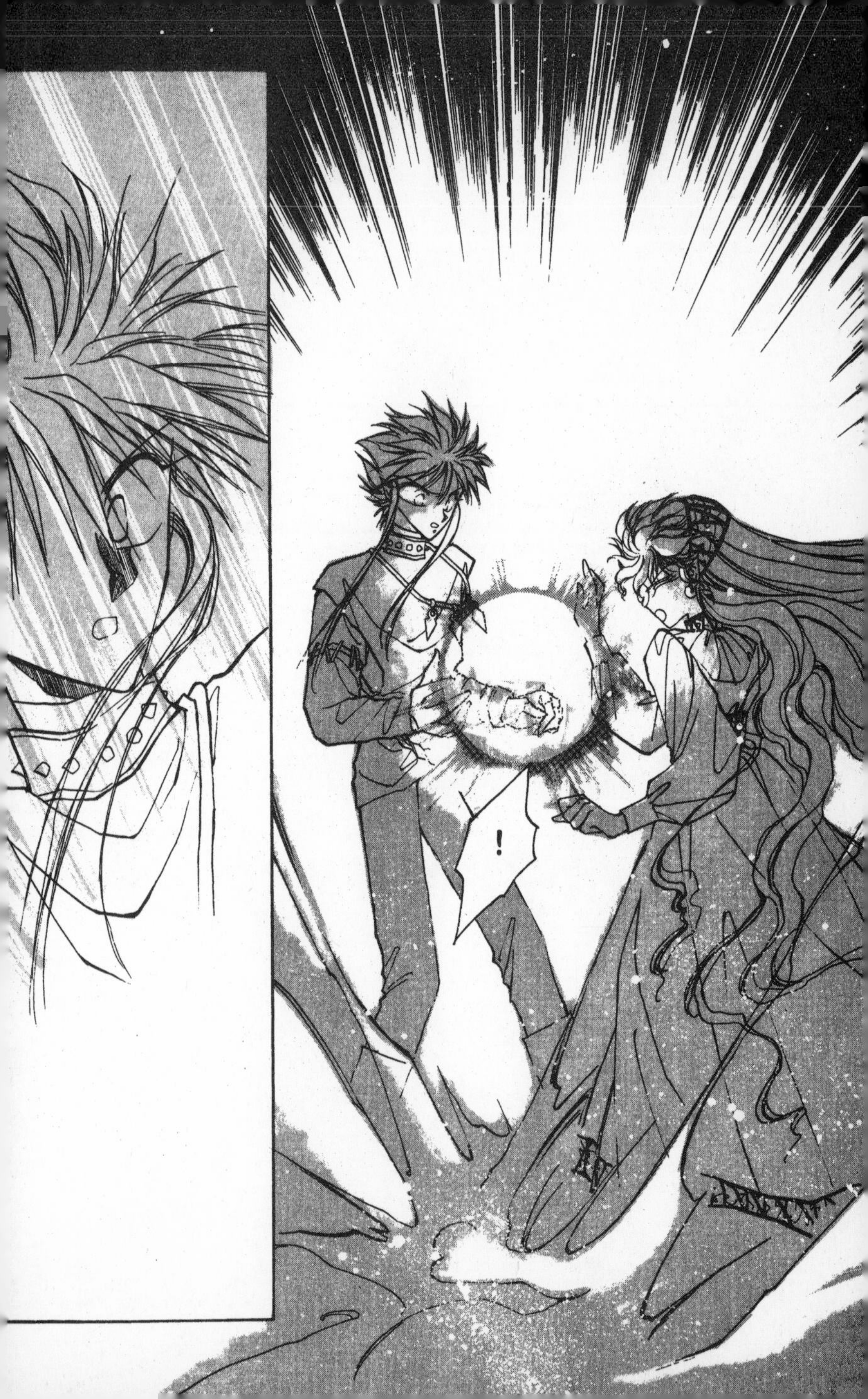
!

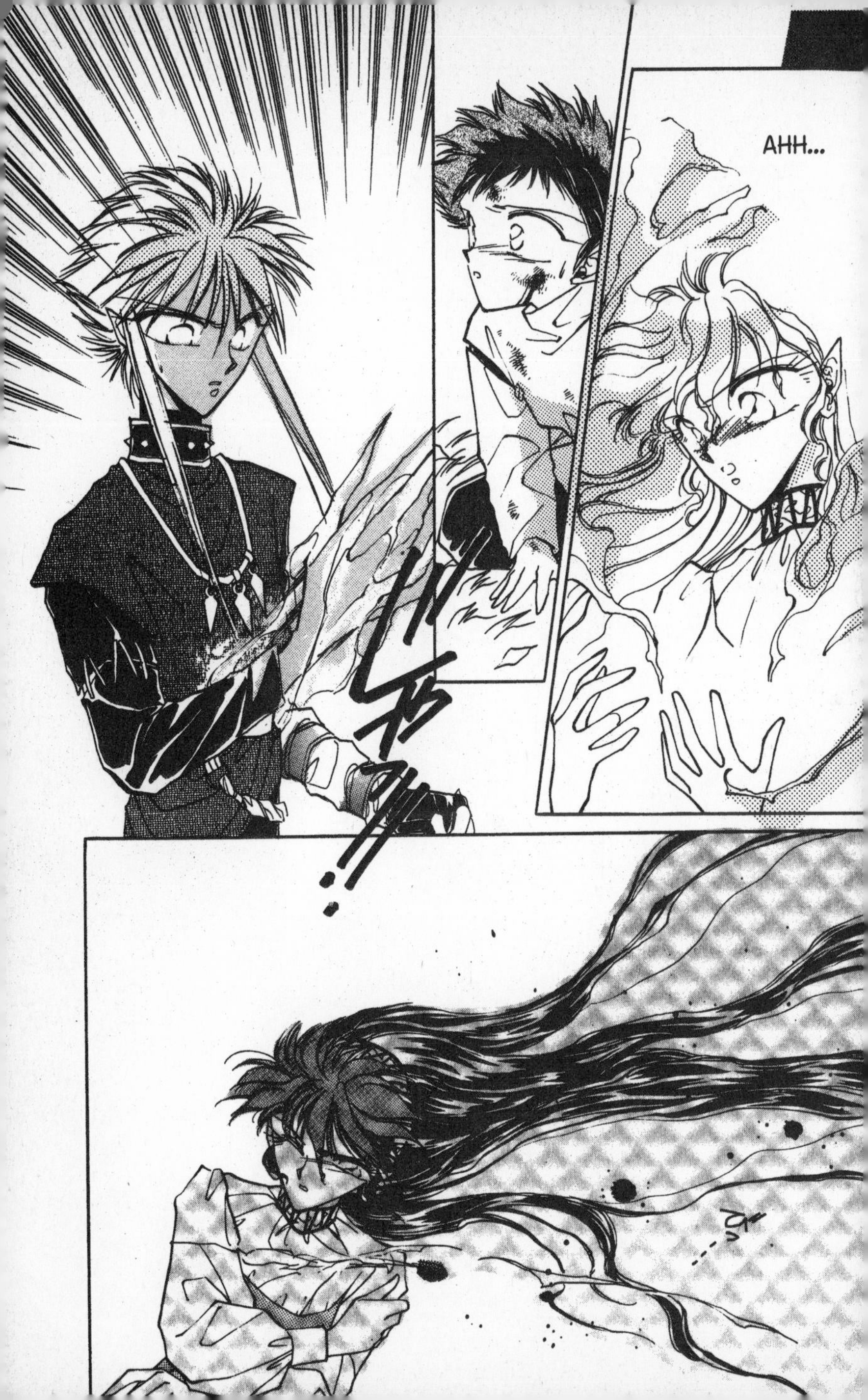
AHH...

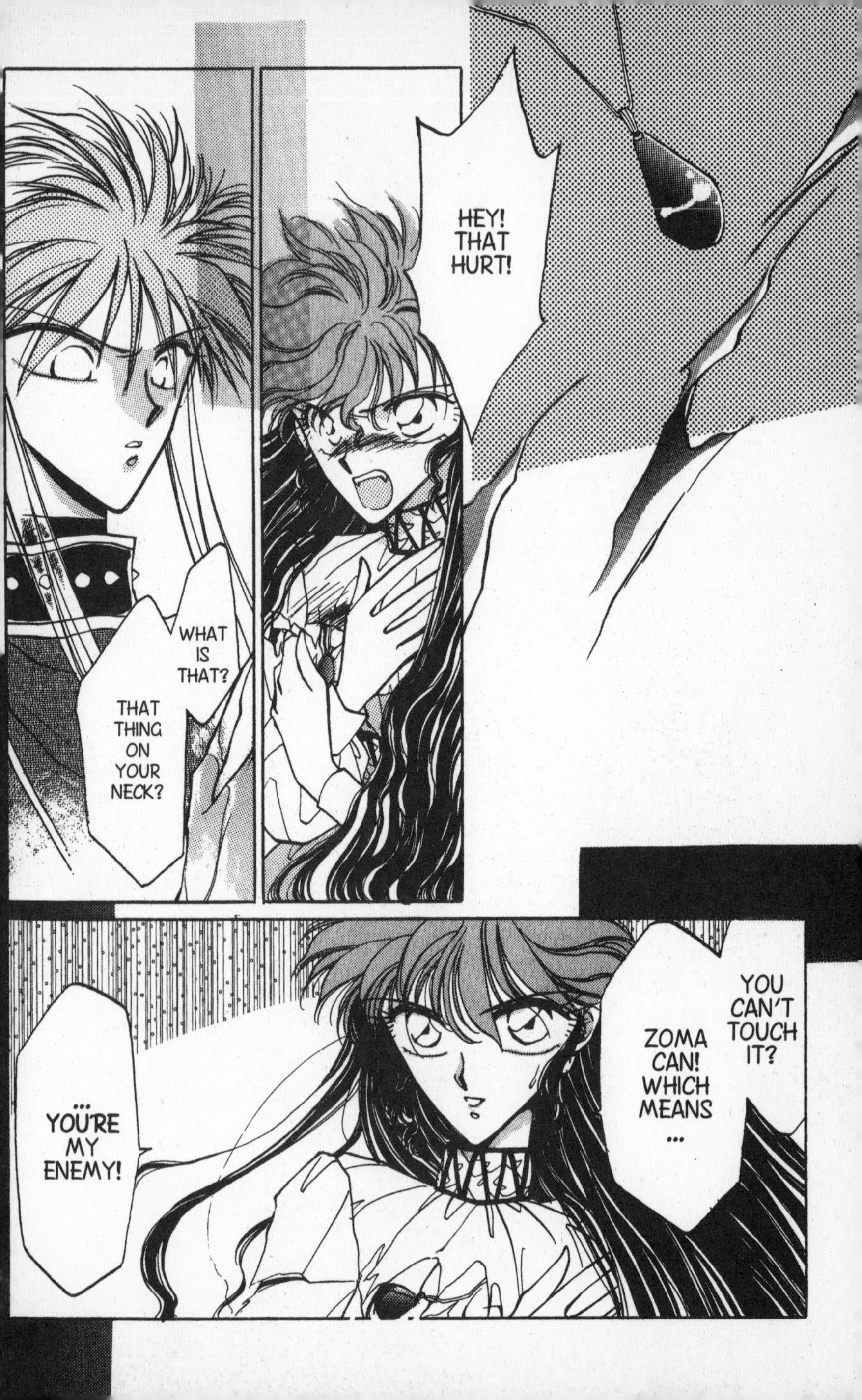
HEY! THAT HURT!
WHAT IS THAT?
THAT THING ON YOUR NECK?
YOU CAN'T TOUCH IT?
ZOMA CAN! WHICH MEANS ...
... YOU'RE MY ENEMY!

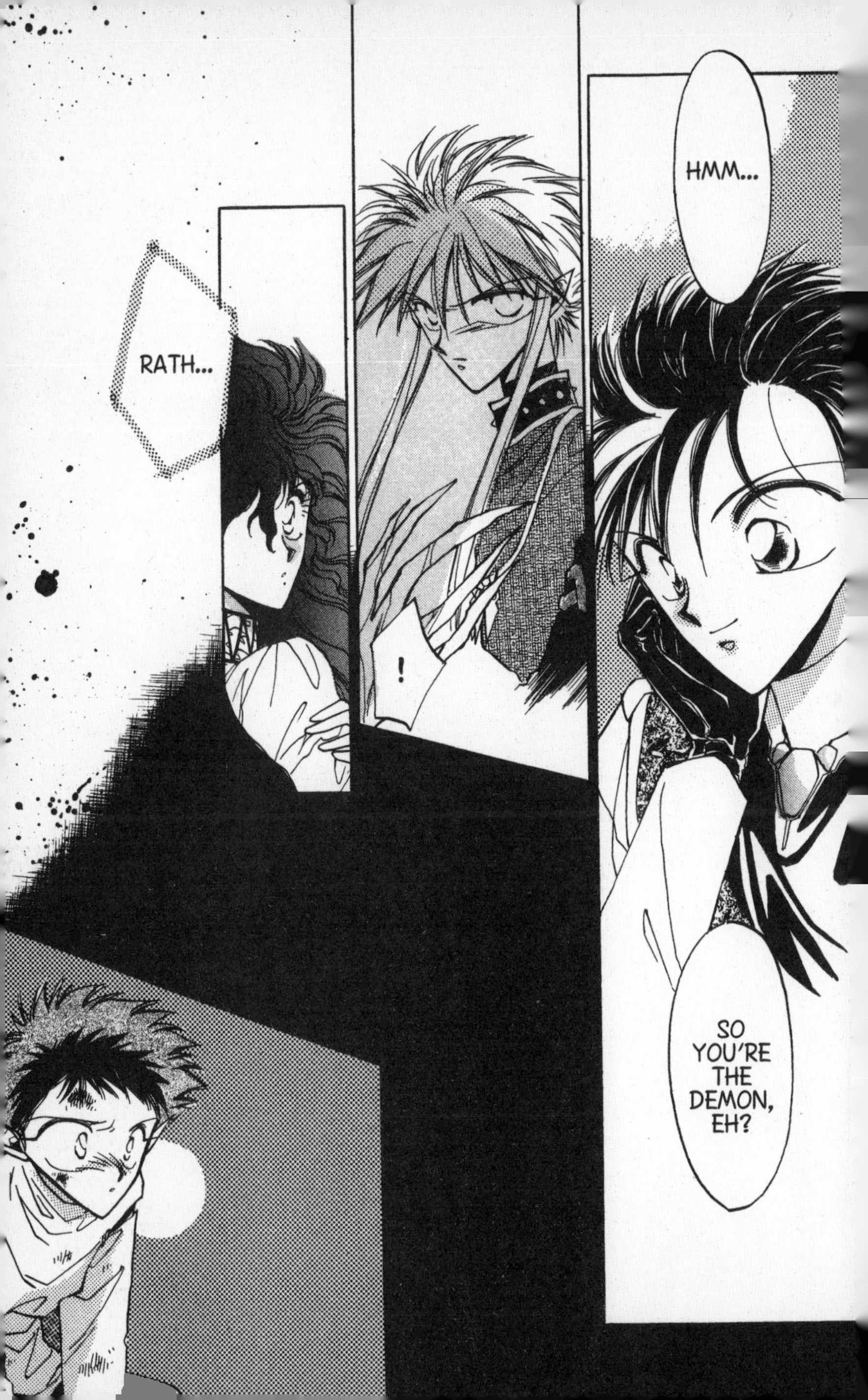
HMM...
SO YOU'RE THE DEMON, EH?
!
RATH...

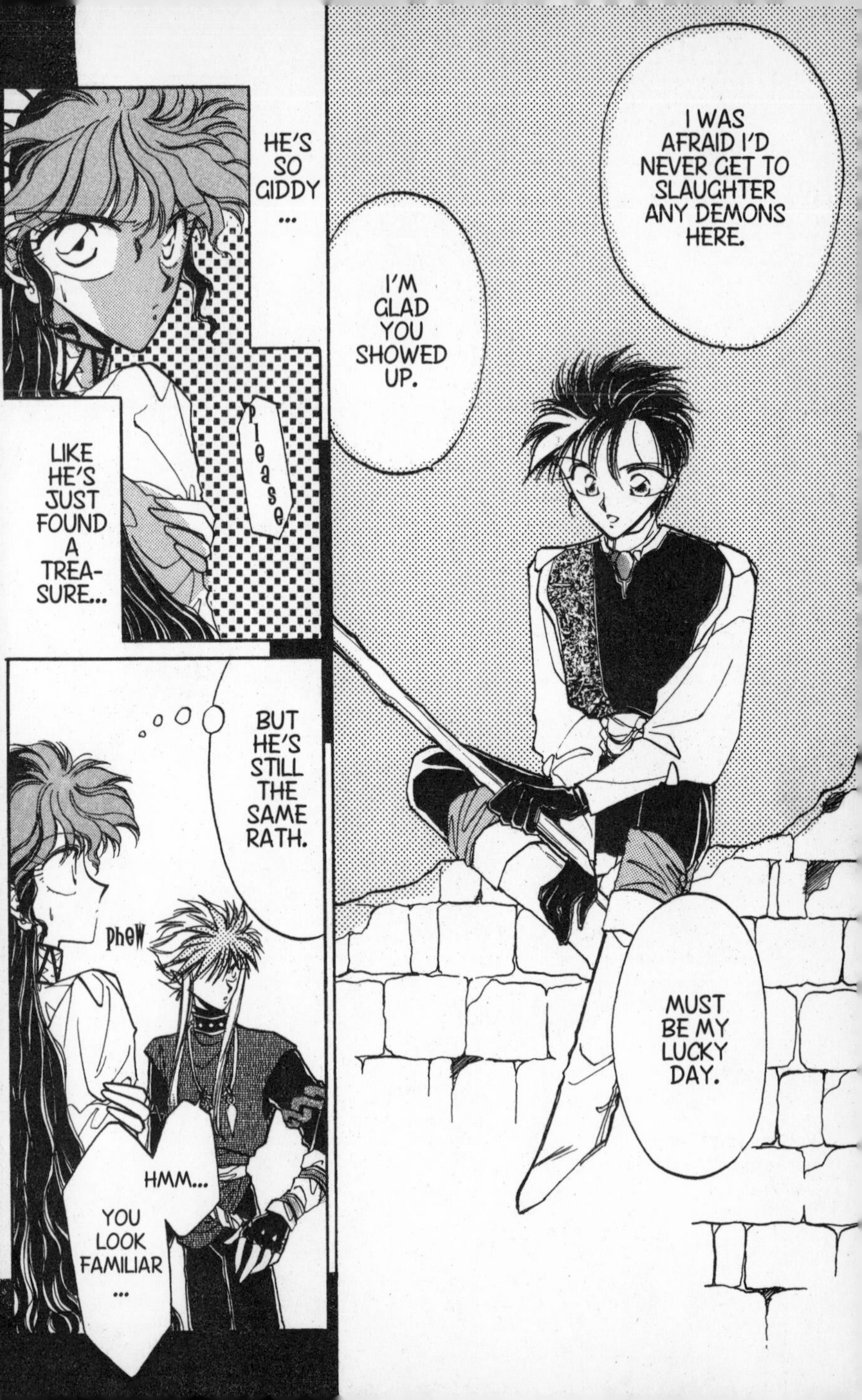
I WAS AFRAID I'D NEVER GET TO SLAUGHTER ANY DEMONS HERE.
I'M GLAD YOU SHOWED UP.
MUST BE MY LUCKY DAY.
HE'S SO GIDDY ...
Please
LIKE HE'S JUST FOUND A TREASURE...
BUT HE'S STILL THE SAME RATH.
pheW
HMM... YOU LOOK FAMILIAR ...

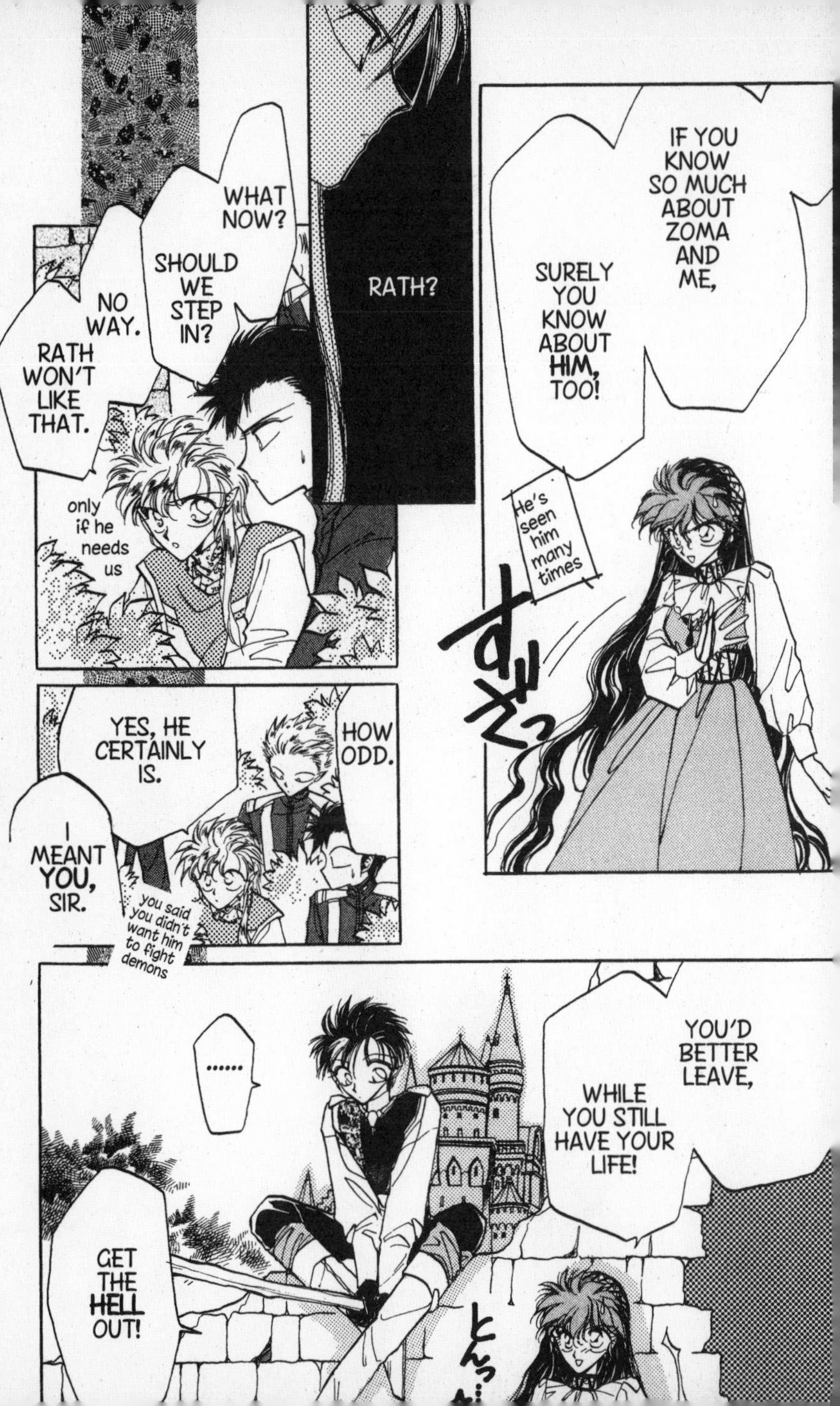

IF YOU KNOW SO MUCH ABOUT ZOMA AND ME,
SURELY YOU KNOW ABOUT **HIM**, TOO!
He's seen him many times
RATH?
WHAT NOW?
SHOULD WE STEP IN?
NO WAY.
RATH WON'T LIKE THAT.
only if he needs us
HOW ODD.
YES, HE CERTAINLY IS.
I MEANT **YOU**, SIR.
you said you didn't want him to fight demons
YOU'D BETTER LEAVE,
WHILE YOU STILL HAVE YOUR LIFE!
......
GET THE **HELL** OUT!

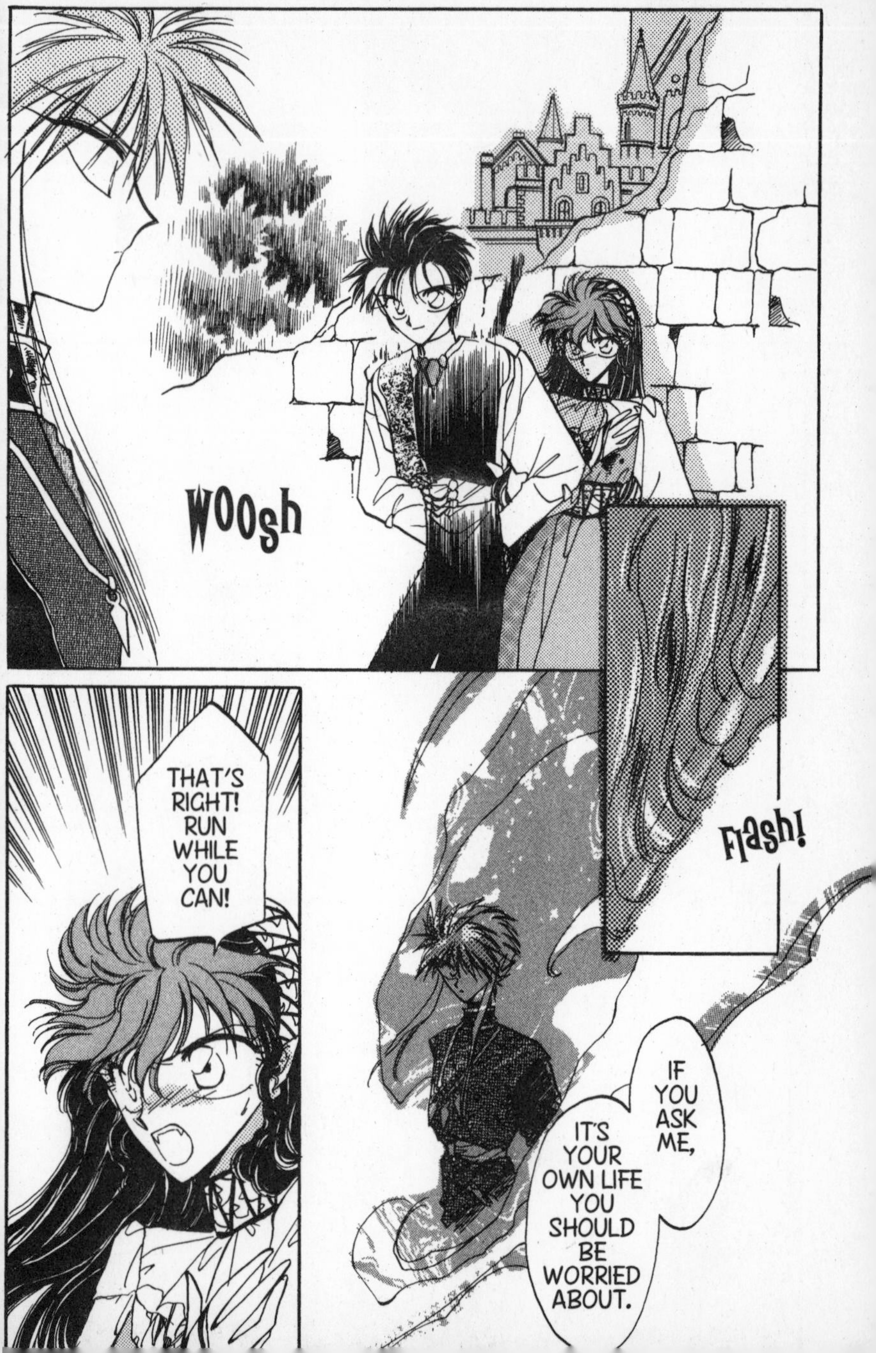
WOOSH
THAT'S RIGHT! RUN WHILE YOU CAN!
FLASH!
IF YOU ASK ME,
IT'S YOUR OWN LIFE YOU SHOULD BE WORRIED ABOUT.

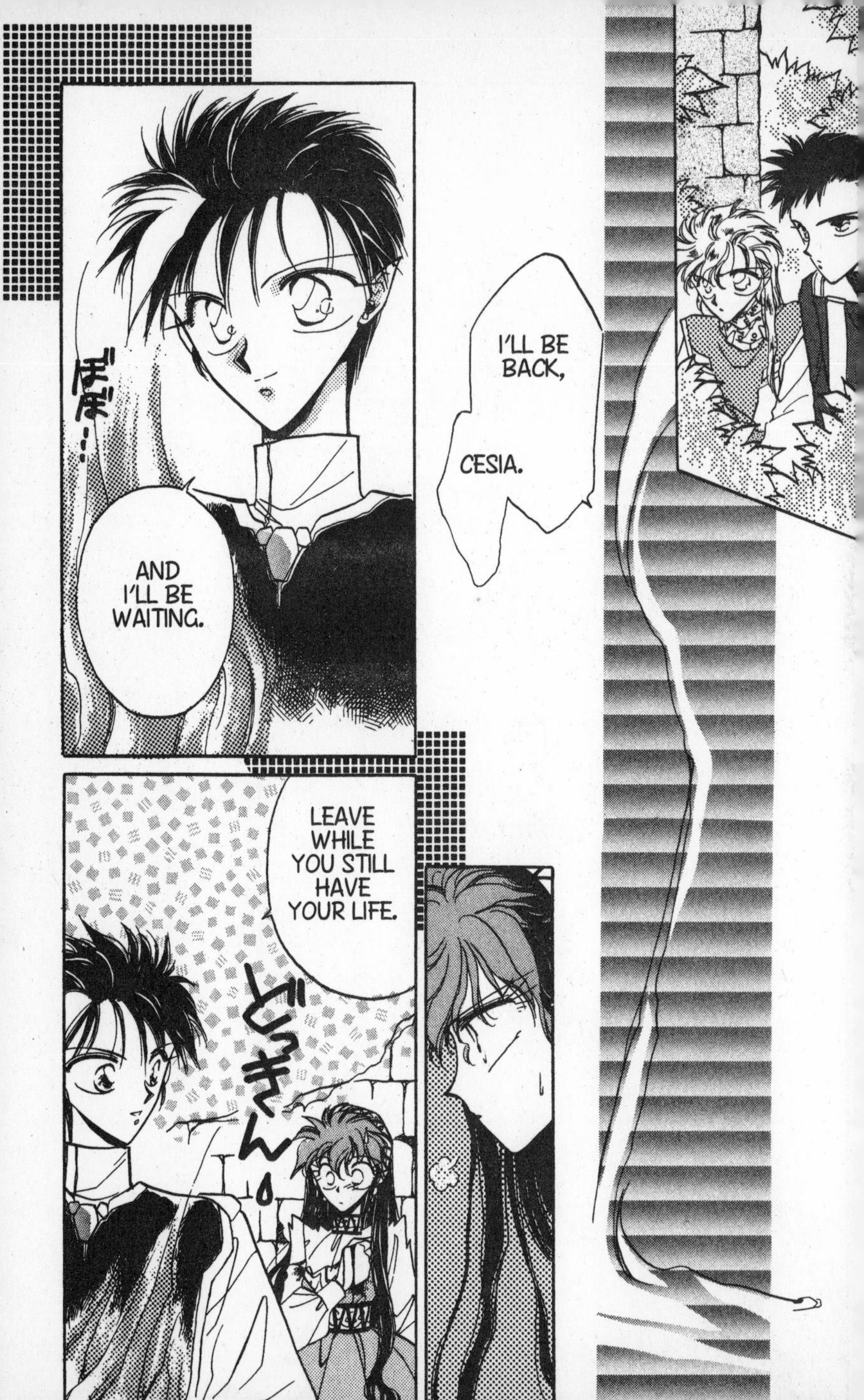
I'LL BE BACK,
CESIA.
ぼぼ…
AND I'LL BE WAITING.
LEAVE WHILE YOU STILL HAVE YOUR LIFE.
どっきん!

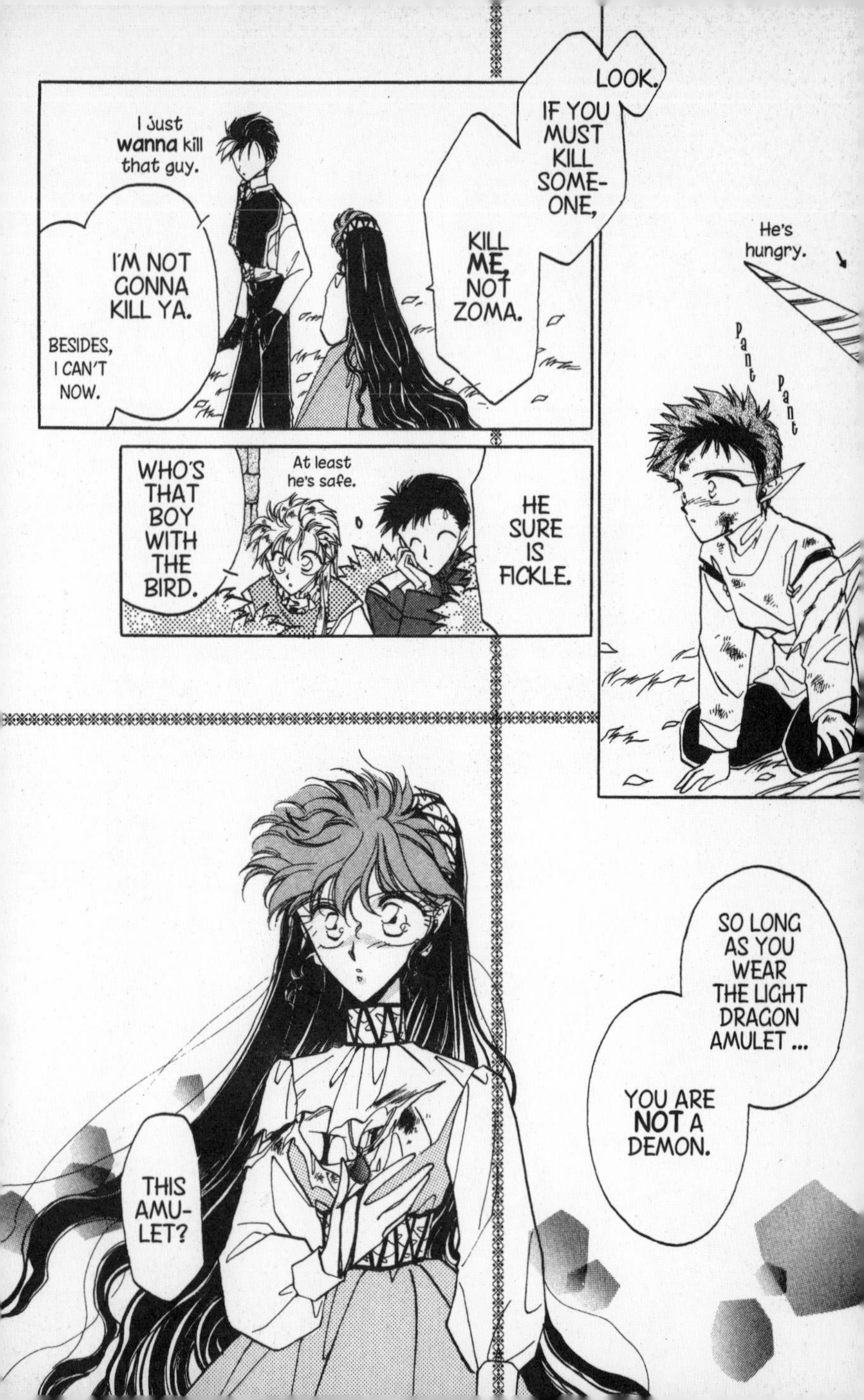
He's hungry.
Pant Pant
LOOK.
IF YOU MUST KILL SOMEONE,
KILL ME, NOT ZOMA.
I just wanna kill that guy.
I'M NOT GONNA KILL YA.
BESIDES, I CAN'T NOW.
HE SURE IS FICKLE.
At least he's safe.
WHO'S THAT BOY WITH THE BIRD.
SO LONG AS YOU WEAR THE LIGHT DRAGON AMULET ...
YOU ARE NOT A DEMON.
THIS AMULET?

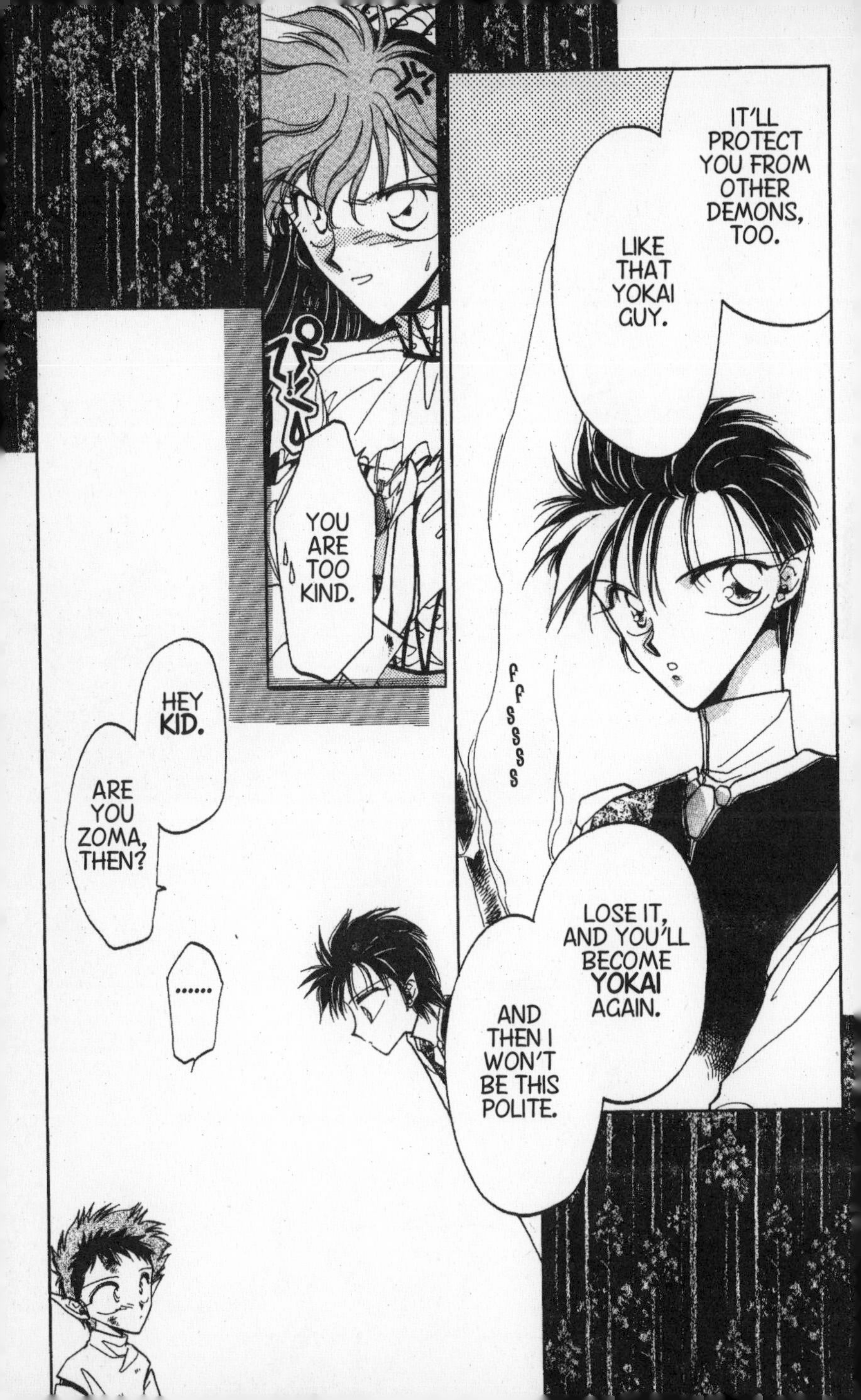
IT'LL PROTECT YOU FROM OTHER DEMONS, TOO.
LIKE THAT YOKAI GUY.
ffssss
LOSE IT, AND YOU'LL BECOME YOKAI AGAIN.
AND THEN I WON'T BE THIS POLITE.
YOU ARE TOO KIND.
HEY KID.
ARE YOU ZOMA, THEN?
....

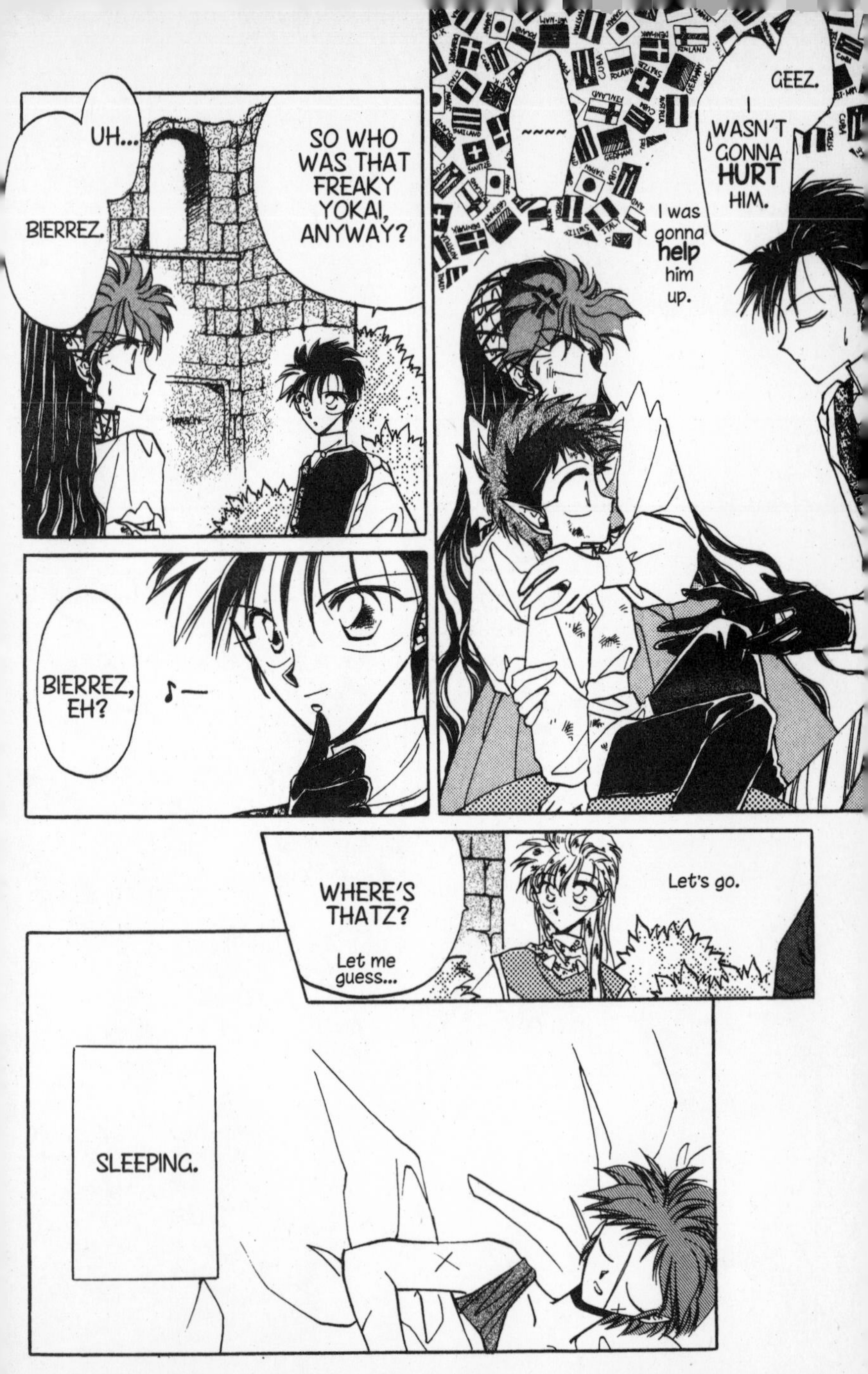

GEEZ. I WASN'T GONNA HURT HIM.
I was gonna help him up.
~~~~
SO WHO WAS THAT FREAKY YOKAI, ANYWAY?
UH... BIERREZ.
♪—
BIERREZ, EH?
Let's go.
WHERE'S THATZ?
Let me guess...
SLEEPING.
~~~~

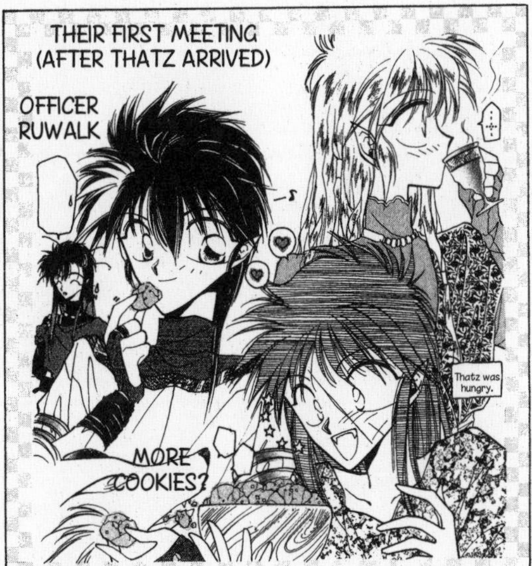
THEIR FIRST MEETING
(AFTER THATZ ARRIVED)
Thatz was hungry.
OFFICER
RUWALK
MORE
COOKIES?

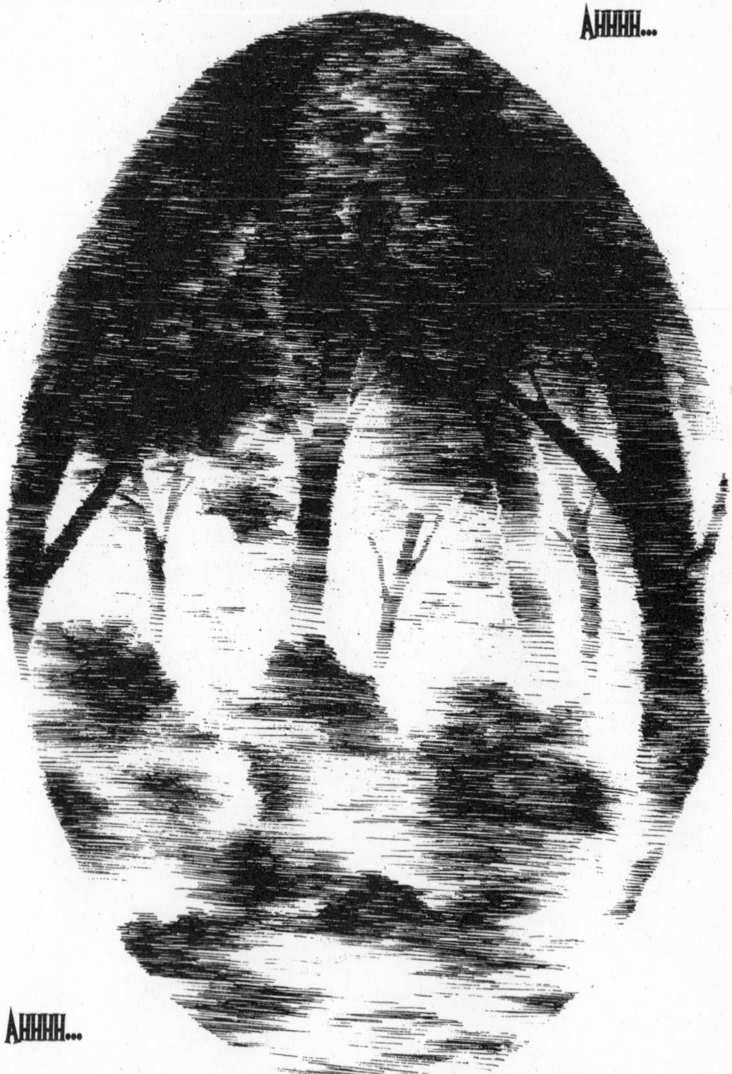
AHHHH...
AHHHH...

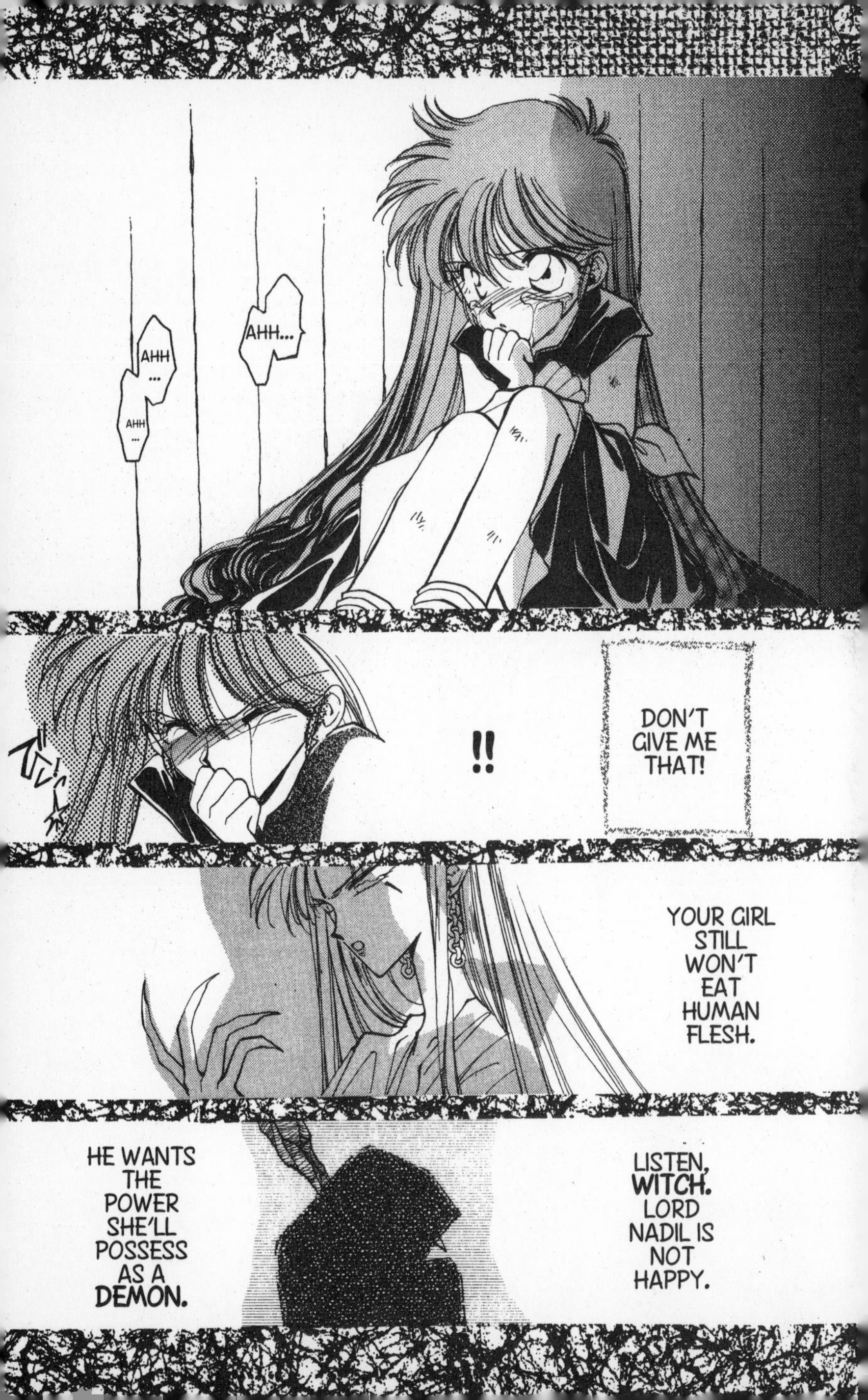
AHH...
AHH ...
AHH ...
DON'T GIVE ME THAT!
!!
YOUR GIRL STILL WON'T EAT HUMAN FLESH.
LISTEN, **WITCH.** LORD NADIL IS NOT HAPPY.
HE WANTS THE POWER SHE'LL POSSESS AS A **DEMON.**

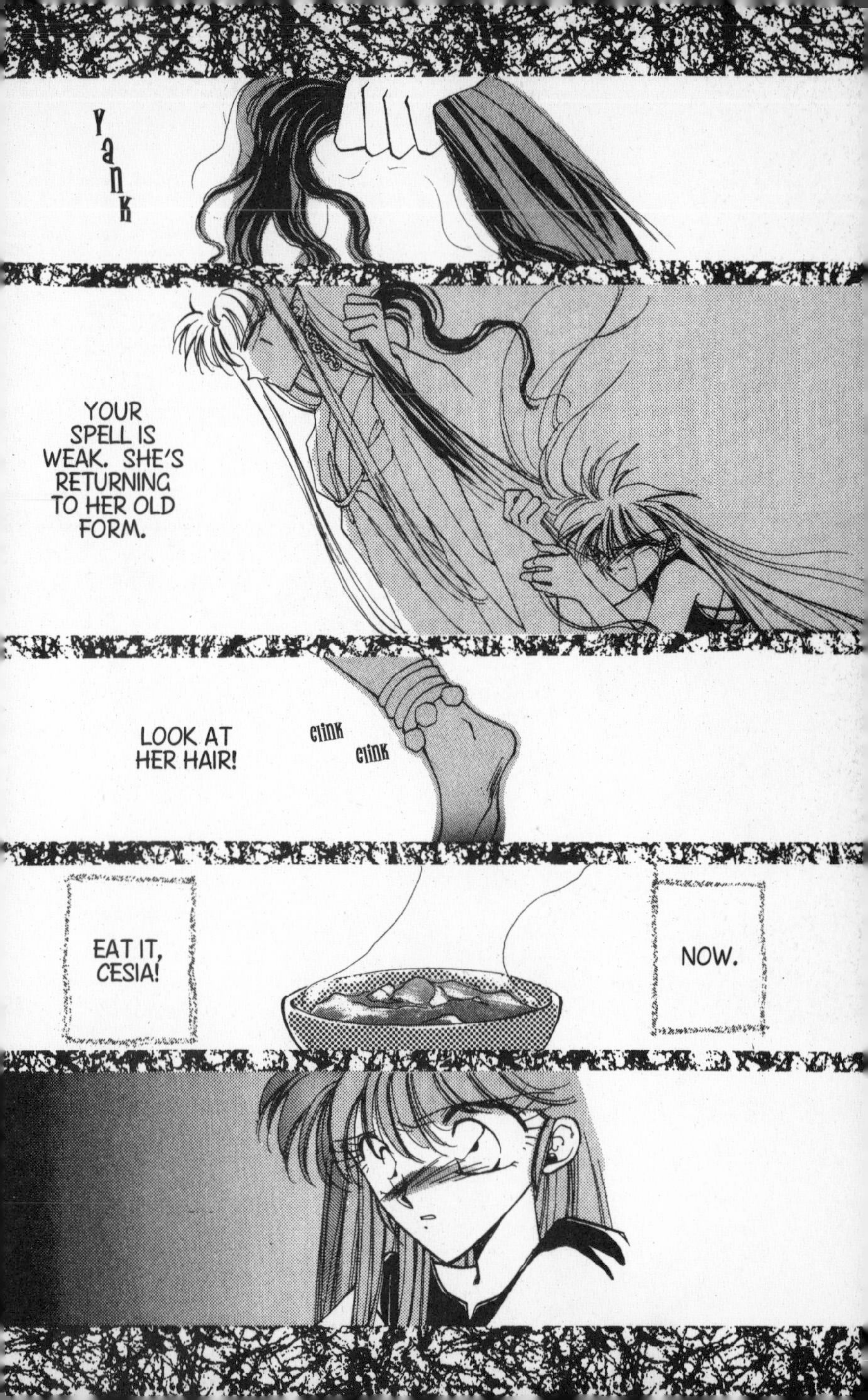
Yank
YOUR SPELL IS WEAK. SHE'S RETURNING TO HER OLD FORM.
Clink
Clink
LOOK AT HER HAIR!
NOW.
EAT IT, CESIA!

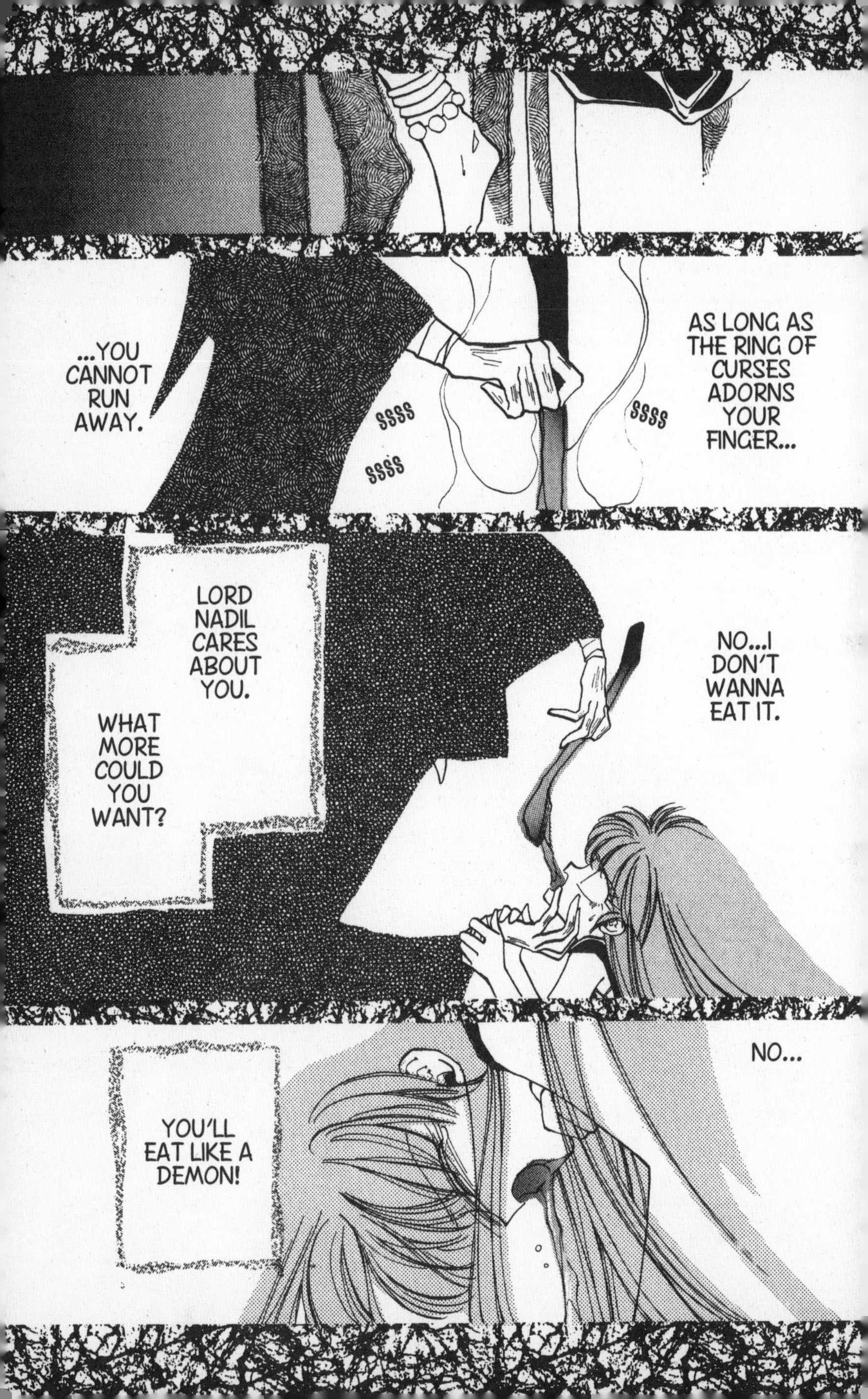
AS LONG AS THE RING OF CURSES ADORNS YOUR FINGER...
...YOU CANNOT RUN AWAY.
SSSS
SSSS
SSSS
NO...I DON'T WANNA EAT IT.
LORD NADIL CARES ABOUT YOU.
WHAT MORE COULD YOU WANT?
NO...
YOU'LL EAT LIKE A DEMON!

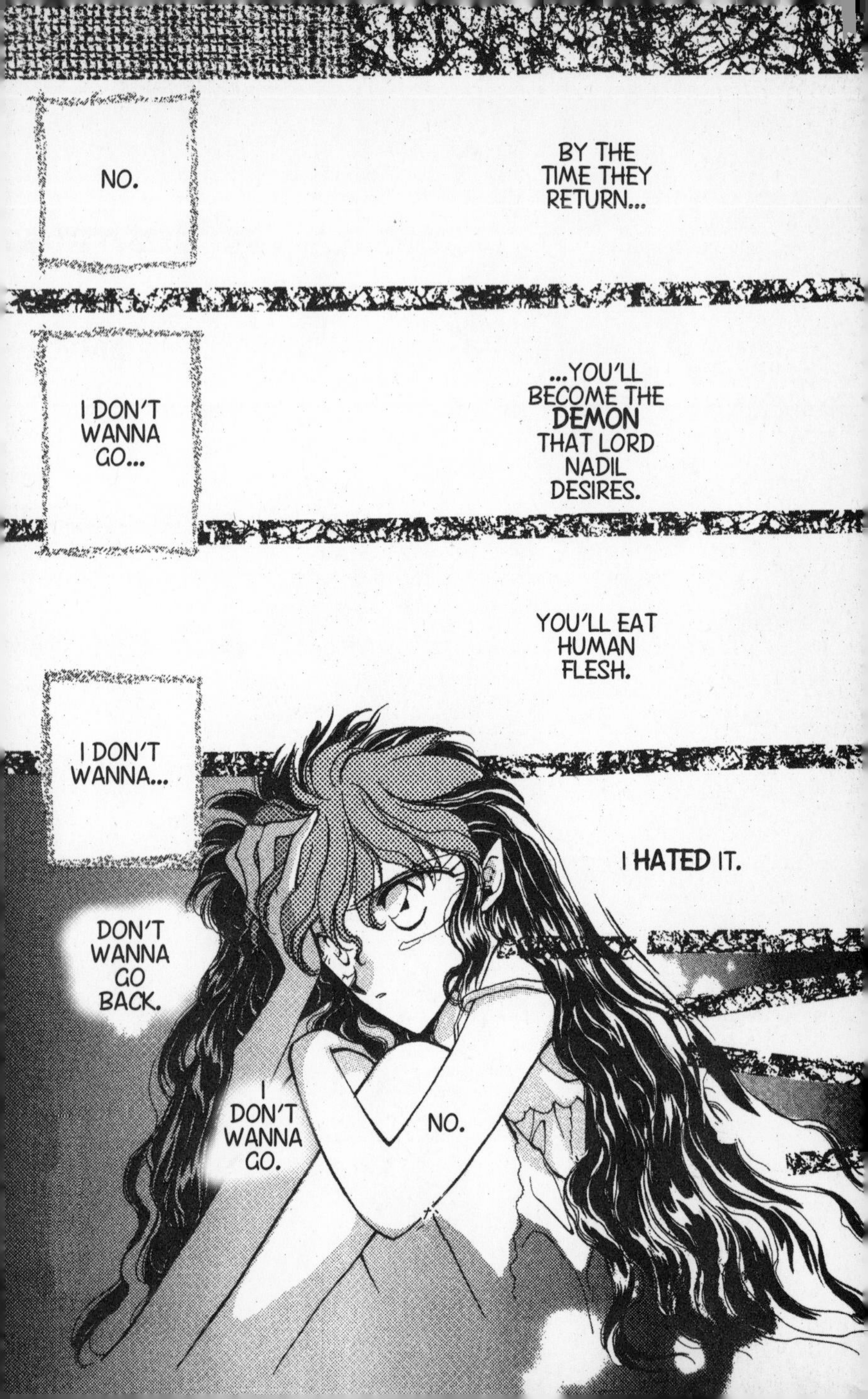
BY THE TIME THEY RETURN...
NO.
...YOU'LL BECOME THE DEMON THAT LORD NADIL DESIRES.
I DON'T WANNA GO...
YOU'LL EAT HUMAN FLESH.
I DON'T WANNA...
I HATED IT.
DON'T WANNA GO BACK.
NO.
I DON'T WANNA GO.

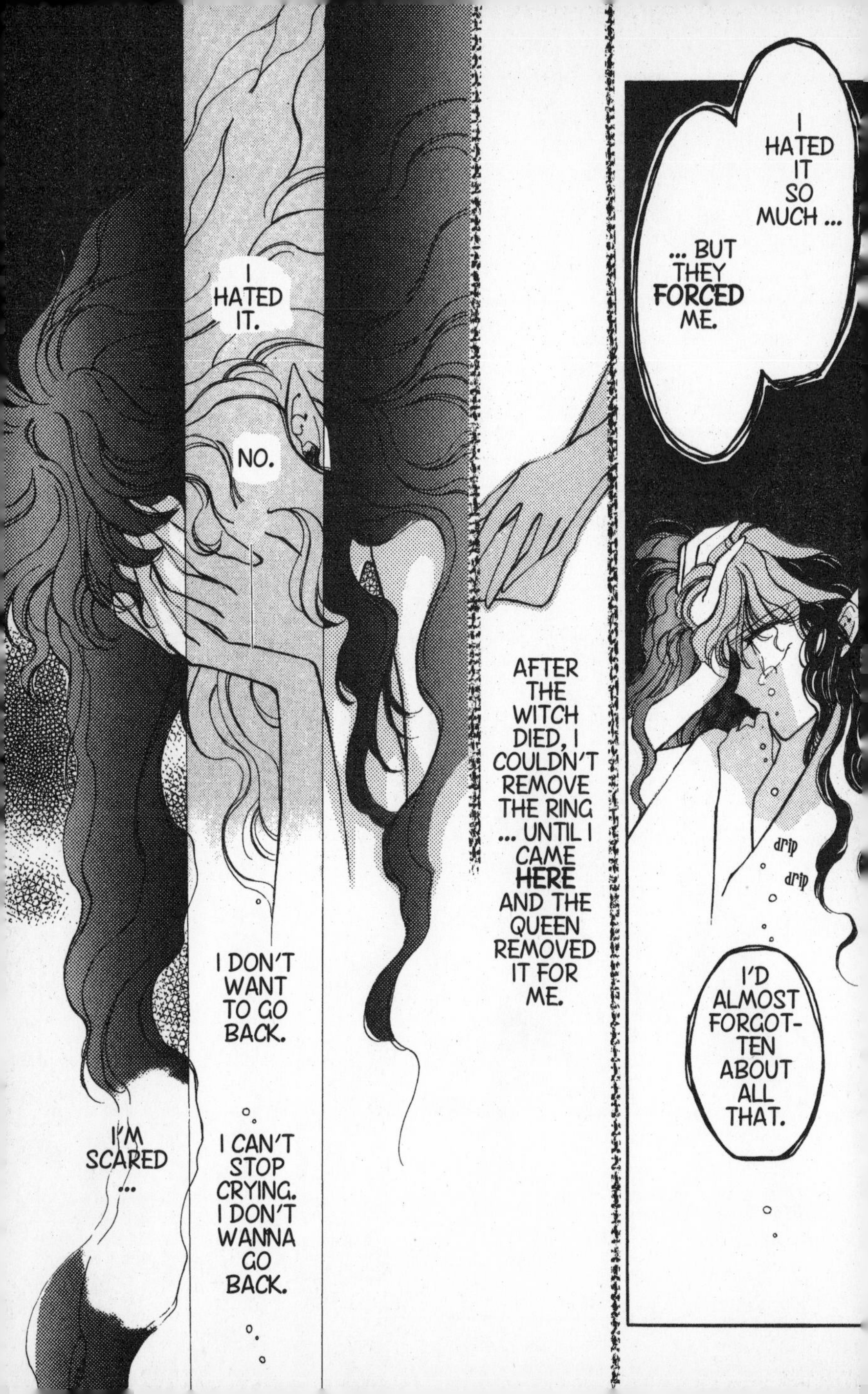
I HATED IT SO MUCH ...
... BUT THEY FORCED ME.
drip
drip
I'D ALMOST FORGOT-TEN ABOUT ALL THAT.
AFTER THE WITCH DIED, I COULDN'T REMOVE THE RING ... UNTIL I CAME HERE AND THE QUEEN REMOVED IT FOR ME.
I HATED IT.
NO.
I DON'T WANT TO GO BACK.
I CAN'T STOP CRYING. I DON'T WANNA GO BACK.
I'M SCARED ...

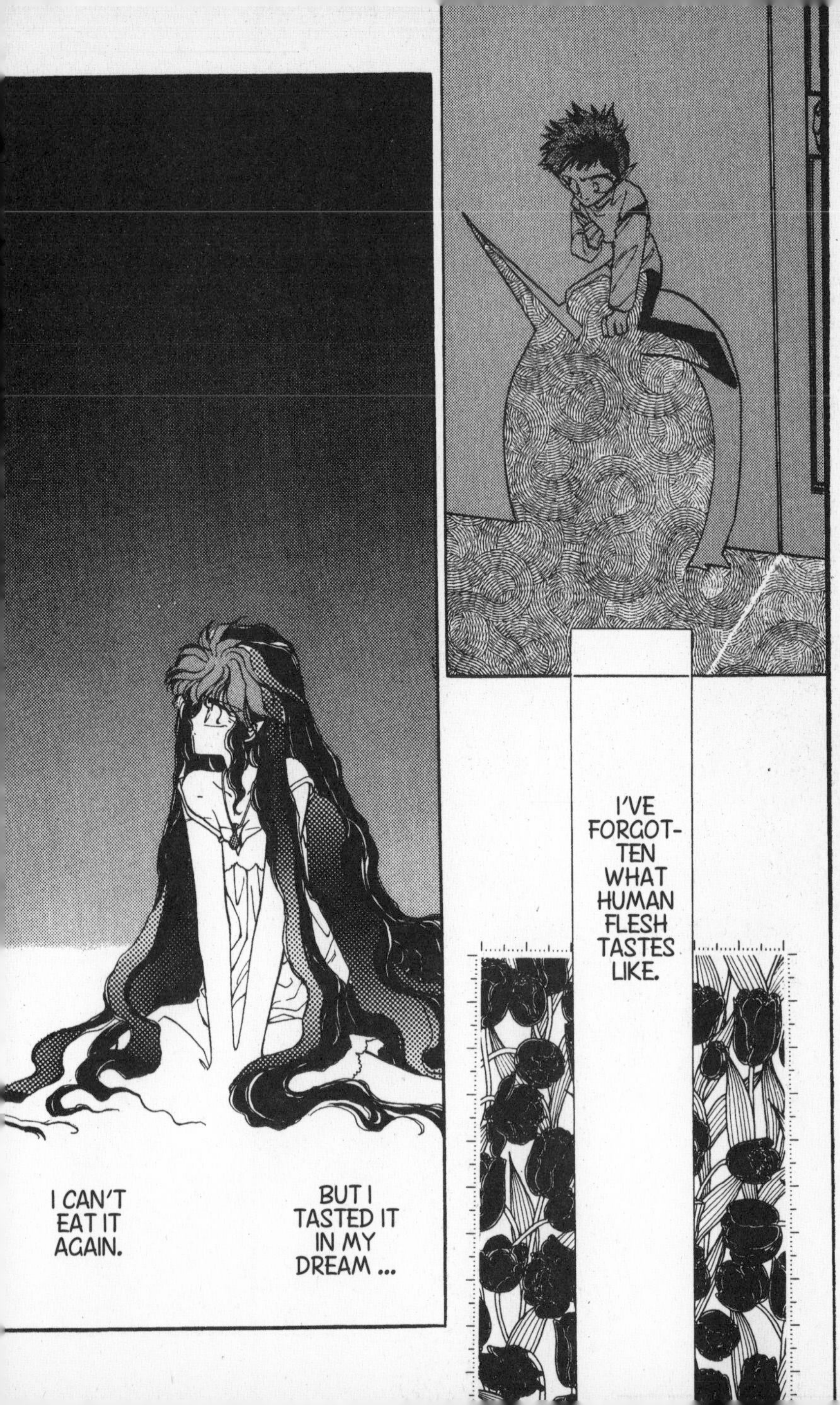
I'VE FORGOT-TEN WHAT HUMAN FLESH TASTES LIKE.
BUT I TASTED IT IN MY DREAM ...
I CAN'T EAT IT AGAIN.

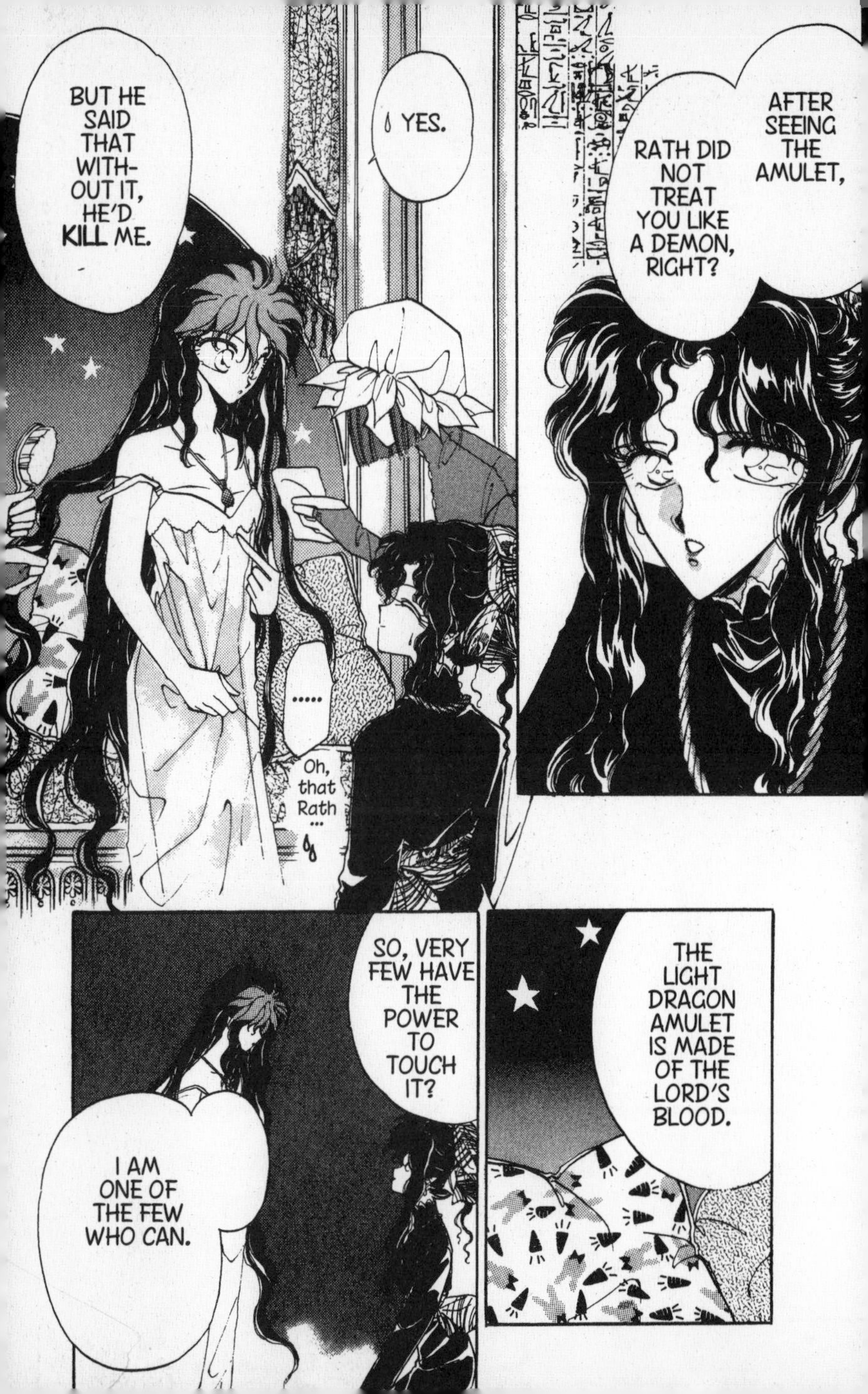
AFTER SEEING THE AMULET,
RATH DID NOT TREAT YOU LIKE A DEMON, RIGHT?
YES.
BUT HE SAID THAT WITH-OUT IT, HE'D KILL ME.
......
Oh, that Rath...
THE LIGHT DRAGON AMULET IS MADE OF THE LORD'S BLOOD.
SO, VERY FEW HAVE THE POWER TO TOUCH IT?
I AM ONE OF THE FEW WHO CAN.

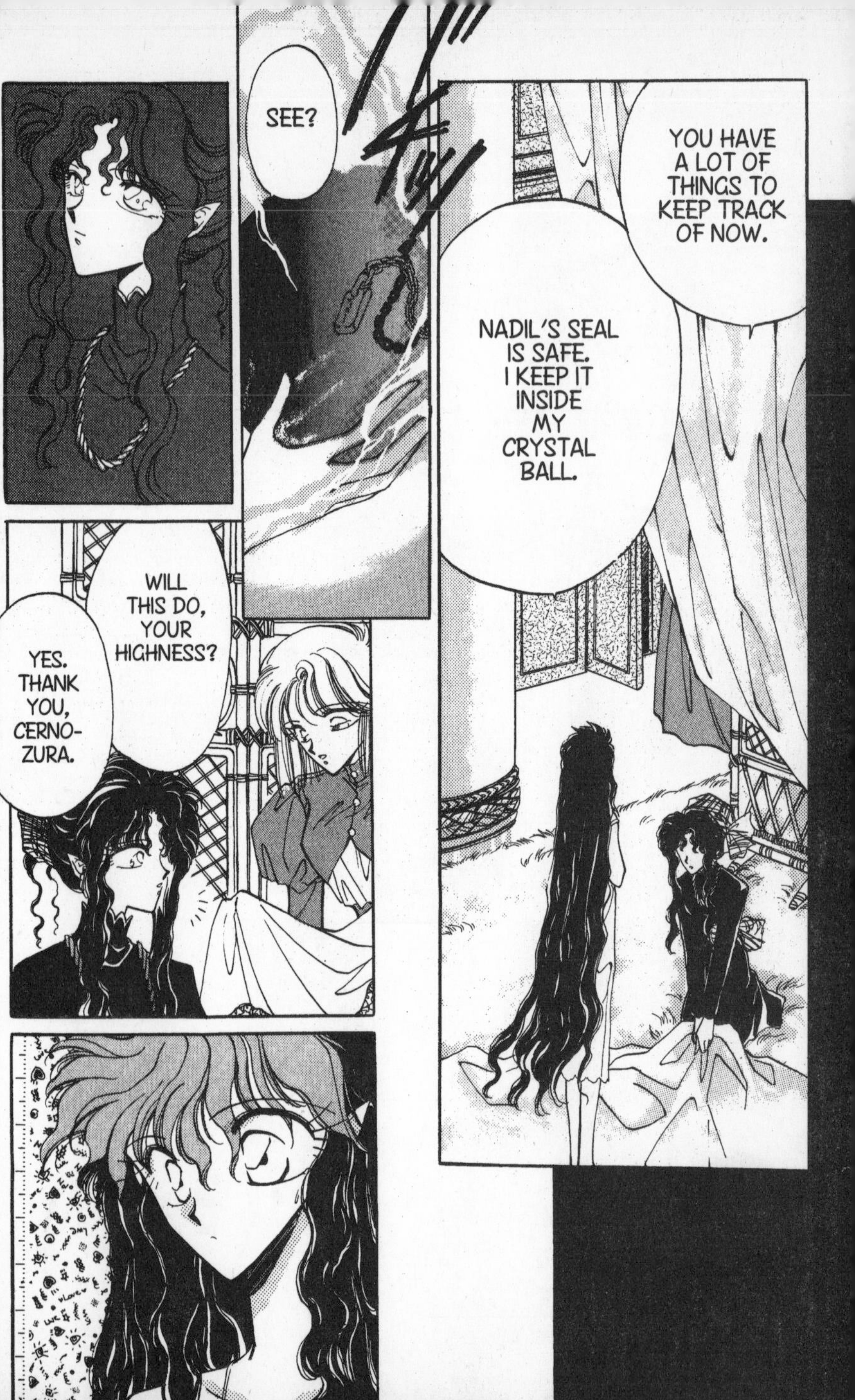
YOU HAVE A LOT OF THINGS TO KEEP TRACK OF NOW.
NADIL'S SEAL IS SAFE. I KEEP IT INSIDE MY CRYSTAL BALL.
SEE?
WILL THIS DO, YOUR HIGHNESS?
YES. THANK YOU, CERNO-ZURA.

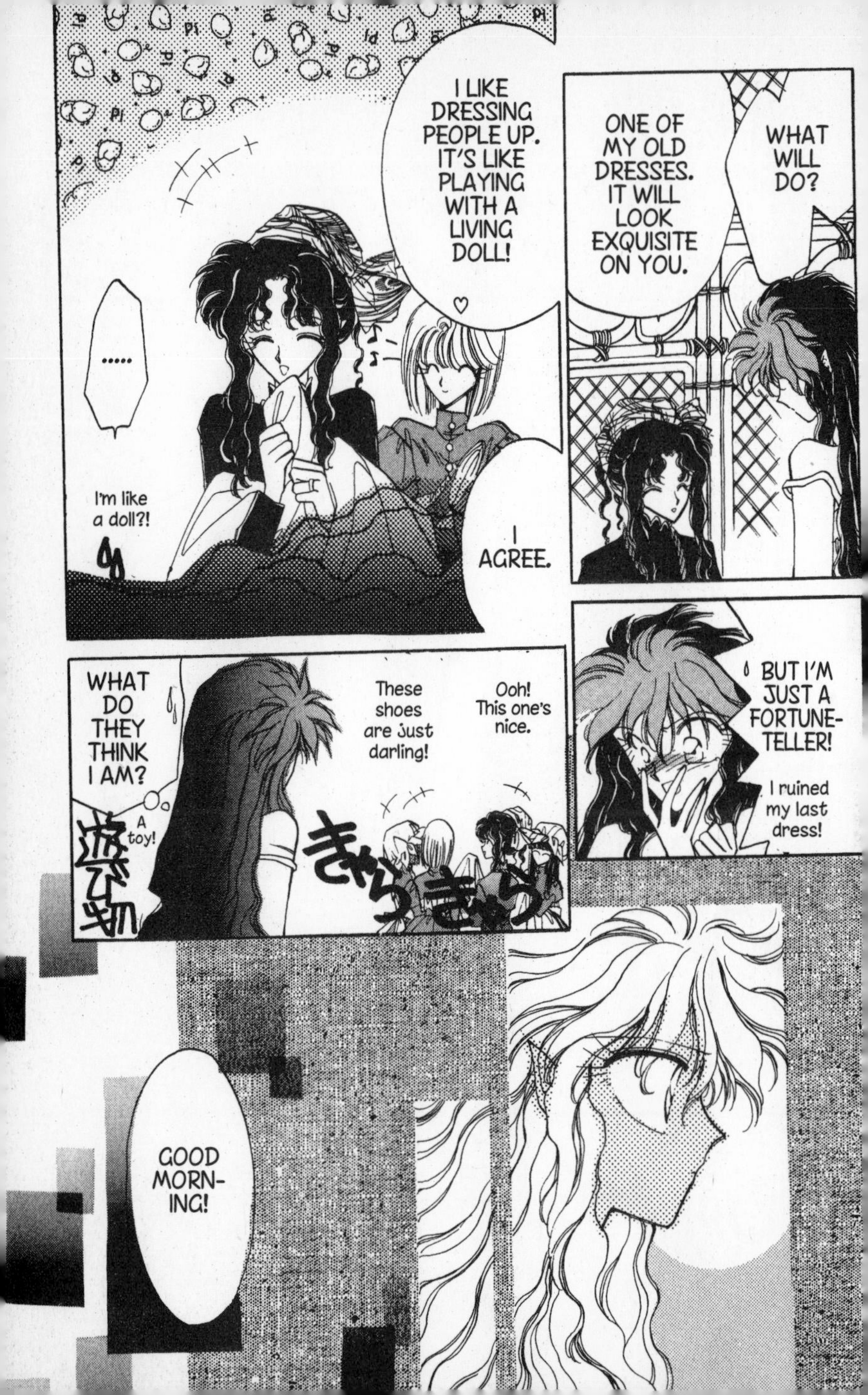
WHAT WILL DO?
ONE OF MY OLD DRESSES. IT WILL LOOK EXQUISITE ON YOU.
I LIKE DRESSING PEOPLE UP. IT'S LIKE PLAYING WITH A LIVING DOLL! ♡
I AGREE.
......
I'm like a doll?!
BUT I'M JUST A FORTUNE-TELLER!
I ruined my last dress!
Ooh! This one's nice.
These shoes are just darling!
WHAT DO THEY THINK I AM?
A toy!
GOOD MORNING!

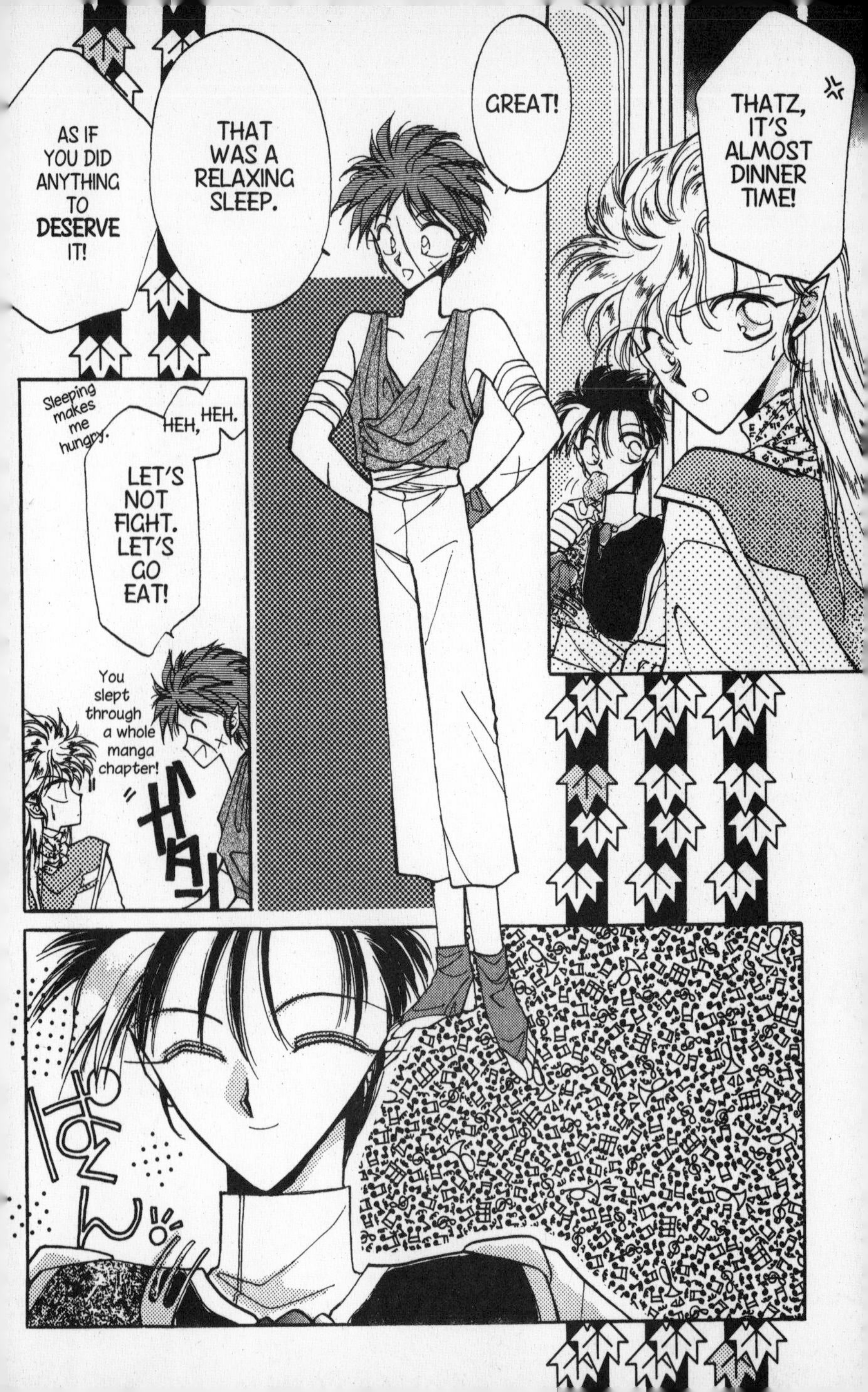
THATZ, IT'S ALMOST DINNER TIME!
GREAT!
THAT WAS A RELAXING SLEEP.
AS IF YOU DID ANYTHING TO DESERVE IT!
HEH, HEH.
Sleeping makes me hungry.
LET'S NOT FIGHT. LET'S GO EAT!
You slept through a whole manga chapter!
ほわん

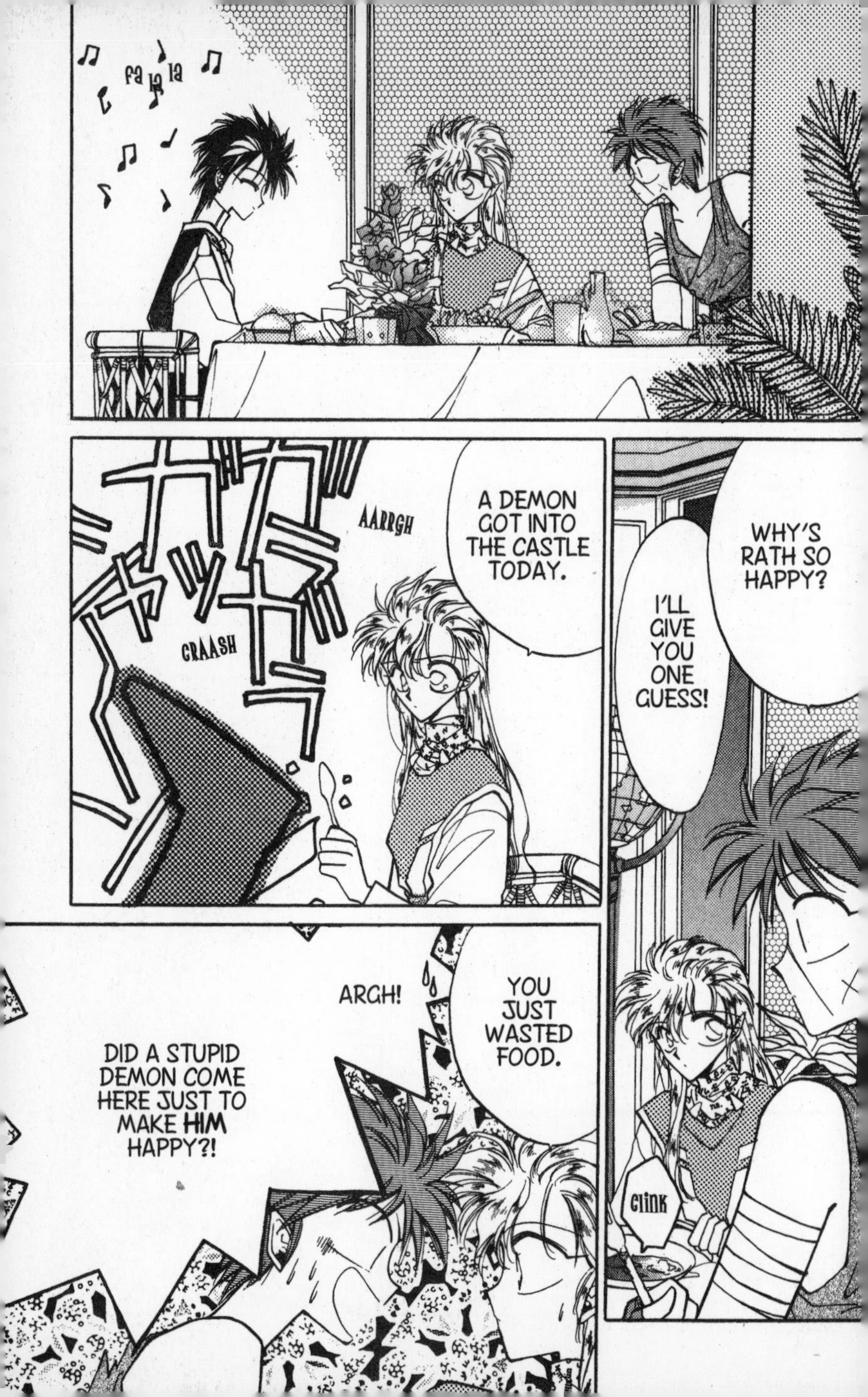

fa la la
WHY'S RATH SO HAPPY?
I'LL GIVE YOU ONE GUESS!
CLINK
A DEMON GOT INTO THE CASTLE TODAY.
AARRGH
CRAASH
YOU JUST WASTED FOOD.
ARGH!
DID A STUPID DEMON COME HERE JUST TO MAKE HIM HAPPY?!

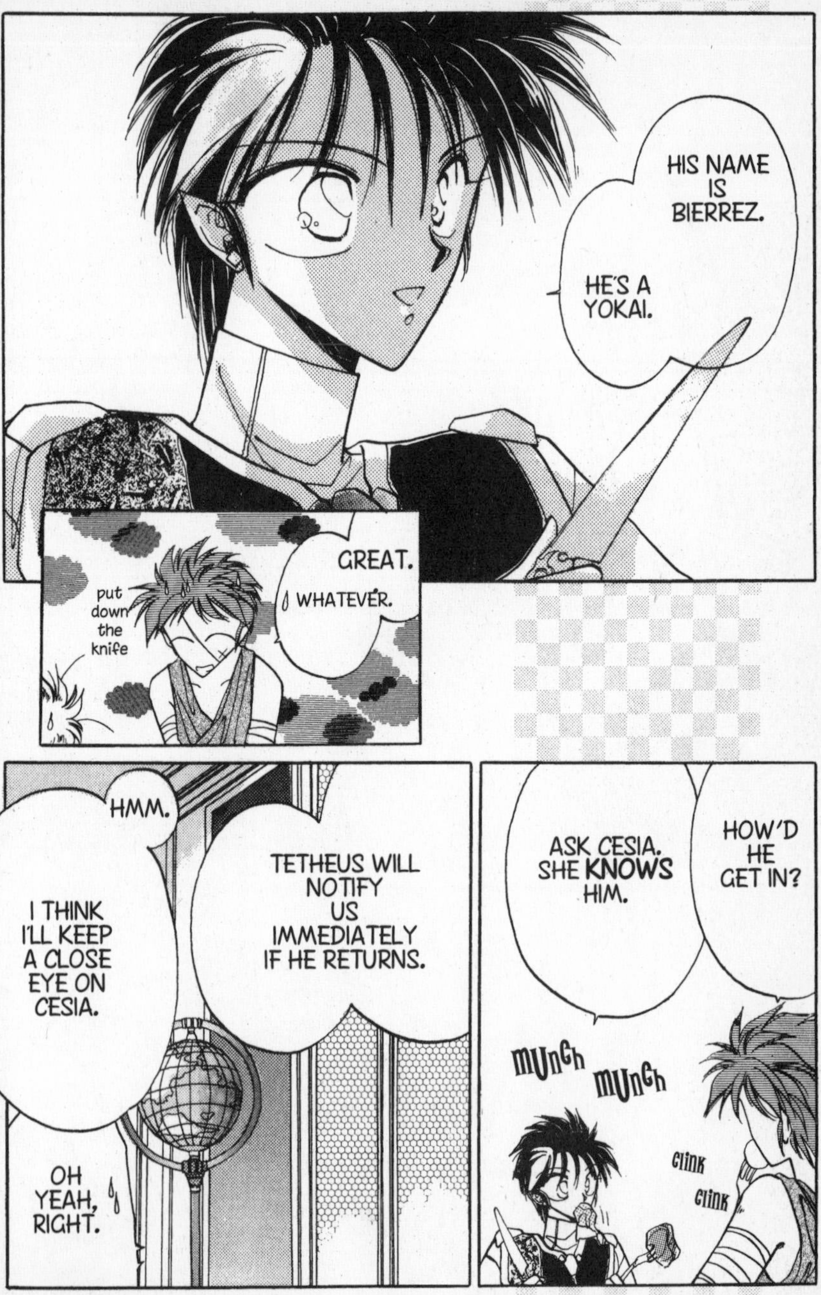
HIS NAME IS BIERREZ.
HE'S A YOKAI.
GREAT.
WHATEVER.
put down the knife
HOW'D HE GET IN?
ASK CESIA. SHE **KNOWS** HIM.
MUNCH
MUNCH
CLINK
CLINK
TETHEUS WILL NOTIFY US IMMEDIATELY IF HE RETURNS.
HMM.
I THINK I'LL KEEP A CLOSE EYE ON CESIA.
OH YEAH, RIGHT.

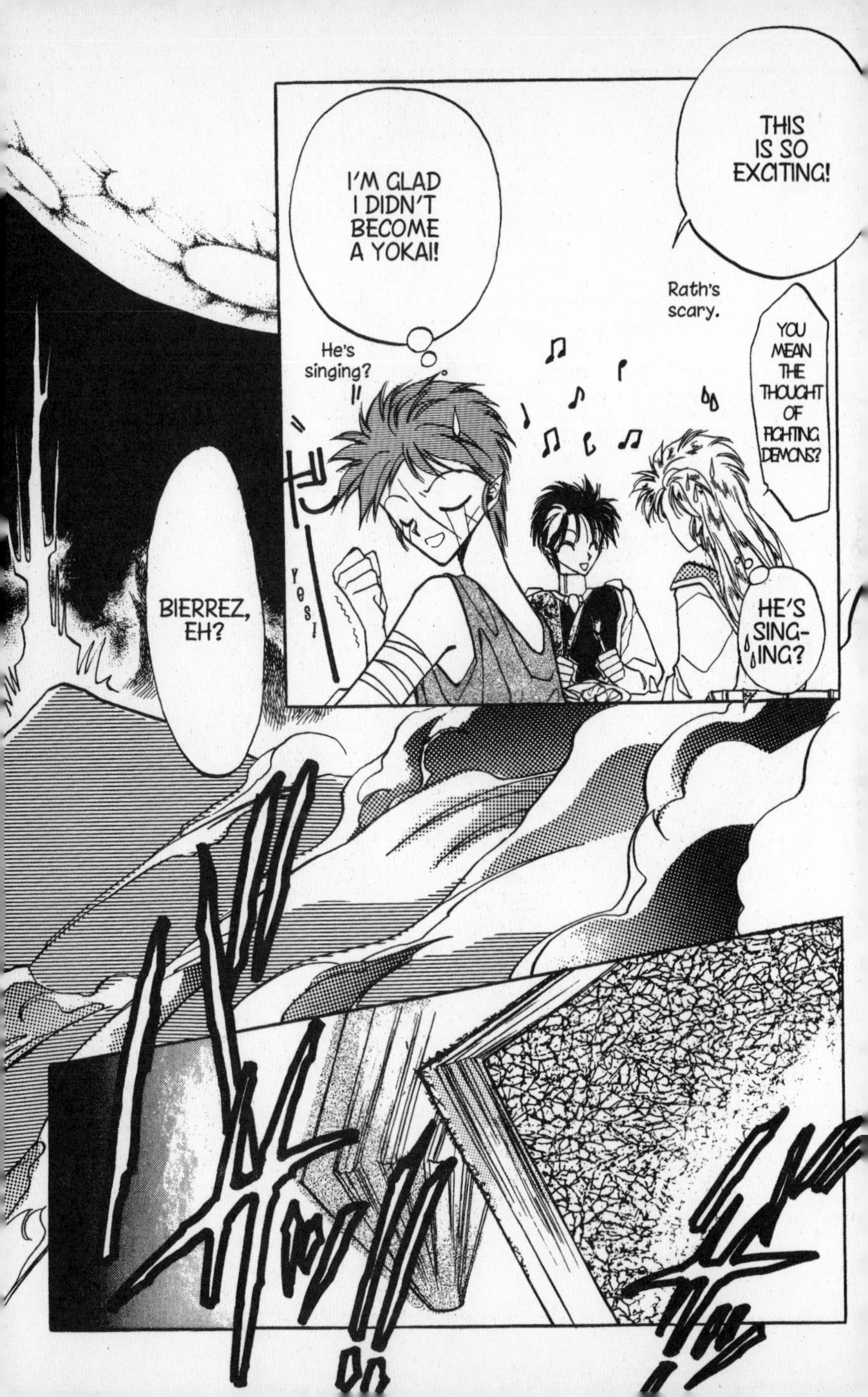
THIS IS SO EXCITING!
I'M GLAD I DIDN'T BECOME A YOKAI!
Rath's scary.
YOU MEAN THE THOUGHT OF FIGHTING DEMONS?
HE'S SINGING?
He's singing?
Yes!
BIERREZ, EH?

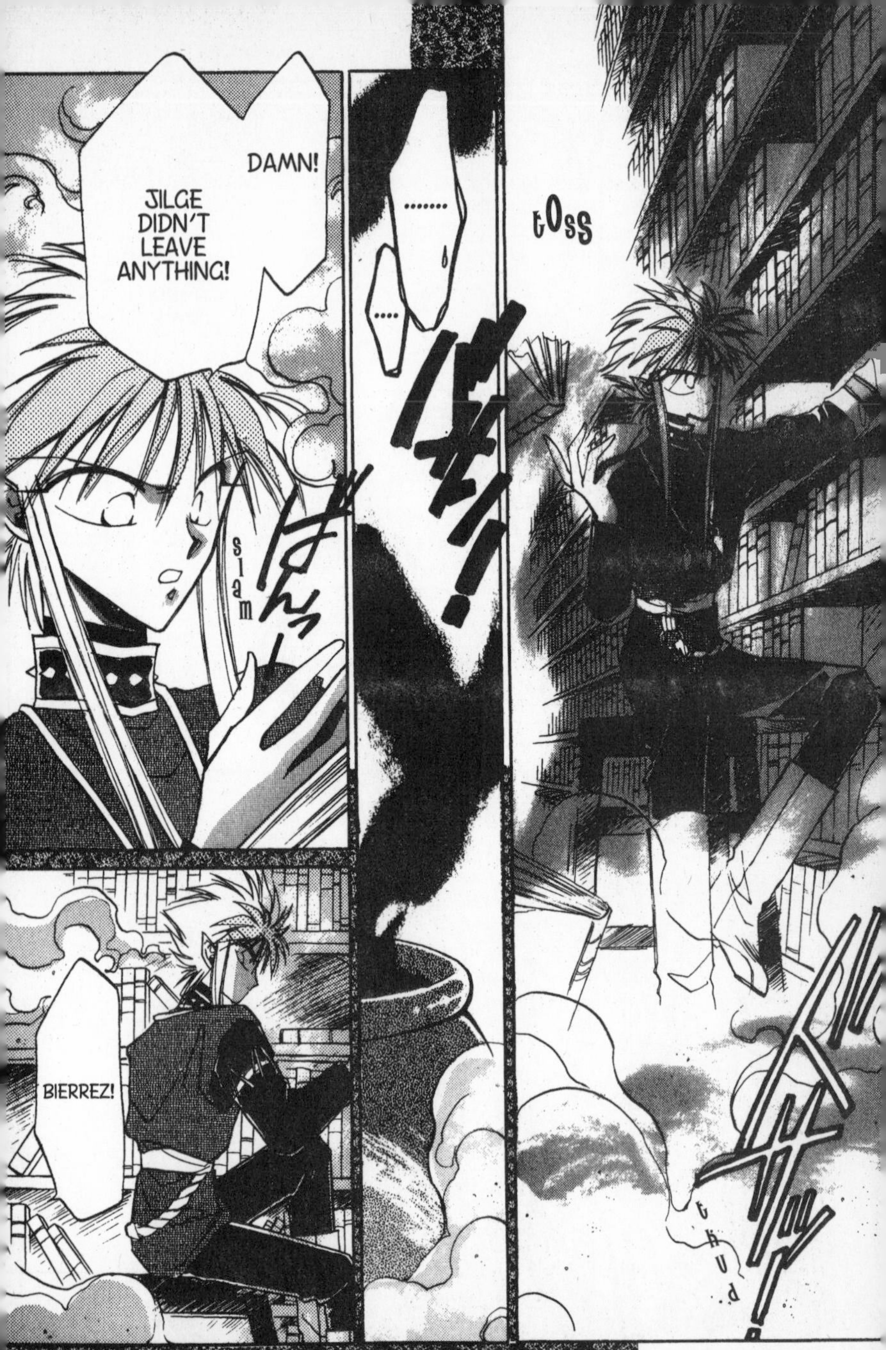
tOss
thud
....
....
DAMN!
JILGE DIDN'T LEAVE ANYTHING!
slam
BIERREZ!

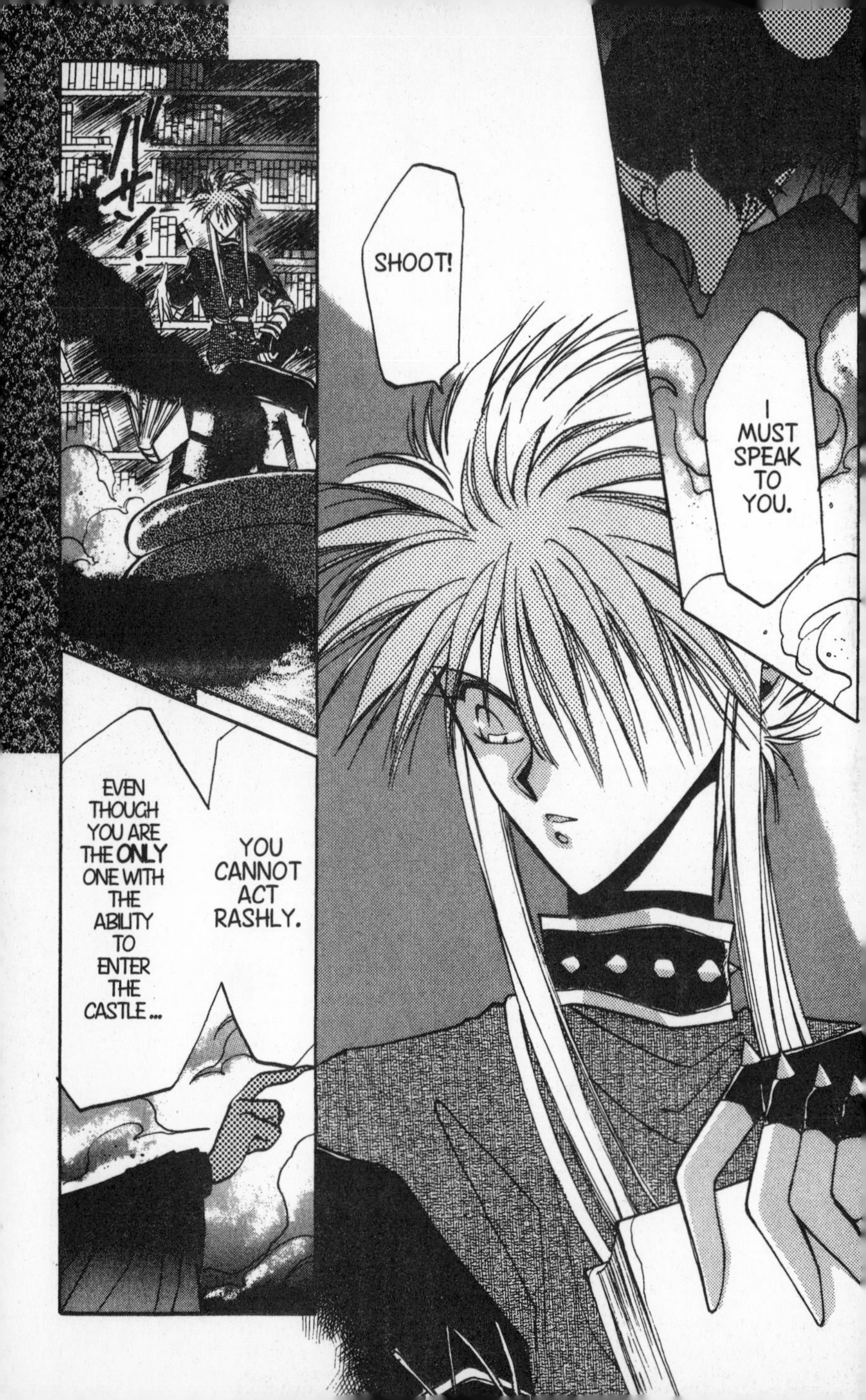
I MUST SPEAK TO YOU.
SHOOT!
YOU CANNOT ACT RASHLY.
EVEN THOUGH YOU ARE THE ONLY ONE WITH THE ABILITY TO ENTER THE CASTLE...

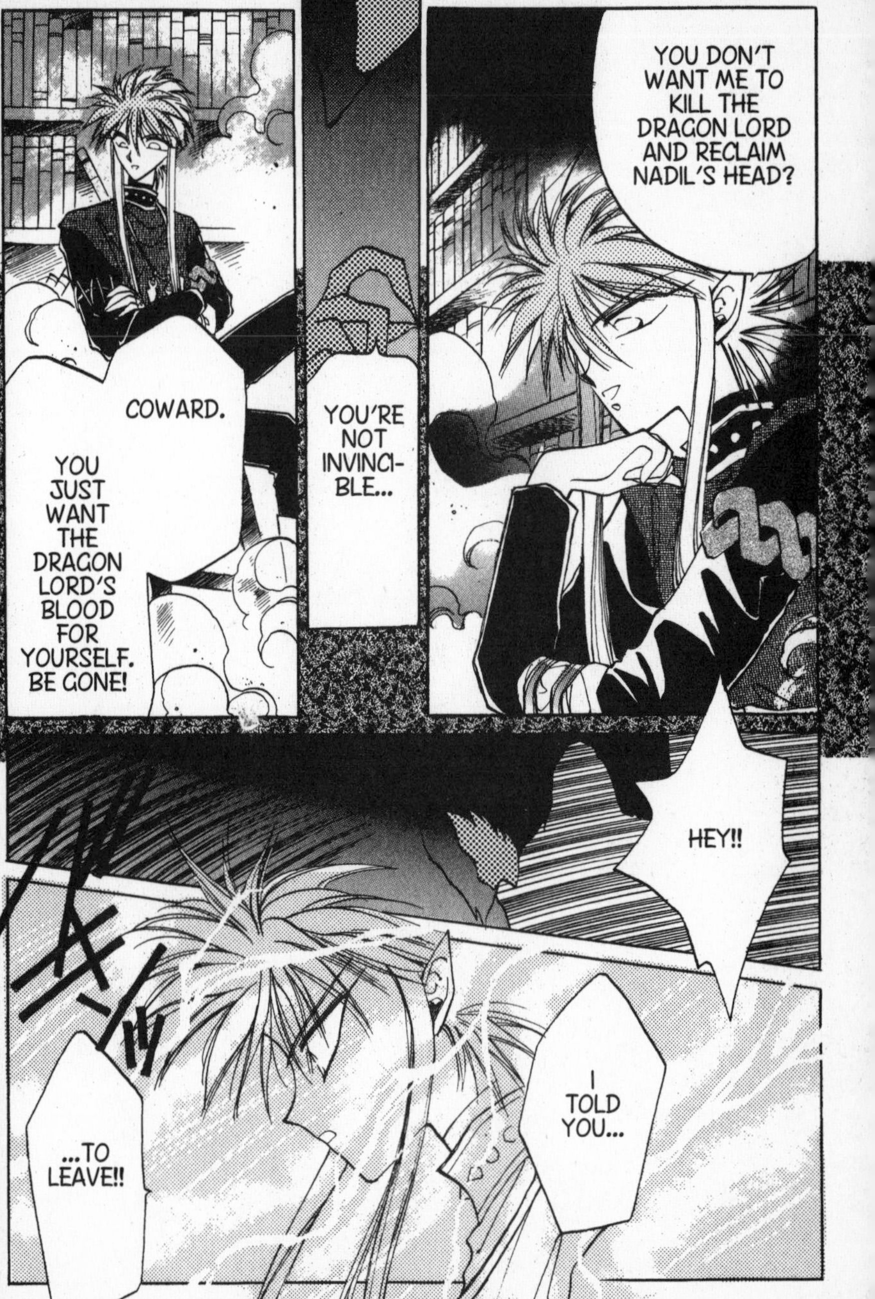
YOU DON'T WANT ME TO KILL THE DRAGON LORD AND RECLAIM NADIL'S HEAD?
YOU'RE NOT INVINCIBLE...
COWARD.
YOU JUST WANT THE DRAGON LORD'S BLOOD FOR YOURSELF. BE GONE!
HEY!!
I TOLD YOU...
...TO LEAVE!!

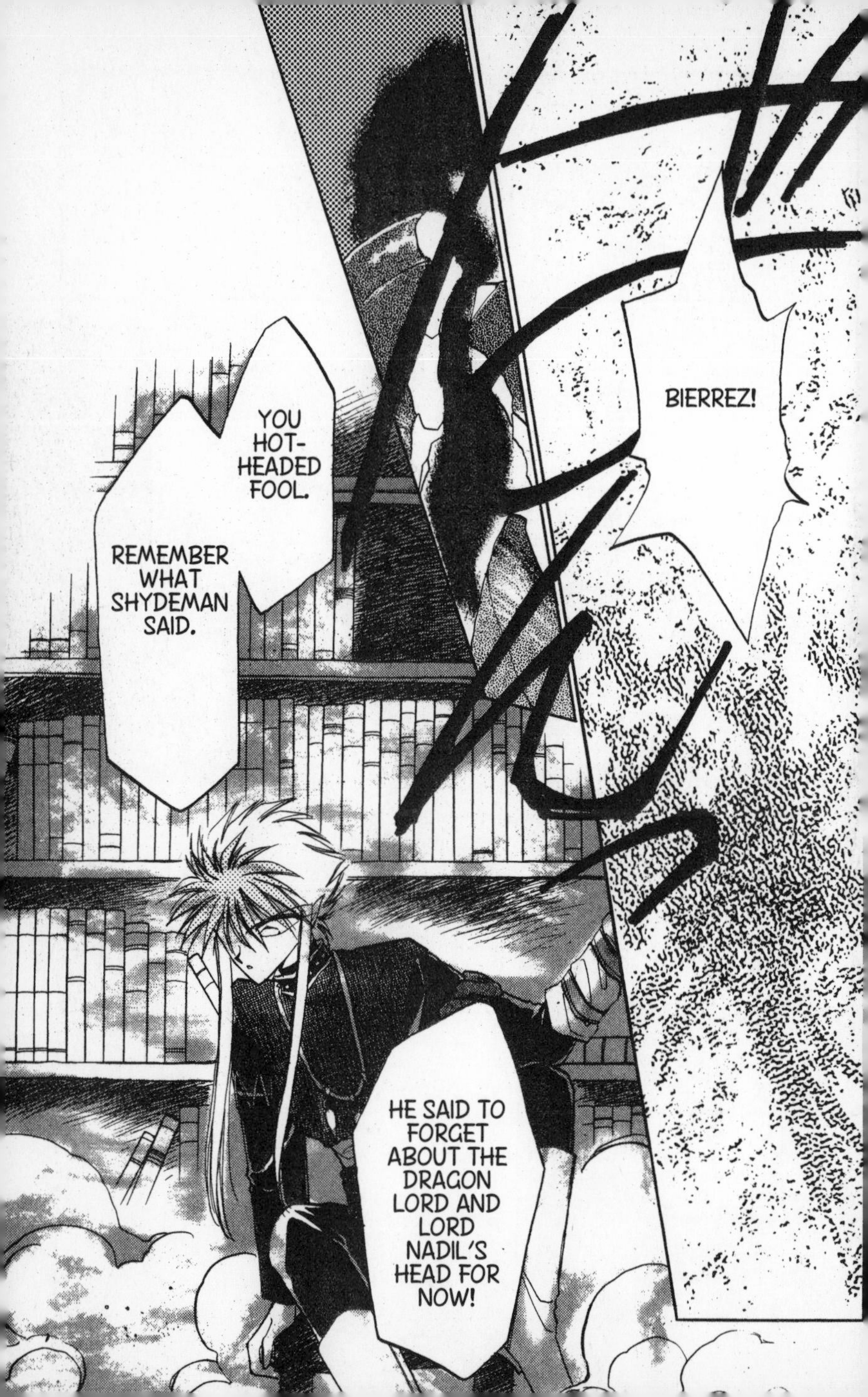
BIERREZ!
YOU HOT-HEADED FOOL.
REMEMBER WHAT SHYDEMAN SAID.
HE SAID TO FORGET ABOUT THE DRAGON LORD AND LORD NADIL'S HEAD FOR NOW!

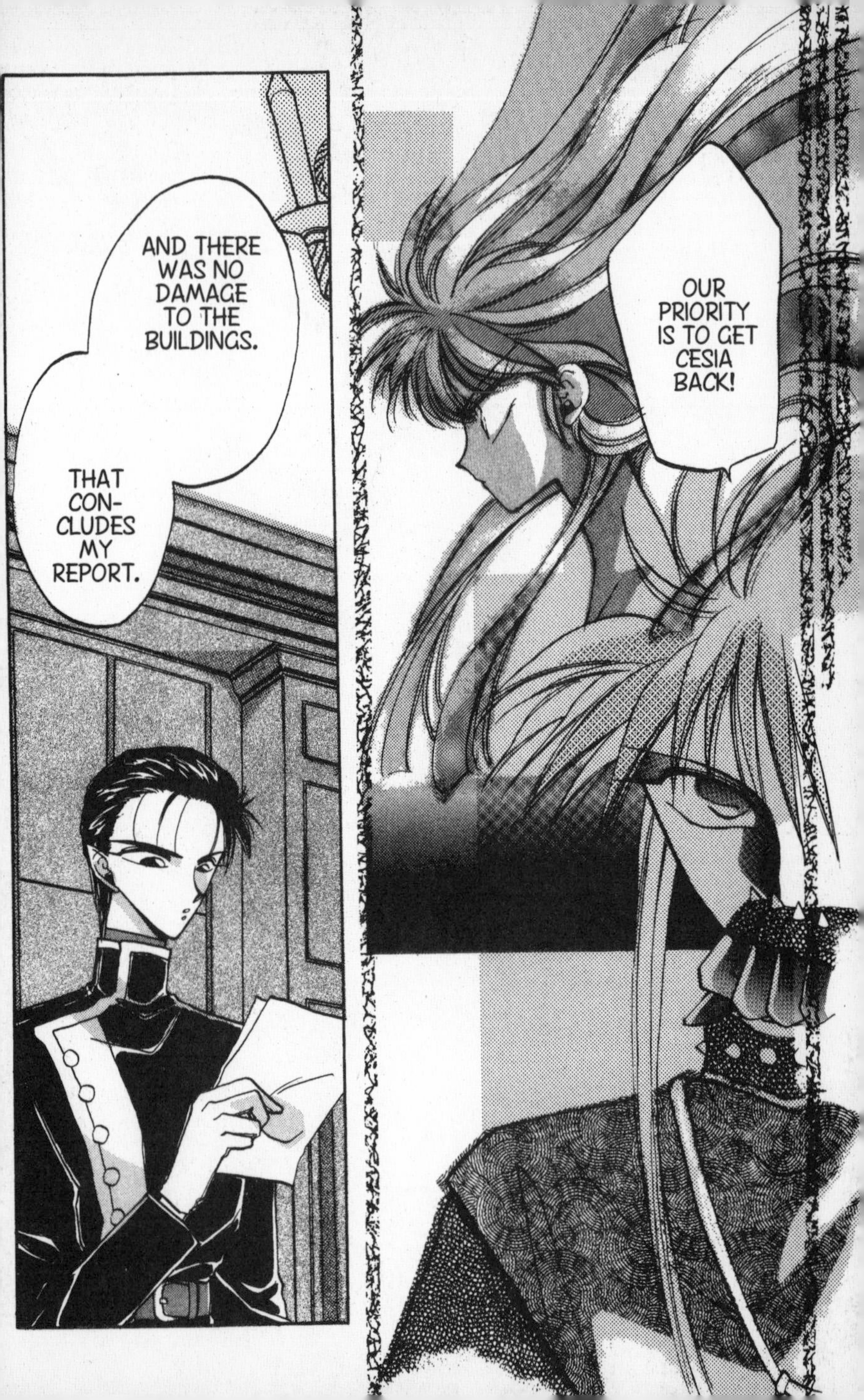
OUR PRIORITY IS TO GET CESIA BACK!
AND THERE WAS NO DAMAGE TO THE BUILDINGS.
THAT CON-CLUDES MY REPORT.

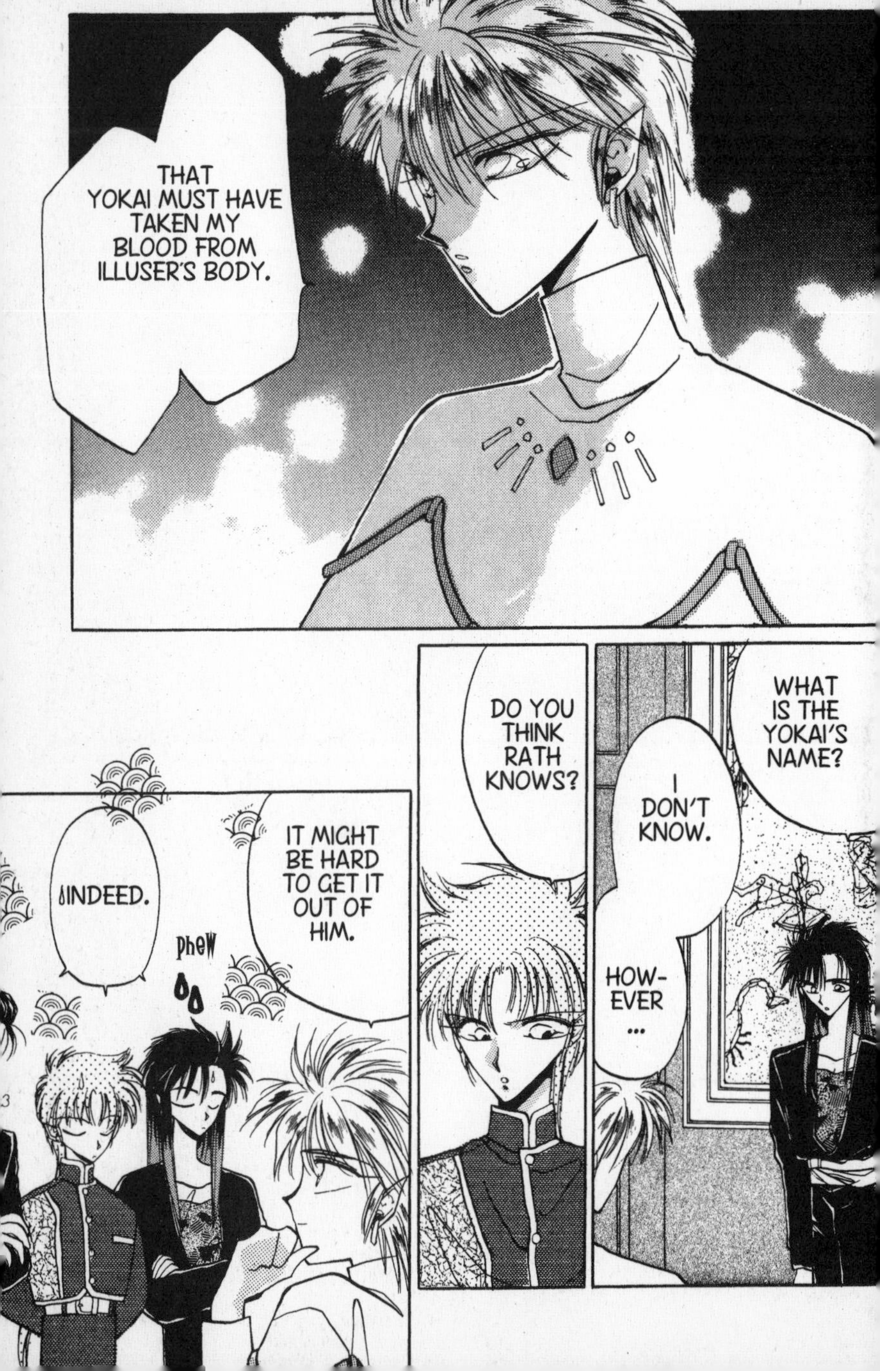
THAT YOKAI MUST HAVE TAKEN MY BLOOD FROM ILLUSER'S BODY.
WHAT IS THE YOKAI'S NAME?
I DON'T KNOW.
HOW-EVER ...
DO YOU THINK RATH KNOWS?
IT MIGHT BE HARD TO GET IT OUT OF HIM.
INDEED.
phew

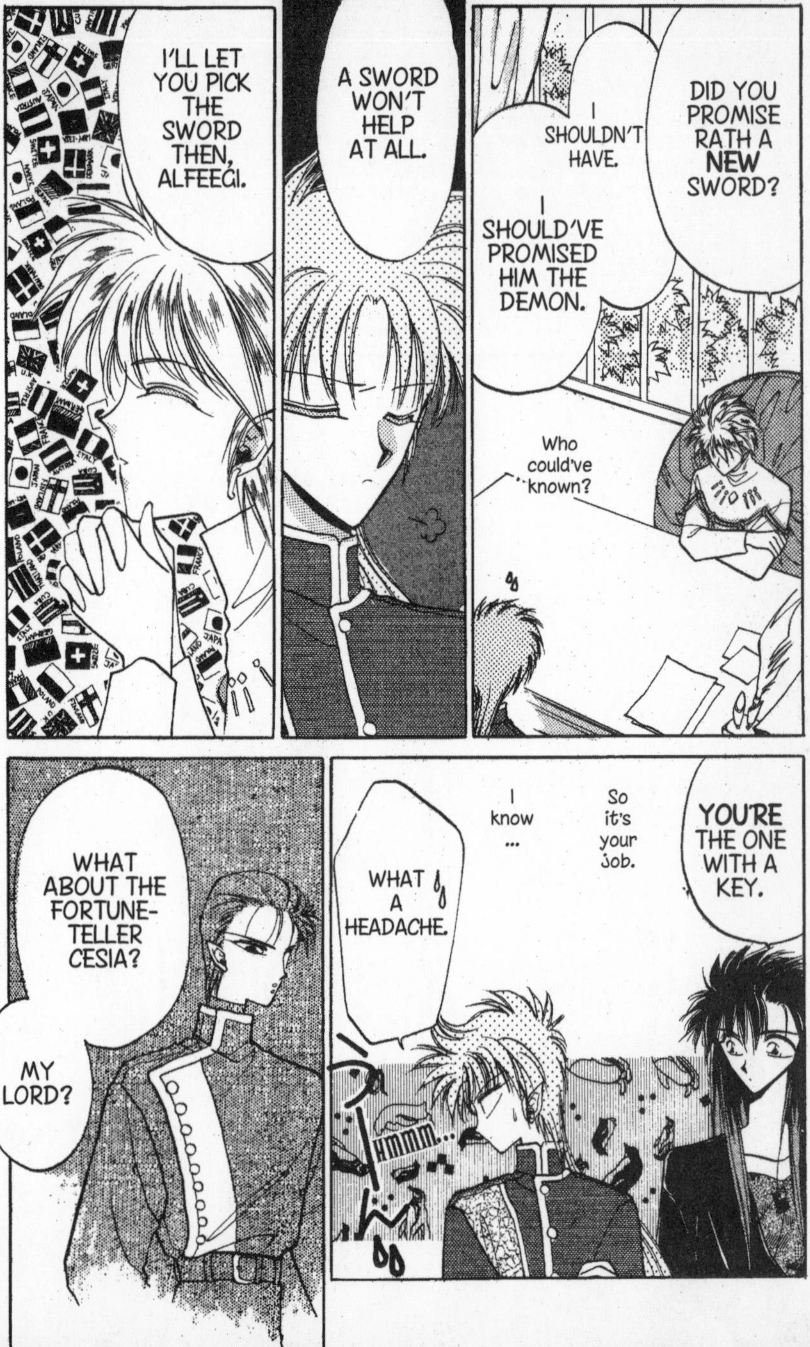
DID YOU PROMISE RATH A **NEW** SWORD?
I SHOULDN'T HAVE.
I SHOULD'VE PROMISED HIM THE DEMON.
Who could've known?
A SWORD WON'T HELP AT ALL.
I'LL LET YOU PICK THE SWORD THEN, ALFEEGI.
YOU'RE THE ONE WITH A KEY.
So it's your job.
I know...
WHAT A HEADACHE.
HMMM...
WHAT ABOUT THE FORTUNE-TELLER CESIA?
MY LORD?

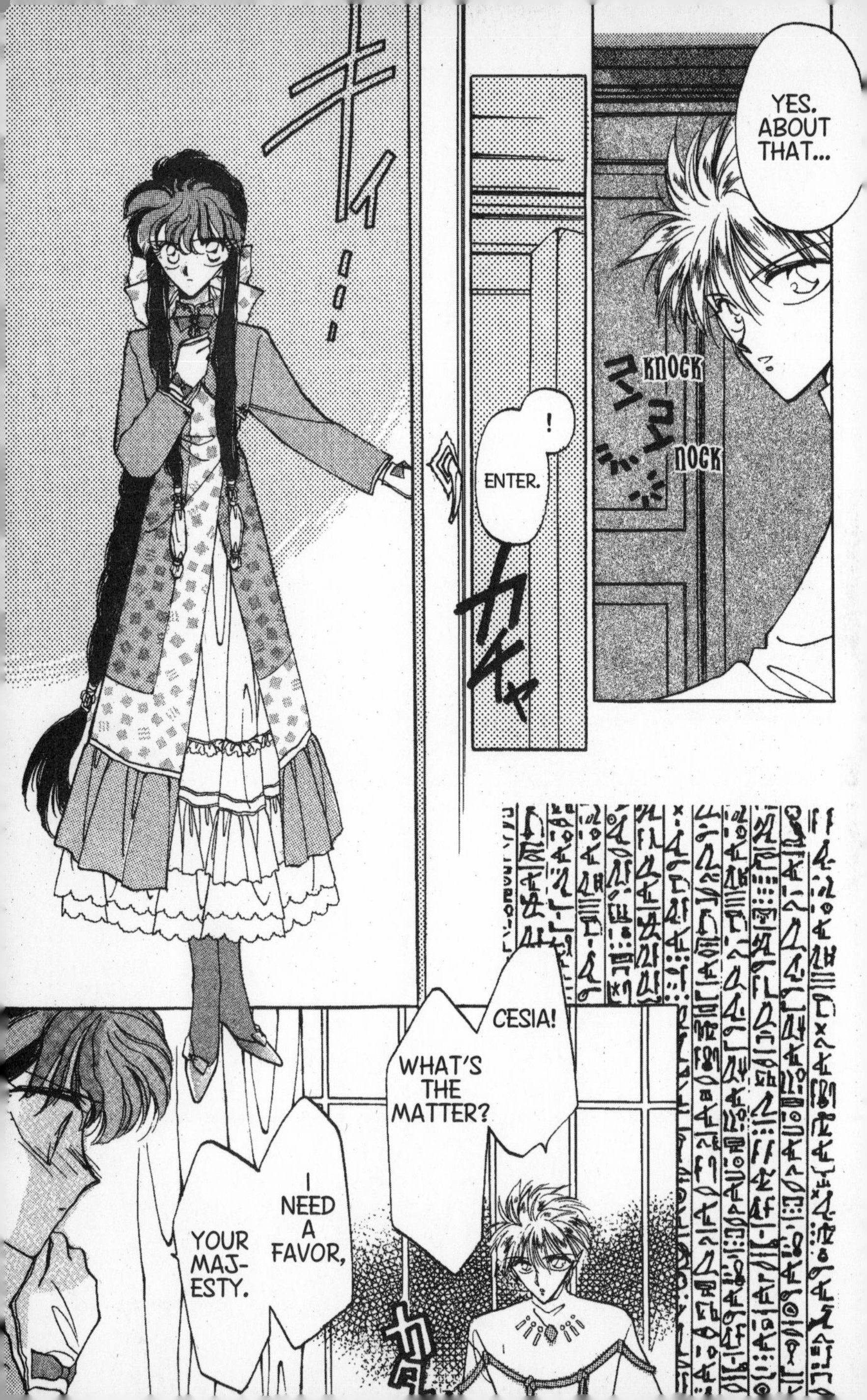
YES. ABOUT THAT...
KNOCK
NOCK
!
ENTER.
CESIA!
WHAT'S THE MATTER?
I NEED A FAVOR, YOUR MAJESTY.

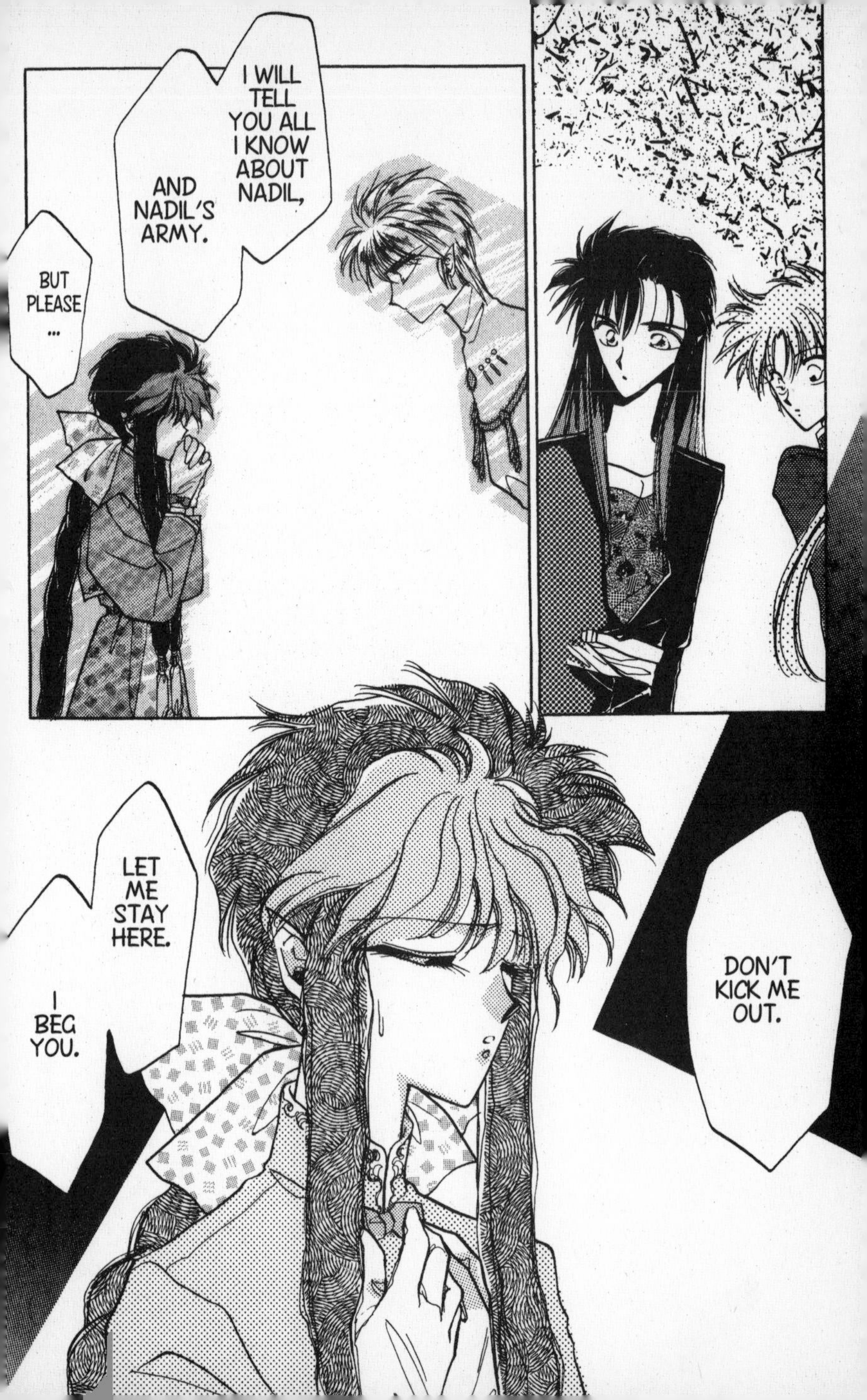
I WILL TELL YOU ALL I KNOW ABOUT NADIL,
AND NADIL'S ARMY.
BUT PLEASE ...
DON'T KICK ME OUT.
LET ME STAY HERE.
I BEG YOU.

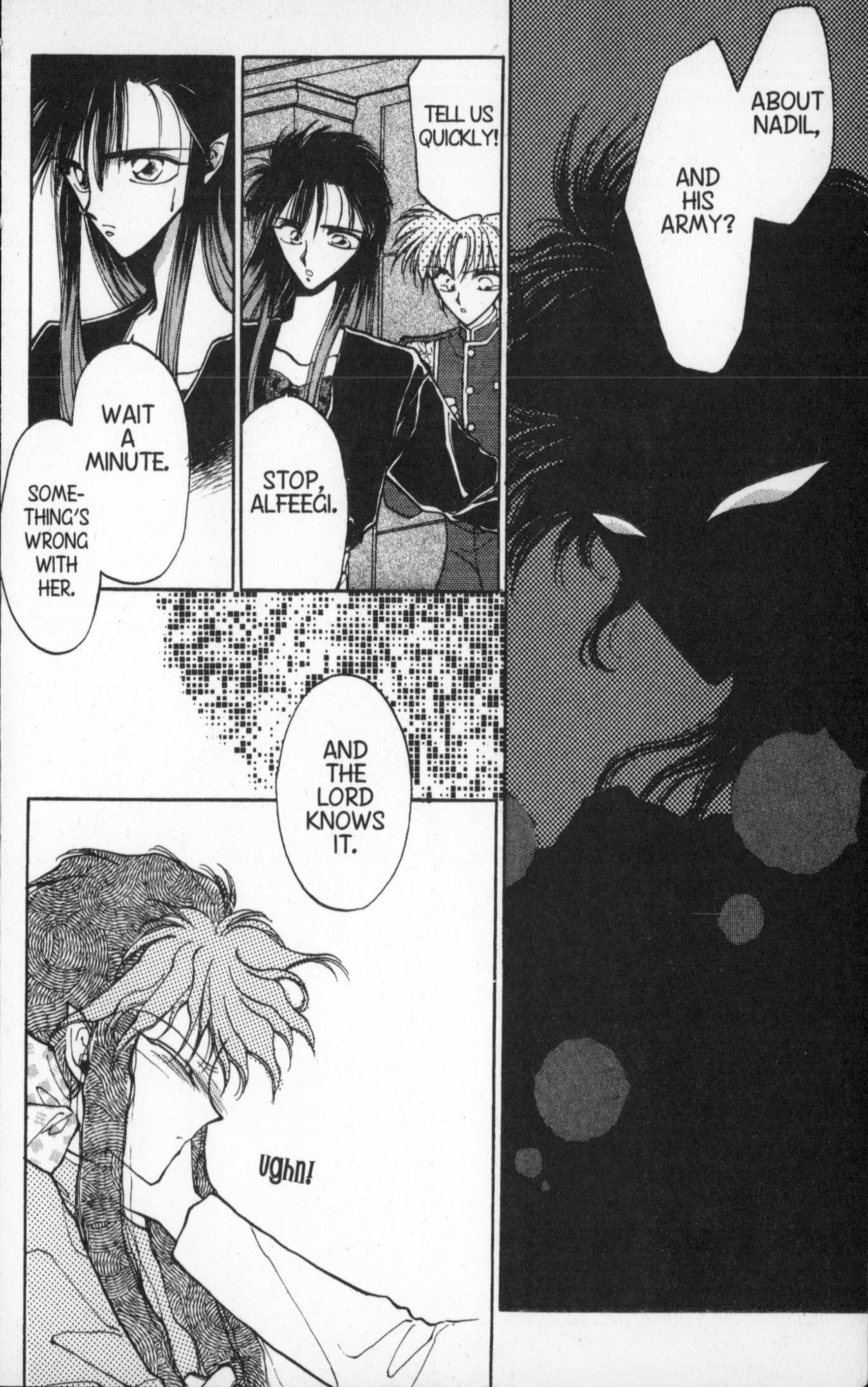
ABOUT NADIL,
AND HIS ARMY?
TELL US QUICKLY!
STOP, ALFEEGI.
WAIT A MINUTE.
SOME-THING'S WRONG WITH HER.
AND THE LORD KNOWS IT.
Ughn!

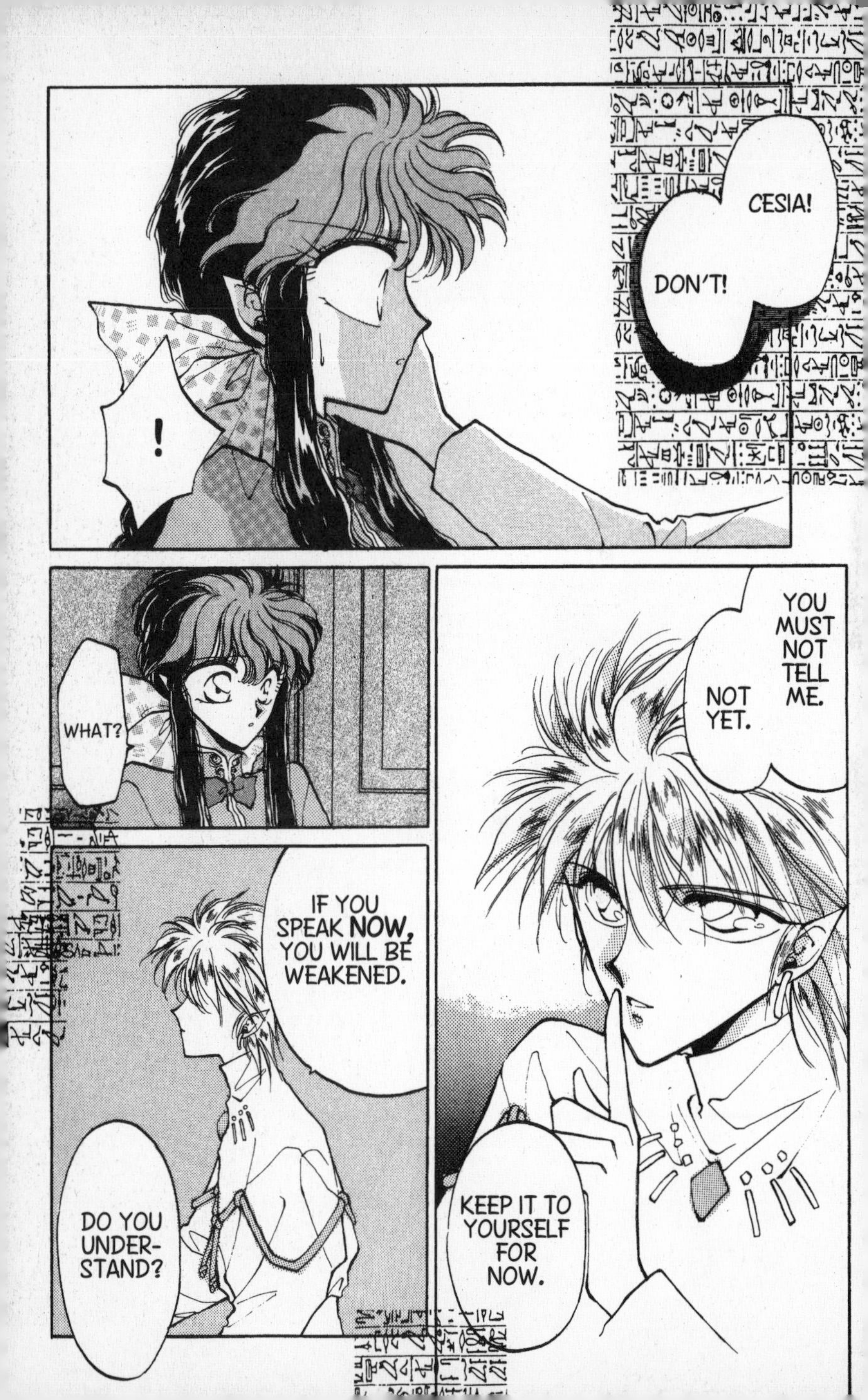
CESIA! DON'T!
!
YOU MUST NOT TELL ME. NOT YET.
KEEP IT TO YOURSELF FOR NOW.
WHAT?
IF YOU SPEAK NOW, YOU WILL BE WEAKENED.
DO YOU UNDER-STAND?

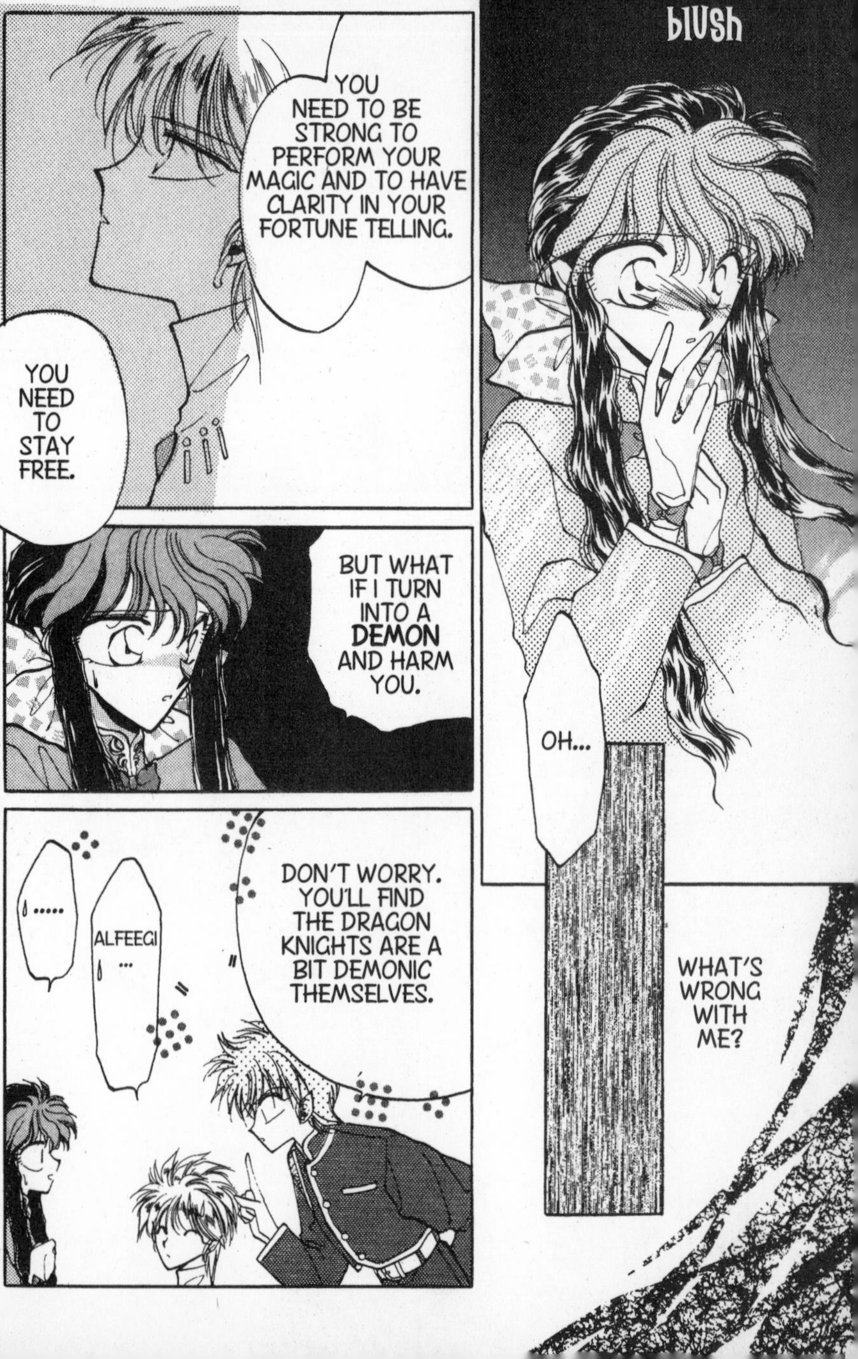

blush
OH...
WHAT'S WRONG WITH ME?
YOU NEED TO BE STRONG TO PERFORM YOUR MAGIC AND TO HAVE CLARITY IN YOUR FORTUNE TELLING.
YOU NEED TO STAY FREE.
BUT WHAT IF I TURN INTO A **DEMON** AND HARM YOU.
DON'T WORRY. YOU'LL FIND THE DRAGON KNIGHTS ARE A BIT DEMONIC THEMSELVES.
ALFEEGI ...
......

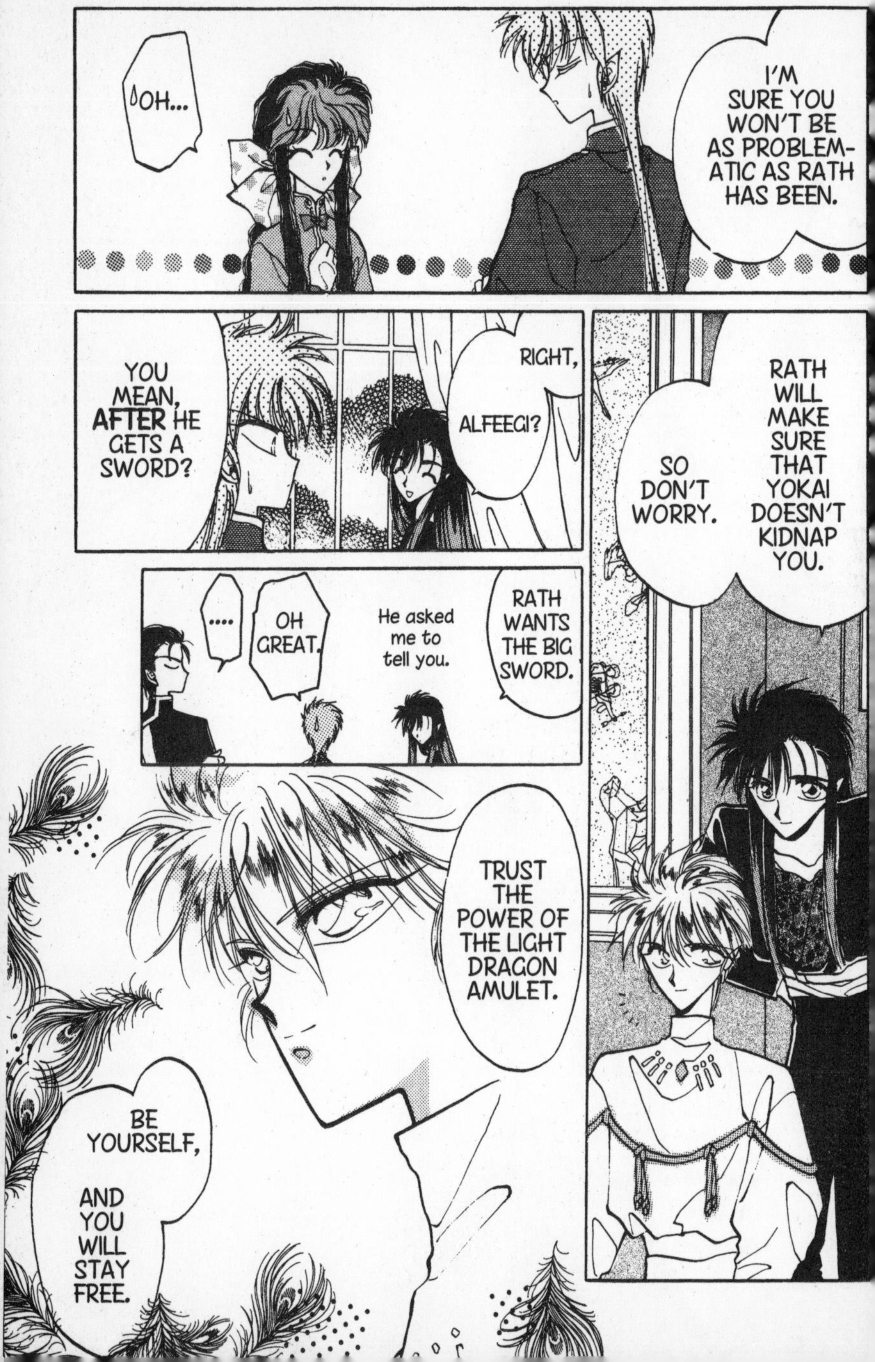
I'M SURE YOU WON'T BE AS PROBLEM-ATIC AS RATH HAS BEEN.
OH...
RATH WILL MAKE SURE THAT YOKAI DOESN'T KIDNAP YOU.
SO DON'T WORRY.
RIGHT,
ALFEEGI?
YOU MEAN, AFTER HE GETS A SWORD?
RATH WANTS THE BIG SWORD.
He asked me to tell you.
OH GREAT.
....
TRUST THE POWER OF THE LIGHT DRAGON AMULET.
BE YOURSELF,
AND YOU WILL STAY FREE.

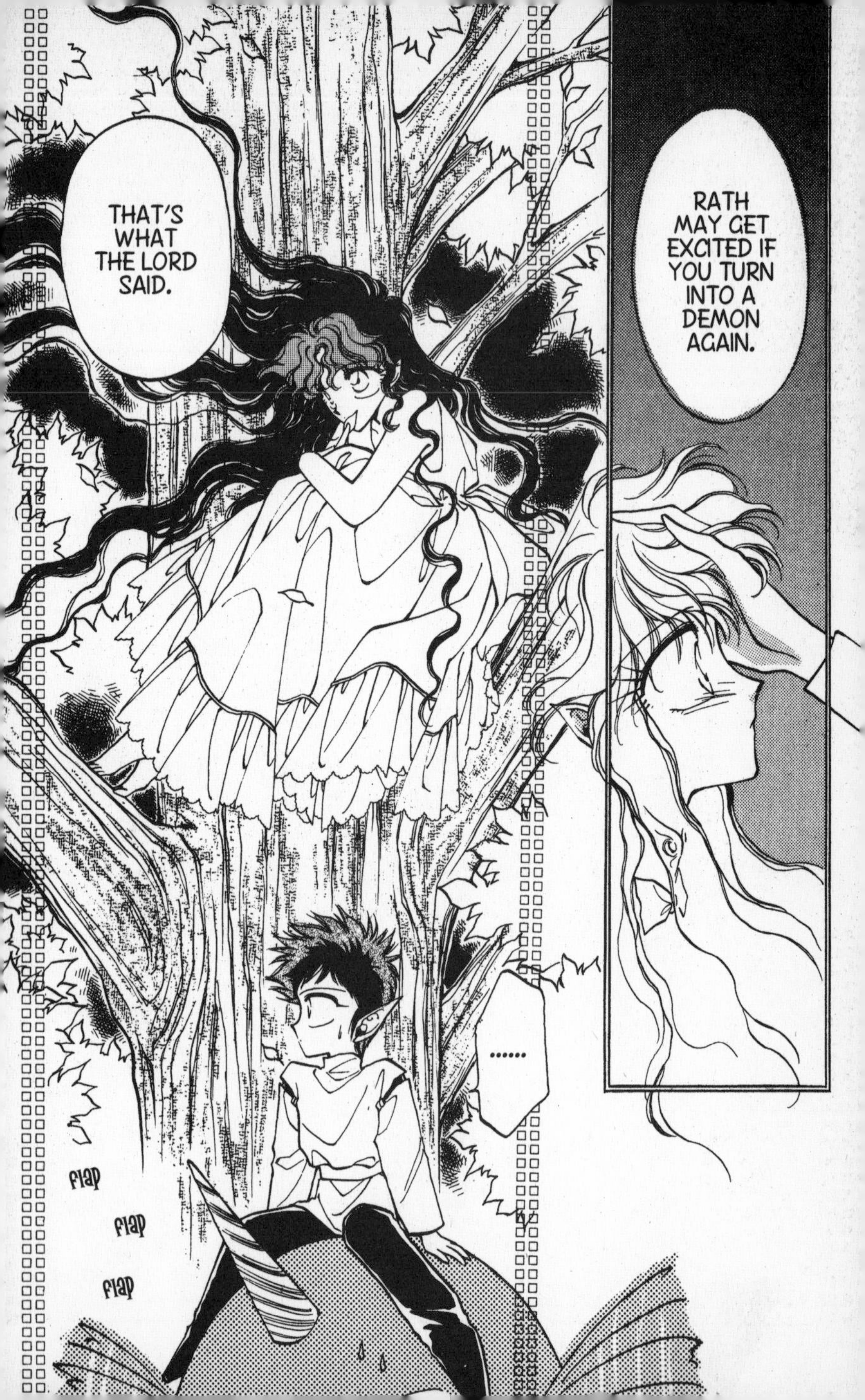
RATH MAY GET EXCITED IF YOU TURN INTO A DEMON AGAIN.
THAT'S WHAT THE LORD SAID.
......
flap
flap
flap

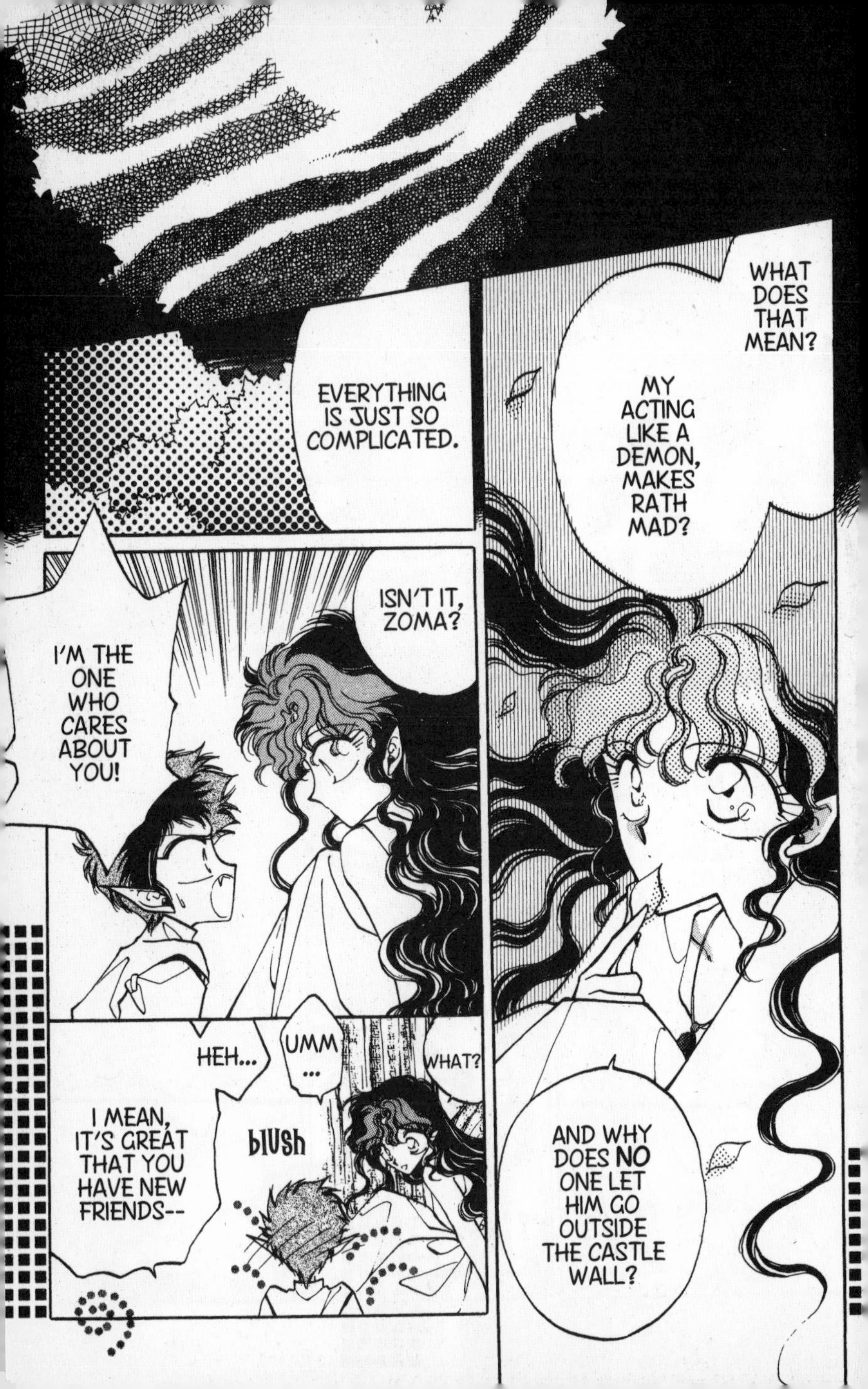
WHAT DOES THAT MEAN?
MY ACTING LIKE A DEMON, MAKES RATH MAD?
AND WHY DOES NO ONE LET HIM GO OUTSIDE THE CASTLE WALL?
EVERYTHING IS JUST SO COMPLICATED.
ISN'T IT, ZOMA?
I'M THE ONE WHO CARES ABOUT YOU!
WHAT?
UMM ...
HEH...
blush
I MEAN, IT'S GREAT THAT YOU HAVE NEW FRIENDS--

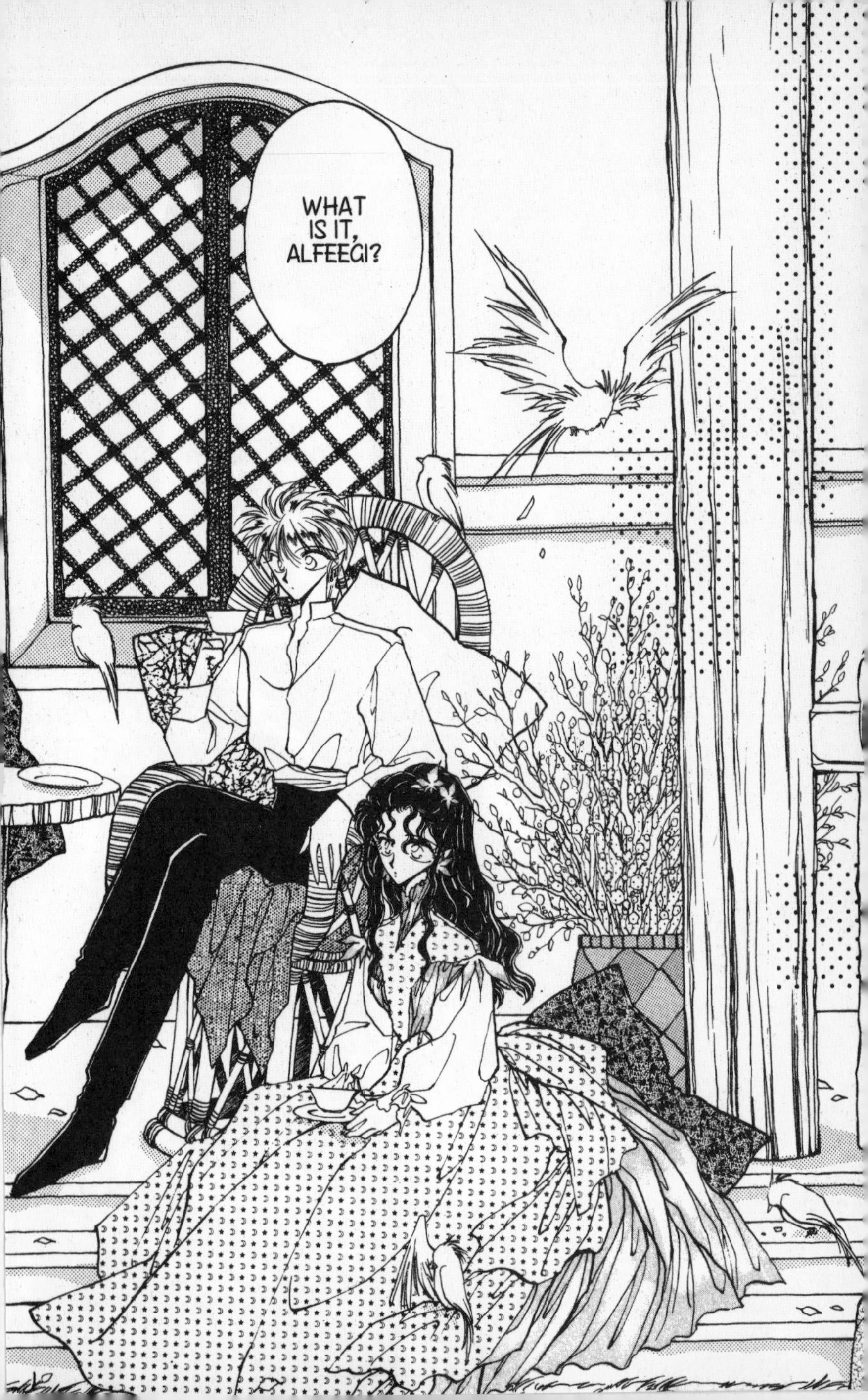
WHAT IS IT, ALFEEGI?

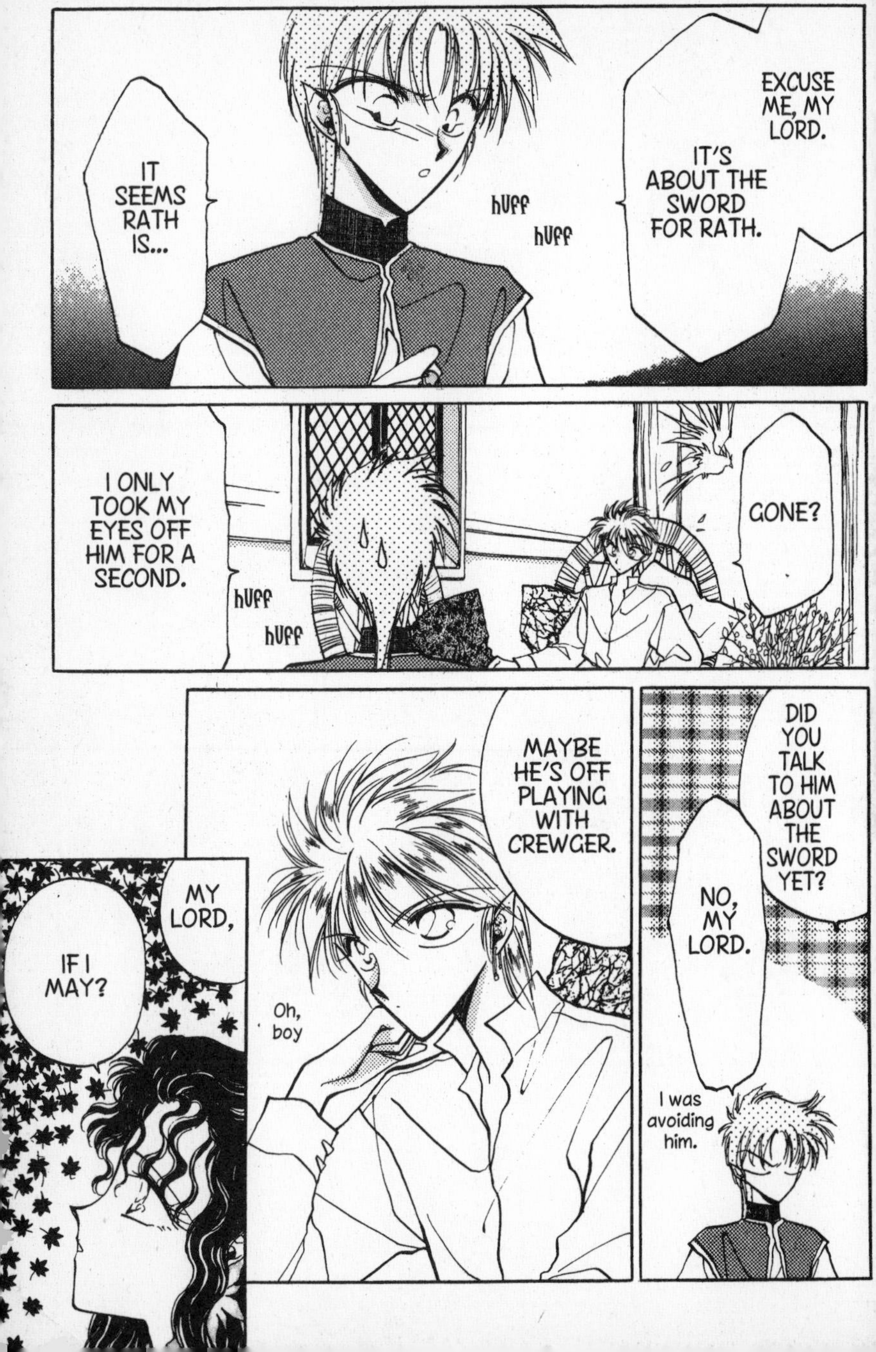
EXCUSE ME, MY LORD.
IT'S ABOUT THE SWORD FOR RATH.
hUFF
hUFF
IT SEEMS RATH IS...
GONE?
I ONLY TOOK MY EYES OFF HIM FOR A SECOND.
hUFF
hUFF
DID YOU TALK TO HIM ABOUT THE SWORD YET?
NO, MY LORD.
I was avoiding him.
MAYBE HE'S OFF PLAYING WITH CREWGER.
Oh, boy
MY LORD,
IF I MAY?

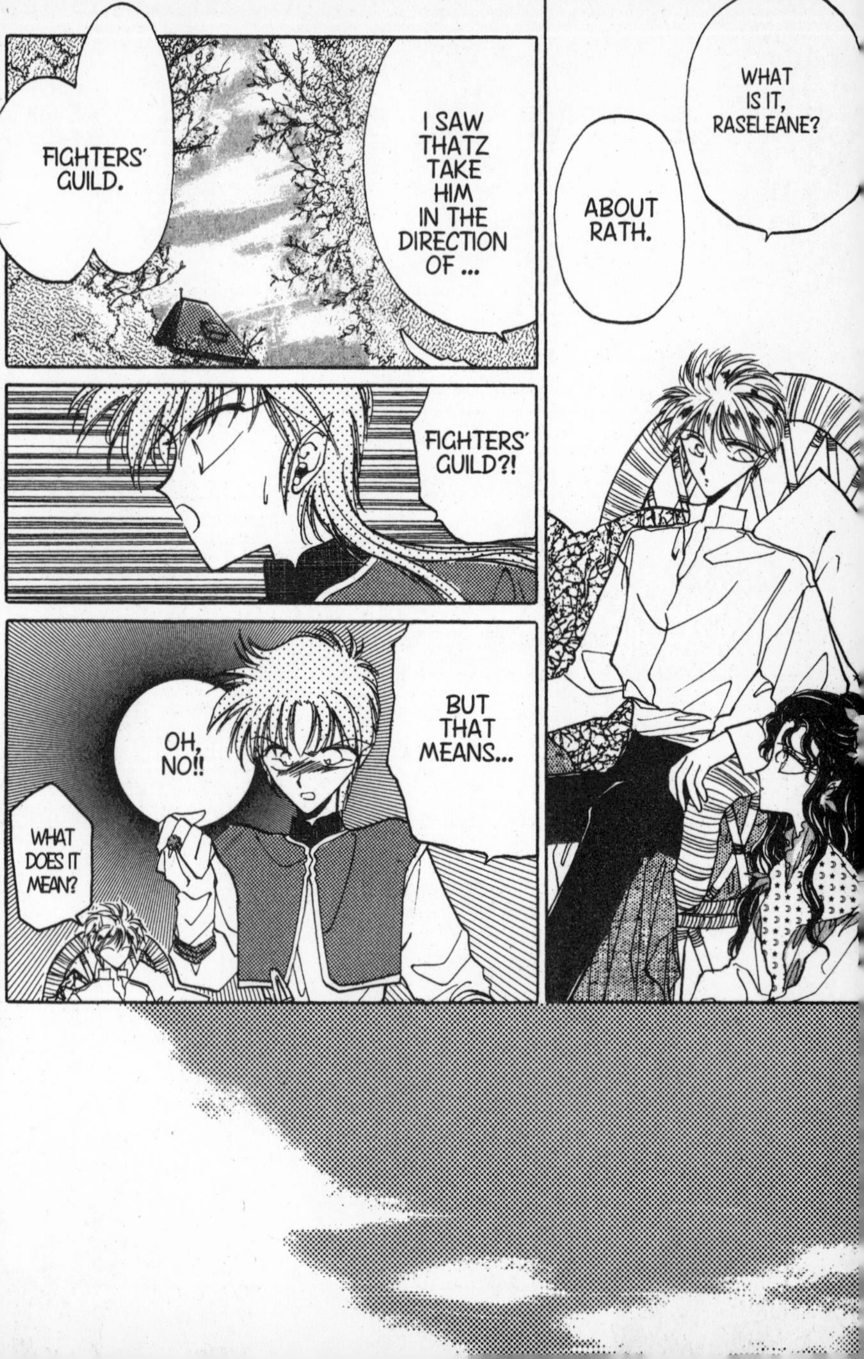
WHAT IS IT, RASELEANE?
ABOUT RATH.
I SAW THATZ TAKE HIM IN THE DIRECTION OF ...
FIGHTERS' GUILD.
FIGHTERS' GUILD?!
BUT THAT MEANS...
OH, NO!!
WHAT DOES IT MEAN?

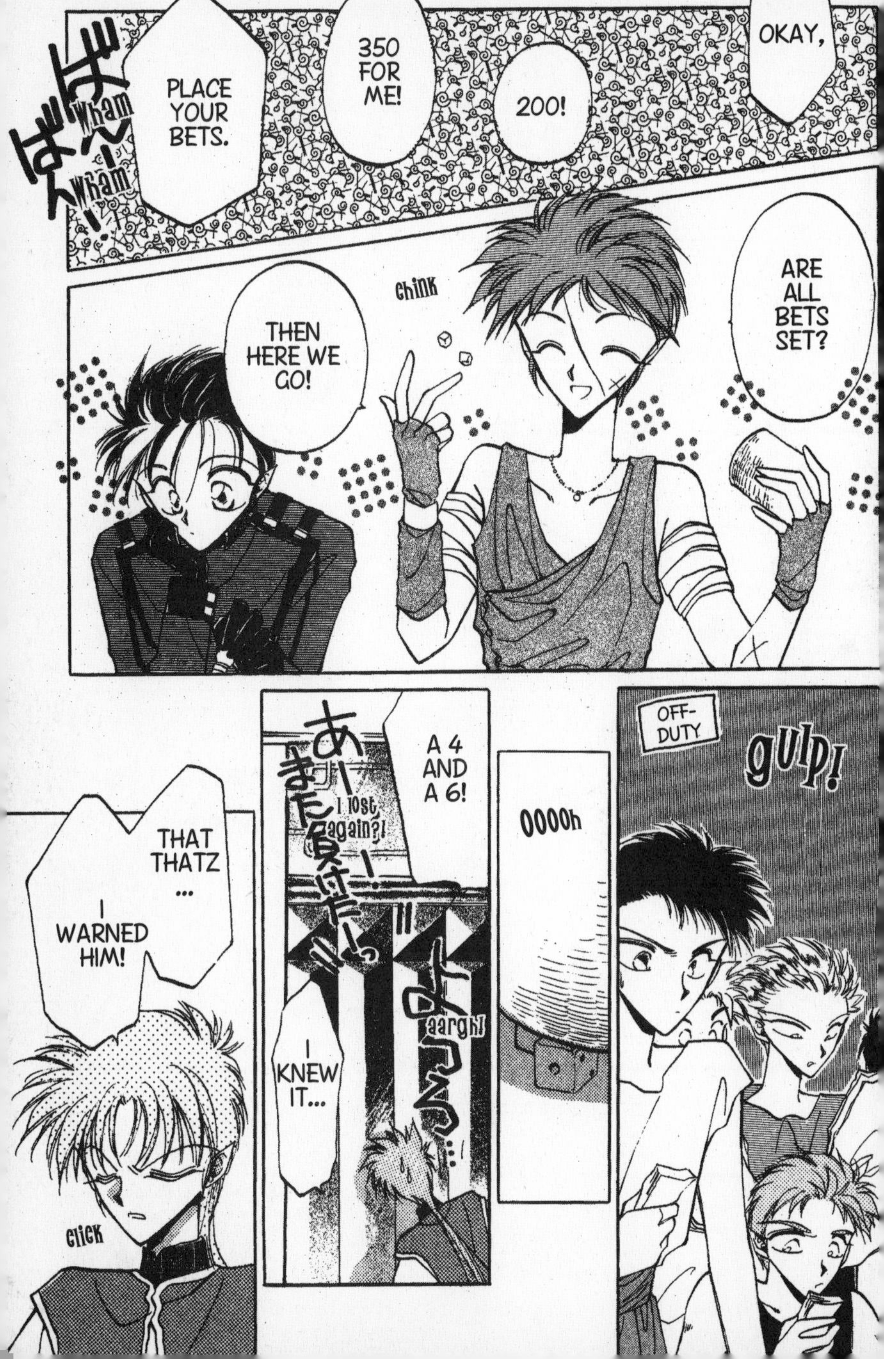
OKAY,
200!
350 FOR ME!
PLACE YOUR BETS.
Wham Wham
ARE ALL BETS SET?
Chink
THEN HERE WE GO!
OFF-DUTY
gulp!
0000h
A 4 AND A 6!
あーまた負けたーっ
I lost again?!
aargh!
I KNEW IT...
THAT THATZ ...
I WARNED HIM!
click

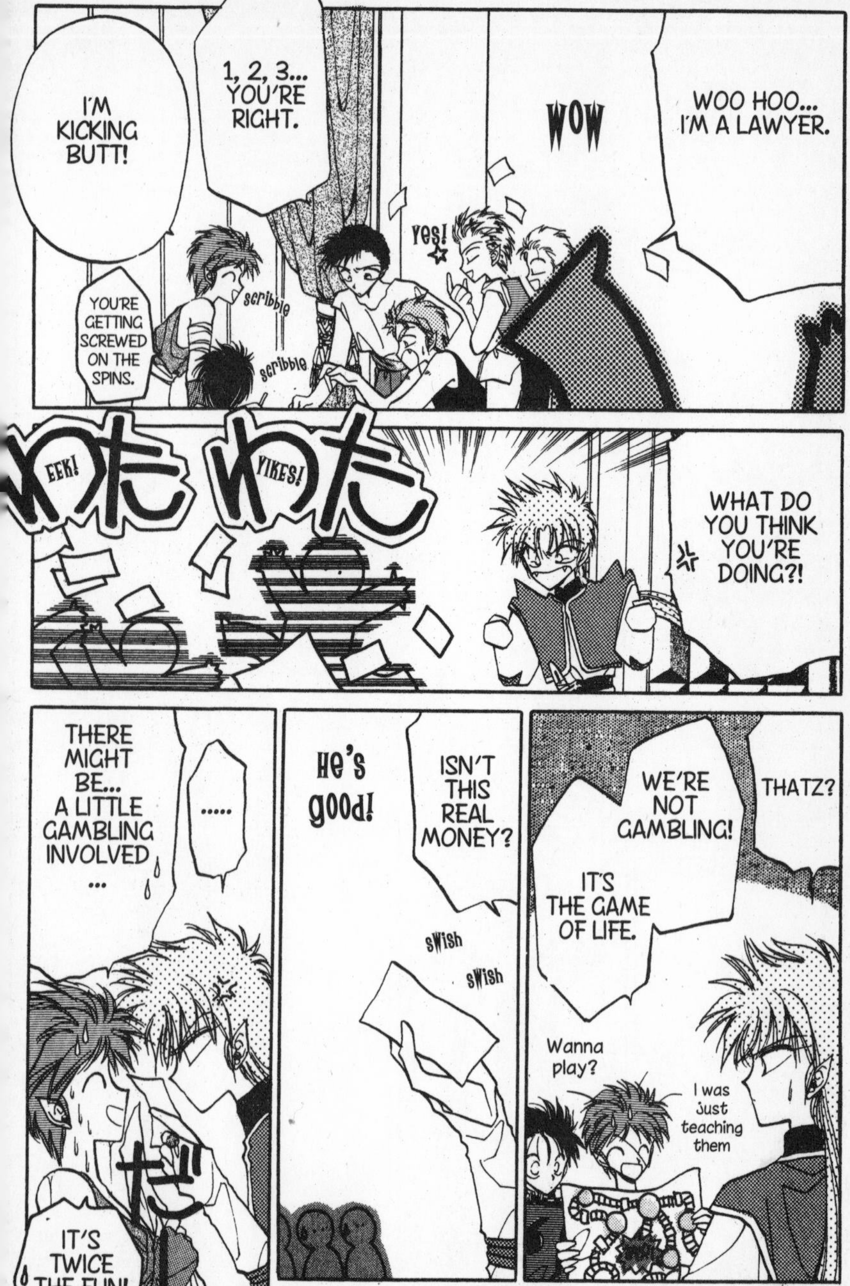
WOO HOO... I'M A LAWYER.
WOW
yes!
1, 2, 3... YOU'RE RIGHT.
I'M KICKING BUTT!
scribble
YOU'RE GETTING SCREWED ON THE SPINS.
scribble
WHAT DO YOU THINK YOU'RE DOING?!
わた わた
YIKES!
EEK!
THATZ?
WE'RE NOT GAMBLING!
IT'S THE GAME OF LIFE.
I was just teaching them
Wanna play?
ISN'T THIS REAL MONEY?
He's good!
swish
swish
.....
THERE MIGHT BE... A LITTLE GAMBLING INVOLVED ...
IT'S TWICE THE FUN!

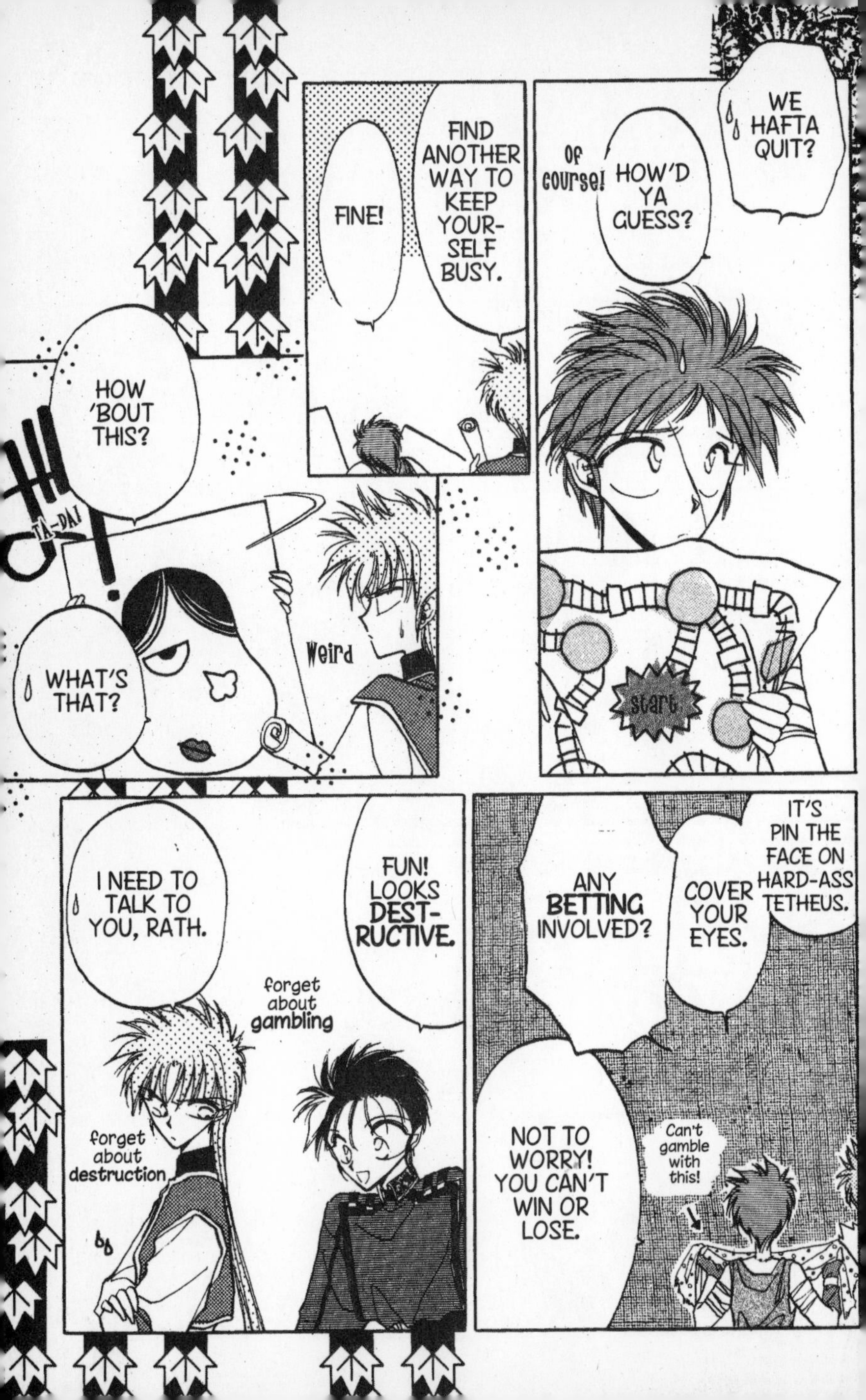
WE HAFTA QUIT?
HOW'D YA GUESS?
Of course!
start
FIND ANOTHER WAY TO KEEP YOUR-SELF BUSY.
FINE!
HOW 'BOUT THIS?
TA-DA!
WHAT'S THAT?
Weird
IT'S PIN THE FACE ON HARD-ASS TETHEUS.
COVER YOUR EYES.
ANY BETTING INVOLVED?
NOT TO WORRY! YOU CAN'T WIN OR LOSE.
Can't gamble with this!
FUN! LOOKS DEST-RUCTIVE.
I NEED TO TALK TO YOU, RATH.
forget about gambling
forget about destruction

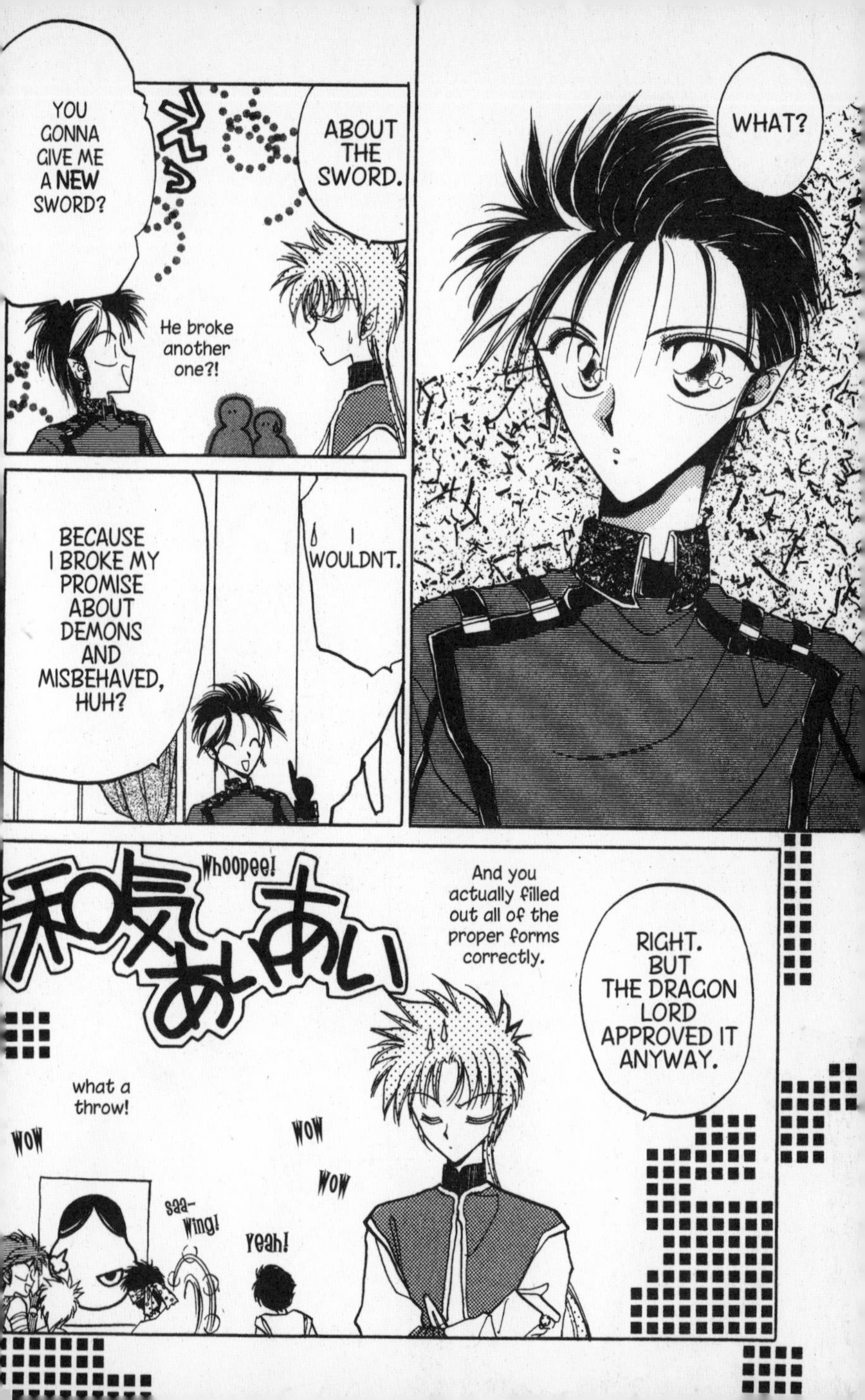
WHAT?
ABOUT THE SWORD.
YOU GONNA GIVE ME A NEW SWORD?
He broke another one?!
I WOULDN'T.
BECAUSE I BROKE MY PROMISE ABOUT DEMONS AND MISBEHAVED, HUH?
RIGHT. BUT THE DRAGON LORD APPROVED IT ANYWAY.
And you actually filled out all of the proper forms correctly.
Whoopee!
和気あいあい
what a throw!
WOW
WOW
WOW
saa-wing!
yeah!

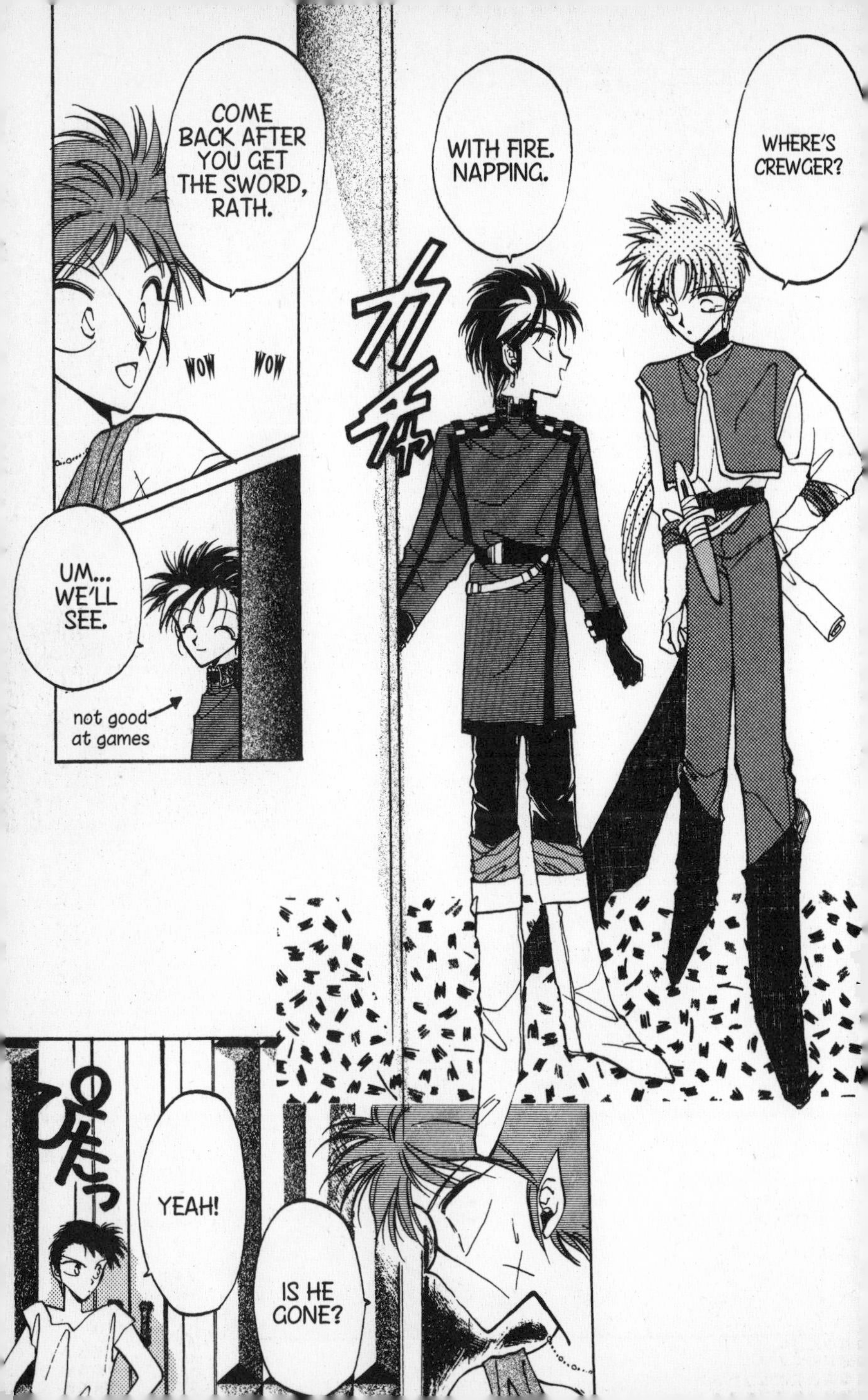
WHERE'S CREWGER?
WITH FIRE. NAPPING.
COME BACK AFTER YOU GET THE SWORD, RATH.
WOW WOW
UM... WE'LL SEE.
not good at games
IS HE GONE?
YEAH!

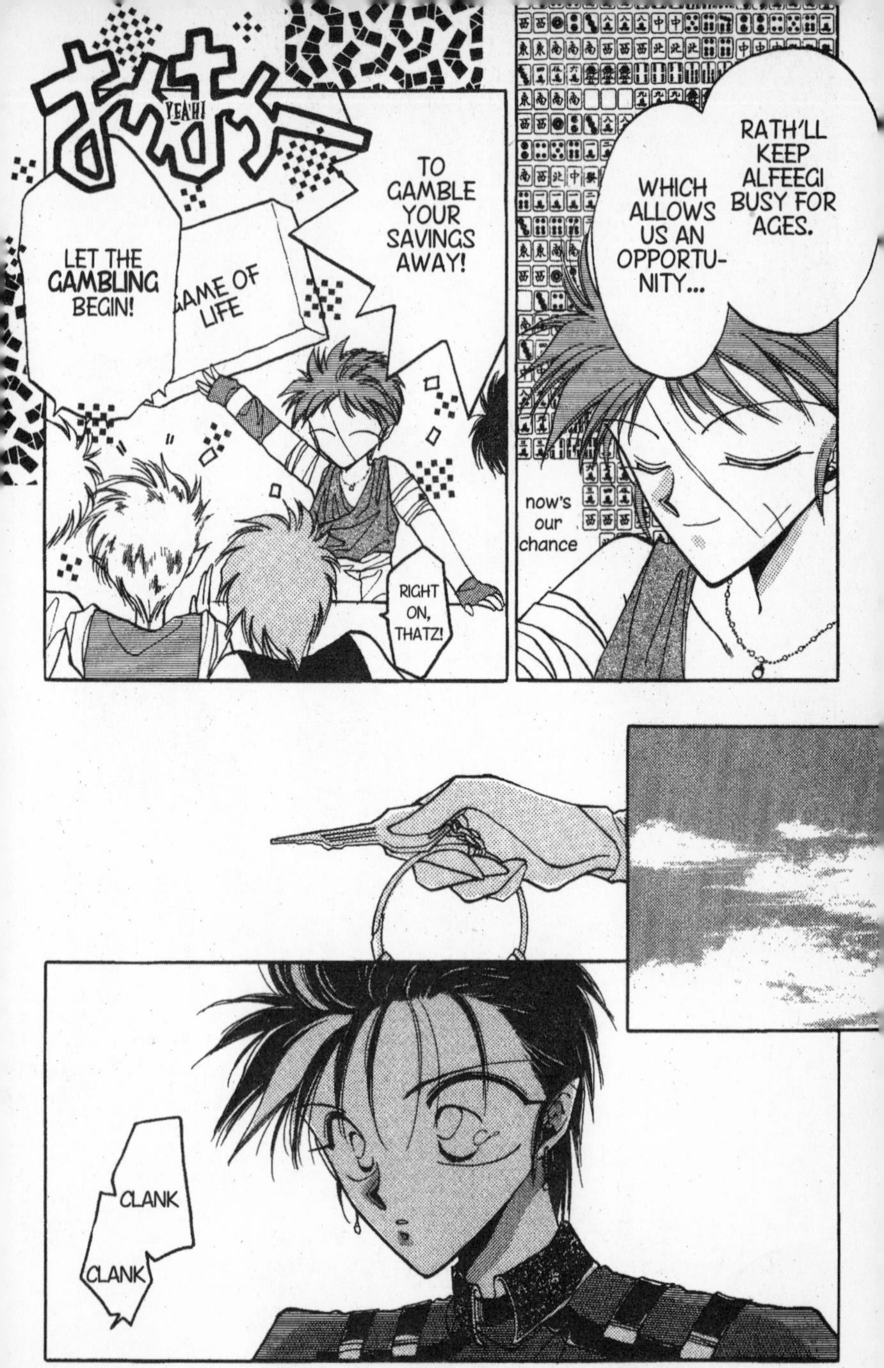
RATH'LL KEEP ALFEEGI BUSY FOR AGES.
WHICH ALLOWS US AN OPPORTU-NITY...
now's our chance
YEAH!
LET THE GAMBLING BEGIN!
GAME OF LIFE
TO GAMBLE YOUR SAVINGS AWAY!
RIGHT ON, THATZ!
CLANK
CLANK

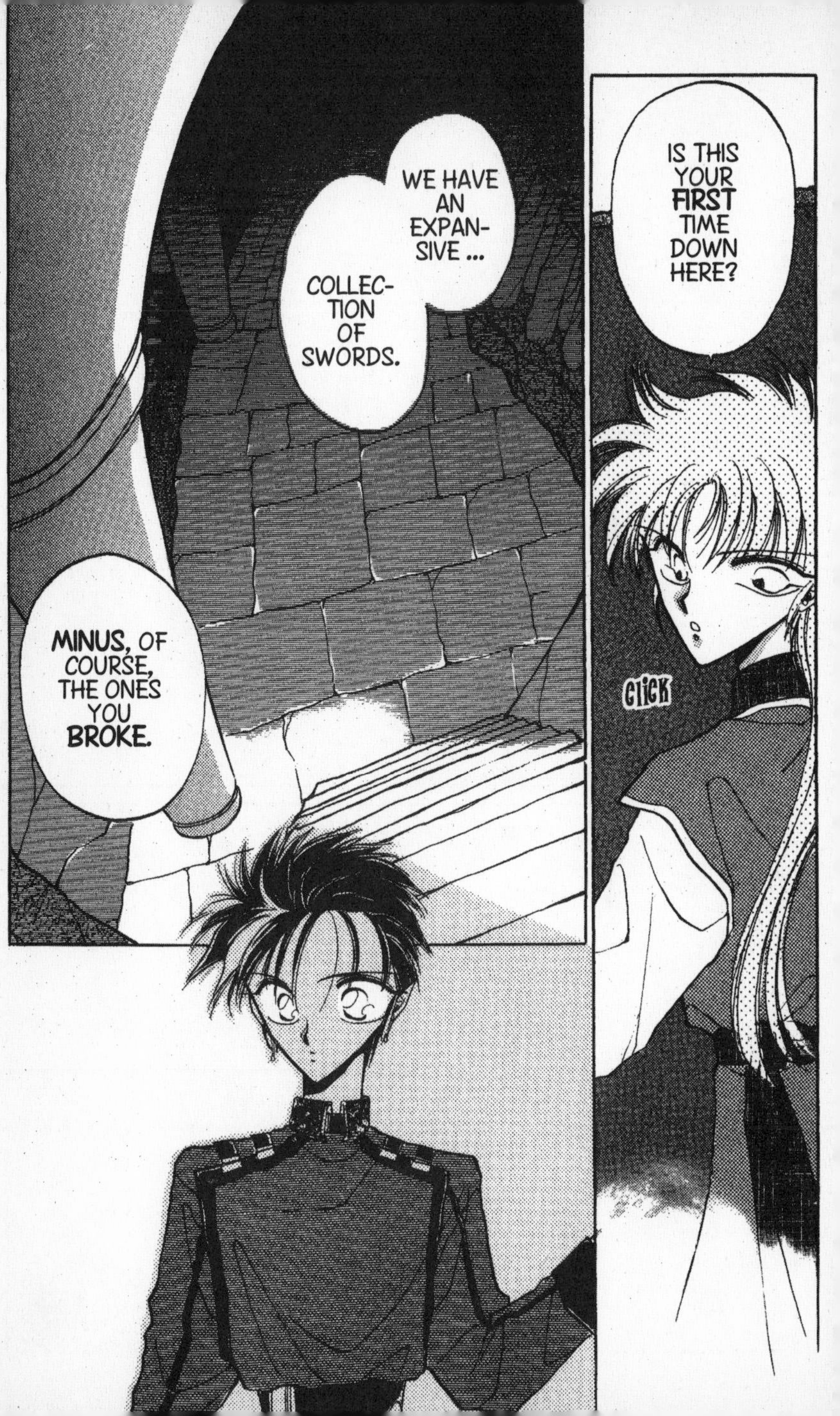
IS THIS YOUR FIRST TIME DOWN HERE?
CLICK
WE HAVE AN EXPANSIVE ...
COLLECTION OF SWORDS.
MINUS, OF COURSE, THE ONES YOU BROKE.

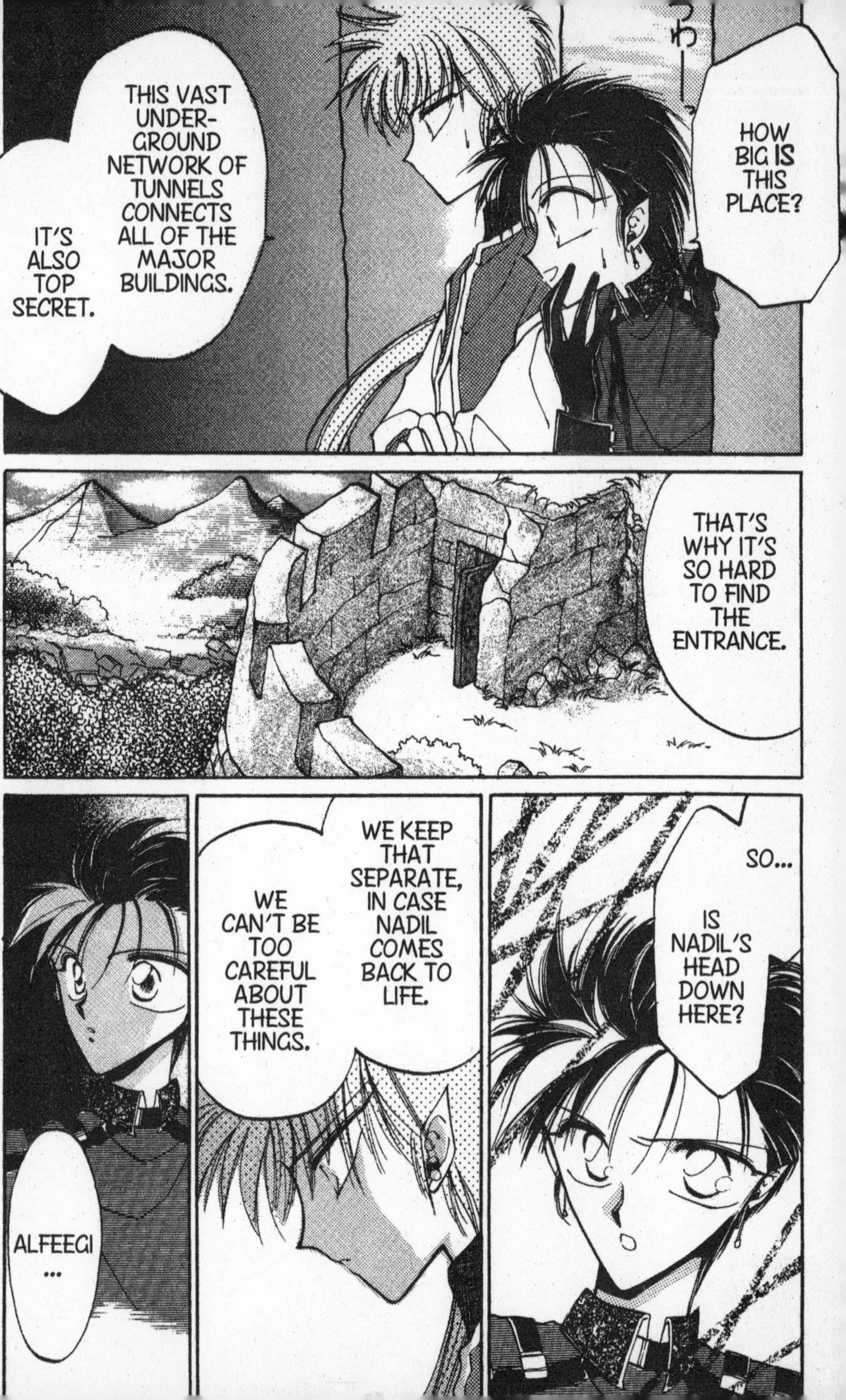
HOW BIG IS THIS PLACE?
THIS VAST UNDER-GROUND NETWORK OF TUNNELS CONNECTS ALL OF THE MAJOR BUILDINGS.
IT'S ALSO TOP SECRET.
THAT'S WHY IT'S SO HARD TO FIND THE ENTRANCE.
SO...
IS NADIL'S HEAD DOWN HERE?
WE KEEP THAT SEPARATE, IN CASE NADIL COMES BACK TO LIFE.
WE CAN'T BE TOO CAREFUL ABOUT THESE THINGS.
ALFEEGI ...

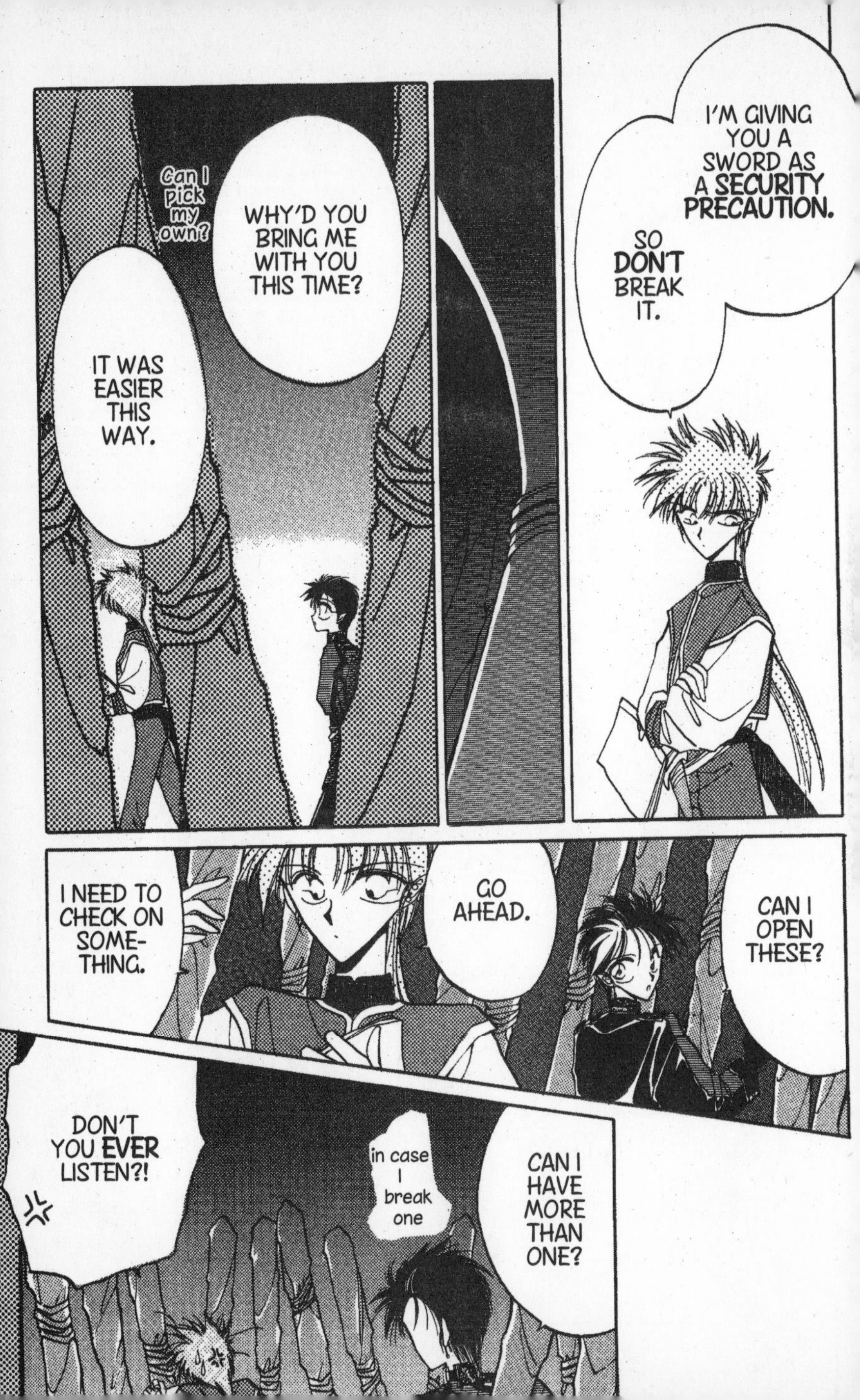
I'M GIVING YOU A SWORD AS A **SECURITY PRECAUTION.**
SO **DON'T** BREAK IT.
WHY'D YOU BRING ME WITH YOU THIS TIME?
Can I pick my own?
IT WAS EASIER THIS WAY.
CAN I OPEN THESE?
GO AHEAD.
I NEED TO CHECK ON SOME-THING.
CAN I HAVE MORE THAN ONE?
in case I break one
DON'T YOU **EVER** LISTEN?!

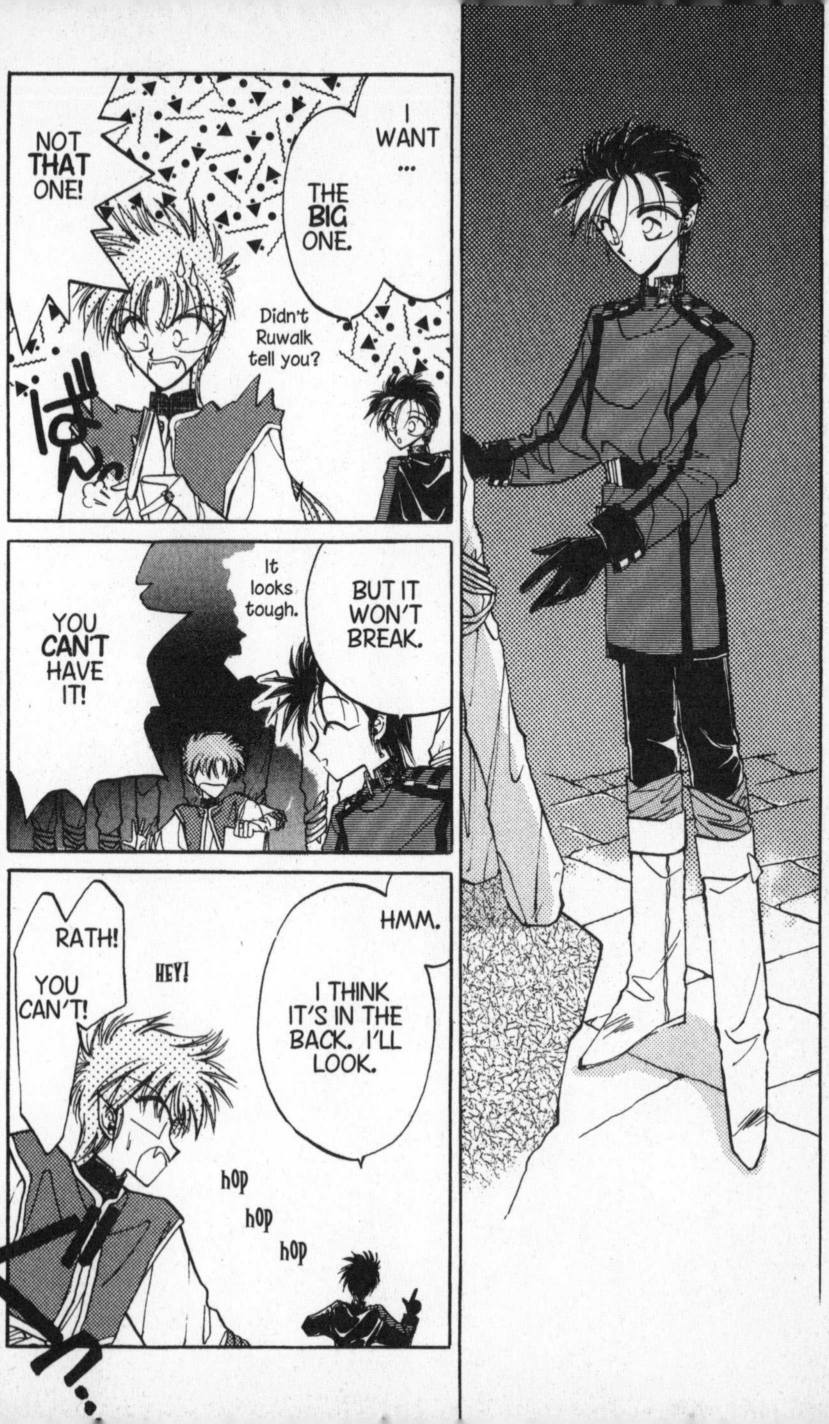
I WANT ...
THE BIG ONE.
NOT THAT ONE!
Didn't Ruwalk tell you?
ばん
BUT IT WON'T BREAK.
It looks tough.
YOU CAN'T HAVE IT!
HMM.
I THINK IT'S IN THE BACK. I'LL LOOK.
HEY!
RATH!
YOU CAN'T!
hop
hop
hop

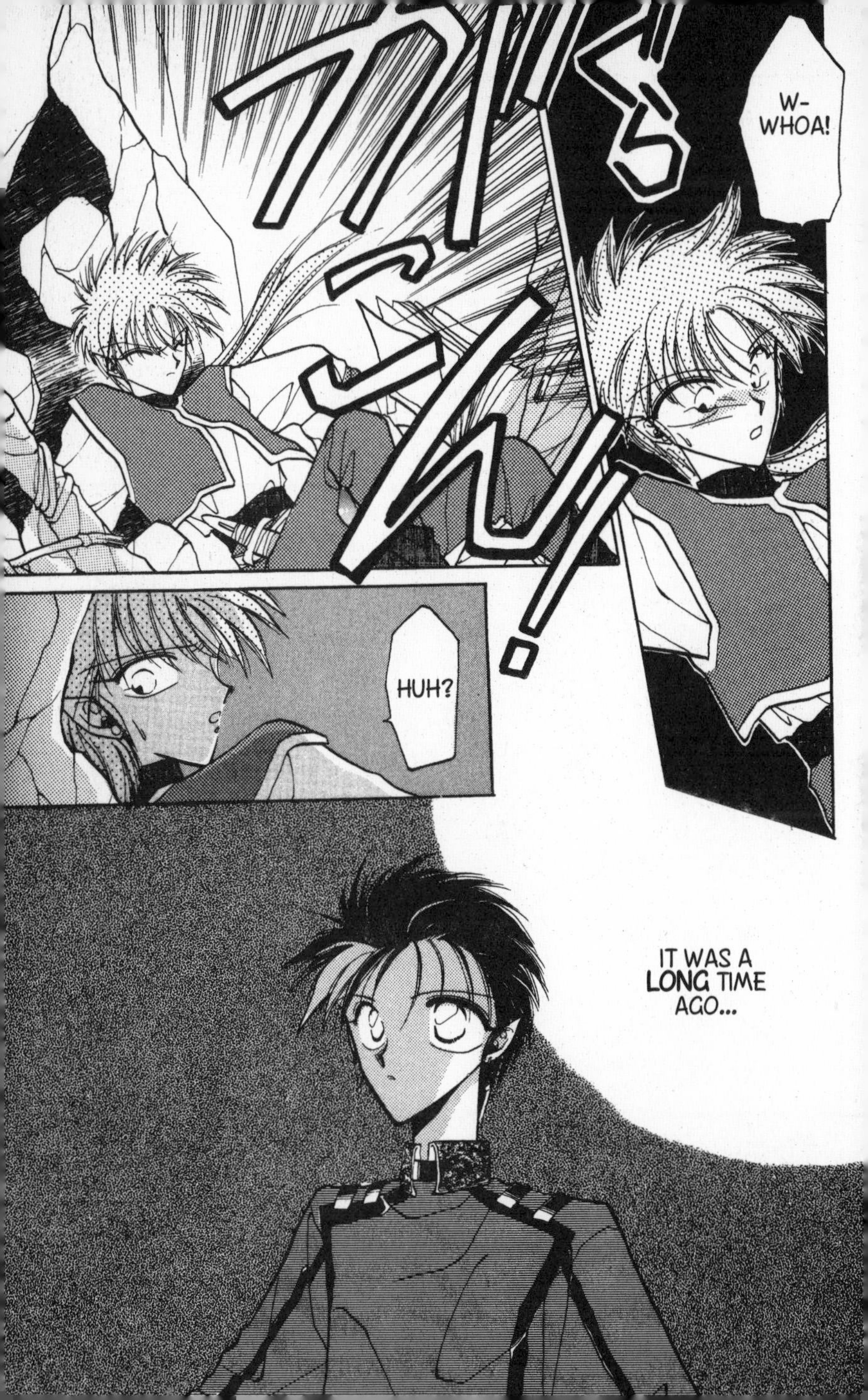
W-
WHOA!
HUH?
IT WAS A **LONG** TIME AGO...

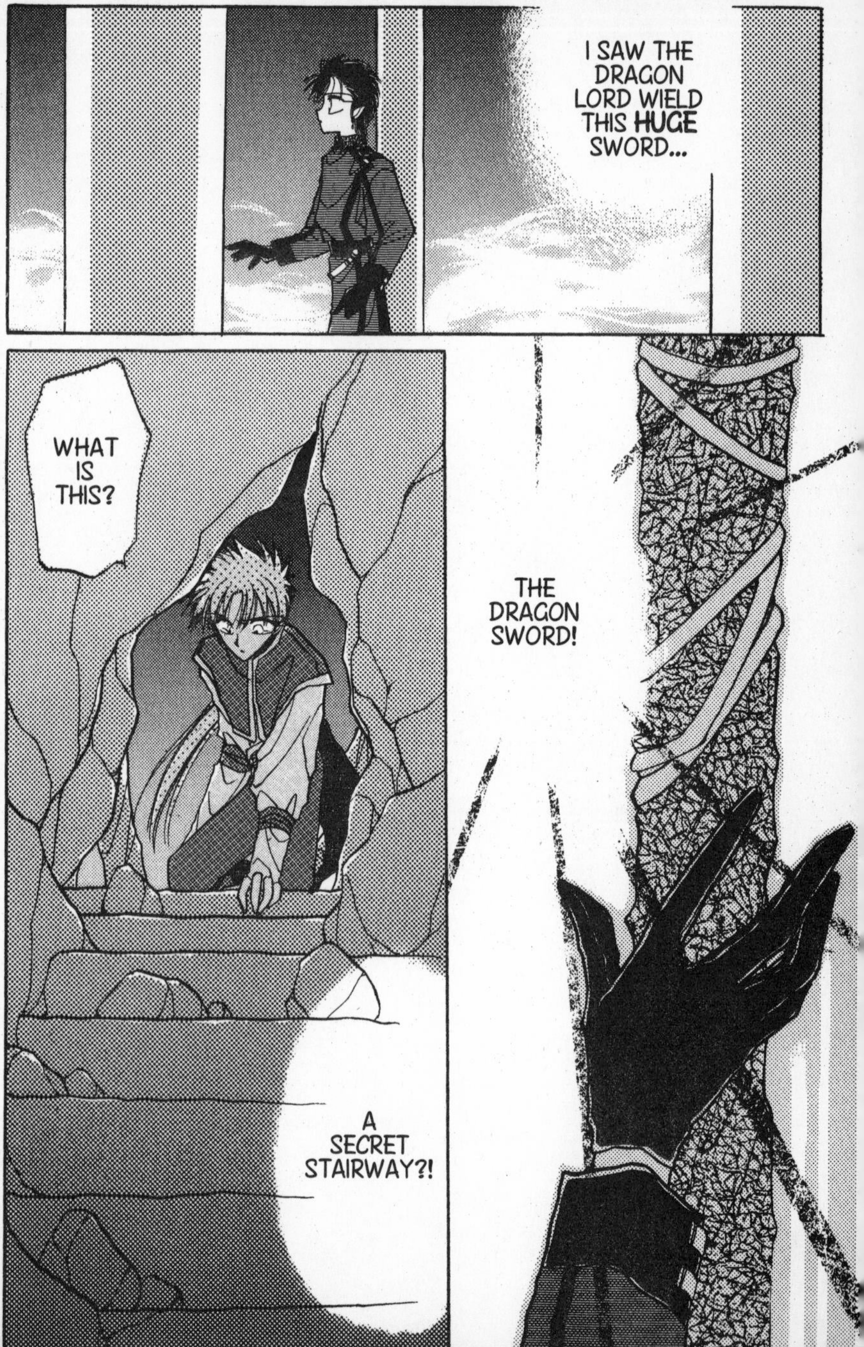
I SAW THE DRAGON LORD WIELD THIS HUGE SWORD...
THE DRAGON SWORD!
WHAT IS THIS?
A SECRET STAIRWAY?!

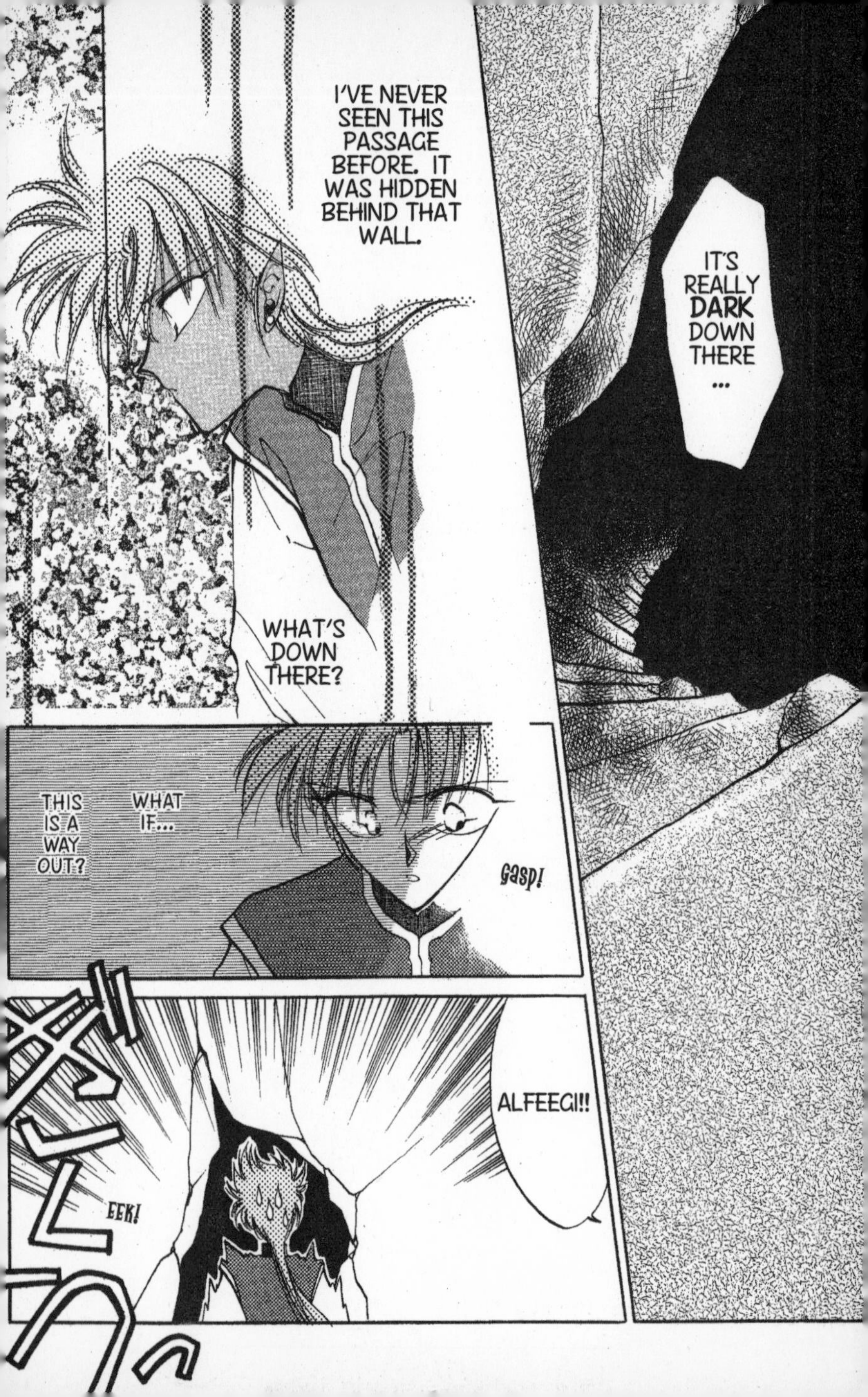
IT'S REALLY **DARK** DOWN THERE ...
I'VE NEVER SEEN THIS PASSAGE BEFORE. IT WAS HIDDEN BEHIND THAT WALL.
WHAT'S DOWN THERE?
GASP!
WHAT IF...
THIS IS A WAY OUT?
ALFEEG!!
EEK!

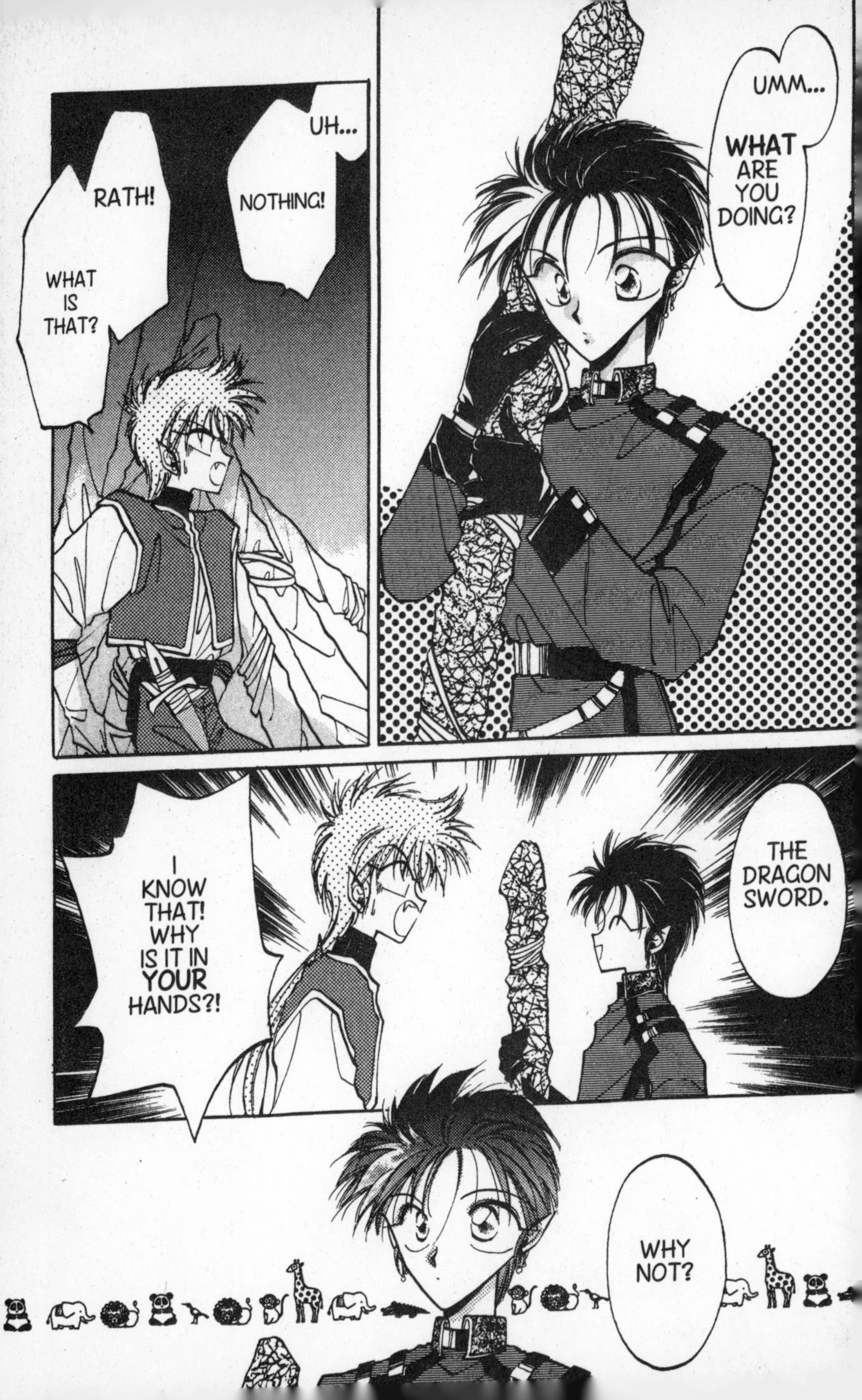
UMM... WHAT ARE YOU DOING?
RATH! WHAT IS THAT?
UH... NOTHING!
THE DRAGON SWORD.
I KNOW THAT! WHY IS IT IN YOUR HANDS?!
WHY NOT?

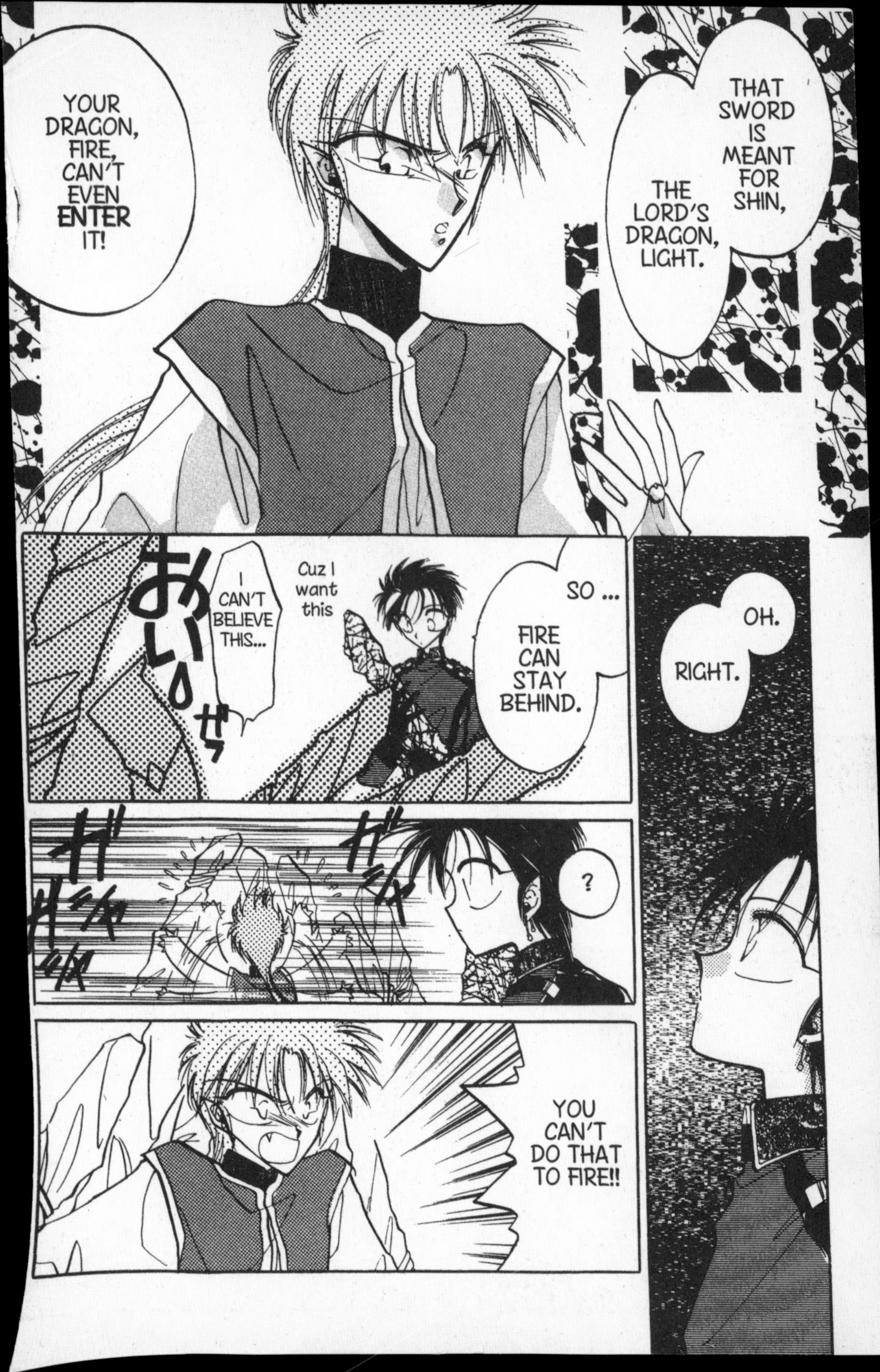
THAT SWORD IS MEANT FOR SHIN,
THE LORD'S DRAGON, LIGHT.
YOUR DRAGON, FIRE, CAN'T EVEN ENTER IT!
OH.
RIGHT.
SO ...
FIRE CAN STAY BEHIND.
Cuz I want this
I CAN'T BELIEVE THIS...
?
YOU CAN'T DO THAT TO FIRE!!

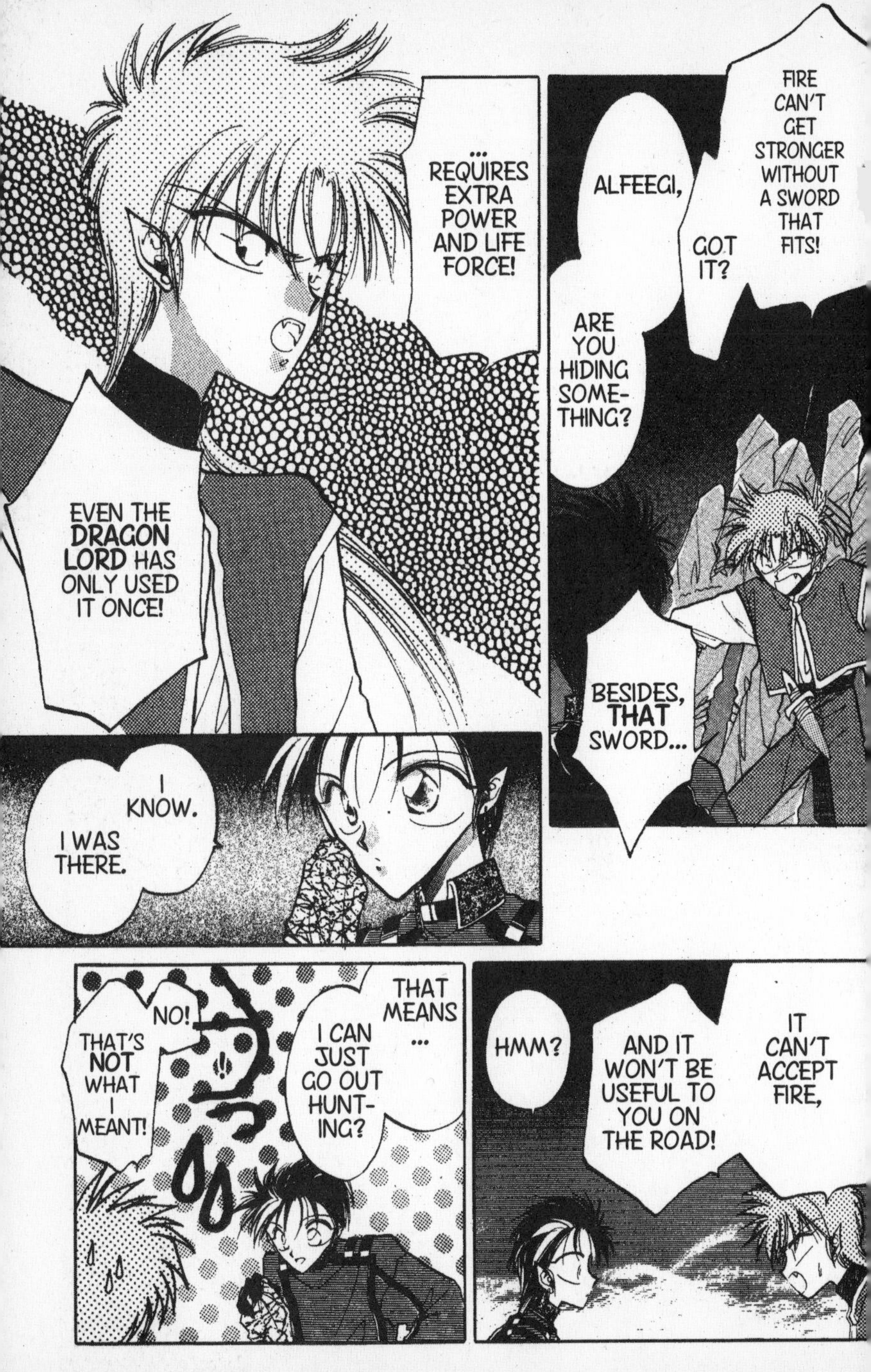
FIRE CAN'T GET STRONGER WITHOUT A SWORD THAT FITS!
GOT IT?
ALFEEGI,
ARE YOU HIDING SOMETHING?
BESIDES, THAT SWORD...
...REQUIRES EXTRA POWER AND LIFE FORCE!
EVEN THE DRAGON LORD HAS ONLY USED IT ONCE!
I KNOW.
I WAS THERE.
IT CAN'T ACCEPT FIRE,
AND IT WON'T BE USEFUL TO YOU ON THE ROAD!
HMM?
THAT MEANS...
I CAN JUST GO OUT HUNTING?
NO!
THAT'S NOT WHAT I MEANT!

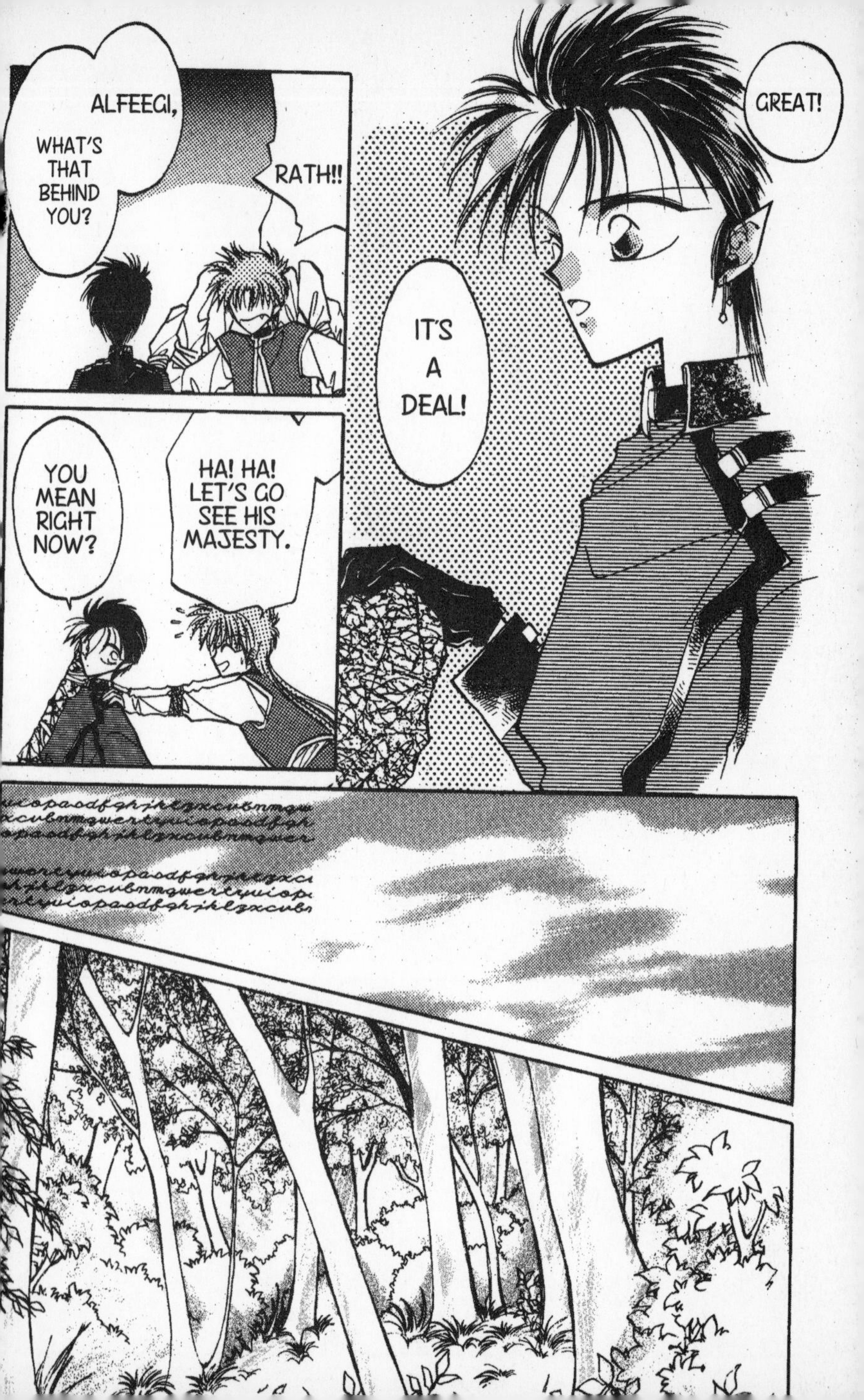
GREAT!
IT'S A DEAL!
ALFEEGI, WHAT'S THAT BEHIND YOU?
RATH!!
HA! HA! LET'S GO SEE HIS MAJESTY.
YOU MEAN RIGHT NOW?

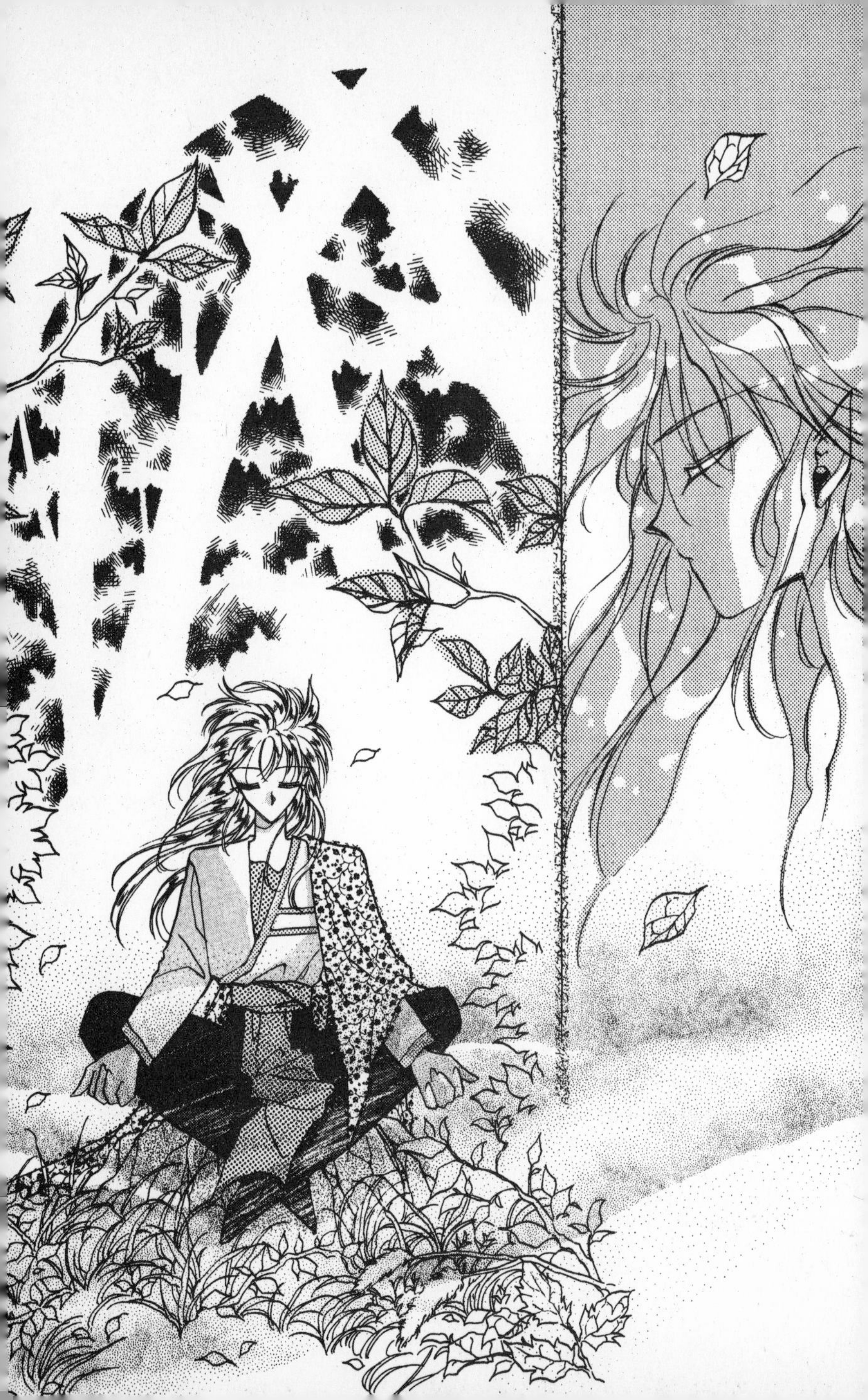

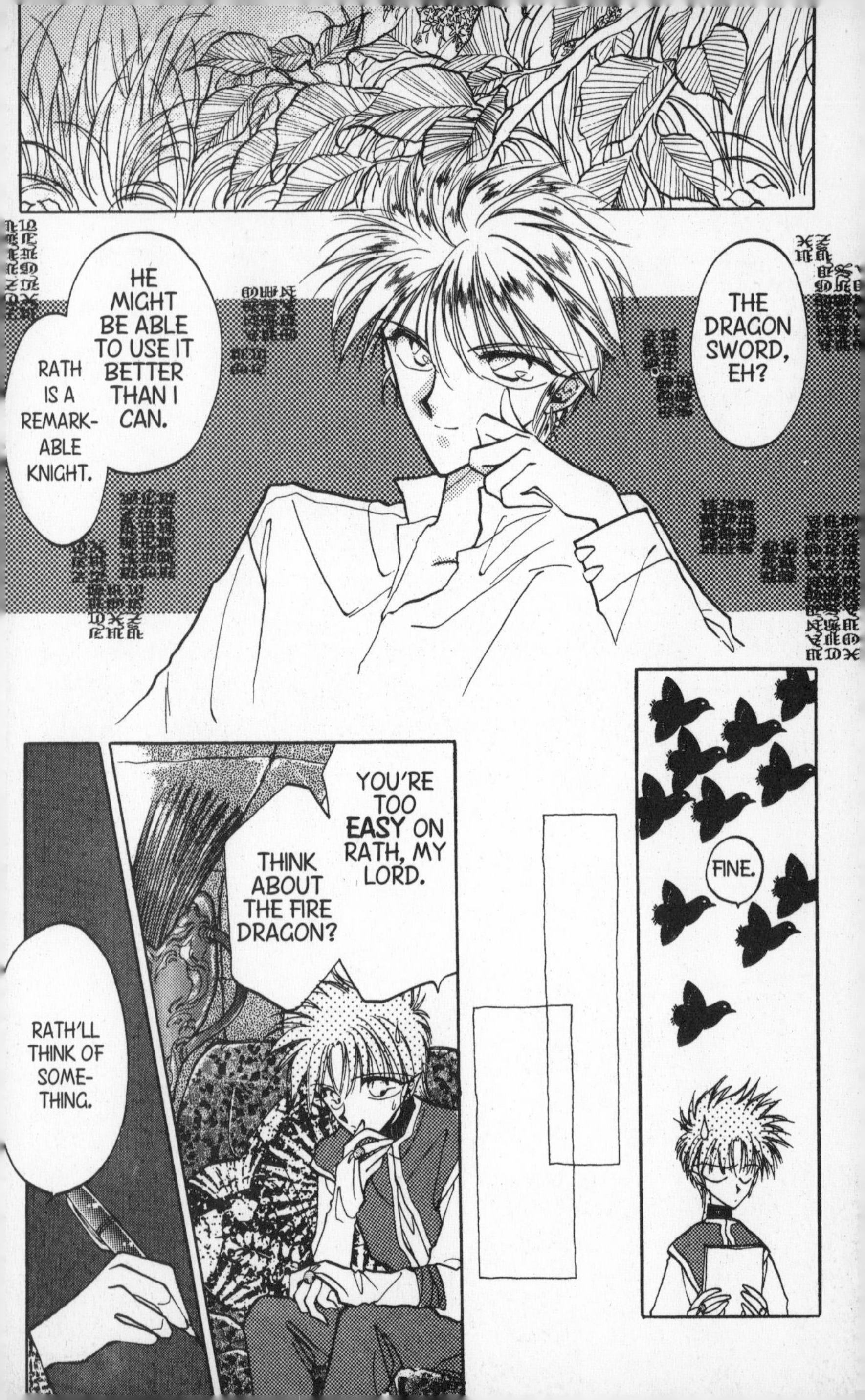
THE DRAGON SWORD, EH?
HE MIGHT BE ABLE TO USE IT BETTER THAN I CAN.
RATH IS A REMARKABLE KNIGHT.
FINE.
YOU'RE TOO **EASY** ON RATH, MY LORD.
THINK ABOUT THE FIRE DRAGON?
RATH'LL THINK OF SOMETHING.

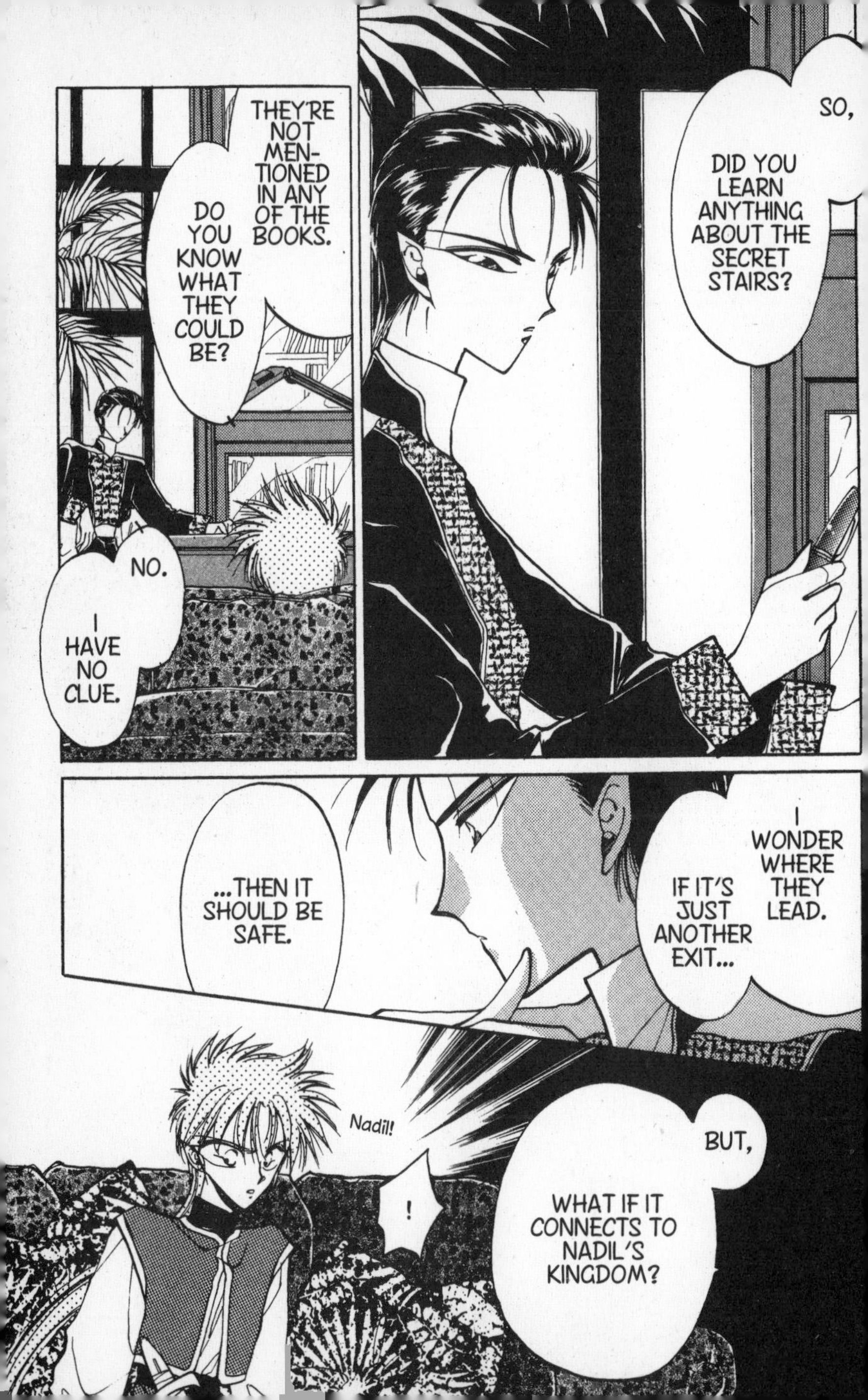
SO,
DID YOU LEARN ANYTHING ABOUT THE SECRET STAIRS?
THEY'RE NOT MEN-TIONED IN ANY OF THE BOOKS.
DO YOU KNOW WHAT THEY COULD BE?
NO.
I HAVE NO CLUE.
I WONDER WHERE THEY LEAD.
IF IT'S JUST ANOTHER EXIT...
...THEN IT SHOULD BE SAFE.
BUT,
WHAT IF IT CONNECTS TO NADIL'S KINGDOM?
!
Nadil!

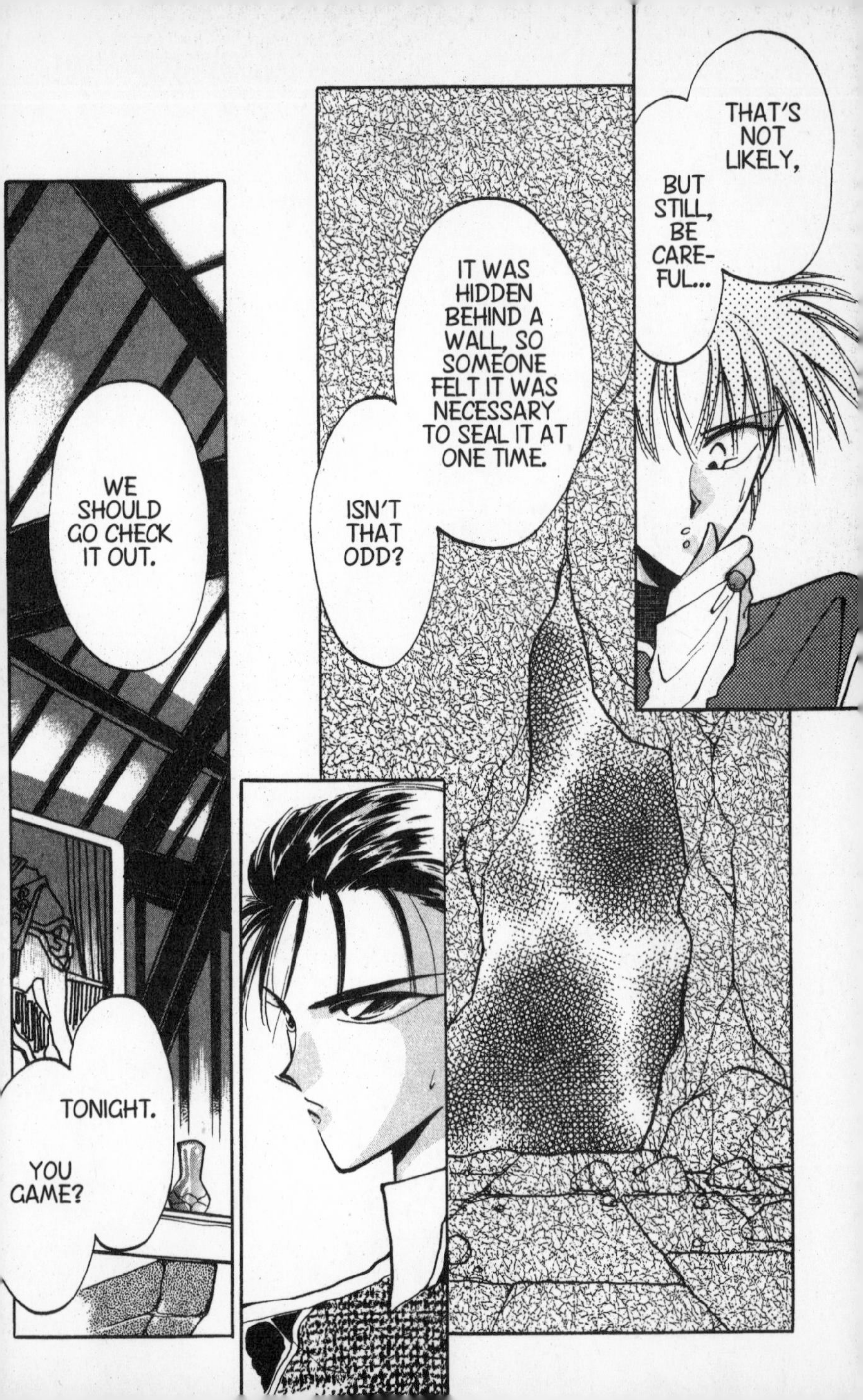
THAT'S NOT LIKELY,
BUT STILL, BE CARE-FUL...
IT WAS HIDDEN BEHIND A WALL, SO SOMEONE FELT IT WAS NECESSARY TO SEAL IT AT ONE TIME.
ISN'T THAT ODD?
WE SHOULD GO CHECK IT OUT.
TONIGHT.
YOU GAME?

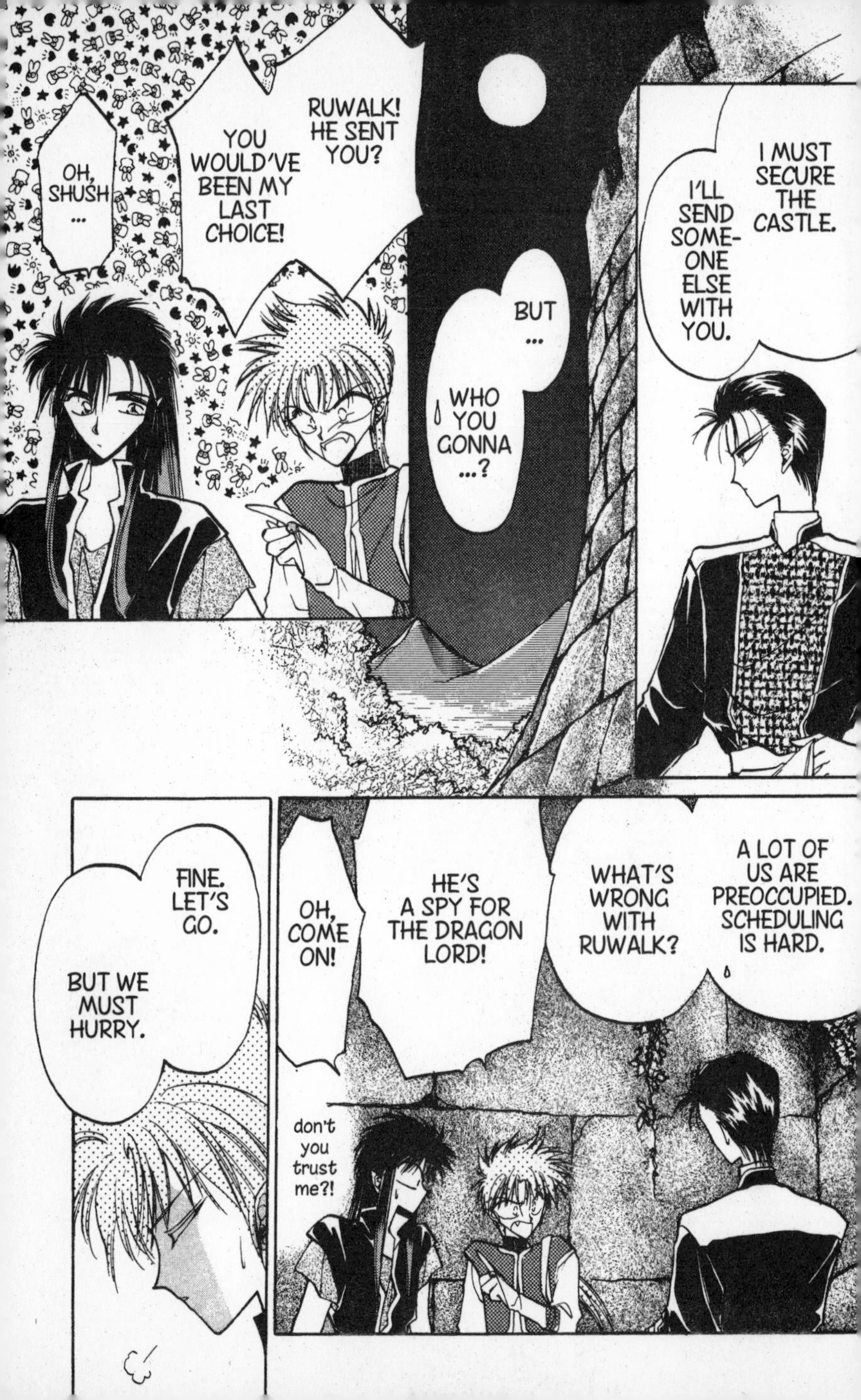
I MUST SECURE THE CASTLE.
I'LL SEND SOME-ONE ELSE WITH YOU.
BUT ...
WHO YOU GONNA ...?
RUWALK! HE SENT YOU?
YOU WOULD'VE BEEN MY LAST CHOICE!
OH, SHUSH ...
A LOT OF US ARE PREOCCUPIED. SCHEDULING IS HARD.
WHAT'S WRONG WITH RUWALK?
HE'S A SPY FOR THE DRAGON LORD!
OH, COME ON!
don't you trust me?!
FINE. LET'S GO.
BUT WE MUST HURRY.

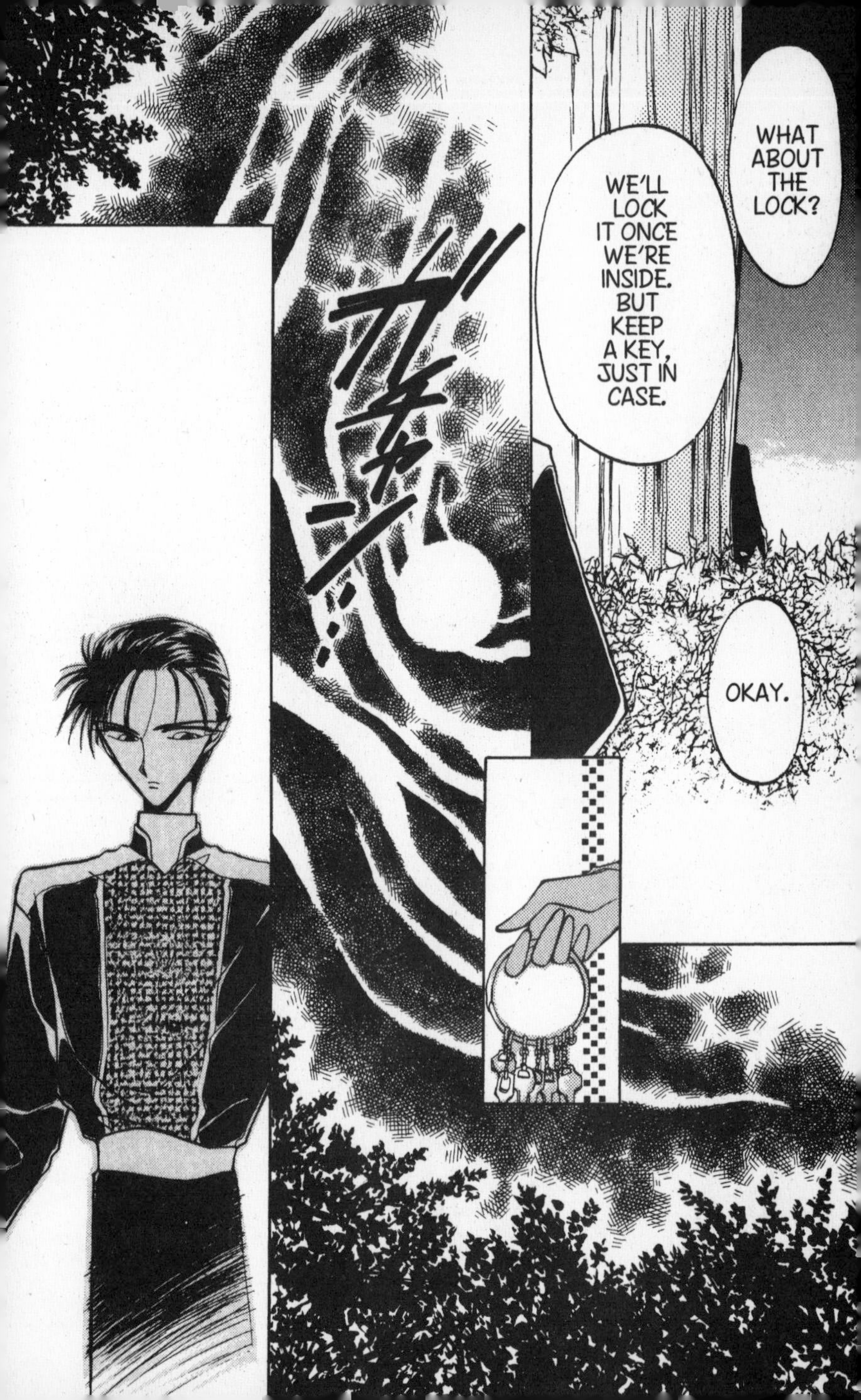
WHAT ABOUT THE LOCK?
WE'LL LOCK IT ONCE WE'RE INSIDE. BUT KEEP A KEY, JUST IN CASE.
OKAY.
ガチャン…

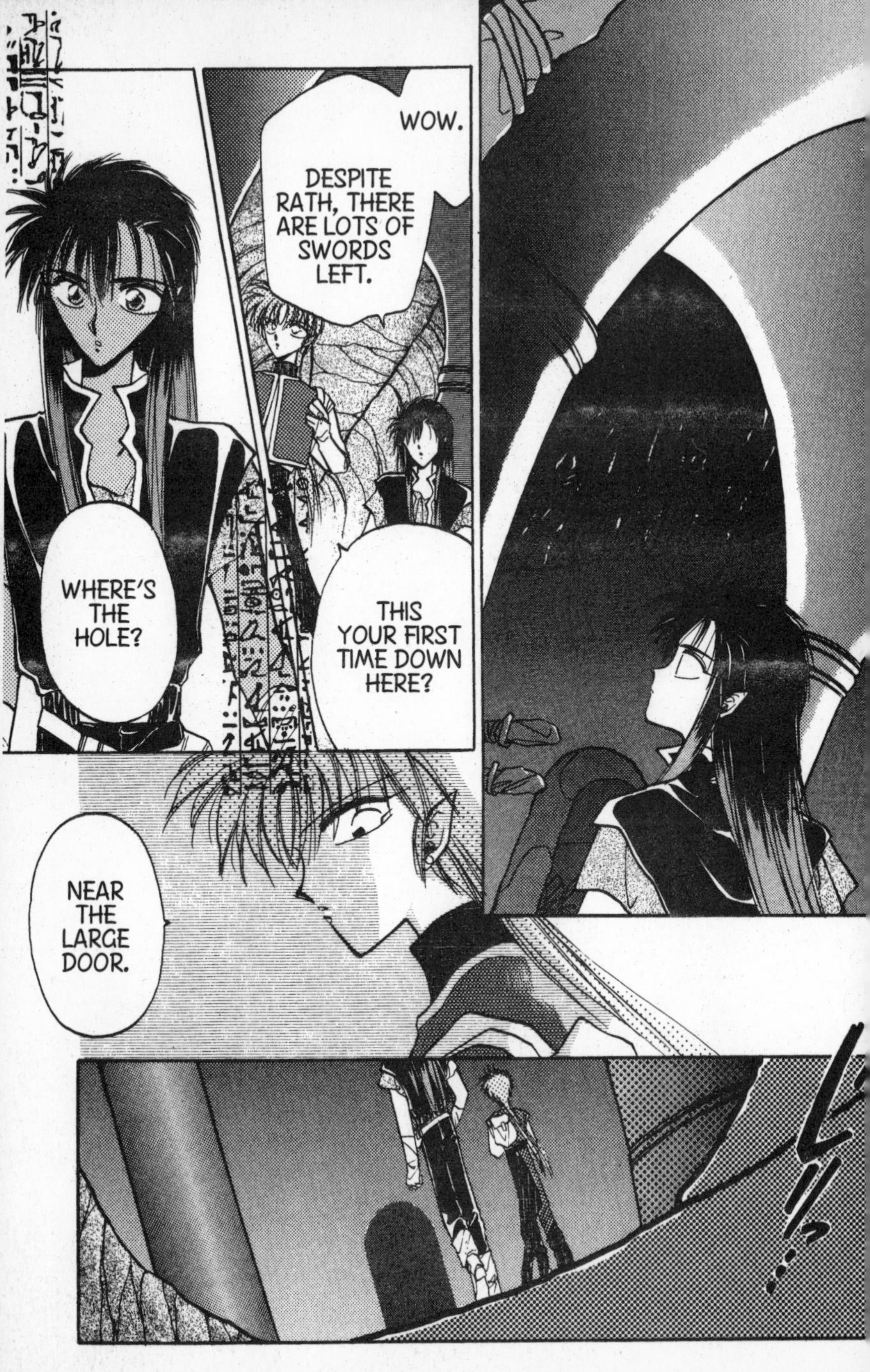
WOW.
DESPITE RATH, THERE ARE LOTS OF SWORDS LEFT.
THIS YOUR FIRST TIME DOWN HERE?
WHERE'S THE HOLE?
NEAR THE LARGE DOOR.

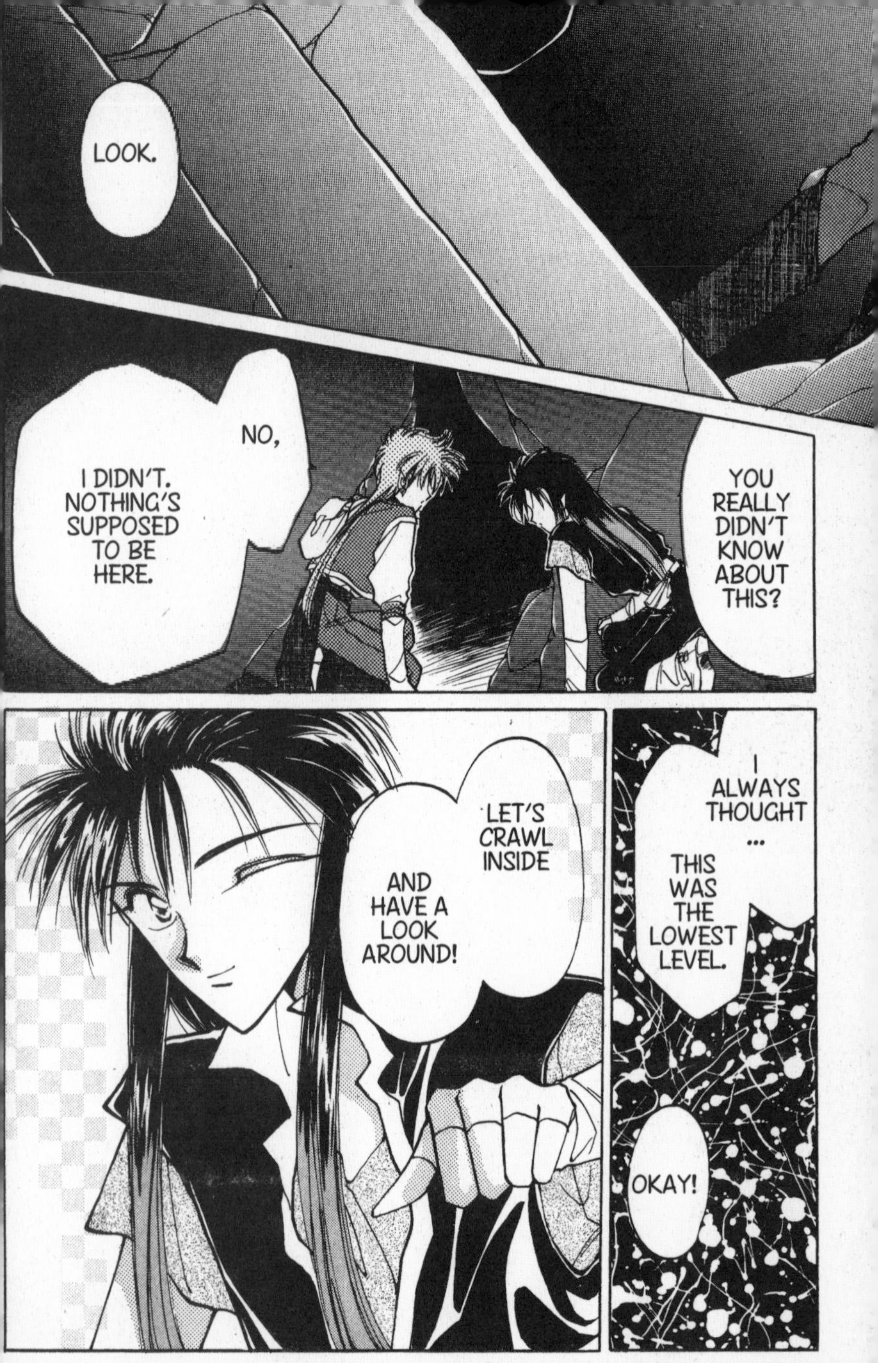
LOOK.
YOU REALLY DIDN'T KNOW ABOUT THIS?
NO,
I DIDN'T. NOTHING'S SUPPOSED TO BE HERE.
I ALWAYS THOUGHT ...
THIS WAS THE LOWEST LEVEL.
OKAY!
LET'S CRAWL INSIDE
AND HAVE A LOOK AROUND!

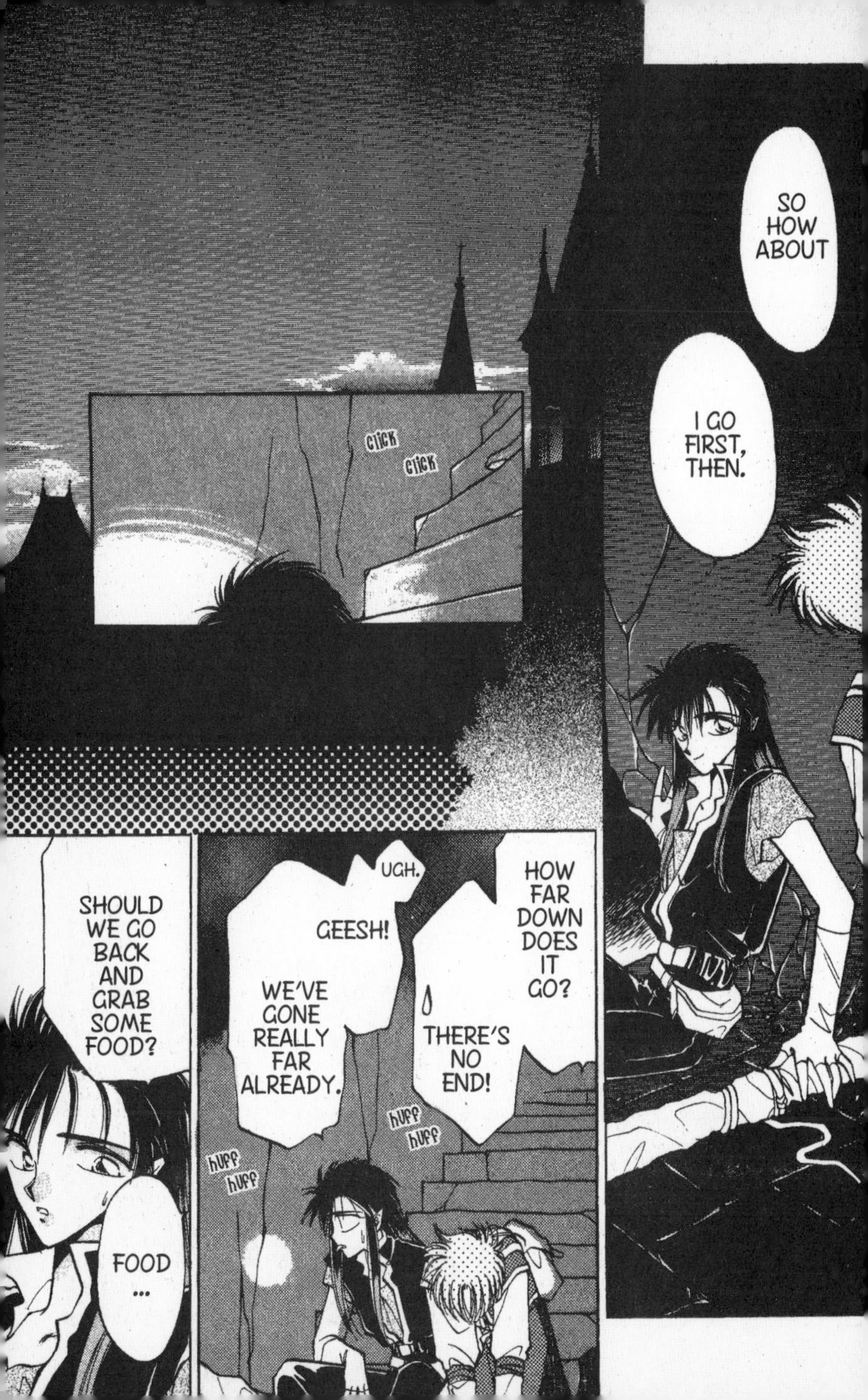
SO HOW ABOUT
I GO FIRST, THEN.
click
click
HOW FAR DOWN DOES IT GO?
UGH.
GEESH!
THERE'S NO END!
WE'VE GONE REALLY FAR ALREADY.
huff
huff
huff
huff
SHOULD WE GO BACK AND GRAB SOME FOOD?
FOOD ...

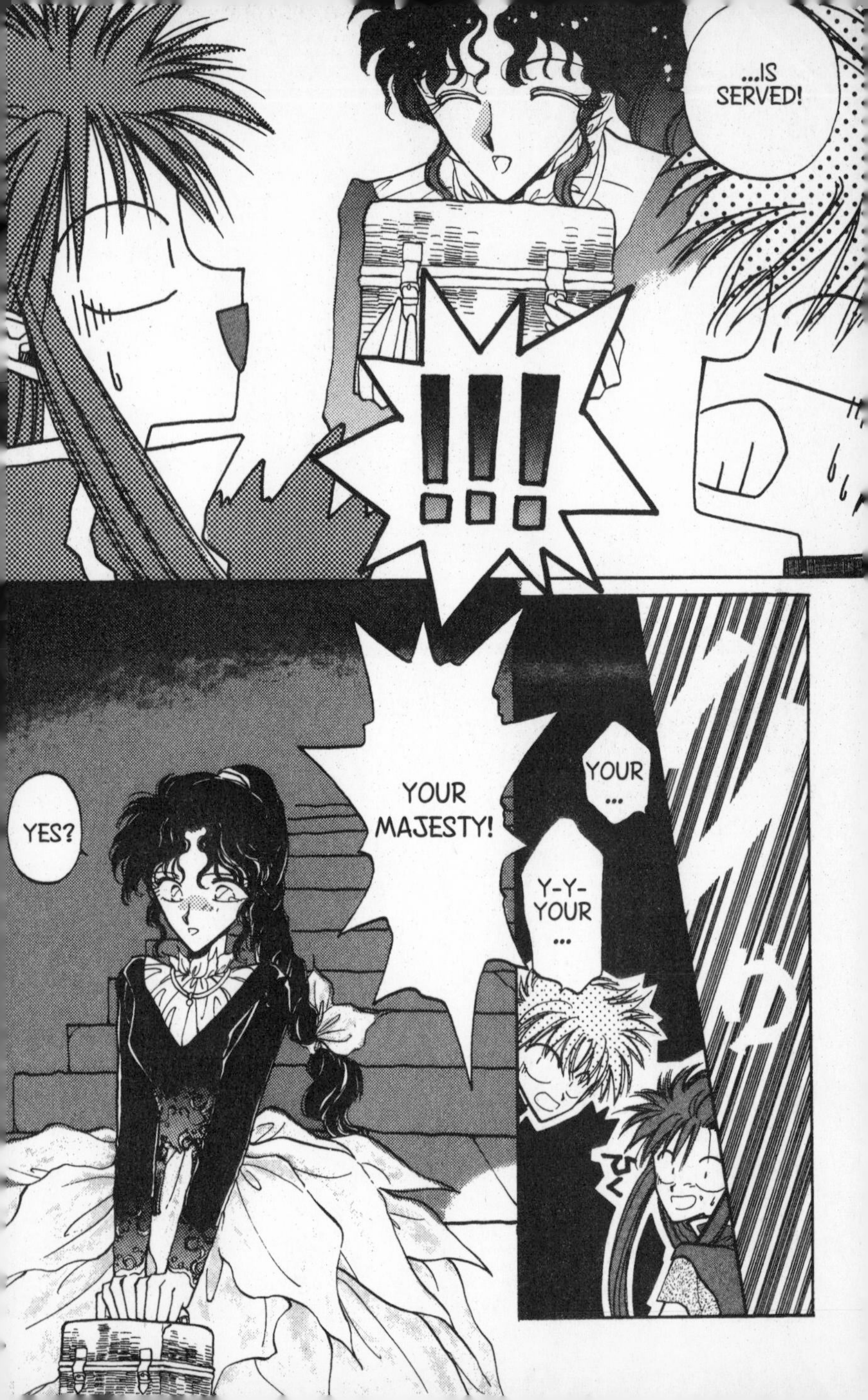
...IS SERVED!
!!!
YOUR ...
Y-Y-YOUR ...
YOUR MAJESTY!
YES?

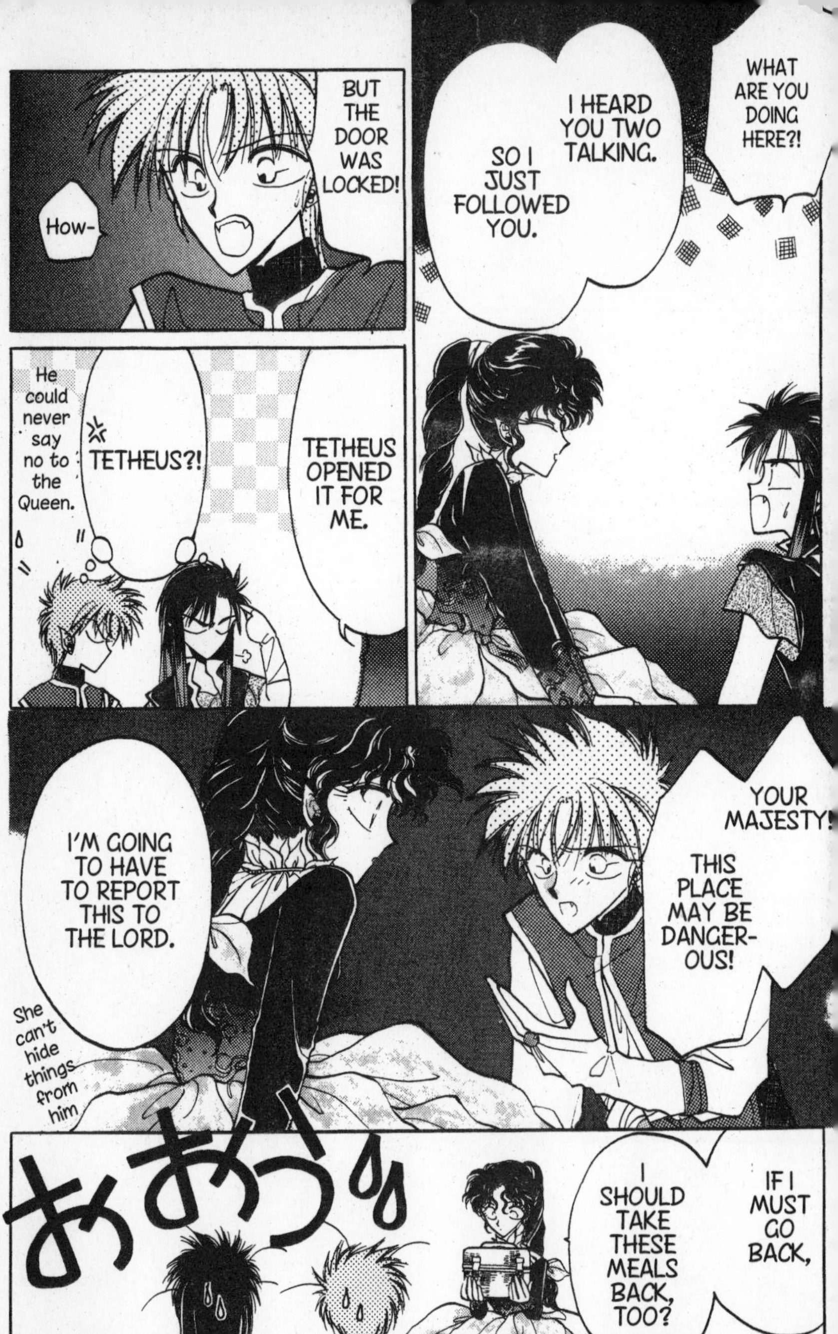
WHAT ARE YOU DOING HERE?!
I HEARD YOU TWO TALKING.
SO I JUST FOLLOWED YOU.
BUT THE DOOR WAS LOCKED!
How-
TETHEUS OPENED IT FOR ME.
TETHEUS?!
He could never say no to the Queen.
YOUR MAJESTY!
THIS PLACE MAY BE DANGER-OUS!
I'M GOING TO HAVE TO REPORT THIS TO THE LORD.
She can't hide things from him
IF I MUST GO BACK,
I SHOULD TAKE THESE MEALS BACK, TOO?

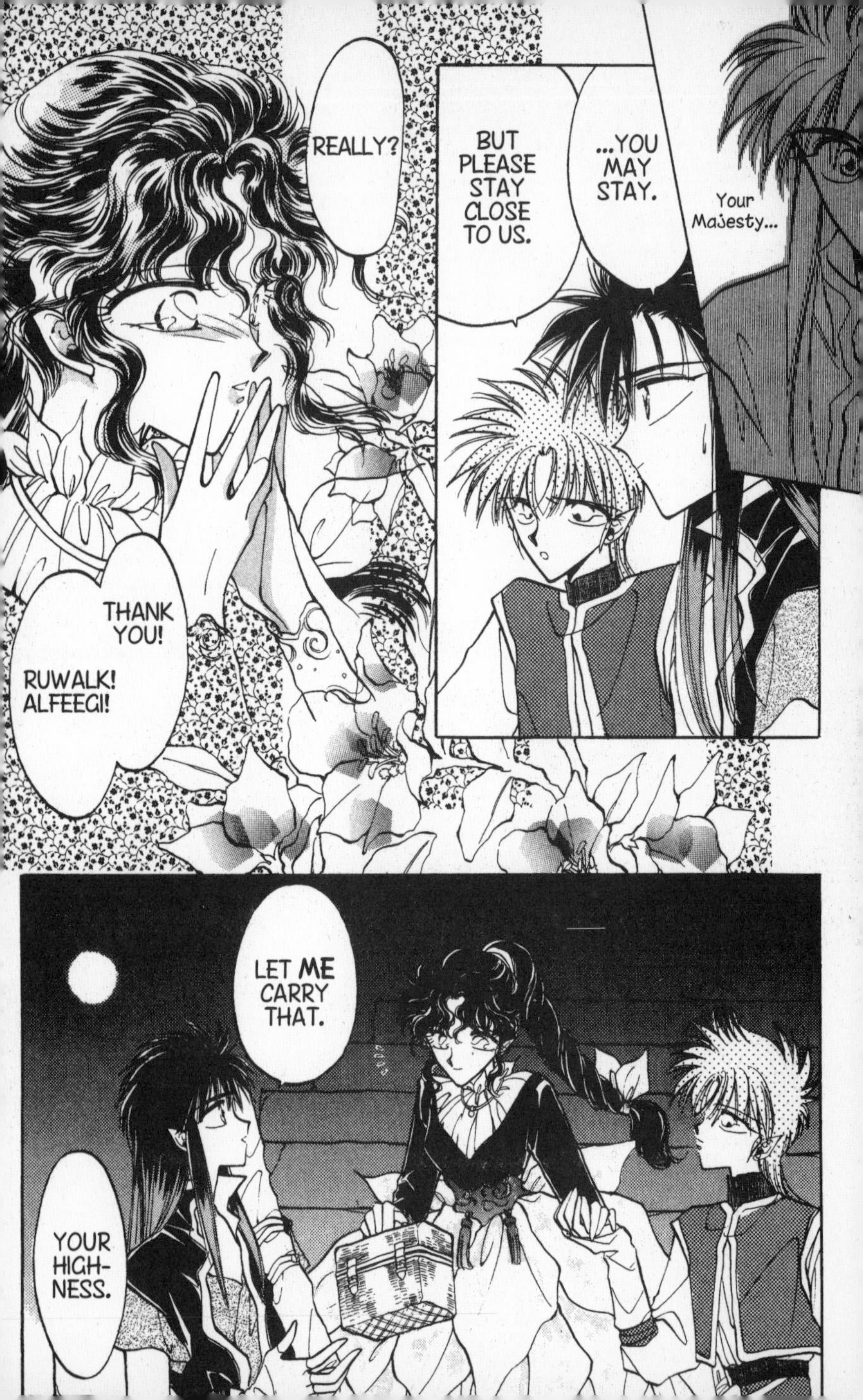
Your Majesty...
...YOU MAY STAY.
BUT PLEASE STAY CLOSE TO US.
REALLY?
THANK YOU!
RUWALK! ALFEEGI!
LET ME CARRY THAT.
YOUR HIGHNESS.

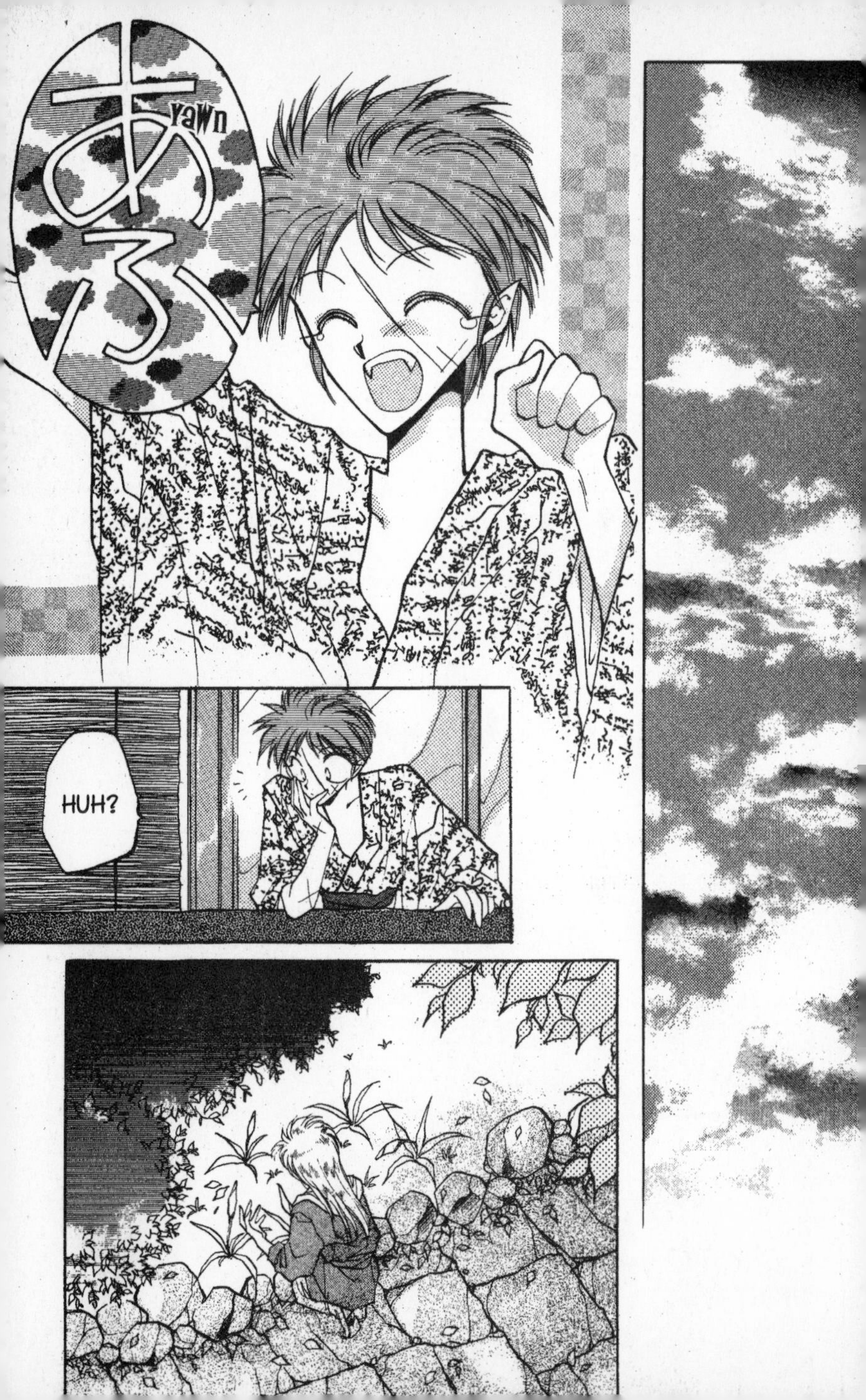
あ〜ふ
yawn
HUH?

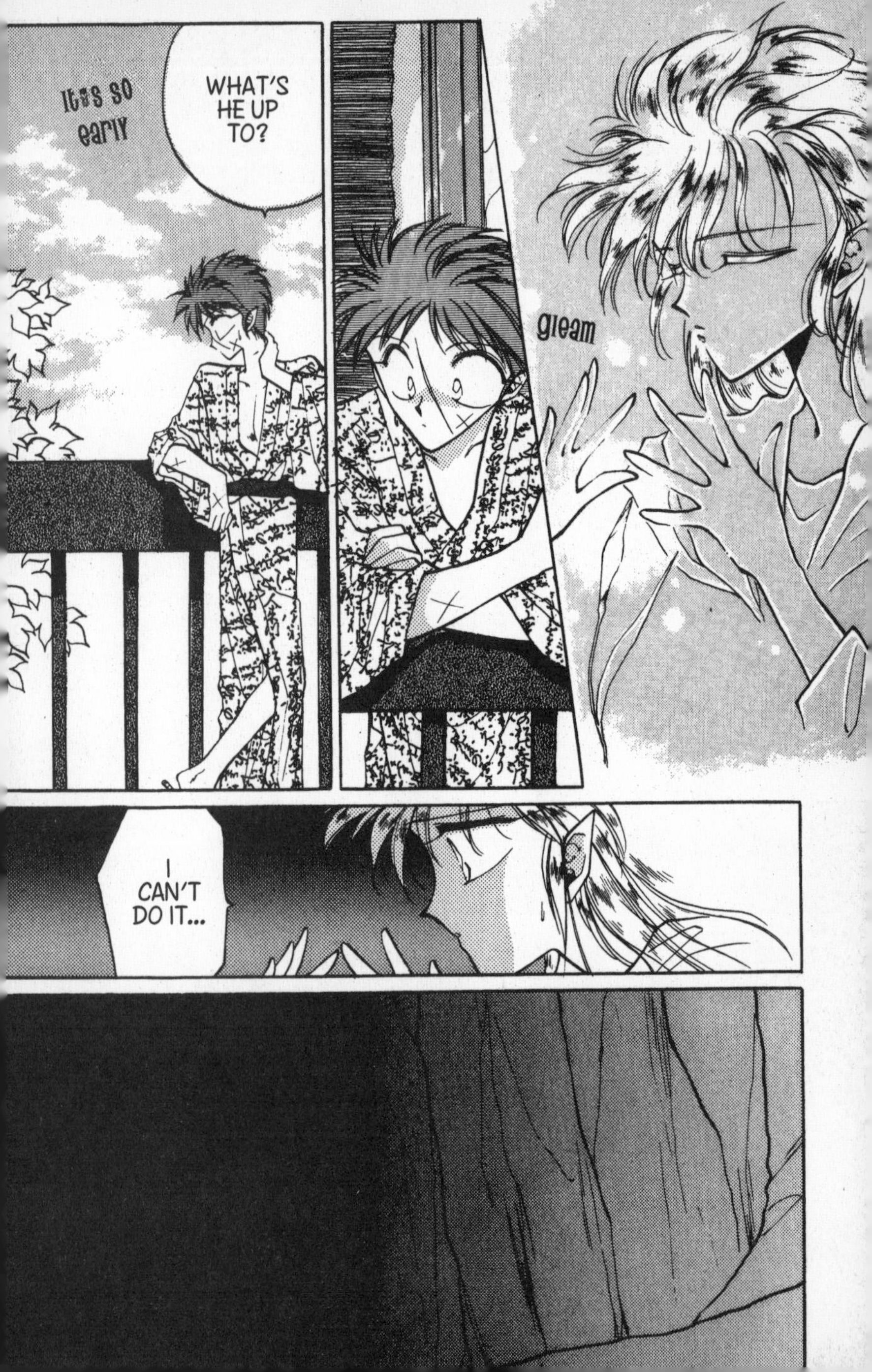
gleam
WHAT'S HE UP TO?
It's so early
I CAN'T DO IT...

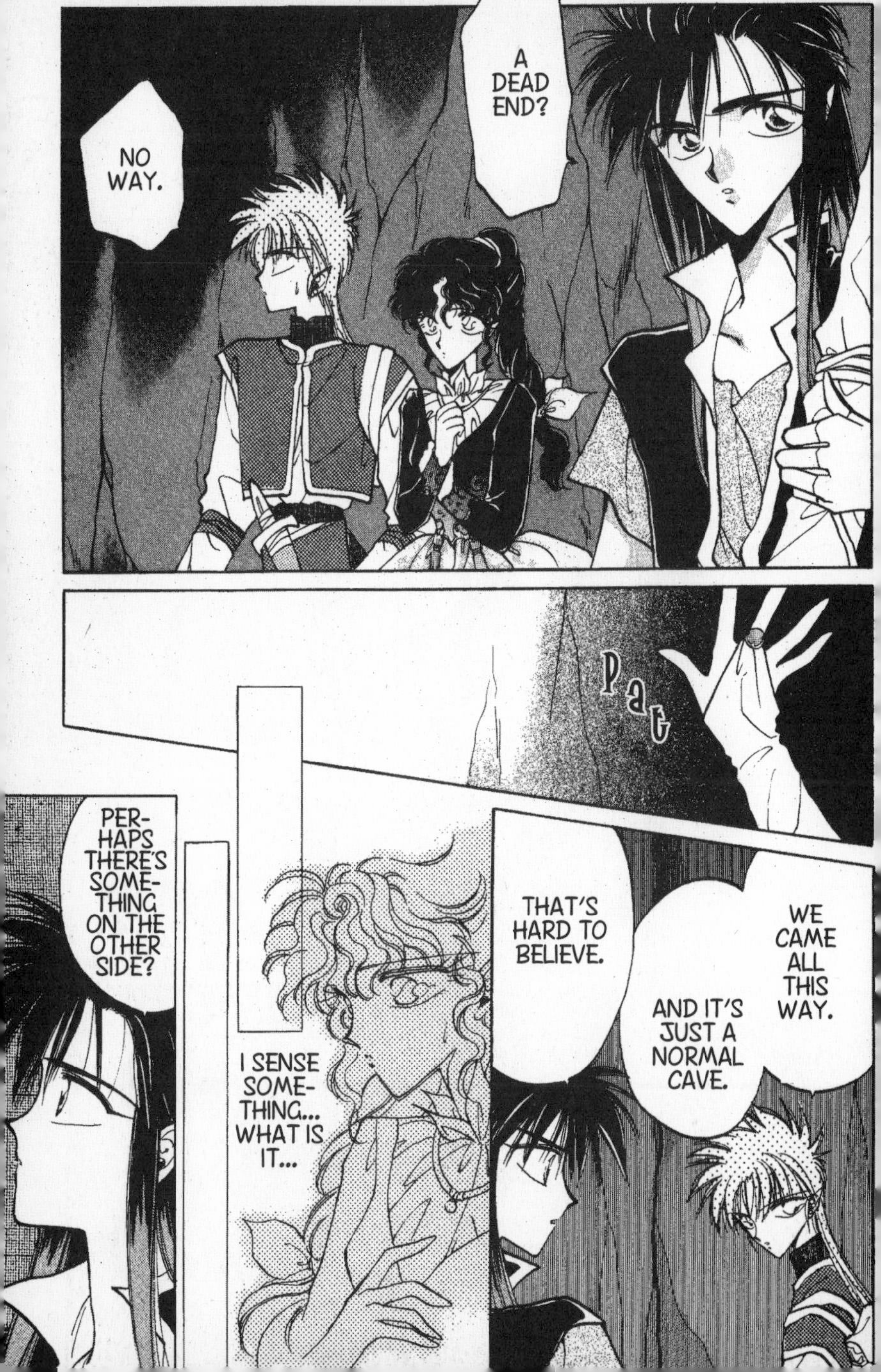
A DEAD END?
NO WAY.
Pat
WE CAME ALL THIS WAY.
AND IT'S JUST A NORMAL CAVE.
THAT'S HARD TO BELIEVE.
I SENSE SOMETHING... WHAT IS IT...
PERHAPS THERE'S SOMETHING ON THE OTHER SIDE?

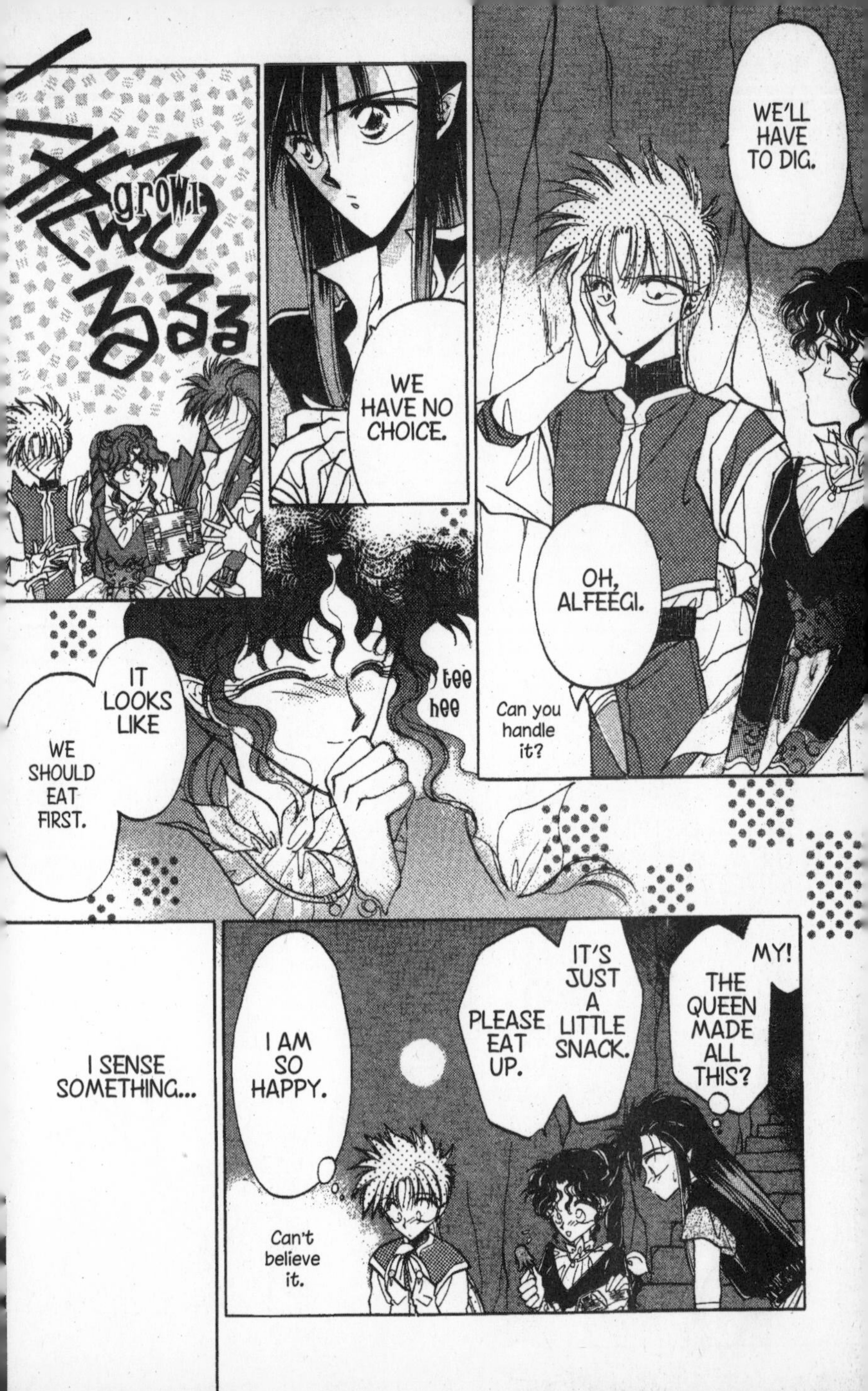
WE'LL HAVE TO DIG.
OH, ALFEEGI.
Can you handle it?
WE HAVE NO CHOICE.
growl
tee hee
IT LOOKS LIKE WE SHOULD EAT FIRST.
MY! THE QUEEN MADE ALL THIS?
IT'S JUST A LITTLE SNACK.
PLEASE EAT UP.
I AM SO HAPPY.
Can't believe it.
I SENSE SOMETHING...

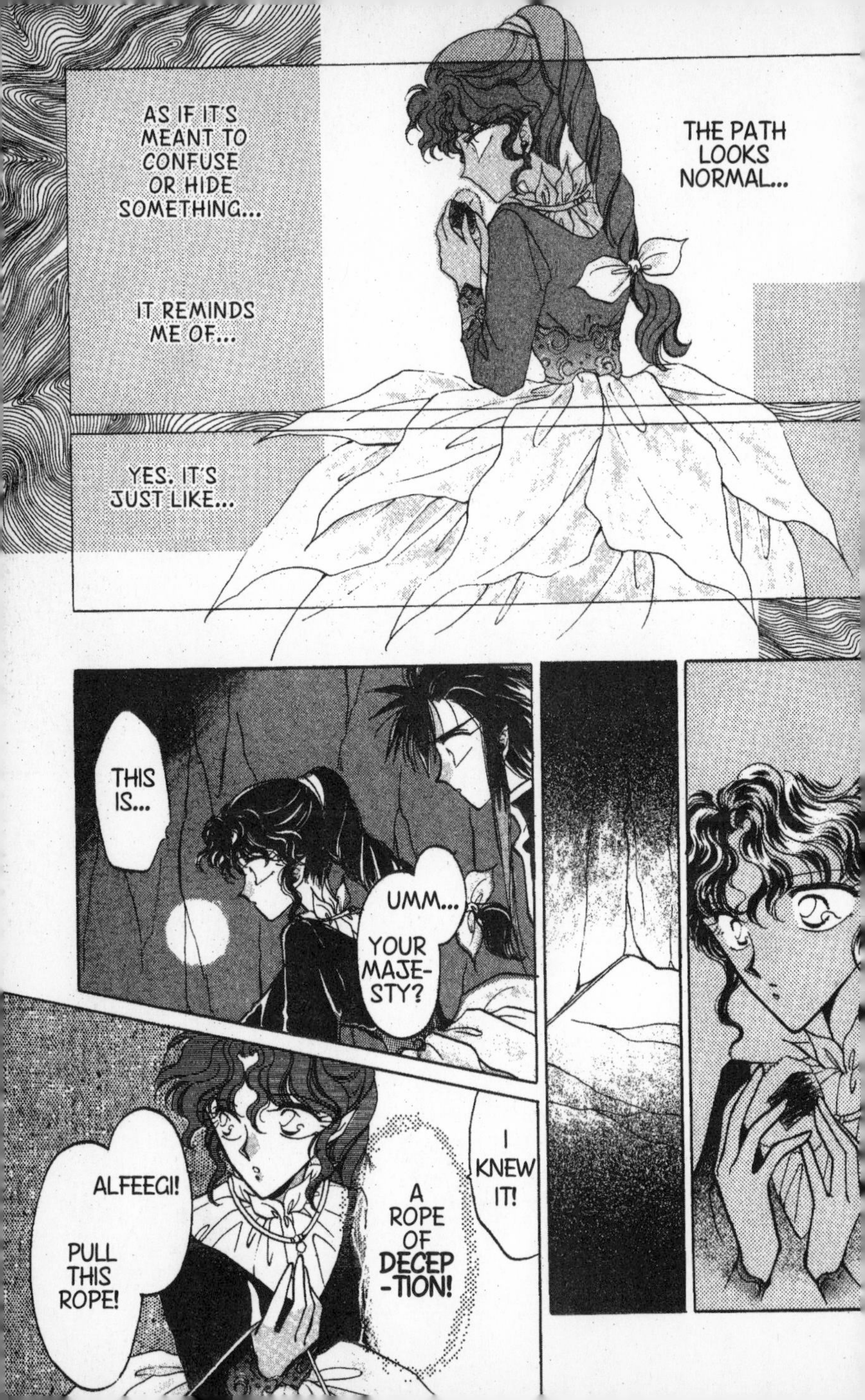
THE PATH LOOKS NORMAL...
AS IF IT'S MEANT TO CONFUSE OR HIDE SOMETHING...
IT REMINDS ME OF...
YES. IT'S JUST LIKE...
THIS IS...
UMM... YOUR MAJESTY?
I KNEW IT!
A ROPE OF DECEPTION!
ALFEEGI!
PULL THIS ROPE!

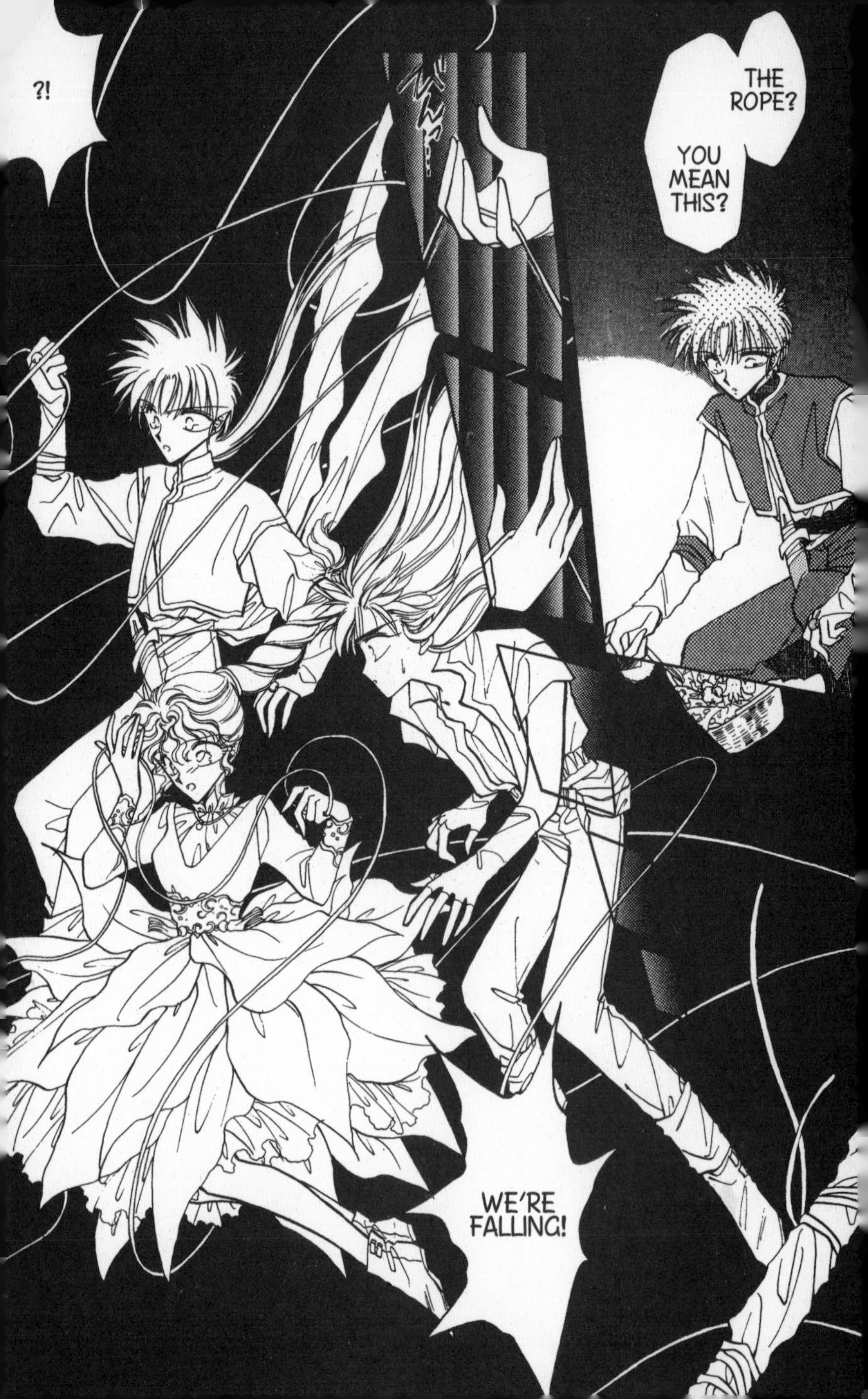
THE ROPE?
YOU MEAN THIS?
?!
WE'RE FALLING!

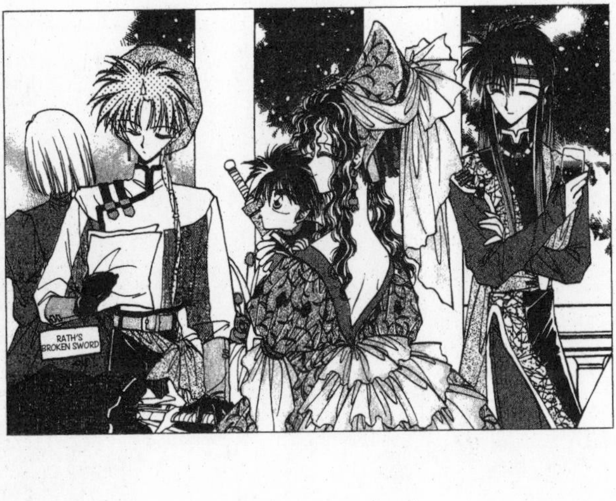
RATH'S
BROKEN SWORD

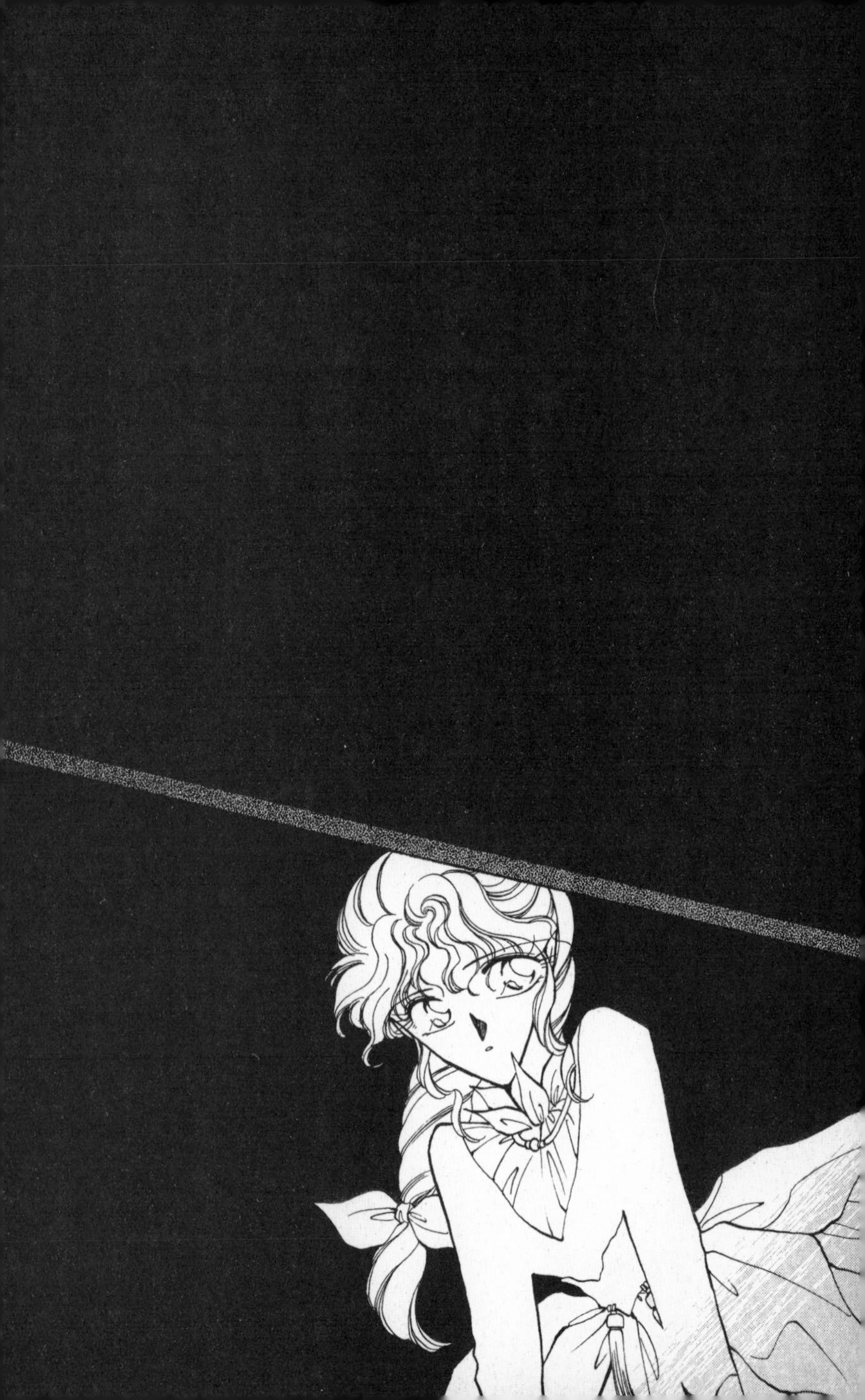

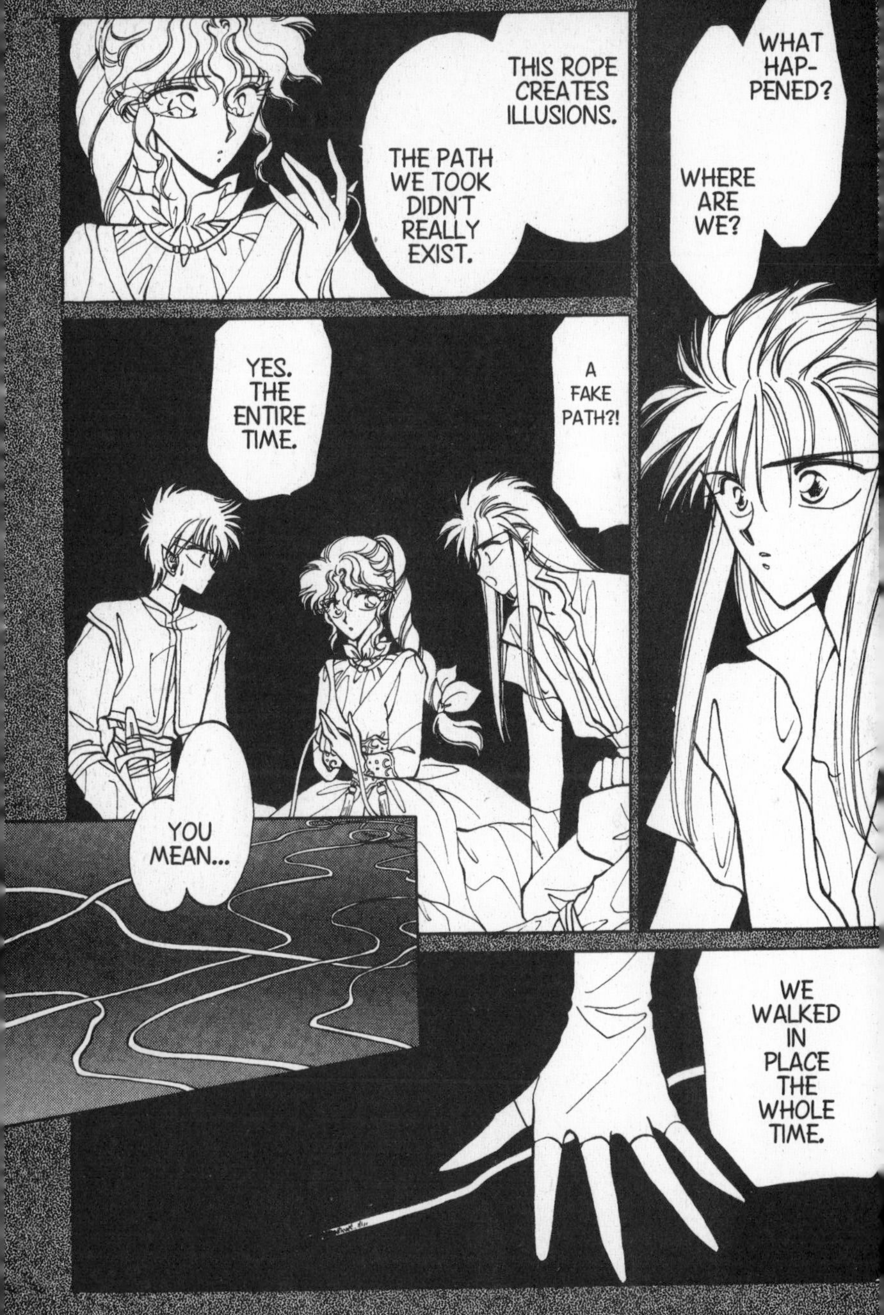
WHAT HAP-PENED?
WHERE ARE WE?
THIS ROPE CREATES ILLUSIONS.
THE PATH WE TOOK DIDN'T REALLY EXIST.
A FAKE PATH?!
YES. THE ENTIRE TIME.
YOU MEAN...
WE WALKED IN PLACE THE WHOLE TIME.

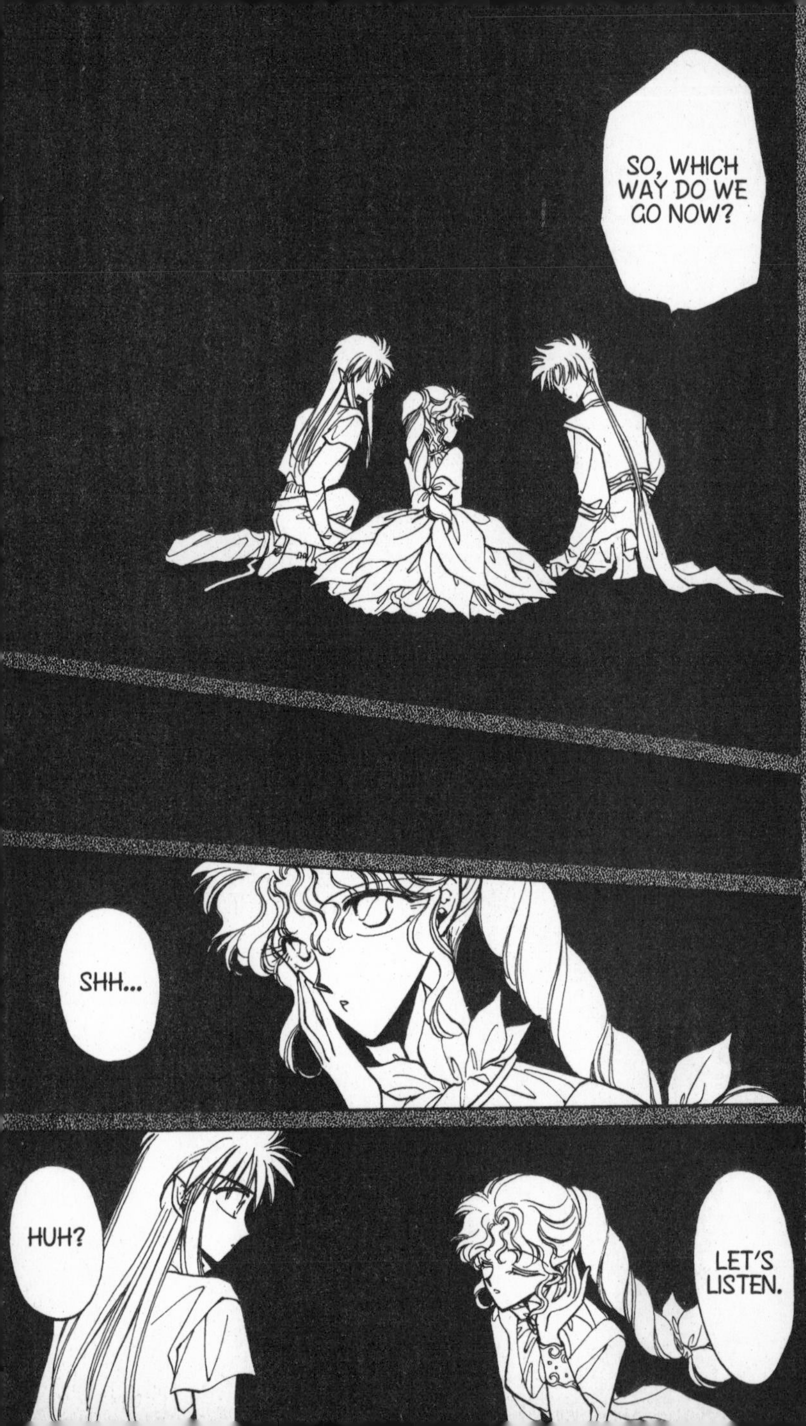
SO, WHICH WAY DO WE GO NOW?
SHH...
LET'S LISTEN.
HUH?

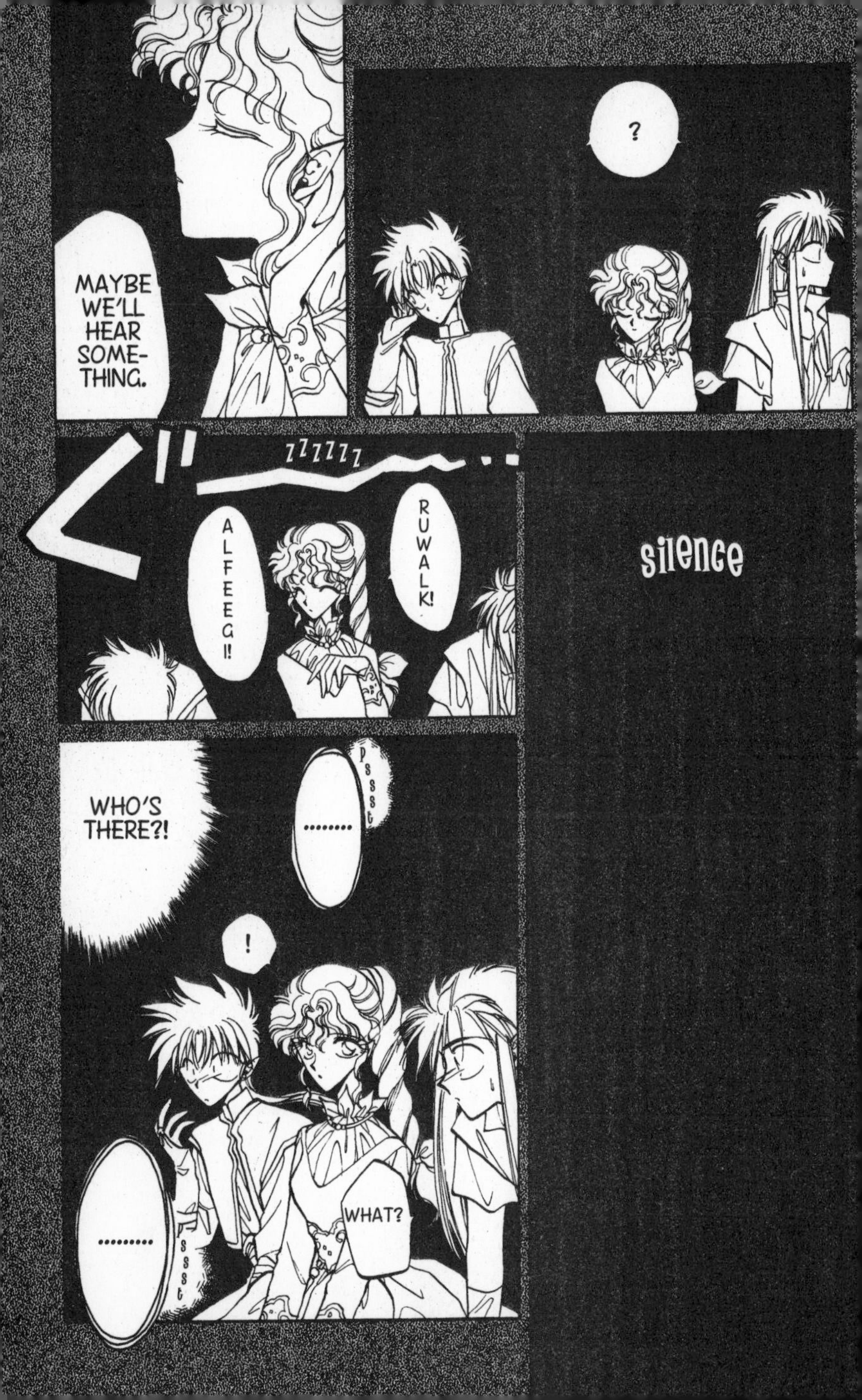
?
MAYBE WE'LL HEAR SOMETHING.
silence
ZZZZZZ
RUWALK!
ALFEEGI!
Pssst
....
WHO'S THERE?!
!
WHAT?
....
Pssst

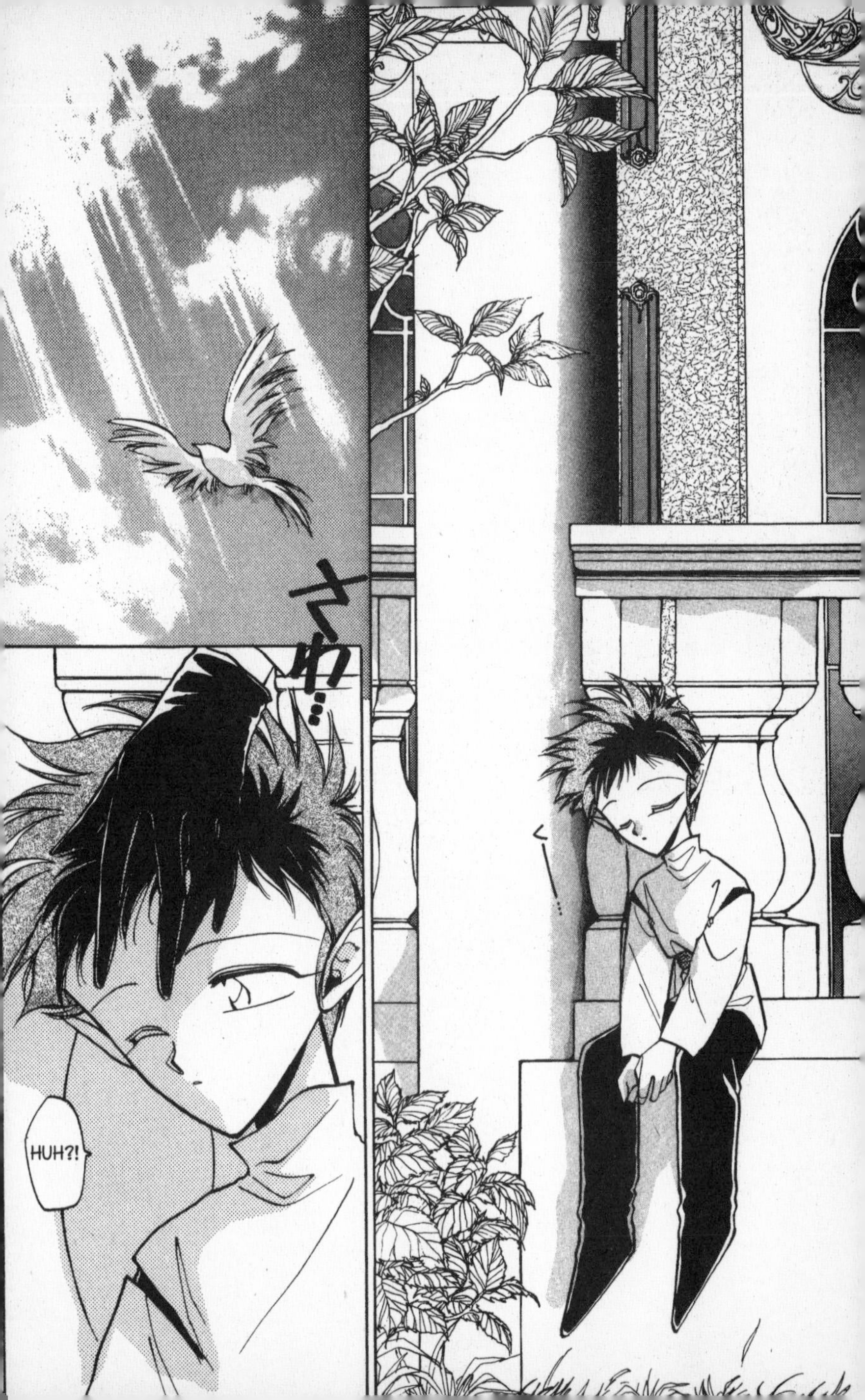
く―…
さわ…
HUH?!

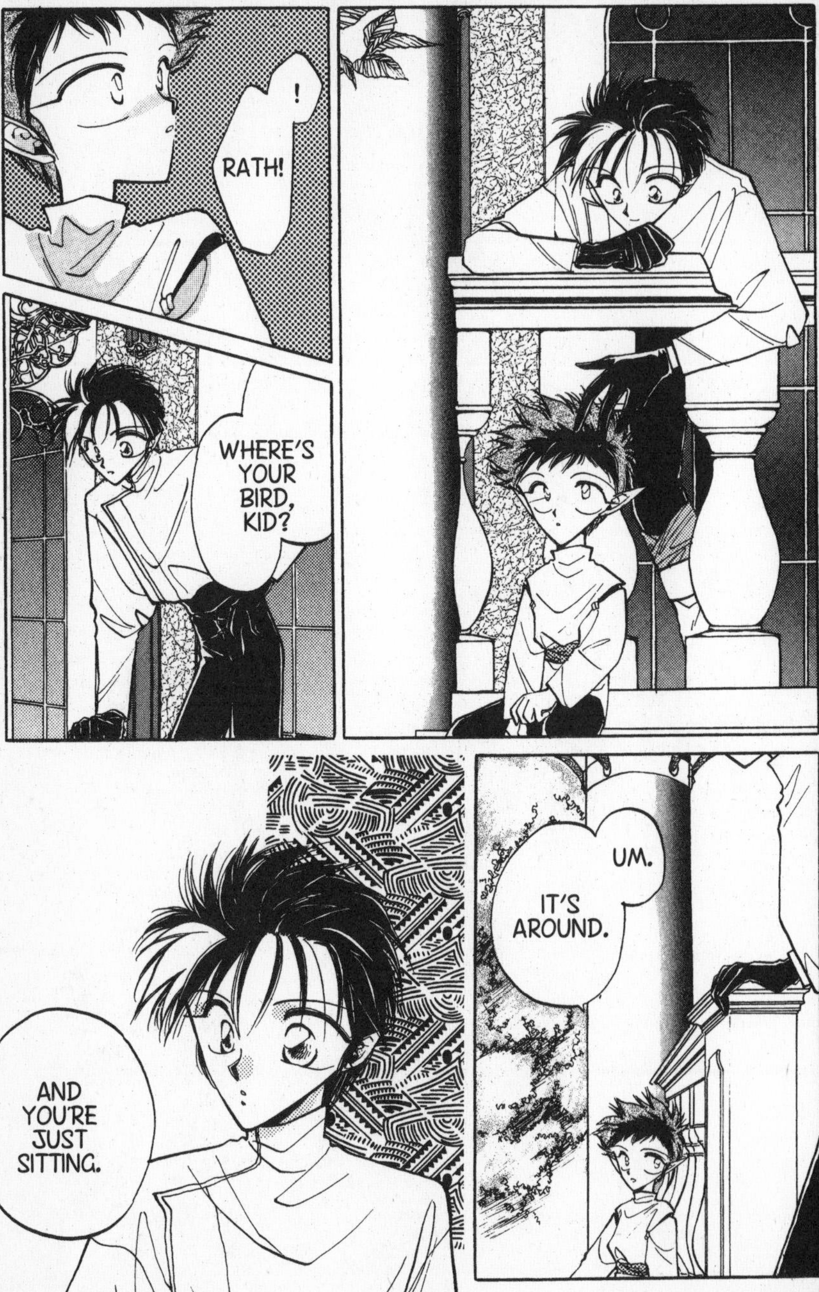
!
RATH!
WHERE'S YOUR BIRD, KID?
UM.
IT'S AROUND.
AND YOU'RE JUST SITTING.

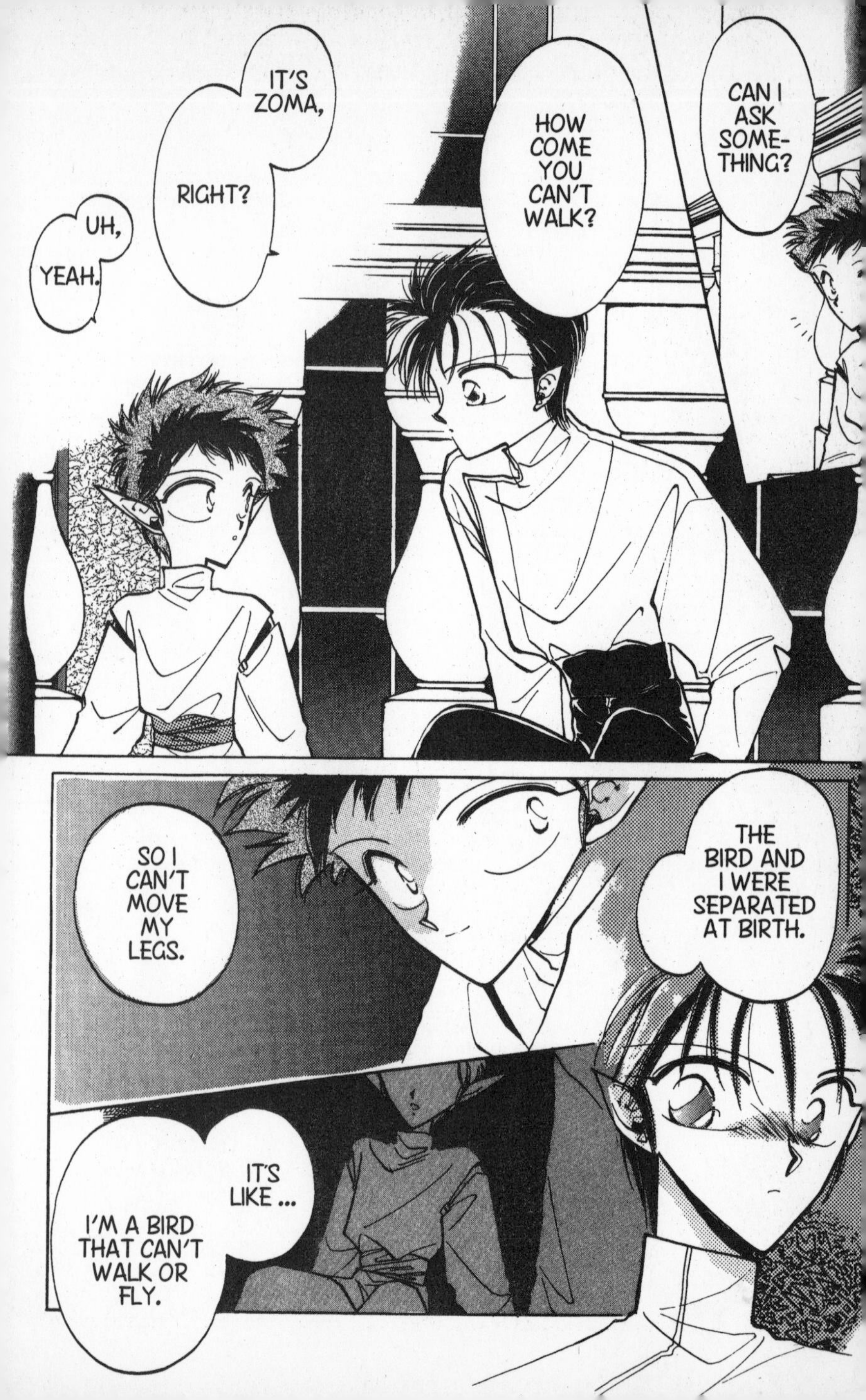
CAN I ASK SOMETHING?
HOW COME YOU CAN'T WALK?
IT'S ZOMA,
RIGHT?
UH,
YEAH.
THE BIRD AND I WERE SEPARATED AT BIRTH.
SO I CAN'T MOVE MY LEGS.
IT'S LIKE ...
I'M A BIRD THAT CAN'T WALK OR FLY.

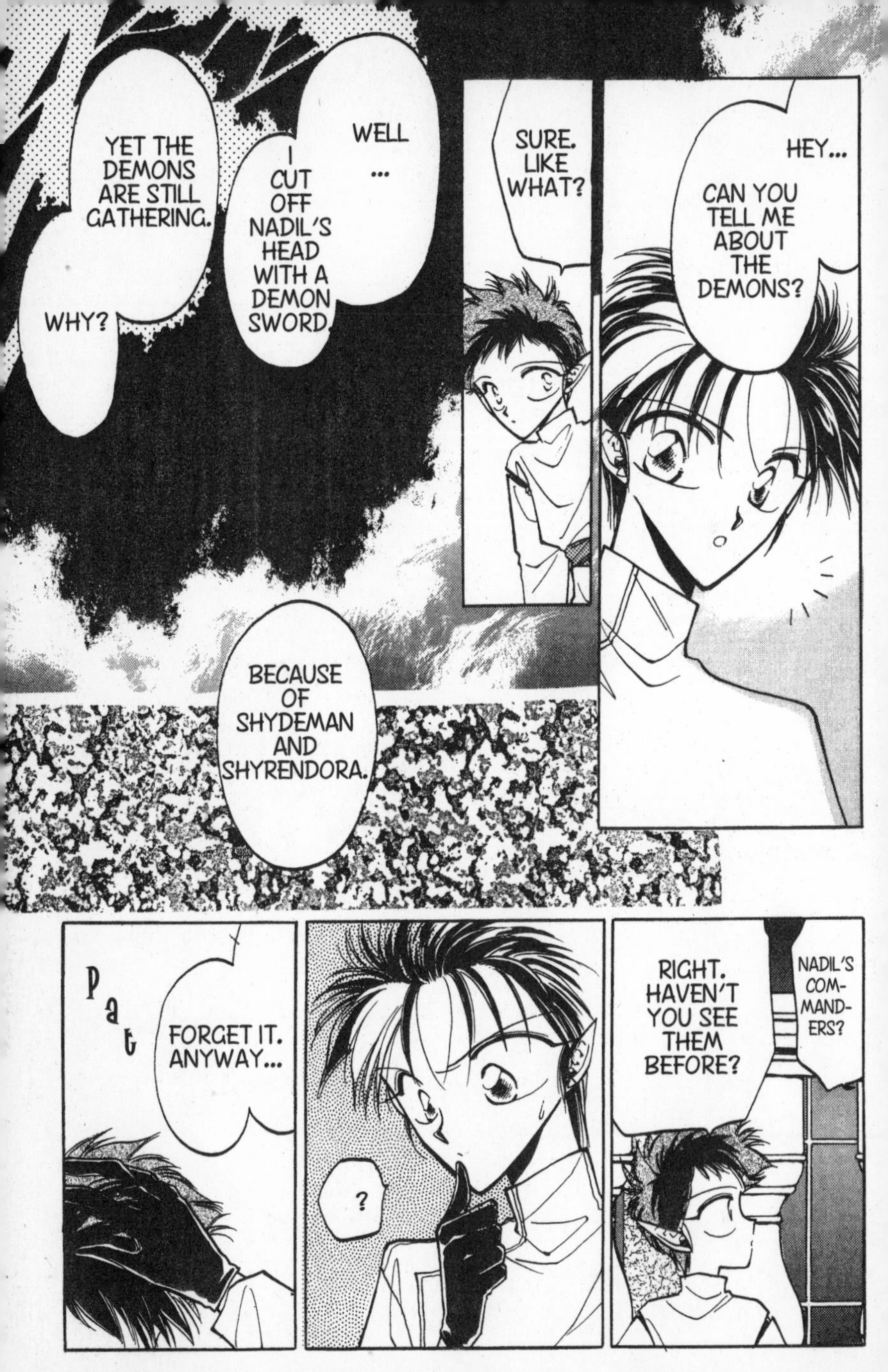
HEY...
CAN YOU TELL ME ABOUT THE DEMONS?
SURE. LIKE WHAT?
WELL ...
I CUT OFF NADIL'S HEAD WITH A DEMON SWORD.
YET THE DEMONS ARE STILL GATHERING.
WHY?
BECAUSE OF SHYDEMAN AND SHYRENDORA.
NADIL'S COM-MANDERS?
RIGHT. HAVEN'T YOU SEE THEM BEFORE?
?
FORGET IT. ANYWAY...
Pat

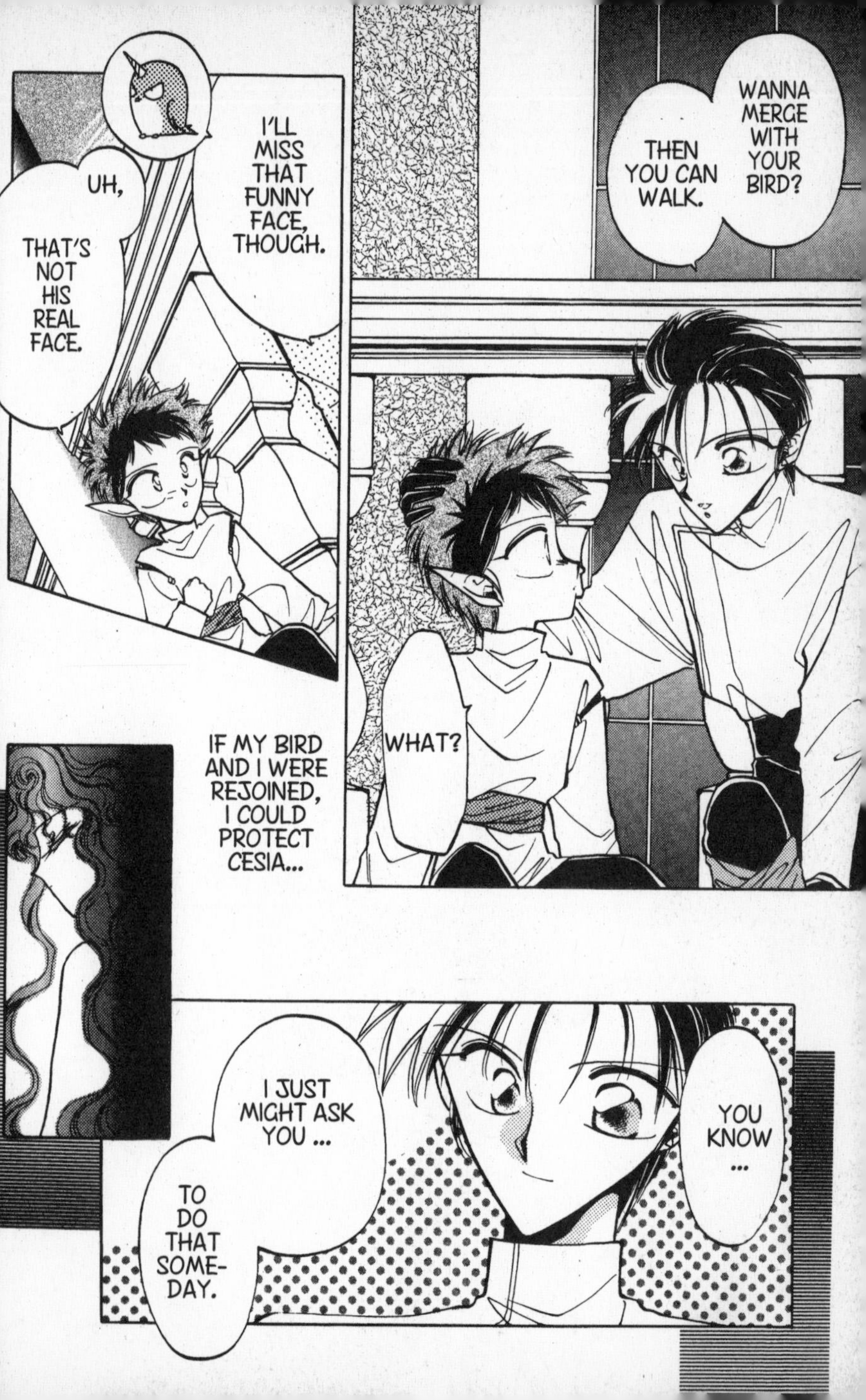
WANNA MERGE WITH YOUR BIRD?
THEN YOU CAN WALK.
WHAT?
I'LL MISS THAT FUNNY FACE, THOUGH.
UH,
THAT'S NOT HIS REAL FACE.
IF MY BIRD AND I WERE REJOINED, I COULD PROTECT CESIA...
YOU KNOW ...
I JUST MIGHT ASK YOU ...
TO DO THAT SOME-DAY.

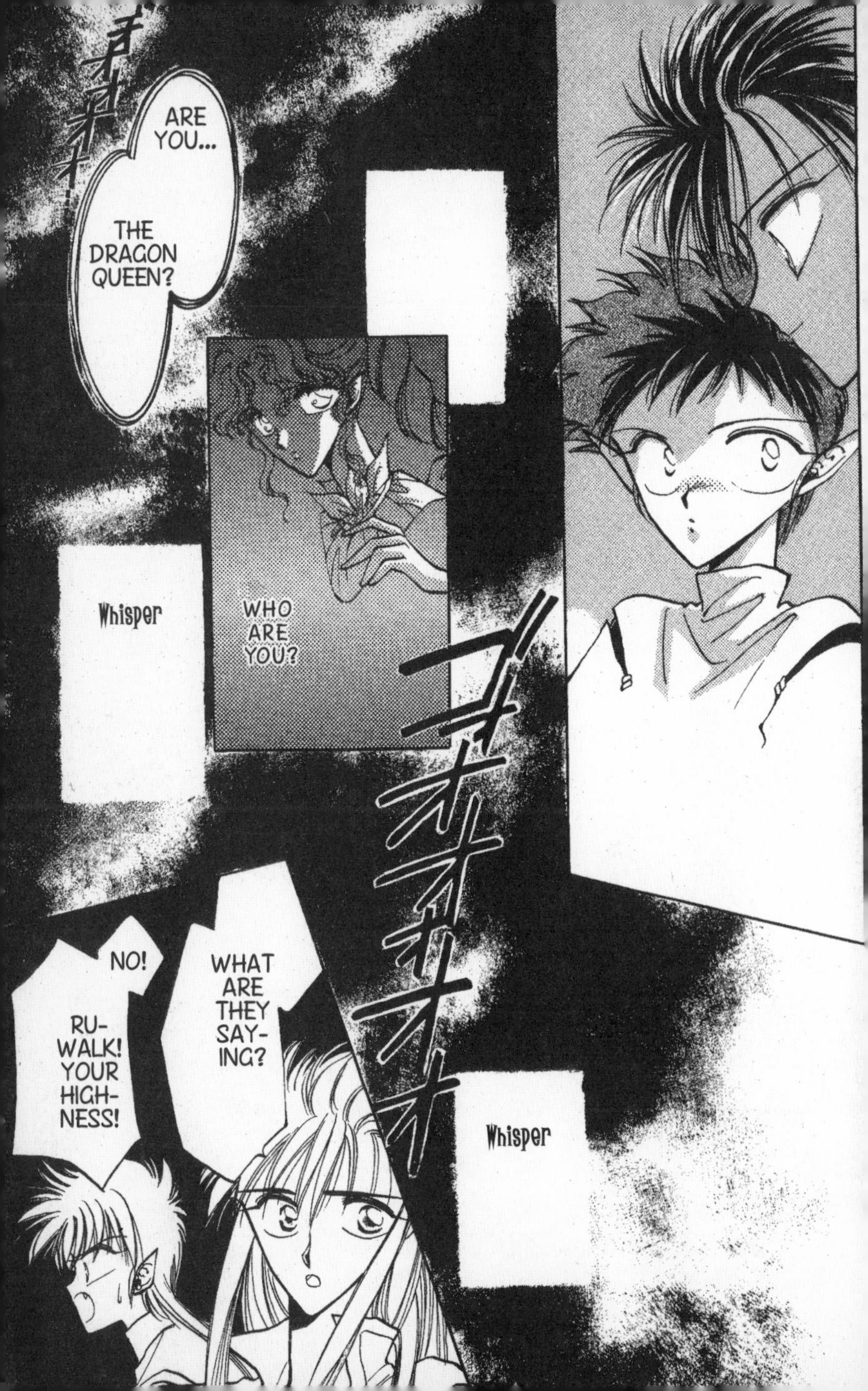
ARE YOU...
THE DRAGON QUEEN?
WHO ARE YOU?
Whisper
Whisper
WHAT ARE THEY SAY-ING?
NO!
RU-WALK! YOUR HIGH-NESS!

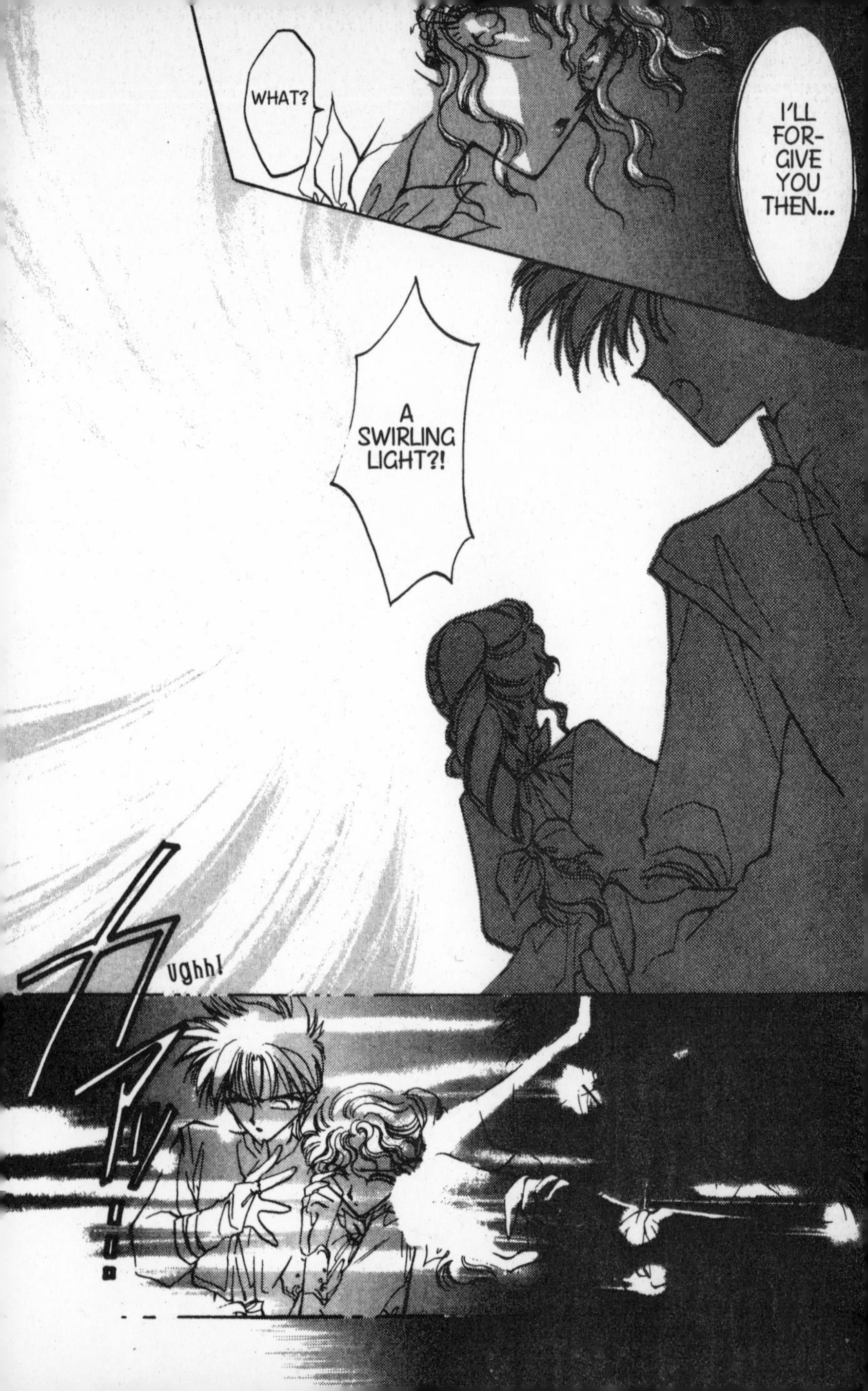
I'LL FOR-GIVE YOU THEN...
WHAT?
A SWIRLING LIGHT?!
Ughh!

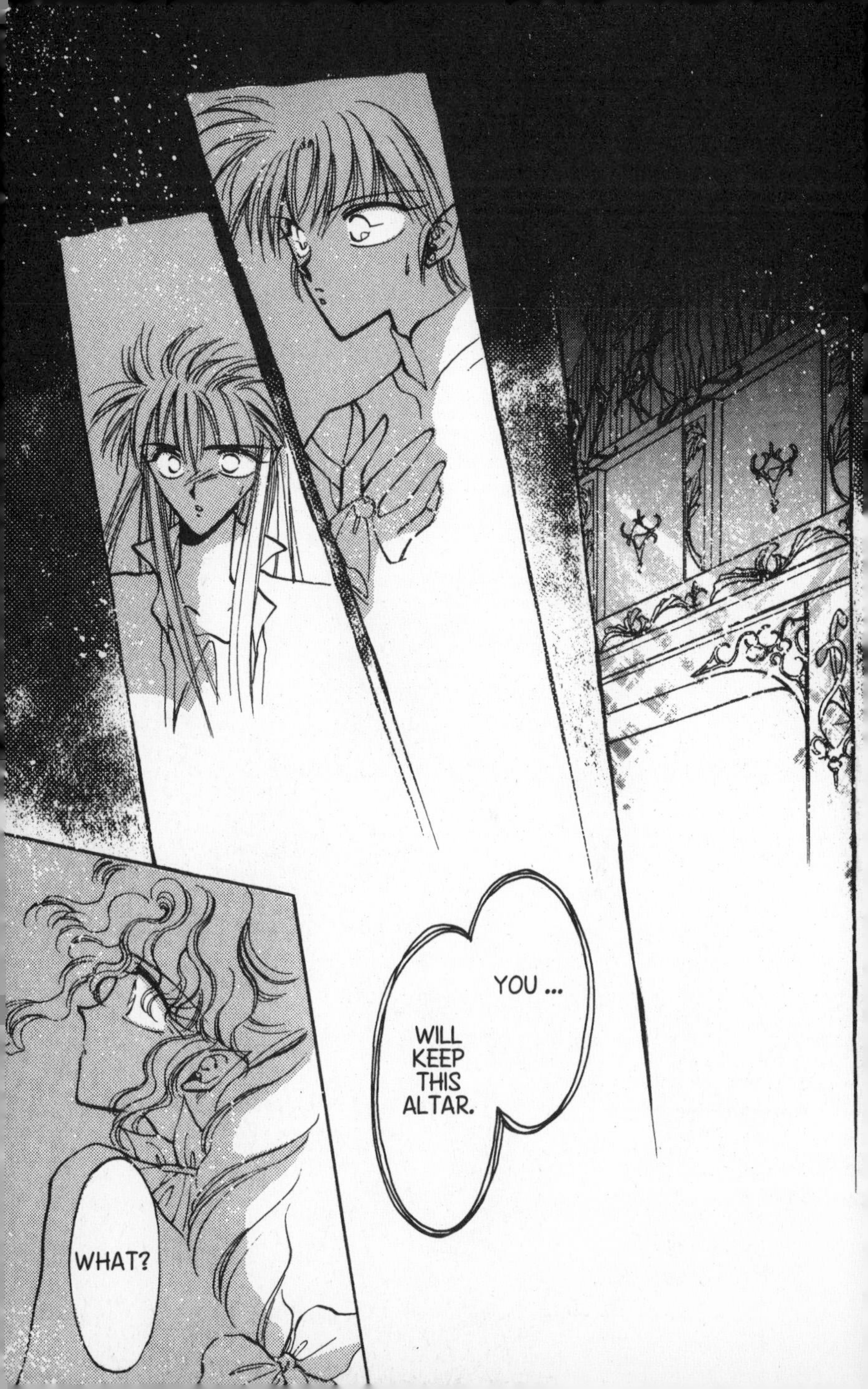
YOU ...
WILL KEEP THIS ALTAR.
WHAT?

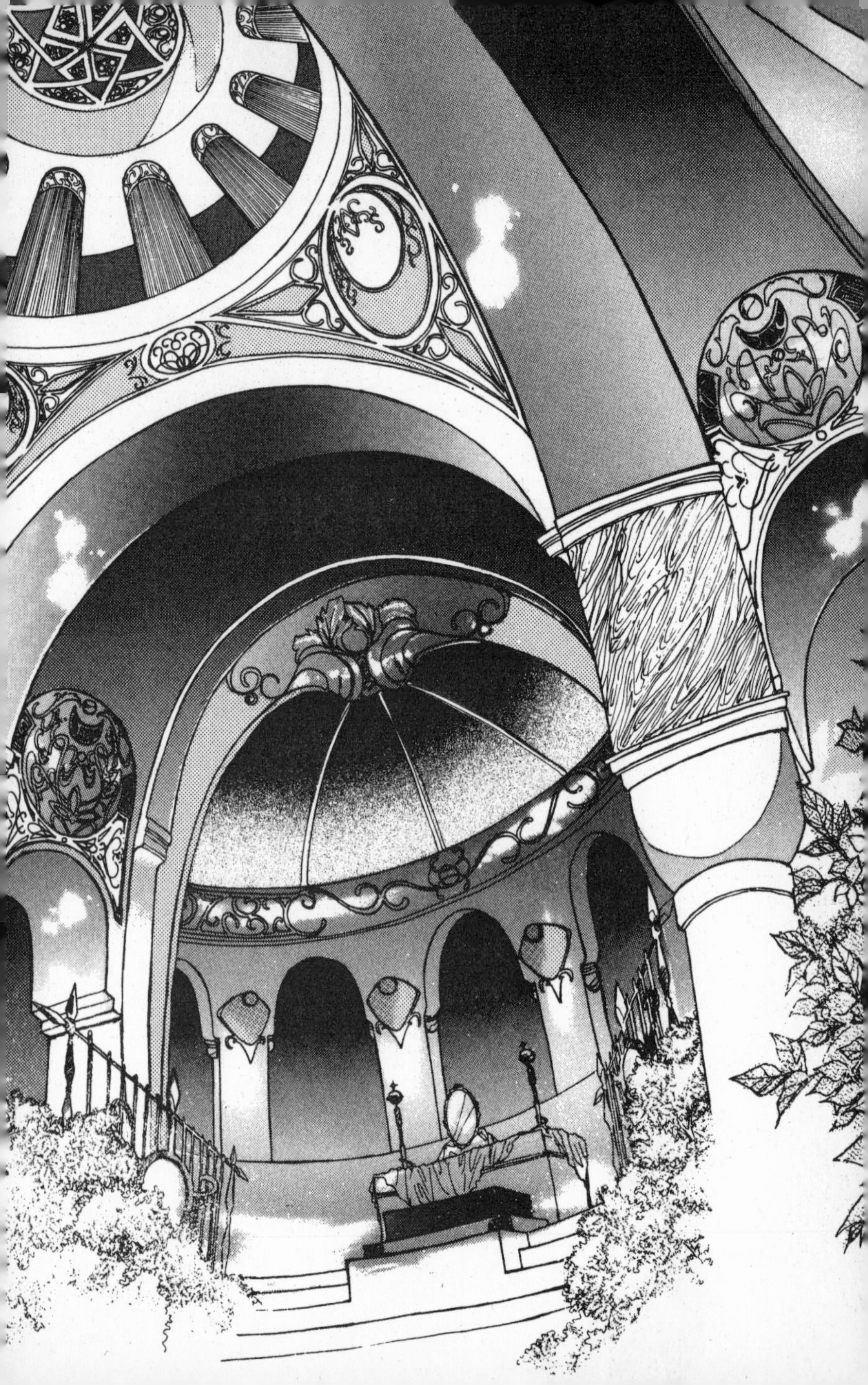

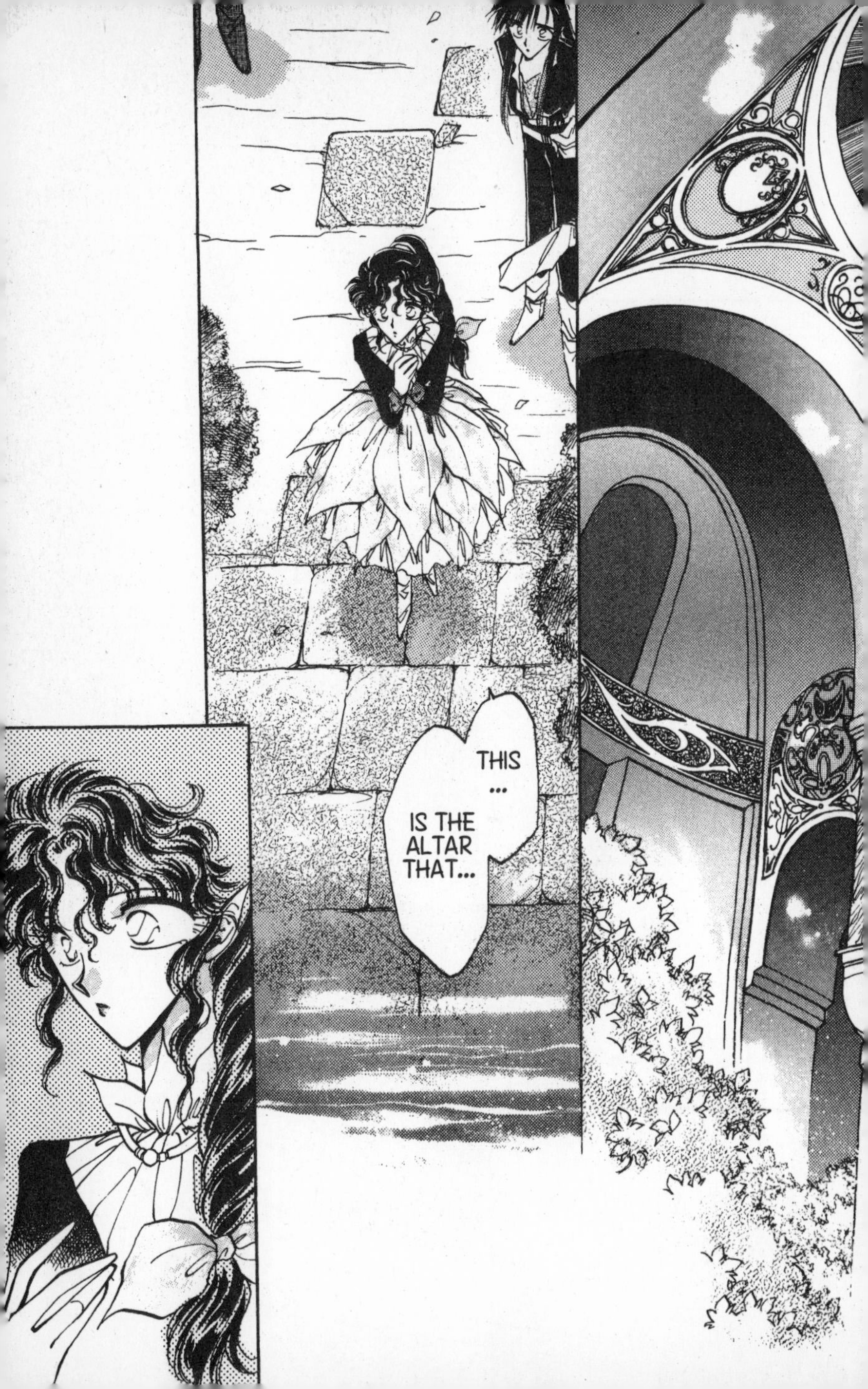
THIS ...
IS THE ALTAR THAT...

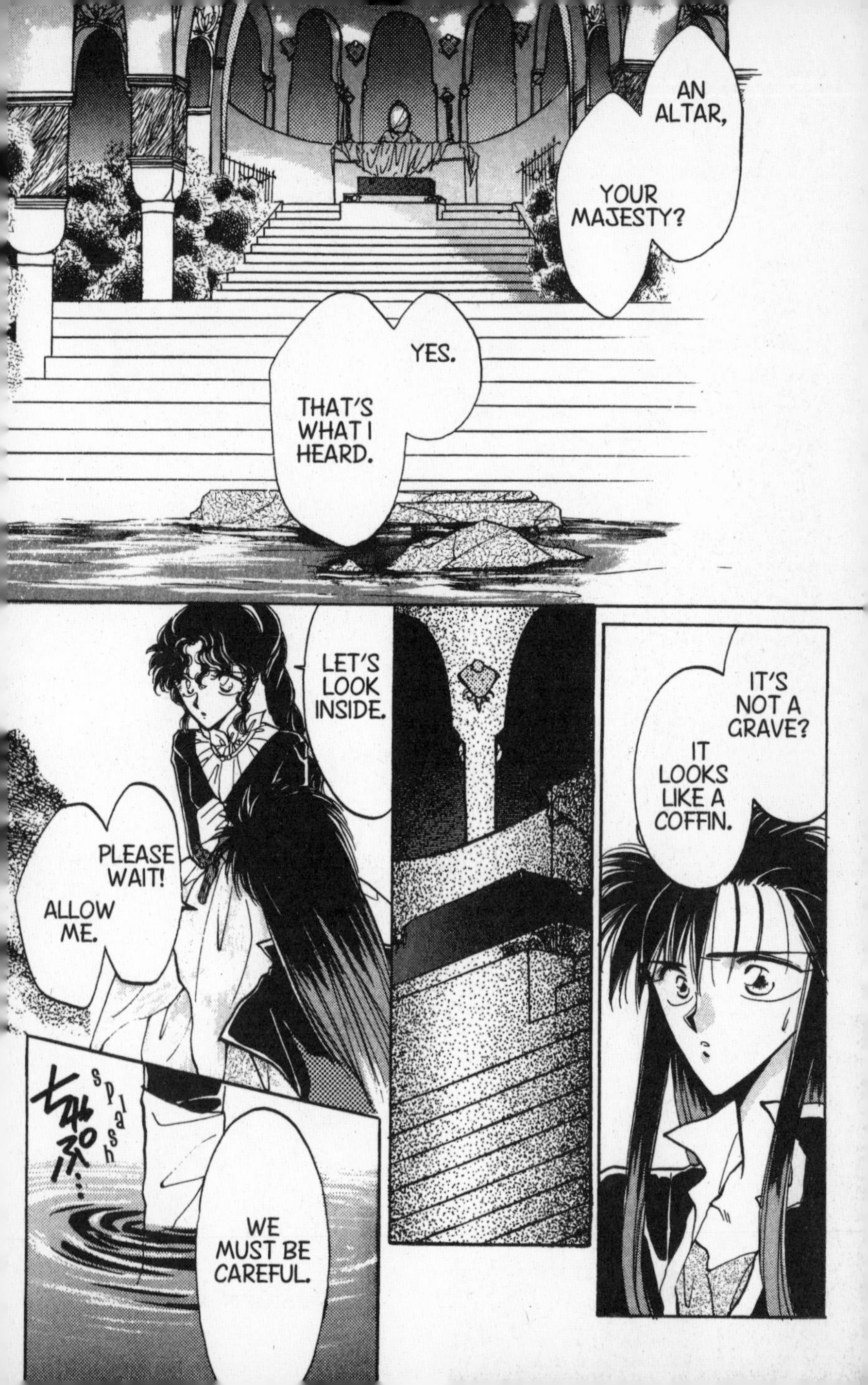
AN ALTAR, YOUR MAJESTY?
YES. THAT'S WHAT I HEARD.
IT'S NOT A GRAVE? IT LOOKS LIKE A COFFIN.
LET'S LOOK INSIDE.
PLEASE WAIT! ALLOW ME.
splash
WE MUST BE CAREFUL.

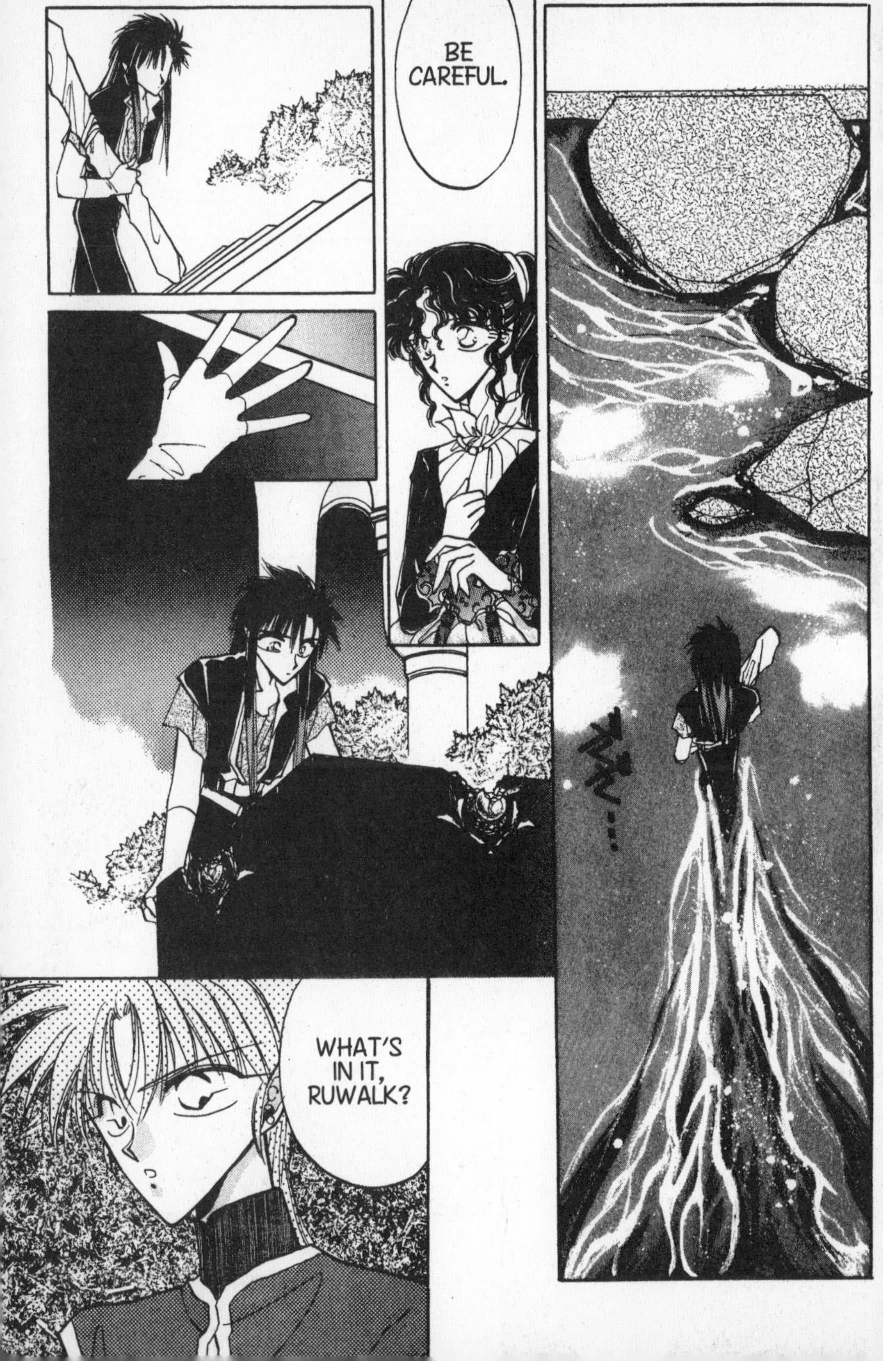
BE CAREFUL.
WHAT'S IN IT, RUWALK?

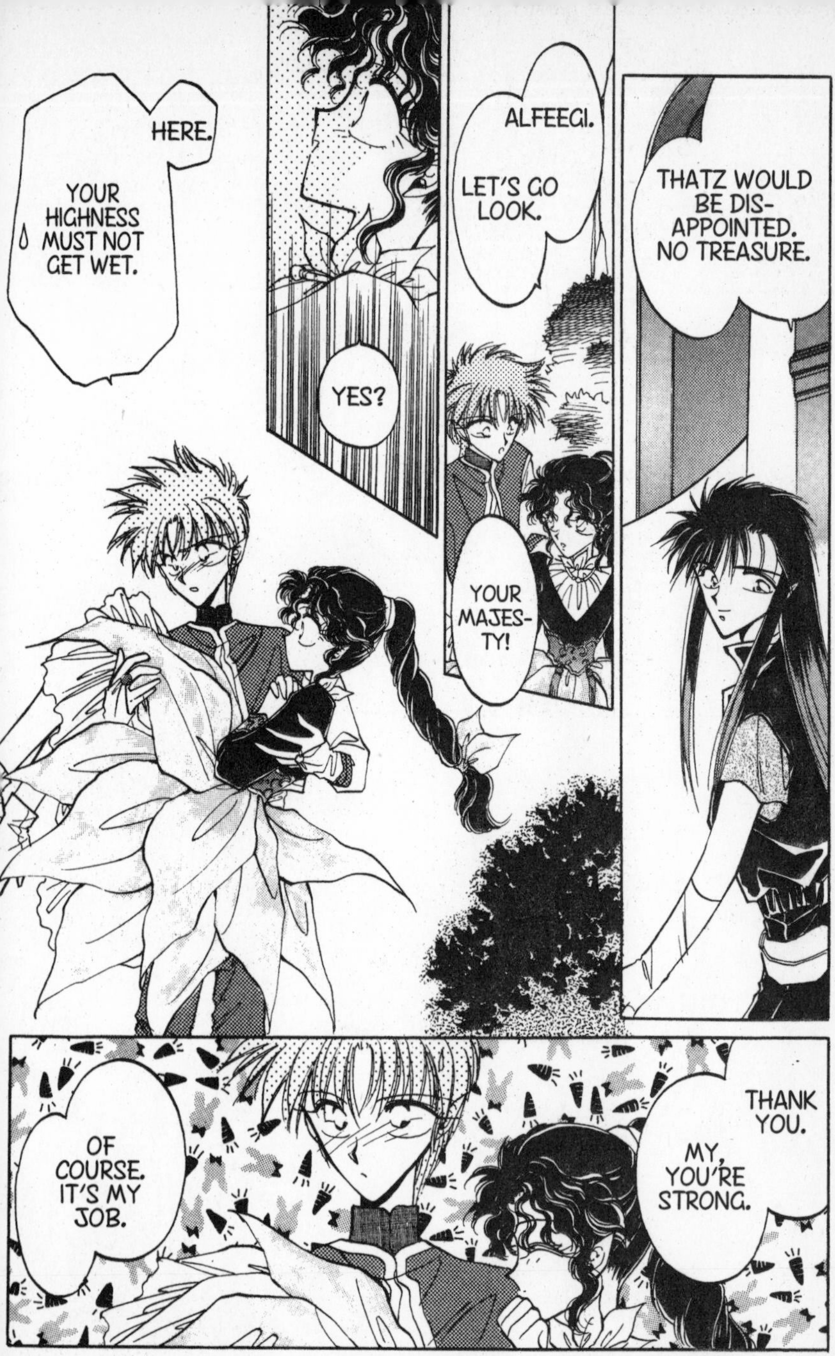
THATZ WOULD BE DIS-APPOINTED. NO TREASURE.
ALFEEGI.
LET'S GO LOOK.
YOUR MAJES-TY!
YES?
HERE.
YOUR HIGHNESS MUST NOT GET WET.
THANK YOU.
MY, YOU'RE STRONG.
OF COURSE. IT'S MY JOB.

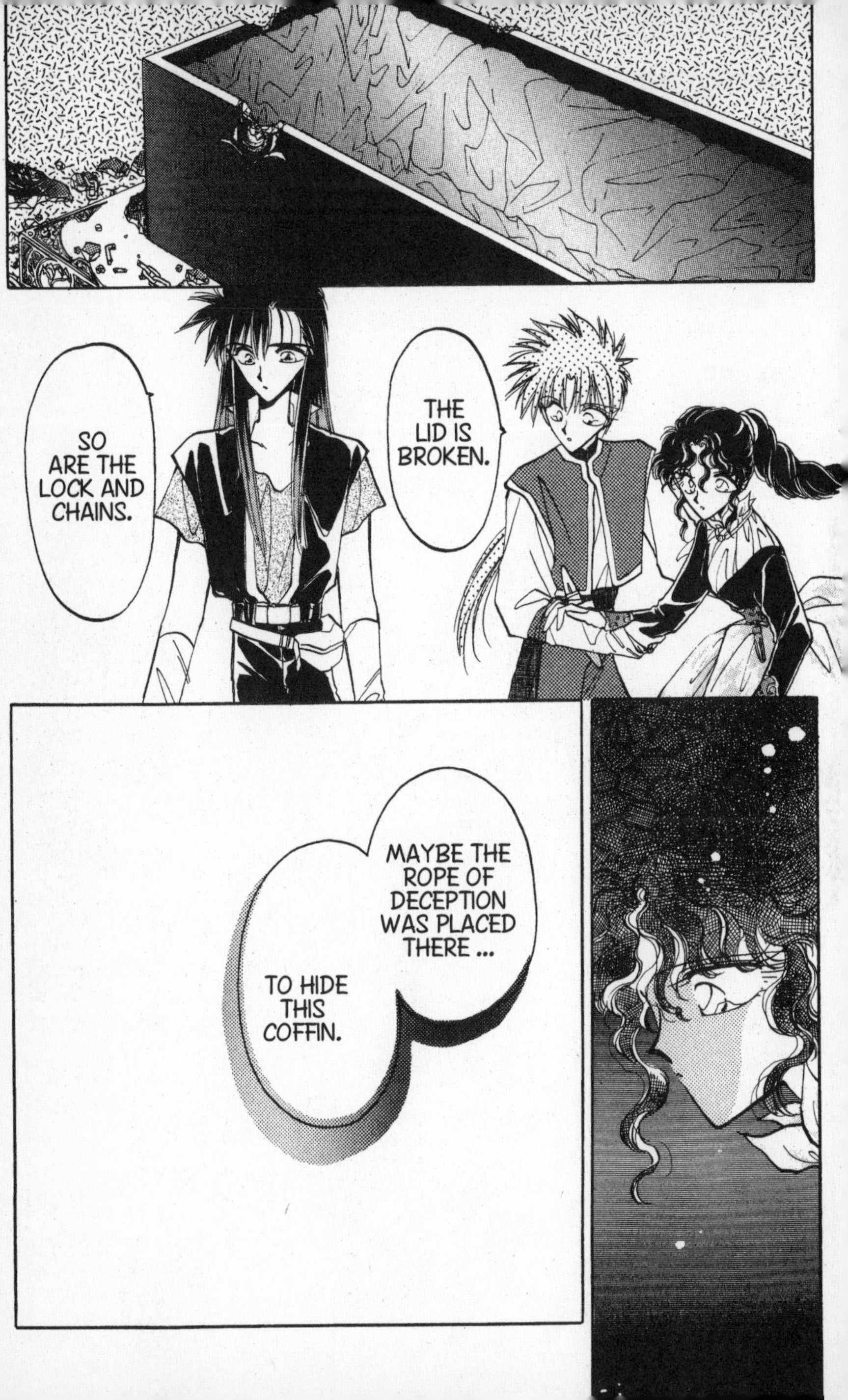
THE LID IS BROKEN.
SO ARE THE LOCK AND CHAINS.
MAYBE THE ROPE OF DECEPTION WAS PLACED THERE ...
TO HIDE THIS COFFIN.

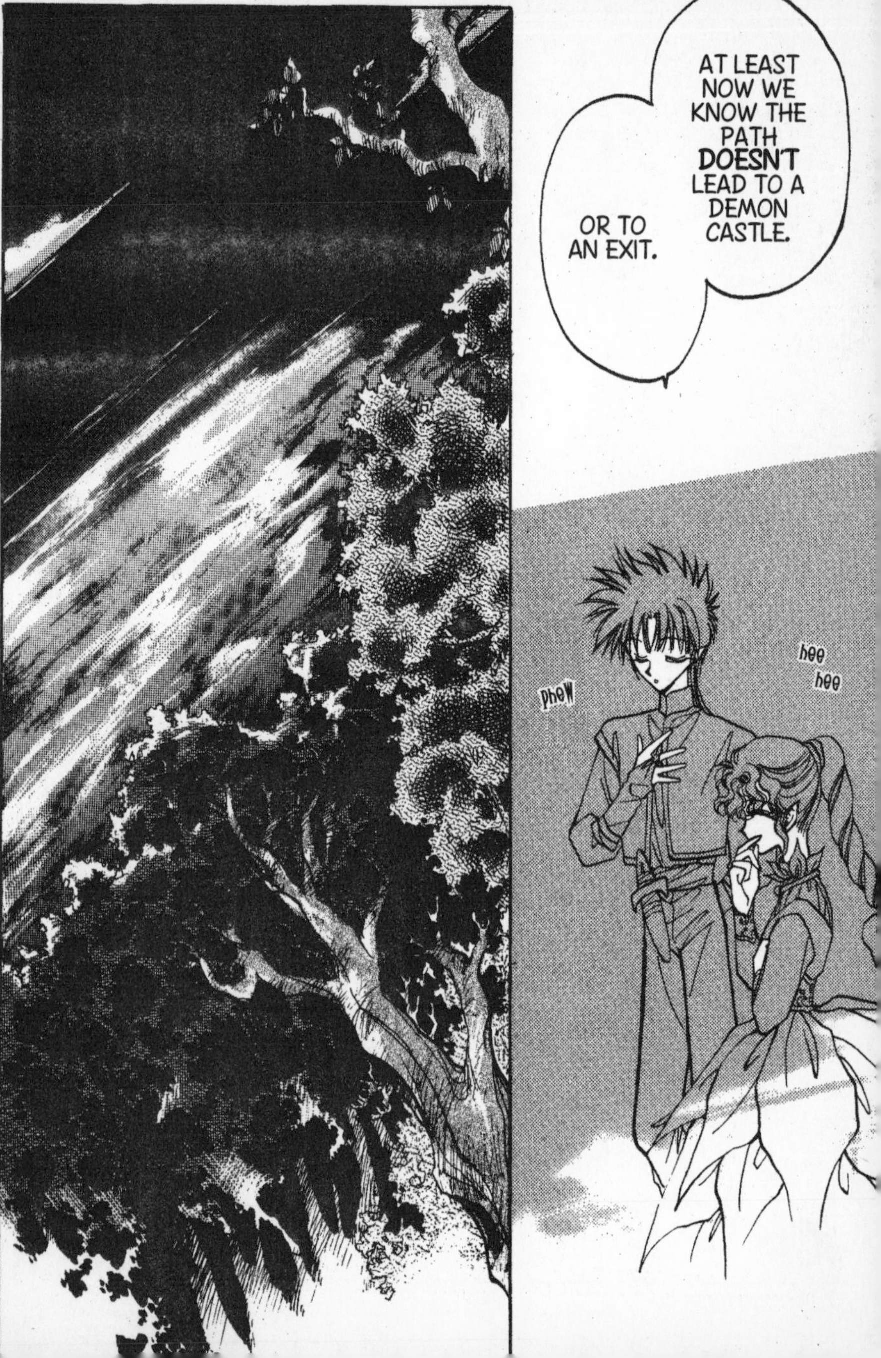
AT LEAST NOW WE KNOW THE PATH **DOESN'T** LEAD TO A DEMON CASTLE.
OR TO AN EXIT.
hee hee
phew

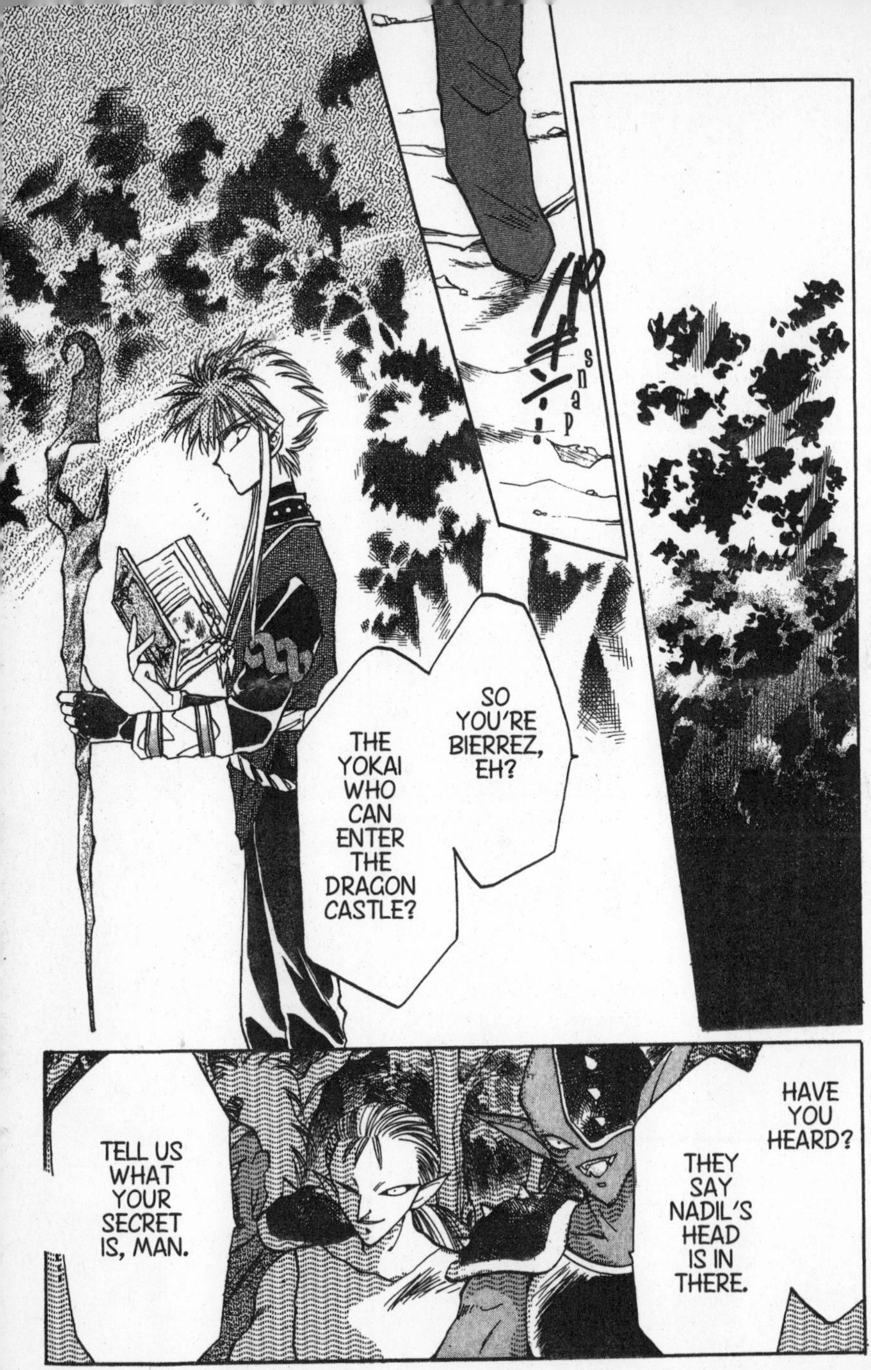
パキン!!
snap
SO YOU'RE BIERREZ, EH?
THE YOKAI WHO CAN ENTER THE DRAGON CASTLE?
HAVE YOU HEARD?
THEY SAY NADIL'S HEAD IS IN THERE.
TELL US WHAT YOUR SECRET IS, MAN.

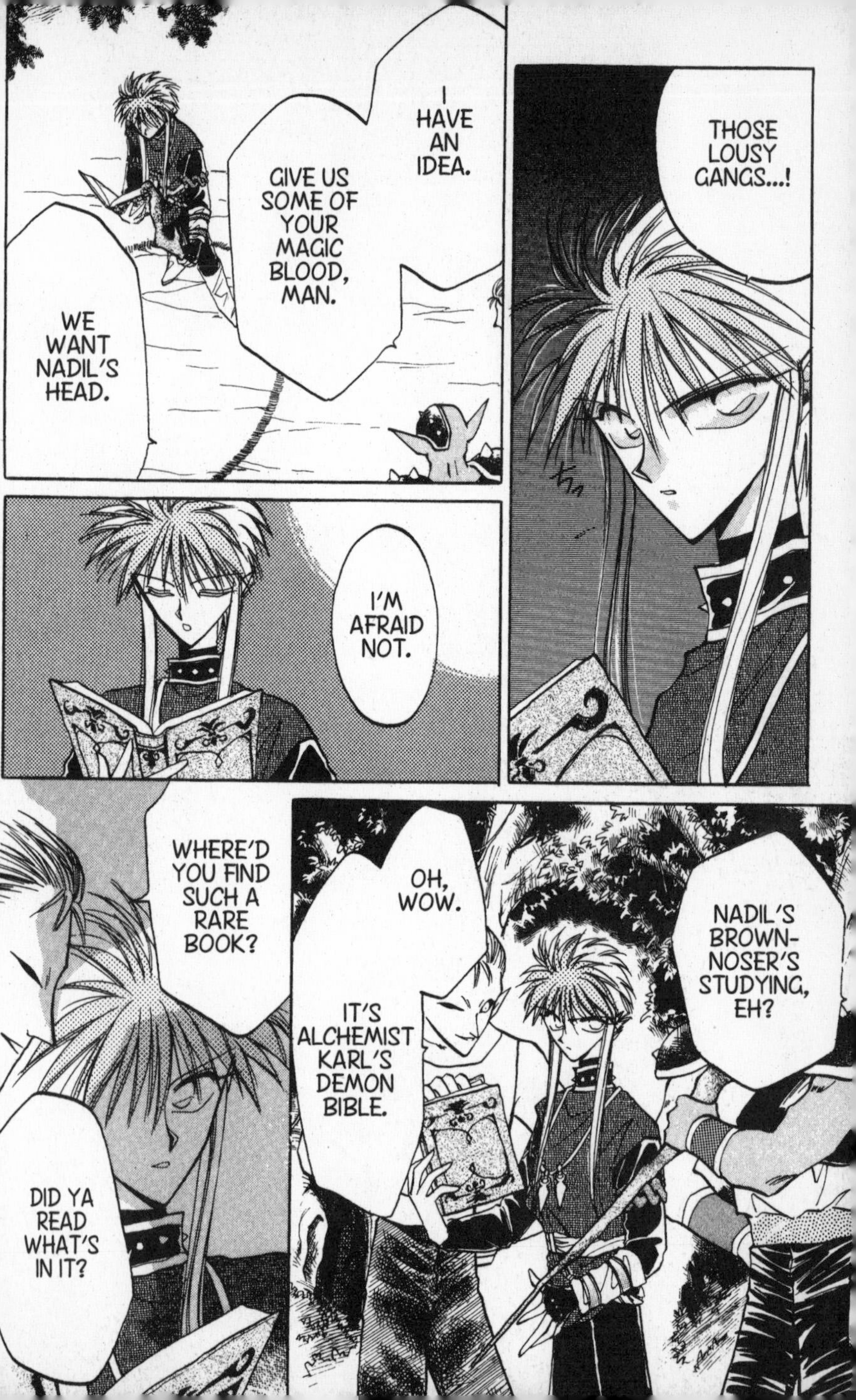
THOSE LOUSY GANGS...!
I HAVE AN IDEA.
GIVE US SOME OF YOUR MAGIC BLOOD, MAN.
WE WANT NADIL'S HEAD.
I'M AFRAID NOT.
NADIL'S BROWN-NOSER'S STUDYING, EH?
OH, WOW.
IT'S ALCHEMIST KARL'S DEMON BIBLE.
WHERE'D YOU FIND SUCH A RARE BOOK?
DID YA READ WHAT'S IN IT?

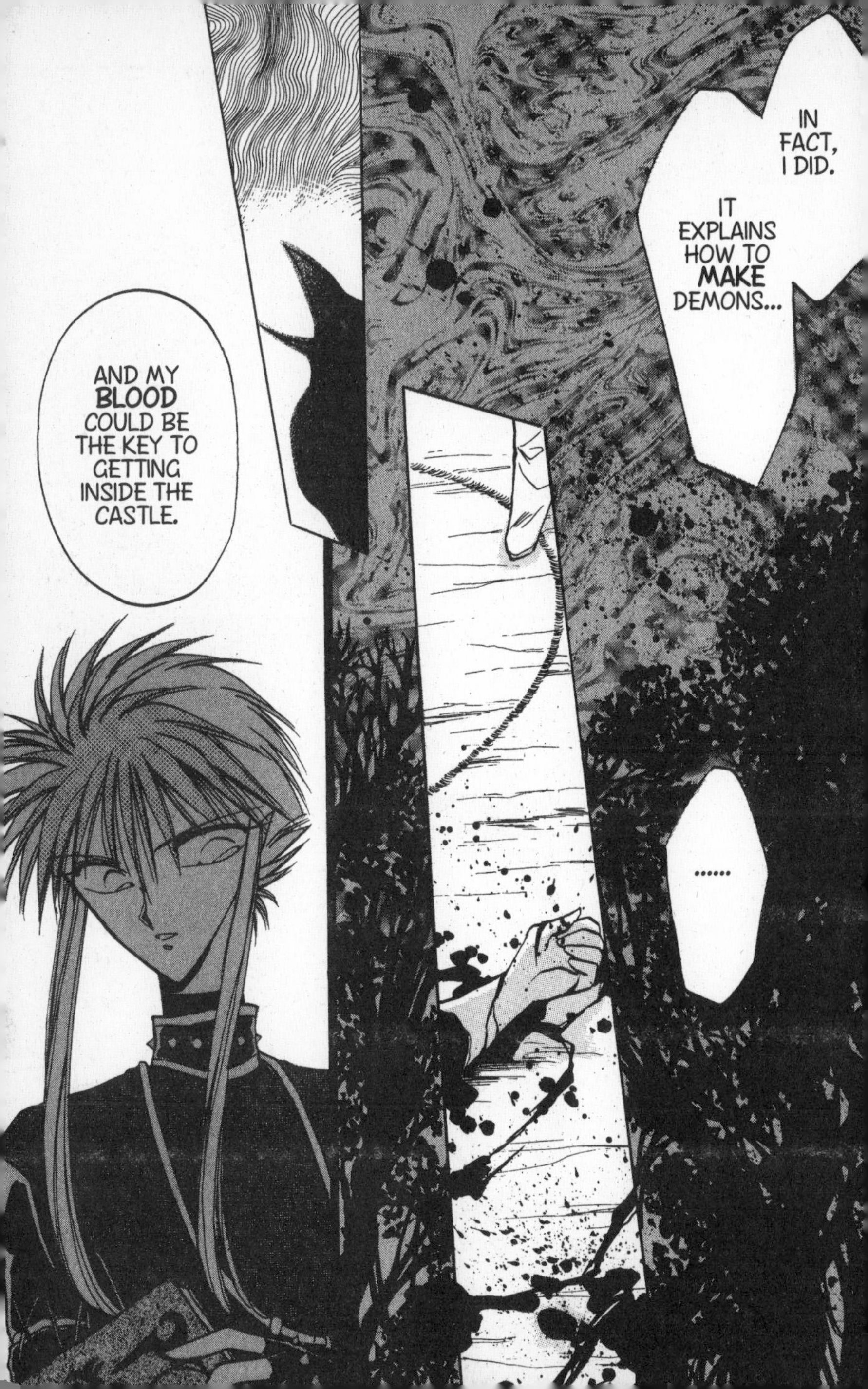
IN FACT, I DID.
IT EXPLAINS HOW TO MAKE DEMONS...
......
AND MY BLOOD COULD BE THE KEY TO GETTING INSIDE THE CASTLE.

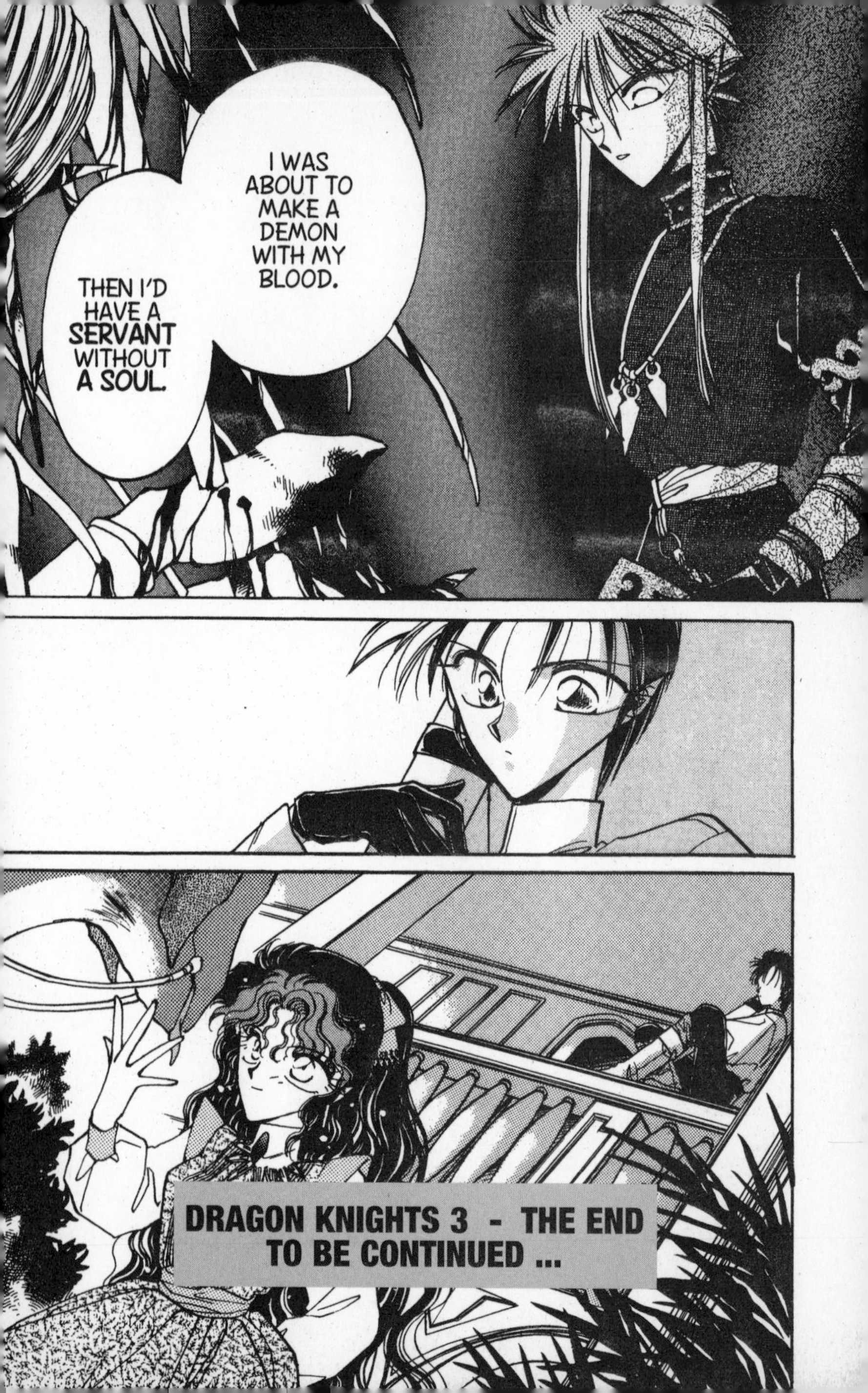
I WAS ABOUT TO MAKE A DEMON WITH MY BLOOD.
THEN I'D HAVE A SERVANT WITHOUT A SOUL.
DRAGON KNIGHTS 3 - THE END
TO BE CONTINUED ...

Dragon Knights

Preview for Vol. 4:
With the Yokai forces amassing to attack the castle, an air of tension has befallen the court – Rath is itching for Bierrez to show his face again, Thatz salivates for treasure and food, and Rune loses himself in a world of self-contemplation, trying to regain the elfin healing powers he lost upon joining the Dragon Tribe. But no matter how disparate their concerns, they must band together with the Dragon Lord Lykouleon and the other Dragon Officers to face Nadil's army. However, Zoma goes missing, Rath may be dying, and the heroes are beginning to show signs of doubt about their chances against a formidable foe.

WELCOME TO THE END OF THE WORLD
Coming in May
from TOKYOPOP®.
RAGNARÖK
English version by New York Times bestselling fantasy writer, Richard A. Knaak.
TOKYOPOP®
© 1992 MYUNG-JIN LEE. All Rights Reserved. First published in Korea in 1992 by Daiwon C.I. Inc.
TOKYOPOP is a registered trademark and TOKYOPOP Manga is a trademark of Mixx Entertainment, Inc.

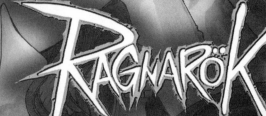

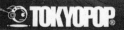

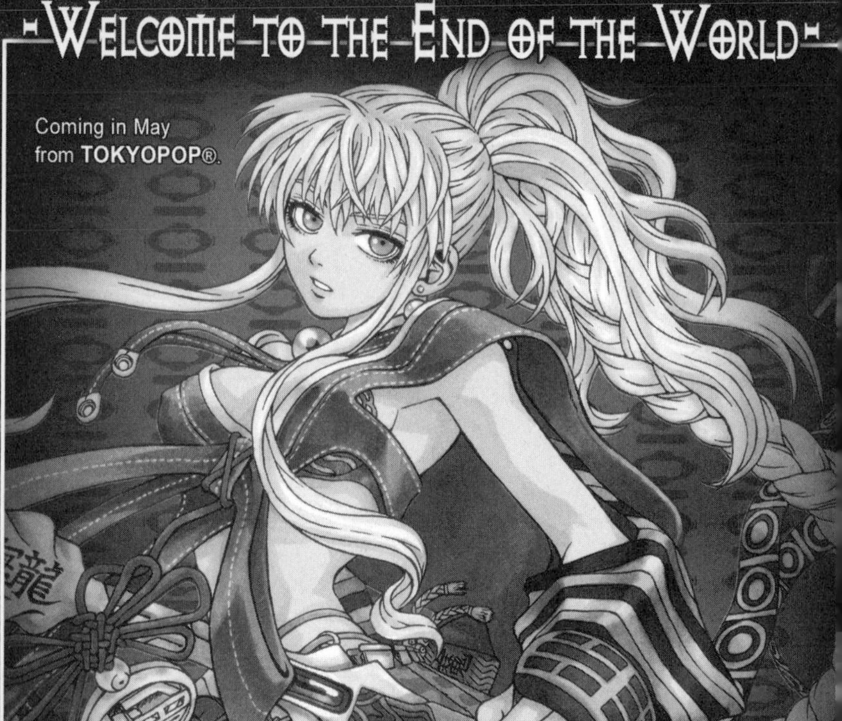

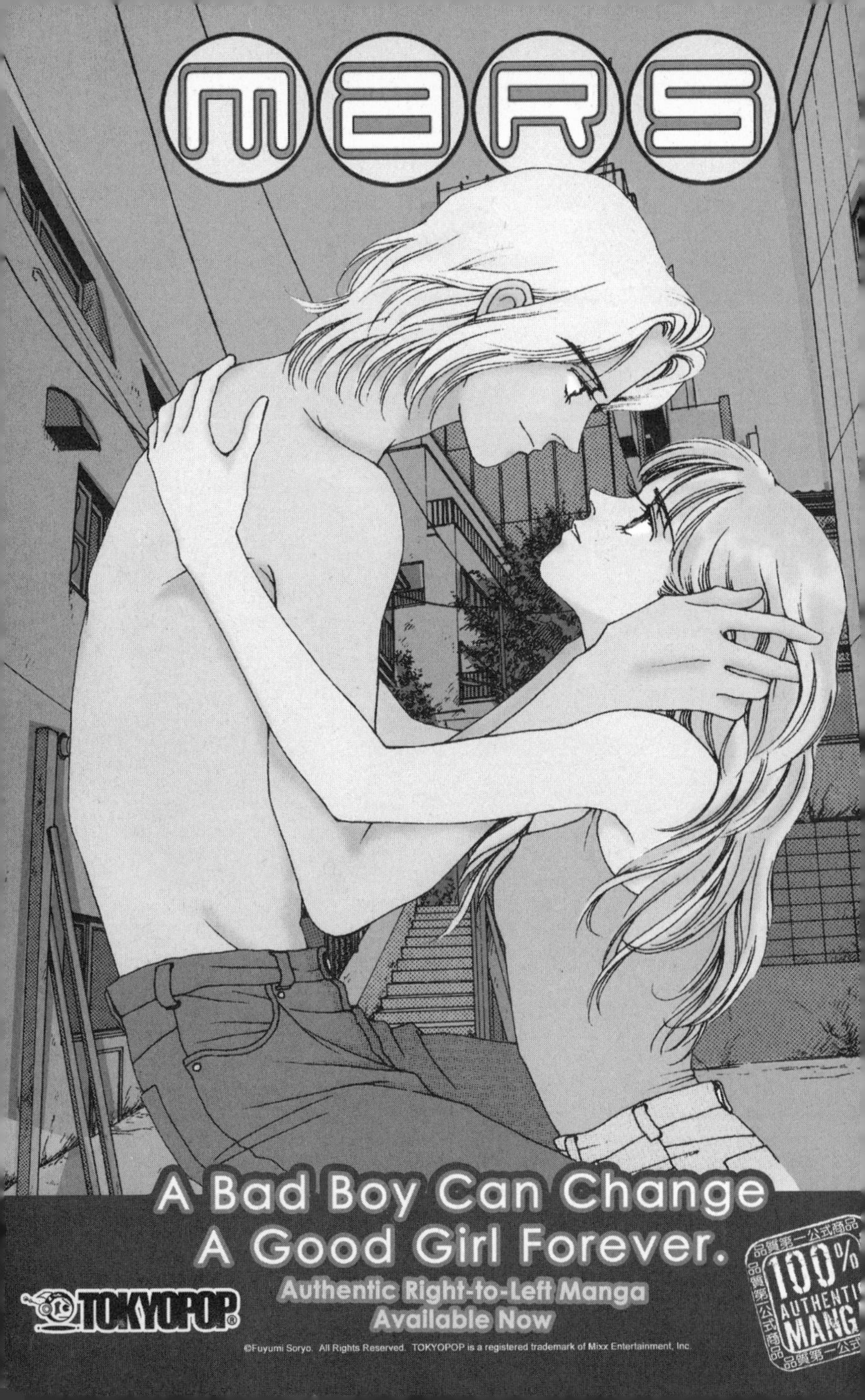
MARS
A Bad Boy Can Change
A Good Girl Forever.
Authentic Right-to-Left Manga
Available Now
TOKYOPOP®
100%
©Fuyumi Soryo. All Rights Reserved. TOKYOPOP is a registered trademark of Mixx Entertainment, Inc.

Chobits

TOKYOPOP®

STOP!

This is the back of the book.
You wouldn't want to spoil a great ending!

This book is printed "manga-style," in the authentic Japanese right-to-left format. Since none of the artwork has been flipped or altered, readers get to experience the story just as the creator intended. You've been asking for it, so TOKYOPOP® delivered: authentic, hot-off-the-press, and far more fun!

DIRECTIONS

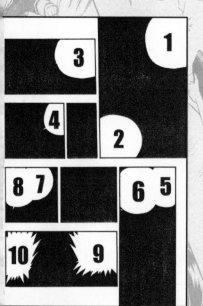

If this is your first time reading manga-style, here's a quick guide to help you understand how it works.

It's easy... just start in the top right panel and follow the numbers. Have fun, and look for more 100% authentic manga from TOKYOPOP®!